ambiguous DISCOURSE

Feminist Narratology & British Women Writers

edited

by

kathy

mezei

The

University

of North

Carolina

Press

Chapel Hill

& London

© 1996
The University of
North Carolina Press
All rights reserved
Manufactured in the
United States of America
The paper in this book meets the
guidelines for permanence and durability
of the Committee on Production Guidelines
for Book Longevity of the Council on
Library Resources.
Library of Congress
Cataloging-in-Publication Data
Ambiguous discourse: feminist narratology
and British women writers / edited by
Kathy Mezei.
    p.   cm.
    Includes bibliographical references
and index.
    ISBN 0-8078-2290-6 (cloth: alk. paper).—
ISBN 0-8078-4599-X (pbk.: alk. paper)
    1. English fiction—Women authors—
History and criticism. 2. Feminism and
literature—Great Britain—History.
3. Women and literature—Great Britain—
History. 4. Discourse analysis, Literary.
5. Narration (Rhetoric).
I. Mezei, Kathy, 1947–
PR830.W6A43   1996
823.009′9287—dc20   95-26584
                     CIP

00 99 98 97 96   5 4 3 2 1

Rachel Blau DuPlessis's "Seismic
Orgasm: Sexual Intercourse and Narrative
Meaning in Mina Loy" has been substantially
revised for this collection; it was previously
published as " 'Seismic Orgasm': Sexual
Intercourse, Gender Narratives, and Lyric
Ideology in Mina Loy," in *Studies in Historical
Change*, ed. Ralph Cohen, 264–91
(Charlottesville: University Press of Virginia,
1992), and is used by permission of the
University Press of Virginia.

An earlier version of Linda Hutcheon's
"Incredulity toward Metanarrative:
Negotiating Postmodernism and Feminisms"
was previously published in *Tessera* 7
(Autumn 1989): 39–44.

Susan S. Lanser's "Queering Narratology" is
based on "Sexing the Narrative: Propriety,
Desire, and the Engendering of
Narratology," first published in *Narrative* 3.1
(January 1995). Copyright © 1995 Ohio
State University Press. All rights reserved.

Robyn Warhol's article, "The Look, the
Body, and the Heroine of *Persuasion*: A
Feminist-Narratological View of Jane
Austen," was published in a slightly different
form in *NOVEL: A Forum on Fiction* 26.1
(Fall 1991). Copyright © 1992 *NOVEL*
Corp. Reprinted with permission.

contents

acknowledgments

For financial assistance with this project, I gratefully acknowledge the President's Research Grant, the Social Sciences and Humanities Research Council Small Grants, and the University Publications Fund Grant awarded by Simon Fraser University.

The generous support of the English Department at Simon Fraser University and in particular the assistance of my secretary, Nancy Burnham, made this project possible.

Anita Mahoney from the Dean of Arts Office skillfully and graciously transformed the original manuscripts into a final polished form, and Jan MacLellan adeptly made the final corrections.

My research assistants Christine Jackman, Helen Takala, Karen Essex, Deborah Blacklock, Lani Vetter, Peter Persad, Tina Kennedy, and Sharon Lo did a wonderful job in preparing bibliographies, undertaking data searches, and organizing all the materials for this book. For reading this manuscript, I thank Susan Knutson and Jill Matus.

To Melba Cuddy-Keane, Linda Hutcheon, Janet Giltrow, and Susan Stanford Friedman I express my warm appreciation for their encouragement and advice.

My thanks, as always, to Bob Anderson, the best of readers.

ambiguous DISCOURSE

introduction

Contextualizing Feminist Narratology

kathy mezei

> *Yes, yes, if you please, no reference to examples in books. Men
> have had every advantage of us in telling their own story. Education
> has been theirs in so much higher a degree; the pen has been in their
> hands. I will not allow books to prove any thing.*
> —*Austen*, Persuasion

Anne Elliot's retort to Captain Harville as they debated the differences between men's and women's "nature" pinpoints the essence of feminist narratology—the *context* of how stories are told, by whom, and for whom.

This collection is the first to gather together essays that combine feminist and narratological readings of women's texts. In their selection of British women writers from Jane Austen to Jeanette Winterson, the contributors focus on writers who are conspicuously self-conscious and iconoclastic in their deployment of narrative techniques. While seeking to decode subversive, evasive, or perplexing narrative strategies in Austen or Woolf or Mina Loy, the contributors recognized the value of a feminist narratology in interpreting these strategies, in proving, as Anne Elliot might say, *some thing*. In 1986 Susan Lanser described the contingent relation between feminism and narratology, which she named "feminist narratology": "My . . . task [is] to ask whether feminist criticism, and particularly the study of narratives by women, might benefit from the methods . . . of narratology and whether narratology, in turn, might be altered by the understandings of feminist criticism and the experience of women's texts" (342). Taking up the "task" in turn, these essays explore and expose "gender's effect on the level of discourse" (Warhol, *Gendered Interventions*, 6). At the same time, the diversity of the contributors' responses reflects both the edgy alliance of feminism and narratology and the evolving, contested histories of feminist literary theory and narratology.

The reader will quickly notice the pervasive theme of ambiguity winding its way through this collection, despite different theoretical positions and texts that range from eighteenth-century domestic realism to postmodern metafiction. Within the texts she had set out to analyze and interpret, each contributor confronted forms of ambiguity. The sites of these ambiguous discourses were located, depending on the individual contributor, within the narrator, the focalizer, the reader, author-ity, subjectivity, historicity, linearity, or specific structures and features of narrative and discourse and their complex interrelations. Feminist narratology, this hybrid of an *ology* (the science of narratives) and an *ism* (the action of being a feminist), then offered the contributors a multilayered stack of tools with which to probe these forms of indirection in convergence with an ideological framework that could account for their singular power and effect. The focus of this volume is to show, through close textual reading, how feminist narratology locates and deconstructs sites of ambiguity, indeterminacy, and transgression in aspects of narrative and in the sexuality and gender of author, narrator, character, and reader.

The his/story of narratology, like any story, rather depends on who the narrator is. If the narrator is Mieke Bal, "narratology" is defined simply as "the theory of narrative texts" (*Narratology*, 3); if he is Gerald Prince, then more fully as a study of "the nature, form, and functioning of narrative ... [which] tries to characterize narrative competence ... [and which] examines what all and only narratives have in common ... as well as what enables them to be different from one another" (*Dictionary*, 65).[1] Perhaps Peter Brooks's phrase describing the Russian formalists' "constructivist" view of literature as one that "so often cuts through thematic material to show the constructed armature that supports it" (14) best visualizes the original intent of narratology to found a science of narrative through a comprehensive study of structures underpinning all narrative. Readers of this collection of essays will undoubtedly be familiar with the emergence of a poetics of narrative through the disparate conduits of structural anthropology, linguistics, Saussurian semiotics, and Russian formalism. Out of these preliminary sources, narratology branched into a grammar of narrative (Todorov, Barthes, Greimas), a discourse of narrative (Genette), and the heteroglossia of novelistic discourse (Bakhtin).

With each narrator-critic plotting trajectories of narratology from different positions, we inevitably end up reading subjective and culturally bound summaries of its history. For example, Ingeborg Hoesterey's 1992 retrospective account places narratology within an evolutionary teleological framework:[2]

> The seminal work of the text-oriented aesthetics of New Criticism marks what might be called the first, "archaic" phase of narratological scholarship. The structuralist-formalist paradigm . . . paved the way for "classical" narratology. . . . During the past decades, certain literary critics have moved away from narratology's almost exclusive focus on the question of what individual texts mean . . . to a heightened awareness of how texts . . . mean, and for whom . . . narratology has provided paradigms and instruments of analysis, even as it has itself undergone critical scrutiny and development. (3)[3]

Wallace Martin, on the other hand, organizes his *Recent Theories of Narrative* (1987) from the point of view of narratives themselves as "modes of explanation" (7); he proceeds through a historical account of theories of the novel via abstract, structural models of narrative analysis to models based on conventions and communication.

As Hoesterey pointed out above, quite predictably, narratology has interrogated its own narrative and story, self-reflexively undergoing "critical scrutiny and development." And so, in "Whatever Happened to Narratology?" (1990), Christine Brooke-Rose quips: "*It got swallowed into story* seems the obvious answer; it slid off the slippery methods of a million structures and became the story of its own functioning" (286). But, as Brooke-Rose reminds us, we continue to pose ancient, elemental questions about stories and their analysis, "not just of representations (stories) in general, but also of the very discourses (stories) that purport to analyse stories, stories of people, stories of people reading stories of people, stories of people reading stories of the world" (283).

In the first of three *Poetics Today* issues featuring papers from the influential 1979 Tel Aviv Symposium 2 on Narrative Theory and Poetics of Fiction, Benjamin Hrushovski had queried: "But what is Narratology? Is it a logical division of Poetics? Does it constitute a clearly-defined discipline with a specific object of study? Or is it a methodology?" (6). Reflecting that "'narratology' . . . is neither one discipline nor one methodology nor a division of Poetics but rather a meeting point, an intersection, of a whole range of problems . . . especially found in works of prose" (208), Hrushovski acknowledged the ever-widening compass of the practice of narratology.

When *Poetics Today* editors Brian McHale and Ruth Ronen decided to revisit narratology in 1989, they canvased the original Symposium 2 participants and other scholars in the field, asking them to consider whether "narratology [has] developed since 1979, or has it stagnated? What new directions of research have emerged, if any? . . . Is narratology a dead-end, or is it still a lively and fruitful direction for research?" (iii–iv). This palpable anxiety about the viability of narratology was vitiated by the considerable response they received.[4] Narratology's continuing vitality, as well as its protean adaptability, is evident in the number of publications in the field; the emergence of a new journal, *Narrative*, in January 1993, edited by James Phelan, Ohio State University; the ongoing *Journal of Narrative Technique*; and the successful annual International Conferences on Narrative Literature, recently held at the University of Nice-Sophia-Antipolis (1991), Vanderbilt University (1992), Simon Fraser University (1994), and the University of Utah (1995). Glancing through tables of contents and conference programs, one notes how narrative analysis embraces not only traditional narratology—the science of narrative (Todorov)—but also a plurality of concepts such as "narrative theory," "narrative poetics" (James Phelan), "narratological criticism" (Gerald Prince),[5] and the inclusive "study of narrative literatures" that calls upon psychoanalysis, deconstruction, postmodernism, or Bakhtin's theories of novelistic discourse. The once "scientific" enterprise has attained a dynamic, if sometimes contested, elasticity. In *Fictions of Discourse: Reading Narrative Theory* (1994), Patrick O'Neill comments on how narratology's "once dominant position in international narrative theory has been . . . challenged . . . by . . . post-narratological theories" (157).

In his reply to McHale and Ronen, "What Can We Learn from Contextualist Narratology," Seymour Chatman signaled a significant shift in narratological studies, one that forms the central assumption behind this collection. He wrote that as of late, "scholars have proposed an approach to narrative which diverges sharply from structuralist narratology" (309). Labeling this new direction "contextualist," Chatman explained that the "Contextualists' chief objection to narratology is that it fails to take into account the actual setting in which literature is situated" (309): in contrast, the contextualist approach is characterized by diversity.

Throughout the two *Poetics Today* special issues on narratology (1990) and in more recent publications by narratologists, the necessity of expanding the parameters of narratology is repeatedly asserted.[6] Inevitably, one of the contexts currently receiving close attention is gender, particularly as expressed through feminist perspectives. Indeed, bringing feminist theory and perspectives into narratology has reoriented narratology. Other gender issues, including sexuality and queer theory, and poststructuralism, post-colonialism, deconstruction, cultural studies, and identity politics, all impinge on the discussion of how narratology functions by querying subject positions, cultural formation, the laws of genre, and the universality and stability of narrative forms. For example, resistance to the laws governing the genre of autobiography have led "to the proliferation of hybrid auto-biographical practices that challenge the laws of genre identified with western notions of traditional autobiography, hybrid practices Caren Kaplan describes as 'out-law' genres" (Smith, 406). Not only has narratology been adapted to historical writing and to historiography (Hayden White), but history, biography, autobiography, and traditionally devalued discourses like gossip, conversation, and silence have expanded our understanding of narrative and representation, pushing the boundaries of narrative analysis. Gossip, as Patricia Meyer Spacks reminds us, "impels plots" (7), and the tentacles of gossip extend narratologically into biography and autobiography as well as impelling the plots of novels such as *Emma*, *Persuasion*, and *Hotel du Lac*. Or, when, for example, Henry Louis Gates Jr. analyzes the rhetorical strategies of black American women writers whose narrative practice invokes the "problematic identity of the speaking subject" (144), there is a radical shift in the comparative values of narrative features: that is, speech and dialect are privileged over writing and "standard" English.

Although narratology obviously has its roots in structuralism, as the essays in this book indicate, poststructuralism—sometimes filtered through feminist theory—has problematized certain features of narratology such as the transparency of language, representation in narrative, and encoding of the self (in narratological terms: author, narrator, focalizer, character, reader) as unified, knowable, and inscribable. As Sidonie Smith and Julie Watson write in *De/Colonizing the Subject*, the "axes of the subject's identifications and experiences are multiple, because locations in gender, class, race, ethnicity, and sexuality complicate one another" (14).

Mieke Bal's response to the debate between ancients and moderns, between formalism and contexualization, summarizes the tension between the two: "Today's options seem to be either regression to earlier positions (Genette 1983), primary focus on application, or rejection of narratology. All three are problematic. . . . More important issues, mainly historical and ideological ones, have taken priority. In my own case feminist concerns have taken the lead but not, I wish to argue, at the cost of more formal narratological issues. Rather, the concern for a reliable model for narrative analysis has more and more been put to the service of other concerns considered more vital for cultural studies" ("Point of Narratology," 728–29). Other feminist critics began to call on narratological models in their own critical readings. When Robyn Warhol published her study of direct address to readers, *Gendered Interventions: Narrative Discourse in the Victorian Novel* (1989), using a model of feminist narratology, she too insisted that "nothing prohibits us from asking, among other questions about the role of social factors in shaping narrative strategies, what part the writer's gender plays in the kinds of interventions he or she uses in narrative" (5). Bal's emphasis on the importance of feminist concerns to narratology and Warhol's insistence on the practical application of what she sees as the productive interaction between gender and narrative invite us to trace the recent but contentious history of feminist narratology, for whereas feminism has adapted itself to a variety of theoretical positions from psychoanalysis to film theory, narratology has, until more recently, questioned or resisted the advances of feminism.[7]

The term "feminist narratology" begs the question of whether the modifier "feminist" refers to feminist literary theory—with its origins in the work of Kate Millett, Elaine Showalter, Ellen Moers, Hélène Cixous, and Luce Irigaray—or to feminism(s)—a movement, an ideology, a political position. Judging by the practice of the critics in this collection, the feminisms that negotiate with narratology resist codification. They range from an assimilation of male critics such as Bakhtin and Genette to French feminist theory, materialist feminism, feminist film theory as it interrogates the gaze, poststructuralism, and queer theory. For just as narratology shifts, evolves, and resists easy definition and houses many narratives, so too are there many feminism(s) and feminist literary theories.

Feminist theory has learned to resist the homogeneity that marked the urgency of its beginnings and to accommodate and indeed celebrate difference in its practice. As Elizabeth Flynn and Patrocinio Schweickart point out in their introduction to *Gender and Reading*, "Gender is a significant determinant of the interaction between text and reader . . . [and] gender-related differences are multifaceted and overdetermined" (xxviii).

It is possible that feminist narratology has some kinship with what Elaine Showalter described as "gynocriticism"—"the study of women *as writers*, and its subjects are the history, styles, themes, genres, and structures of writing by women" (184)—but what emerges from the following essays is a complex mix of interrogations about gender and its narratorial representation. For argument's sake, let's adopt Warhol's concise definition of feminist narratology as "the study of narrative structures and strategies in the context of cultural constructions of gender." In this way, we acknowledge contextualization yet retain narratology's formalism—a fluid formalism, however, that reflects the eclectic approach of the essays that follow.

Ingeborg Hoesterey, in the introduction to *Neverending Stories*, perceives narratology evolving through the incorporation of feminist studies: "The field of feminist studies has celebrated a syncretic mode for some time, borrowing from French poststructuralist writing . . . and adding semiotics and Bakhtinian concepts through the work of Julia Kristeva. This syncretism has facilitated the rise of a feminist narratology, by definition the conflation of an orientation toward form with a political agenda—an approach that has destabilized the formalism/antiformalism opposition" (10–11). Nevertheless, the road to a feminist narratology has been a rocky one, for as Susan Lanser concedes, "the two concepts I have been describing—the feminist and the narratological—have entailed separate inquiries of antithetical tendency: the one general, mimetic, and political, the other specific, semiotic, and technical" (*Fictions of Authority*, 4).

Where do we then locate those moments along the critical path where feminist critics recognized and articulated the necessity of conversing with narratology or vice versa? Certainly, women writers have been cognizant of the need to match their subject matter and subjectivity to an appropriate narrative technique, as Ann Ardis reminds us in her discussion of the new women novelists: "Issues of female identity fueled tremendous experimentation with narrative form in the 1890s" (169). From Austen's retorting through Anne Elliot that the pen has been in the hands of men to Woolf's musing that "the first thing" a woman writer would find "setting pen to paper, was that there was no common sentence ready for her use" (76), the constraints on "telling their story" have simultaneously hampered and inspired women writers. Thus, they have developed ingenious strategies to tell their story, such as Austen's invoking irony and indirection or Woolf's decentering the authorial narrator. We have been made aware how women writers sought to rewrite conventional or master plots, to write, in the words of Rachel Blau DuPlessis, beyond the ending.[8]

One of the first essays to incorporate feminist narratology was Mária Minich Brewer's 1984 "A Loosening of Tongues: From Narrative Economy to Women Writing" (to which Lanser refers in "Toward a Feminist Narratology"). Brewer addressed the relation between narrativity and women's writing, asserting that "certain critical discourses have discerned the taut web of relationships that exist between narrativity on the one hand, and power, desire, and knowledge on the other. Women's writing and its theories are essential elements in both the crisis and the generalization of narrative" (1141). Concerned about the limits placed on textual analyses, Brewer anticipated the condemnation by Chatman, Bal, and Lanser of formalist narratology's refusal of contextualization: "When narratology does attempt to account for the contextual, it does so in terms of narrative conventions and codes. Yet their capacity to account for social, historical or contextual differences always remains limited by the original formalist closure within which such codes and conventions are defined" (1143). She analyzed women's positionality in and through narrative, focusing on the fiction theories of Hélène Cixous, Annie Leclerc, Madeleine Gagnon, and Luce Irigaray, who exposed the "ideological narrativizing of women" (1146).

But it was Lanser who in 1986 first named and outlined a form of inquiry that feminist critics had been gesturing toward, calling for a feminist narratology that would examine the role of gender in the construction of narrative theory.[9] I still remember my elation when I first read Lanser's article.

Lanser was strongly rebuked, however, by Nilli Diengott (1988), who insisted that narrative categories like focalization are abstract concepts "totally indifferent to gender" and that Lanser was falling over the precipice into dangerous territory—the category of interpretation (45); Diengott claimed that Lanser's analysis was based on a confusion of theoretical poetics with other fields within the study of literature such as interpretation, historical poetics, or criticism. To Diengott, narratology is a science and "focuses only on systematic questions about the system" (48).[10] In her subsequent rebuttal of Diengott, "Shifting the Paradigm: Feminism and Narratology," Lanser replied that Diengott was trapped by the paradigm of a particular theory, reiterating the necessity for narratology to be " 'interested in' any element of discourse that contributes appreciably and regularly to the structure of narrative texts" (56). In response to this debate, Prince commented that because "one of the goals of narratology is to explain the *functioning* of narrative, narratologists must not only characterize the general pragmatic/contextual principles affecting this functioning but also devise ways of testing the possible influence of factors like gender on narrative production and processing" ("Narratology, Narratological Criticism, and Gender," 7).[11]

By 1989, feminist narratology had entered another important stage, which saw the transformation of theory and theoretical positioning into praxis. Detailed narratological analyses of women's writing had been slow to surface, for although crucial, groundbreaking thematic studies of women's narratives such as Gilbert and Gubar's *The Madwoman in the Attic* (1979) had been published, few considered the ideological implications of structure. As Warhol remarked in *Gendered Interventions*, although feminist critics expressing interest in narrative strategies (Nancy K. Miller, Rachel Blau DuPlessis, Marianne Hirsch) have looked at how "gender colors the production of *story* in narrative" (ix), "no feminist critic has taken a detailed look into gender's effect on the level of discourse in fiction" (6).

That same year, the editorial collective of *Tessera*, a journal specializing in feminist literary theory in English-Canadian and Québécois women's writing, published the special issue "Vers une narratologie féministe/Toward Feminist Narratology." Introducing this issue, a combination of theoretical and creative work, Susan Knutson argued that "feminist narratology can identify gender-determined forms in traditional narrative and analyze feminist revision of narrative grammar" ("For Feminist Narratology," 10). In accordance with the contextualist approach to narratology, she suggested that "ultimately, feminist narratology may help correct the ethnocentrism of narratology itself by clarifying that a certain dominant sense of story is culturally determined" (10).

In her 1990 essay "Bakhtin and Feminism: The Chronotopic Female Imagination," Marianne Cave summarized the Lanser-Diengott debate, agreeing with Lanser that, since context and meaning are important in narrative, feminist issues form a necessary element of narratology. She then turned to the practical application of narrative theory from a feminist perspective. Acknowledging the popularity of Bakhtin's paradigms of heteroglossia and polyphonia in the merging of feminist criticism and narratology, she engaged a Bakhtinian chronotope to read Kate Chopin's *The Awakening* and Virginia Woolf's *To the Lighthouse*. Adapting the contextualist rationale, Cave remarked, "Within current feminist criticism, then, there is a new movement to read narratives dialogically, to illuminate the embedded narrative structure which resists any simple thematic signification which threatens to limit the text to one class and race and ignores ideological tension" (118).

In her 1991 book, *Engendering the Subject: Gender and Self-Representation in Contemporary Women's Fiction*, Sally Robinson tackled feminist narratology from a different perspective. Under the subsection "Toward a Contestatory Practice of Narrative" of her introduction, Robinson explained that "most feminist accounts of the narrative production of gender have stressed the masculinist orientation of narrative and narrative theory" (17). She herself examined novels by Doris Lessing, Angela Carter, and Gayl Jones, novels that model a contestatory practice of reading. In a lengthy footnote, she contextualized her particular narrative approach within a feminist narratology: "There have been some attempts to devise a feminist narrative theory and feminist theories of reading, although none have taken quite the tack I take here. . . . Perhaps because, like Warhol, Lanser is invested in a structuralist account of narrative, she does not ask the questions about narrative's construction of gender that I am asking here. . . . I am concerned with how gender is produced *through* narrative processes, not prior to them" (198 n. 23; emphasis in original). Robinson thus extends the affective relation between narrative and gender to the construction of gender in the text and in the reader, a topic that is addressed and further developed by a number of the contributors to this volume.

In intersecting with poststructuralism, feminist narratology can shed light on the elusive or decentered subject. Because it no longer assumes (in the form of narrators, focalizers, readers, authors) a unitary subject or fixed subject position, a feminist narratological reading of postmodern texts can fold back the layers of this subject and expose ambiguities and indeterminacies in a methodical way (see Lee's and Lanser's essays). For example, in *Virginia Woolf and Postmodernism* (1991), Pamela Caughie recognized the contingent relation between narrative form and feminist ideology, noting "*that Woolf's experiments with narrative forms and functions engender certain ideological assumptions and political strategies, and thereby enable a feminist ideology to take shape*" (19; emphasis in original).

Elaborating the feminist poetics of narrative set out in "Toward a Feminist Narratology," in her 1992 *Fictions of Authority*, Lanser examined "certain configurations of textual voice" in a number of women writers, including Jane Austen, George Eliot, Virginia Woolf, Toni Morrison, and Monique Wittig. Lanser distinguished three narrative modes of voice—authorial, personal, and communal (collective)—and considered how these writers react to issues of public voice and authority. Stressing the necessary convergence of narrative form with social identity and ideology, she demonstrated how the female voice is a "site of ideological tension made visible in textual practices" (6).

This "rise of a feminist narratology" is evident in insightful articles on nineteenth-century British women writers by Beth Newman, Robyn Warhol, and Susan Winnett published over the last few years in *PMLA*. The 1994 International Conference on Narrative Literature, "Nativity and Narrativity," presented a panel discussion entitled "Why a Feminist Narratology?" Speaking from quite different perspectives, several contributors to this book (Melba Cuddy-Keane, Susan Stanford Friedman, Janet Giltrow, Kathy Mezei, and Robyn Warhol) debated how feminist narratology has contributed to their critical practice and reading.

As we trace the trajectory of feminist narratology over the last ten years, at first in theory, now in practice, we see the gradual appearance of a distinct though far from hegemonic critical enterprise. Whereas earlier theorizing about narrative was gender blind or androcentric, an emerging feminist narratology begins to critique the androcentrism of earlier stages and paradigms of narratology. Just as feminist psychoanalytic critics have objected to the male bias in theories of psychoanalysis or feminist readers have challenged the "universality" of reading in reader response criticism, we need to interrogate Genette's models, for example, and to determine whether his typologies are as gender-neutral as presumed. In *Gendered Interventions*, Warhol pointed out the gender blindness of narratology, and in "Coming Unstrung: Women, Men, Narrative, and Principles of Pleasure" (1990), Susan Winnett challenged the "gender bias of contemporary narratology" by arguing that a narratology—such as practiced by Peter Brooks and Robert Scholes—"based on the oedipal model would have to be profoundly and vulnerably male in its assumptions about what constitutes pleasure" (506). Susan Lanser in *Fictions of Authority* reminded us that "the canon on which narrative theory is grounded has been relentlessly if not intentionally man-made" (6). In "The Authorial Mind and the Question of Gender," Ina Schabert surveyed how critics have responded to the issue of gender in the authorial narrator. Rachel Blau DuPlessis, in her contribution to this volume, also queries the claim of universality implicit in Roland Barthes's and Peter Brooks's "masterplots" and their association of narrative design with male sexual trajectory and orgasm, offering an alternative narratology in her reading of "seismic orgasm" in Mina Loy's poetry. In a similar deconstruction, Christine Roulston considers Bakhtin's erasure of gender from his analysis of the sentimental novel through the perspective of Jane Austen's *Emma*.

Feminist narratology helps us understand our response to the narratives we read and to the role that gender plays in our reading. The essays here show just how diverse and complex gender's role in fictional and poetic narratives is as it incorporates gender identity, sex roles, sexual activity, and sexual preference (Delphy, 202).

In her discussion of *Persuasion*, Robyn Warhol considers "the gendered implications of the way Austen puts a novel together," presenting a "gender-conscious look at Austen's management of focalization." Warhol reveals the pervasiveness of the gaze as a narrative device and suggests that the gaze as practiced by Anne Elliot and on Anne Elliot, particularly in relation to the body, implies a "feminine form of language," an alternative to explicitly verbal discourse. Opposing the trend of many feminist critiques of Austen, Warhol shows us how "a close look at the narrative discourse of *Persuasion* yields an alternate view of Austen's literary feminism, discernible in her text's representation of a heroine's access to knowledge (through the act of looking) and to pleasure (through textual consciousness of the body)."

Whereas Warhol envisions Anne Elliot as exemplifying solidarity with other women, suggesting that Austen's heroine obtains "access to power through the feminine language of looking," Christine Roulston argues that Emma's assertion of her position of class privilege "ties her to male structures of class over and above a potential female solidarity." Roulston reads Jane Austen's *Emma* across Bakhtin to engage questions of class and gender, claiming that "Austen assumes and essentializes class difference, whereas Bakhtin silences and erases gender difference as a possible way of analyzing conflictual structures in the novel." By locating occurrences of dialogism and heteroglossia within the narrative structures and strategies of *Emma*, Roulston links Bakhtin's theories of novelistic discourse to the practice of narratology. In her analysis of the different discourses in *Emma*, by highlighting gossip in relation to private and public space, female subjectivity and empowerment, Roulston exposes the ambiguity of Austen's text, for, as she reminds us, "we cannot but question whether Austen is using gender-based discourse as a form of social critique or as means of confirming the *status quo*." When, as a new ideal heroine, Emma herself valorizes the ability to communicate over innate virtue, we begin to recognize her enduring appeal to us. By reading across Bakhtin to *Emma*, Roulston enacts the way narratology reads across feminism to give us a valuable entry into an opaque text.

Reaching back to Austen and forward to Woolf through the intermediary of Forster's interrogation of narratorial authority in *Howards End*, Kathy Mezei locates the site of gender and textual ambiguity within a specific discourse—free indirect discourse (FID). Through FID Austen allows her heroine to achieve a certain independence from the status quo and from authority in the form of the narrator. Like Roulston, Mezei notes the ironic parallels between the narrator's and Emma's plotting and matchmaking, but she locates the site of Emma's struggle for (narratorial) control within instances of FID where Emma's discourse vies with that of the narrator. A similar struggle for control between character and narrator, between male power and female desire, and between fixed gender roles assigned to the figure of the narrator is waged within FID in *Howards End* and *Mrs. Dalloway*.

Because Virginia Woolf wrote so incisively and passionately about the importance of breaking the sentence and the sequence in recognition of writing "like a woman" (81, 91), and about the patriarchal hold over women's lives and over the novel form, she rests at the center of this collection, with five contributors focusing on her novels and essays. Denise Delorey discusses the narratological and feminist implications of the "paradox of containment" in *Jacob's Room, Mrs. Dalloway*, and *To the Lighthouse*, suggesting that Woolf's "strategic focus on the parenthetical [is] a feminist narrative principle." Through the parenthetical, Woolf shifts the focus/locus of what is perceived as significant, thereby deflating masculine metanarratives, opening up space for the private and the domestic, and allowing Woolf to displace the (feminine) subject. Once again, the reader is alerted to the narratological representation of paradox and ambiguity, this time by means of a feature of discourse—the parenthetical.

Susan Stanford Friedman's reading of Woolf's first novel, *The Voyage Out*, presents a "spatialized reading strategy." Contrary to most critics' interpretation of the relation between early and final drafts, Friedman proposes that the final draft reveals Woolf's own ambivalence about marriage, sexuality, and the traditional romantic closure of the novel form more frankly than the more explicit earlier draft. Adapting Kristeva's model of spatialization in *Desire in Language* and Bakhtin's double chronotopes in *The Dialogic Imagination*, Friedman charts *The Voyage Out*'s narrative axis in order to plumb the different (repressed) stories embedded within the narrative. By diagramming the interweaving of the novel's vertical axis (literary, historical, and psychic, including the draft *Melymbrosia*) with its horizontal axis (space-time chronotope, represented world, and characters), Friedman seeks to expose the two main and paradoxical narratives of defeat (Rachel's) and victory (Woolf the writer's). What Friedman calls a "dissonant narrative" of the bildungsroman (she also cites Brontë's *Villette* as an example) is another term for what I describe here as ambiguous discourse or the indeterminacy of narrative.

Turning to Woolf's often enigmatic essays, Melba Cuddy-Keane reveals how Woolf deliberately instills indeterminacy or ambiguity into the discourse of these essays; she analyzes the rhetorical mode of conversation, which is "particularly well suited to a woman writer who seeks an alternative to the authorial/authoritative dominance of patriarchal discourse." Like Roulston discussing Austen, Cuddy-Keane aligns Woolf with Bakhtin, this time to point out that although Bakhtin has been celebrated for his theory of double-voiced discourse (1929), Woolf had even earlier (1923) "proposed her own version of the dialogic"—conversation. Cuddy-Keane then continues on to show how conversation for Woolf "became the informing trope of her critical prose," how innovative and subversive that trope proved to be, and how unrecognized. As in the previous essays, Cuddy-Keane emphasizes our role as readers both in untangling and in responding to her subject's narrative strategies.

Like Delorey, Patricia Matson is interested in Woolf's conflation of sexuality and textuality and her challenge to the "authority of the humanist subject and the authority of patriarchal value systems." Through detailed textual analyses of moments of discourse, Matson probes the relationship between codes of oppression and the possibilities of transgression and resistance. She decodes the writing of writing as subject and proceeds to show how "writing in and of itself is an act of resistance" and how the "authority of the 'patriarchs and pedagogues' is undercut and challenged at the level of syntax."

Rachel Blau DuPlessis is the only one to discuss a poet—the modernist Mina Loy—providing us with insight into *poetic* narrative strategies. DuPlessis reminds us (via Dorothy Richardson) how intensely the ideological link between narrative and sexual conventions was debated in early modernist writing. In her personal advocacy of the contextualist approach of narratology, she firmly insists on completing narrative poetics with a "sociological poetics." DuPlessis discusses Loy's "Feminist Manifesto" and her long poem "Love Songs to Joannes" in terms of reading "sexual intercourse as a site wherein various agents and cultural processes are exposed," contrasting Loy's narrative trajectory of sexual intercourse—seismic orgasm—with that of D. H. Lawrence's in *Lady Chatterley's Lover*. For Loy, "seismic orgasm" is "the only site in which gender binaries are rendered inoperable," the "only point at which the interests of the sexes merge."

In "Ironies of Politeness in Anita Brookner's *Hotel du Lac*," Janet Giltrow approaches textuality in an equally radical way. Like Matson, Giltrow emphasizes the importance of penetrating beyond narratological surfaces into the deep structures of syntax and semantics; like Roulston, Warhol, and Mezei, she is intrigued by the narratological (and discursive) and gendered implications of irony (and gossip). By setting out before us specific features of discourse—presupposing and agentless expressions, modalities such as "naturally," "of course," and projection—as materials of politeness, as an encoding of ordered social relations, Giltrow shows us that Brookner, as do Austen and Woolf, mounts a (coded) attack on the institution of marriage as closure and as the "conclusive social relation."

Alison Lee's reading of Angela Carter's *The Passion of New Eve*, in which the narrator transforms from a male into a female voice, presents us with a text that concretely and ironically engages gender and narrativity. The hints of gender ambiguity that Mezei had observed in Austen, Forster, and Woolf become the subject of Carter's novel. As Lee indicates, because the narrator's gender shifts and because texts are narrated in time, difficulties beset a reader in pinning down the gender of the narrative voice at specific moments in the novel; focalization is indeterminate; it is as difficult to distinguish between the narrating and the experiencing self as between male and female language and voice. This is indeterminacy and dissonance rendered graphically narratological, though Lee reminds us, "Gender does not determine narrative; it makes narrative identity as complex as gender identity." Focalization, as other contributors have noted in Austen, Woolf, and Loy, "creates a political framework," and the significance of looking— or what Lee, echoing Carter, calls "persistence of vision"—constructs the gendered subjectivity. Lee suggests that it is the "heteroglossia, the multiplicity, the undermining of binaries that make a text like Carter's feminist in both its narrative structure and its story."

Who better to close this discussion of the discourses of ambiguity than Susan Lanser, who, by naming feminist narratology, was the impetus for the book? Lee begins her discussion of gender and narrativity with Jeanette Winterson's *Written on the Body*; here, Lanser explores *Written on the Body* as the embodiment of the complicated relations between sex, gender, sexuality, and narrative. "Queering Narratology" argues for the inclusion of sex, gender, and sexuality in narrative analysis and questions the relegating of these essential elements to the margins of narratology. Marking or unmarking the sex and gender of the heterodiegetic, autodiegetic, or homodiegetic narrator matters and has always mattered—as several other contributors point out. In the context of Jeanette Winterson's *Written on the Body*, where the narrator's sex is deliberately elided from the text and where his/her sexuality is ambiguous, Lanser looks at how this deliberate silence or absence drives narratives and implicates readers. It is time, she suggests, to introduce gender, sex, and sexuality, along with contextuality and interpretation, into narrative poetics and to begin the process of queering and querying narratology.

As a coda to the preceding examples of feminist narratology, Linda Hutcheon's essay sets out some of the issues surrounding (meta)narrative, postmodernism, and feminisms. In recognition of the variety of narrative systems, she expands the concept of narrative to include metanarrative, pointing to moments of conflation between postmodernism and feminisms as both, for example, offer parodic representations in their critique of metanarrative. Whereas feminisms seek to effect real social change and therefore foreground their political agenda, postmodernism insists on incredulity toward metanarratives, although in response to feminist influences it occasionally incorporates gender into its parodic structures.

Hutcheon's acknowledgment of the paradoxes that arise out of theoretical positions echoes the other contributors' uncovering of contradictions that destabilize readers as they jostle to locate themselves in relation to textual evasions. And so feminism and narratology combine in the praxis of feminist narratology to address these contradictions, evasions, and ambiguities—and to invoke and provoke them.

NOTES

1. The term, according to several critics, was coined by Todorov in 1969: "a science that does not yet exist, let us say, 'narratology,' the science of the narrative" (*Grammaire du Décaméron*, 10).

2. For different "stories" and summaries, see also Shlomith Rimmon-Kenan's *Narrative Fiction: Contemporary Poetics*; Wallace Martin's *Recent Theories of Narrative*; Terry Eagleton's subsection on narratology in *Literary Theory*; chapter 1 of Peter Brooks's *Reading for the Plot*; Ingeborg Hoesterey's historical introduction to *Neverending Stories: Toward a Critical Narratology*; or Thomas Pavel's "Narrative Tectonics," in which he moves onto textual, psychoanalytical, deconstructionist, reader-oriented, and like challenges to the originary formalist views. These summaries reflect the narrators' intellectual backgrounds—Israeli poetics, American Freudian, British Marxist, and German phenomenology.

3. See also Philippe Hamon's version of narratology's evolution: "Narratology has evolved (or is evolving) by dissemination. At first centered around essentially linguistic and oral objects (songs, myths, tales), it rapidly found itself confronted with written literary messages, plurisemiotic objects (films, comic strips, theater), nonlinguistic objects (paintings, photographs, architecture), and even nonsemiotic objects (a 'semantics of human acts,' sketched here or there). Among the most interesting repercussions, and sometimes the most unpredictable, of this scattering (which proves the vitality of the body of axioms and postulates that define narratology), let us point out the semiotics of passion elaborated around Greimas (Jacques Fontanille and A. J. Greimas's *Sémiotique des passions [Semiotics of the Pas-*

sions]), which renews a long rhetorical tradition going back to Aristotle, and the narrative semiotics of biblical texts (probably inaugurated by a collective study in 1971 *Exégèse et herméneutique*—which includes an article by R. Barthes—and then continued by the 'Groupe d'Entrevernes' and the collection 'Parole de Dieu,' published by Seuil), which also renews a long and prestigious tradition, the exegesis and hermeneutics of sacred texts" (364–65).

4. See the two ensuing issues of *Poetics Today*—"Narratology Revisited I" (Summer 1990) and "Narratology Revisited II" (Winter 1990).

5. Prince feels that it is not the function of narratology to engage in interpretation that would fall under the aegis of "narratological criticism."

6. In her 1989 review of Bal's *Narratology*, Ruth Ronen points out that while "researchers in narratology are relatively in agreement as to the definition of basic concepts and procedures: narrative levels, narrative structures, temporal order, causality, perspective, types of narration . . . the a-contextual view of narrative concepts, the belief in the self-sufficiency of texts and the playing down of referentiality, fictionality and readership" create a "discrepancy between the 'ideology' behind the structuralist paradigm and its methodological appeal." The change from structuralist to current narrative theory "is reflected in new conceptions of the interaction between texts and readers" (188–89).

7. See also Lanser's account of how narratology and feminism are perceived differently: "With a few exceptions, feminist criticism does not ordinarily consider the technical aspects of narration, and narrative poetics does not ordinarily consider the social properties and political implications of narrative voice. Formalist poetics may seem to feminists naively empiricist, masking ideology as objective truth, sacrificing significance for precision, incapable of producing distinctions that are textually meaningful" (*Fictions of Authority*, 4–5).

8. See, for example, Alison Booth, *Famous Last Words: Changes in Gender and Narrative Closure*; Rachel Blau DuPlessis, *Writing beyond the Ending: Narrative Strategies of Twentieth-Century Women Writers*; Gayle Greene, *Changing the Story: Feminist Fiction and the Tradition*; Sandra M. Gilbert and Susan Gubar, *The Madwoman in the Attic: The Woman Writer and the Nineteenth-Century Literary Imagination*; Molly Hite, *The Other Side of the Story: Structures and Strategies of Contemporary Feminist Narrative*; Ellen G. Friedman and Miriam Fuchs, *Breaking the Sequence: Women's Experimental Fiction*.

9. Lanser also raised what she felt were two related issues: (1) the status of narrative as mimesis or semiosis ("structuralist narratology has suppressed the representational aspects of fiction and emphasized the semiotic, while feminist criticism has done the opposite" ["Feminist Narratology," 344]); and (2) the importance of context for determining meaning (343). As this introduction shows, Brewer's and Lanser's validation of context was later echoed in Chatman, Bal, Prince, and Warhol.

10. Diengott tries to dismiss Warhol's essay "Toward a Theory of the Engaging Narrator: Earnest Interventions in Gaskell, Stowe, and Eliot," which Lanser cites as an example of feminist narratology in practice. Is it not more important to read texts through narratology than to dispute taxonomies and definitions?

11. See Prince's revised version of this argument, "On Narratology: Criteria, Corpus, Context," *Narrative* 3.1 (January 1995): 73–84. See also Susan Lanser's response to Prince in *Narrative* 3.1, "Sexing the Narrative: Propriety, Desire, and the Engendering of Narratology."

WORKS CITED

Ardis, Ann. *New Women, New Novels: Feminism and Early Modernism*. New Brunswick: Rutgers University Press, 1990.

Austen, Jane. *Persuasion*. Ed. John Davie. Oxford: Oxford University Press, 1991.

Bakhtin, Mikhail. *The Dialogic Imagination: Four Essays*. Ed. Michael Holquist. Trans. Caryl Emerson and Michael Holquist. Austin: University of Texas Press, 1981.

Bal, Mieke. *Narratology: Introduction to the Theory of Narrative*. Trans. Christine van Boheemen. Toronto: University of Toronto Press, 1985.

——. "The Point of Narratology." *Poetics Today* 11 (1990): 727–54.

Barthes, Roland. "Introduction to the Structural Analysis of Narratives." *Image-Music-Text*. Trans. Stephen Heath. New York: Hill and Wang, 1977. 79–124.

Booth, Alison, ed. *Famous Last Words: Changes in Gender and Narrative Closure*. Charlottesville: University Press of Virginia, 1993.

Brewer, Mária Minich. "A Loosening of Tongues: From Narrative Economy to Women Writing." *Modern Language Notes* (hereafter abbreviated *MLN*) 99.5 (1984): 1141–61.

Brooke-Rose, Christine. "Whatever Happened to Narratology?" *Poetics Today* 11.2 (Summer 1990): 283–94.

Brooks, Peter. *Reading for the Plot: Design and Intention in Narrative*. New York: Vintage, 1985.

Caughie, Pamela. *Virginia Woolf and Postmodernism: Literature in Quest and Question of Itself*. Urbana: University of Illinois Press, 1991.

Cave, Marianne. "Bakhtin and Feminism: The Chronotopic Female Imagination." *Women's Studies* 18 (1990): 117–27.

Chatman, Seymour. "What Can We Learn from Contextualist Narratology?" *Poetics Today* 11 (1990): 309–28.

Delphy, Christine. "The Invention of French Feminism: An Essential Move." *Yale French Studies* 87 (1995): 190–221.

Diengott, Nilli. "Narratology and Feminism." *Style* 22.1 (1988): 42–51.

DuPlessis, Rachel Blau. *Writing beyond the Ending: Narrative Strategies of Twentieth-Century Women Writers*. Bloomington: Indiana University Press, 1985.

Eagleton, Terry. *Literary Theory: An Introduction*. Oxford: Basil Blackwell, 1985.

Flynn, Elizabeth A., and Patrocinio Schweickart, eds. *Gender and Reading: Essays on Readers, Texts, and Contexts*. Baltimore: Johns Hopkins University Press, 1986.

Friedman, Ellen G., and Miriam Fuchs, eds. *Breaking the Sequence: Women's Experimental Fiction*. Princeton: Princeton University Press, 1989.

Gates, Henry Louis, Jr. "Color Me Zora: Alice Walker's (Re)Writing of the Speakerly Text." In *Intertextuality and Contemporary American Fiction*. Ed. Patrick O'Donnell and Robert Con Davis, 144–67. Baltimore: Johns Hopkins University Press, 1989.

Genette, Gérard. *Narrative Discourse: An Essay in Method*. Trans. Jane E. Lewin. Ithaca: Cornell University Press, 1980.

Gilbert, Sandra M., and Susan Gubar. *The Madwoman in the Attic: The Woman Writer and the Nineteenth-Century Literary Imagination*. New Haven: Yale University Press, 1979.

Greene, Gayle. *Changing the Story: Feminist Fiction and the Tradition*. Bloomington: Indiana University Press, 1991.

Greimas, A. J. "Narrative Grammar: Units and Levels." *MLN* 86.6 (1971): 793–806.

Hamon, Philippe. "Narratology: Status and Outlook." *Style* 26.4 (1992): 362–67.

Hite, Molly. *The Other Side of the Story: Structures and Strategies of Contemporary Feminist Narrative*. Ithaca: Cornell University Press, 1989.

Hoesterey, Ingeborg. Introduction. *Neverending Stories: Toward a Critical Narratology*. Princeton: Princeton University Press, 1992.

Hrushovski, Benjamin. "Theory of Narrative and Poetics of Fiction: Editorial." *Poetics Today* 1 (1980): 5–6, 208.

Knutson, Susan. "For Feminist Narratology." *Tessera* 7 (Fall 1989): 10–14.

Lanser, Susan S. *Fictions of Authority: Women Writers and Narrative Voice*. Ithaca: Cornell University Press, 1992.

——. "Shifting the Paradigm: Feminism and Narratology." *Style* 22.1 (1988): 52–60.

——. "Toward a Feminist Narratology." *Style* 20.3 (1986): 341–63.

McHale, Brian, and Ruth Ronen. "Narratology Revisited I: Editors' Note." *Poetics Today* 11 (1990):iii–iv.

Martin, Wallace. *Recent Theories of Narrative*. Ithaca: Cornell University Press, 1987.

O'Neill, Patrick. *Fictions of Discourse: Reading Narrative Theory*. Toronto: University of Toronto Press, 1994.

Pavel, Thomas G. "Narrative Tectonics." *Poetics Today* 11 (1990): 349–64.

Poetics Today: "Narratology I: Poetics of Fiction," 1 (1980); "Narratology II: The Fictional Text and the Reader," 1 (1980); "Narratology III: Narrators and Voices in Fiction," 2 (1981).

Poetics Today: "Narratology Revisited I," 11 (1990); "Narratology Revisited II," 11 (1990).

Prince, Gerald. *A Dictionary of Narratology*. Lincoln: University of Nebraska Press, 1987.

——. "Narratology, Narratological Criticism, and Gender." Paper delivered in honor of Lubomír Doležel at the colloquium "Fiction and Worlds," University of Toronto. Toronto, 1990. In *Fiction Updated: The Theory of Fictionality and Contemporary Humanities*. Eds. Colin Mihailescu and Walid Harmarneh. Toronto: University of Toronto Press, forthcoming.

Rimmon-Kenan, Shlomith. *Narrative Fiction: Contemporary Poetics*. New York: Methuen, 1983.

Robinson, Sally. *Engendering the Subject: Gender and Self-Representation in Contemporary Women's Fiction*. New York: State University of New York Press, 1991.

Ronen, Ruth. "Review of Mieke Bal's *Narratology: Introduction to the Theory of Narrative.*" *Canadian Review of Comparative Literature* 16.1–2 (March–June 1989): 188–92.

Schabert, Ina. "The Authorial Mind and the Question of Gender." In *Telling Stories: Studies in Honour of Ulrich Broic on the Occasion of His 6oth Birthday*. Eds. Elmar Lehmann and Bernd Lenz. Amsterdam: Grüner, 1992, 312–29.

Showalter, Elaine. "Feminist Criticism in the Wilderness." *Critical Inquiry* 8.2 (1981): 179–206.

Smith, Sidonie. "Who's Talking/Who's Talking Back? The Subject of Personal Narrative." *Signs* 18.2 (Winter 1993): 392–407.

Smith, Sidonie, and Julia Watson, eds. *De/Colonizing the Subject: The Politics of Gender in Women's Autobiography*. Minneapolis: University of Minnesota Press, 1992.

Spacks, Patricia Meyer. *Gossip*. New York: Knopf, 1985.

Todorov, Tzvetan. *Grammaire du Décaméron*. The Hague: Mouton, 1969.

———. "The Grammar of Narrative." In *The Poetics of Prose*. Trans. Richard Howard. Ithaca: Cornell University Press, 1977. 108–19.

"Vers une narratologie féministe/Toward Feminist Narratology." *Tessera* 7 (Fall 1989).

Warhol, Robyn R. *Gendered Interventions: Narrative Discourse in the Victorian Novel*. New Brunswick: Rutgers University Press, 1989.

———. "Toward a Theory of the Engaging Narrator: Earnest Interventions in Gaskell, Stowe, and Eliot." *PMLA* 101 (1986): 811–18.

Winnett, Susan. "Coming Unstrung: Women, Men, Narrative, and Principles of Pleasure." *PMLA* 105 (1990): 505–18.

Woolf, Virginia. *A Room of One's Own*. 1928. Middlesex: Penguin, 1965.

the look, the body, and the

heroine of *persuasion*

A Feminist-Narratological View of Jane Austen

robyn | warhol

ane Austen's *Persuasion* (1818) is a novel constructed around what was, for its time, a radically unusual narrative premise: the love affair that should have culminated in a marriage to end a conventional romance has gone awry, and the heroine of the piece must begin again, eight and a half years later, on her quest for narrative closure. As Nancy Miller pointed out some time ago, the feminocentric text of Austen's period—the novel with a female protagonist—could reach closure in one of two ways: the heroine can get married, or she can die. Either resolution depends on a change of status for the heroine's body: it can cease being virginal, or it can cease to live. For some feminist critics, Austen's apparent willingness to remain locked into this binary conception of the possibilities for heroines has been a problem.[1] Focusing on the heroine's body, however, I read *Persuasion* as a story of oppositions being called into question, as well as a story of lost love regained. Feminist readers in the 1990s may wish, like Anne Elliot, to reclaim an old attachment.

What happens when a feminist resists the powerful temptation to think of Jane Austen's heroines as persons and scrutinizes them as functions of texts instead? Feminist narratology, which is the study of narrative structures and strategies in the context of cultural constructions of gender, provides a method for reclaiming Jane Austen as a feminist novelist. It gives us the analytical tools to distinguish her "story" (*what* happens in a text) from her "discourse" (*how* the story is rendered in language). In Austen, the interplay between *story*, in which the independent heroine must, as some critics have it, "swindle into a wife," and *discourse*, through which traditional power relations can be subverted, carries important implications for feminist literary theory.

A close look at the narrative discourse of *Persuasion* yields an alternate view of Austen's literary feminism, discernible in her text's representation of a heroine's access to knowledge (through the act of looking) and to pleasure (through textual consciousness of the body). Although some non-feminist critical analysis of Austen's narrative techniques has laid a foundation for talking about the forms Austen employs in her fiction—especially free indirect discourse, or what Dorrit Cohn calls "narrated monologue" (109)—feminist narratology can provide a context for politicizing that analysis, for considering the gendered implications of the way Austen puts a novel together.[2]

As an alternative to a story-centered analysis of *Persuasion*, I propose to take a gender-conscious look at Austen's management of focalization, that is, her use of Anne Elliot as the central consciousness through which the story gets transmitted. As Louise Flavin observes, "In no other Austen novel is so much of what happens filtered through a central consciousness" (23); Flavin describes the resulting effect as a "complexity of polyvocality . . . achieved by having a narrator report what a character hears another character say that another character has said" (21). Of course, the characters—Anne included—are textual constructs, not literally "consciousnesses": as Michael Orange puts it, "It might be better to say that the narration filters knowledge of aspects of one part of itself, which it represents as 'Captain Wentworth,' by means almost exclusively of another, labeled 'Anne Elliot.' There is no Captain Wentworth beyond Anne Elliot's point of view until very late in the novel, and no Anne Elliot outside this narration" (66).[3] Still, studies of focalization in this novel typically conclude that the layering of voices in free indirect discourse has the effect of giving "the illusion of depth to character," to use John Dussinger's phrase (99). Yet while everyone grants that "Anne Elliot" seems "deep," no one stops to consider what it means for this focal character to be constructed as female.

At the simplest level, it means that the novel's heroine must be almost obsessed with the act of looking, an activity that—as Claudia Johnson has established and as I will explain below—was not associated with female characters in the novels of Austen's predecessors. This heroine *has* to look, for the conditions of narration depend entirely on her observing everything that ought to be told. Anne's visual perceptions are crucial to the narrative movement, particularly because hers is a world bound by proprieties which dictate that so many things "should not be said" (Austen, 238), or indeed—as Janis Stout has pointed out—a world where verbal language is so limited in its capacity to convey significant feelings. Looking and interpreting others' looks come to function for Austen's last heroine as an alternative language, a means of communication without recourse to words.

Because looking is a physical action, a function of those organs called eyes, representations of the act of looking continually draw attention in this text to the heroine's own body: its placement on the scene she is observing, its visceral reaction to what she sees, and its appearance as mirrored in the remarks of others on Anne's "looks." The female body, therefore, comes into the narrative foreground not just as the vehicle of looking in the novel but also as the object of the gaze of other characters. Anne Elliot has no moment of looking at herself, no glance into a mirror or contemplation of any part of her body she might see—she becomes visible in the text only through the comments others make about how she looks. The first description of Anne is filtered through her father's perspective (although, since Anne is the focal character, I read this passage as her understanding of her father's view of her appearance): "A few years before, Anne Elliot had been a very pretty girl, but her bloom had vanished early; and as even in its height, her father had found little to admire in her, (so totally different were her delicate features and mild dark eyes from his own); there could be nothing in them now that she was faded and thin, to excite his esteem" (37). Later, as Anne's "bloom" begins to return, the narrative continues to convey Anne's appearance through her father's remarks. The narrator reports that "Anne and her father chancing to be alone together, he began to compliment her on her improved looks; he thought her 'less thin in her person, in her cheeks; her skin, her complexion, greatly improved—clearer, fresher'" (158). At no point in the novel does Anne take an unmediated look at her own body; her consciousness registers her appearance only through what others tell her about how she looks.

This heroine's body takes shape, then, in the objectifying view of other characters, especially male characters. When she feels herself to be under someone's scrutiny, Anne reacts with "sensations," sometimes pleasurable, sometimes disagreeable. This focus on looks and looking results in *Persuasion*'s being the most physical, the most literally "sensational," of Austen's novels, in that the heroine's experiences—and the textual transmission of them through her perspective—are thoroughly grounded in the senses.[4]

The female body comes explicitly into the foreground in the famous argument scene between Anne Elliot and Captain Harville over the differences between the sexes. The point under debate is whether men's or women's love lasts longest "when existence or when hope is gone"; Harville argues for men's greater constancy, on the grounds of " 'a true analogy between our bodily frames and our mental; . . . as our bodies are the strongest, so are our feelings' " (236). Anne counters that if men's feelings are strongest, " 'the same spirit of analogy will authorise me to assert that ours are the most tender.' " In this physical connection, "tenderness" implies soreness, sensitivity, and susceptibility to pain, and Anne's position as focal character—as much as her experience as heroine—puts her in a peculiar position of authority to speak of such physical vulnerability. By making Anne's the central consciousness and by placing her body always on the narrative scene no matter how "painful" or "agitating" to Anne the circumstances, the novelist subjects her heroine's body to a kind of textual violence. Early in the novel and throughout her period of uncertainty about Wentworth's marital intentions, Anne is markedly uncomfortable in her body, uncomfortable with the female body in general and particularly with the "large, fat" person of Mrs. Musgrove. But by gradually bringing together Anne's capacity for looking (and its attendant power to gain knowledge within the public realm) with the heroine's growing appreciation for the life of the body (and its intensely private set of significances), the text blurs the strictly binary divisions between external appearance and intrinsic value, between seeing and being seen, and between the public and the private realism that have operated under patriarchy (in Jane Austen's time as in ours) to keep women oppressed. The feminism of Austen's last novel resides not so much in the heroine's marrying the man of her choice as in the text's dismantling those oppositions which it represents as making life in the female body so painful.

Before looking more closely at the female body in *Persuasion*, though, I want to return to the question of "looking" itself, especially in its function here as a narrative device. On the level of narrative discourse, I will be concentrating here on the "focalization" of Austen's text in the sense proposed by Gérard Genette and defined in Gerald Prince's *Dictionary of Narratology*: "The perspective in terms of which the narrated situations and events are presented; the perceptual or conceptual position in terms of which they are rendered" (31). To find the focal character of a passage of narration, one asks whether there are different answers to the questions, Who is speaking? and Who is seeing? In this novel the nameless narrator speaks, but Anne generally is the one who sees. *Persuasion* is, therefore, structured by "internal focalization" (to use Genette's term), because the perspective is—as Prince puts it—"locatable (in one character or another) and entails conceptual or perceptual restrictions (with what is presented being governed by one character's or another's perspective)" (32). Genette's concept of focalization closely resembles what film theorists call the "gaze" in visual texts.

It seems to me that narratology has not made as much use as it might of the notion of the "gaze" as it has developed in film studies. Just as the gaze in film and the focalization of verbal texts are similar in their function, they might also resemble each other in their potential for carrying connotations of gender. Feminist film theorists (notably Laura Mulvey and Mary Ann Doane) have argued from a psychoanalytic perspective that the position of spectatorship in Hollywood movies is always male; some commentators, such as John Berger, extend this observation into culture at large: "*Men act and women appear*. Men look at women. Women watch themselves being looked at" (47). Whether this is invariably true of the gaze in popular culture has become debatable, leading some feminists to posit a female viewing position that is not, as Mulvey's and Doane's work suggests, a kind of cross-dressing or adoption of a masculine subject position but something distinct. Suzanne Moore has suggested that a distinctly "female gaze" might exist and that if it does, "it does not simply replicate a monolithic and masculinized stare, but instead involves a whole variety of looks and glances—an interplay of possibilities" (Moore in Gamman and Marshment, 59). Moore, very careful to avoid implying that gendered positions are "fixed outside social conditions," offers a liberation from what some see as an essentializing tendency in the more properly psychoanalytic theory of the gaze. Feminist narratology might begin from Moore's position, arguing that in a given text the focalization represents a feminine perspective. In fiction there is no structural reason why the position of spectatorship must necessarily be male. What *Persuasion* does is to distinguish among kinds of looking, juxtaposing the feminine focalization that relies on the heroine's viewpoint with the objectifying gaze—often associated in this novel with male characters—which others in the text direct at the heroine's body.

In verbal narration, as in film, the "gaze" and the "look" are distinct from each other, though often related: the first occurs in the realm of the "extra-diegetic," outside the world of the story, whereas the second can be located inside, as something exchanged among characters "intradiegetically."[5] The extradiegetic gaze frames the reader's view of what is happening in the fictional world, whereas the intradiegetic look is one among the thousands of events that are represented as occurring there. When a novel is as carefully focalized through one character as is *Persuasion*, the gaze imitates that of the focal character; in this novel, then, the extradiegetic gaze and Anne's intradiegetic look are often identical. Far from placing Anne in a male subject position, this arrangement (working together with certain ethical structures within the story, which I will outline below) functions to gender looking as a feminine activity. The result is to overturn the tradition of the gaze that Claudia Johnson has so persuasively traced through eighteenth-century novels of sensibility.

In a discussion of Austen's relation to the politics of sensibility, Johnson asserts, "Sentimental moral theory of the eighteenth century is essentially spectatorial, exploring the moralizing effects of seeing ourselves beheld in the gaze of others" (169). Commenting on Marianne Dashwood's physical decline in *Sense and Sensibility* as part of the tradition of heroines who fade out or die in sentimental novels, Johnson explains that such novels emphasize the emotions inspired in men (such as Col. Brandon and Willoughby) by the spectacle of the heroine's suffering body. "What is emphasized in this literature," according to Johnson, "is the feeling of the onlooker, not the feeling of the sufferer," and she argues convincingly that this pattern is reproduced in Austen's first published novel (169).

As Johnson sees it, the tradition "locks women within an objective status, as things wept over" by men of sensibility. "Women, for their part, rarely look," she says. "Usually they are too insane—like Sterne's mad Maria or Burney's 'idiot' woman—to return a lucid gaze; too ashamed—like Goldsmith's Olivia—to meet a looker's eyes; or too delirious—like Marianne Dashwood—to care" (169). Given that Marianne fits the pattern of the fading heroine, a look at Anne Elliot will reveal that she represents a significant break with this model of heroism. Anne, unlike Marianne (and unlike Marianne's foil, her sister Elinor) begins the novel in a physically "faded and thin" state, for "her bloom had vanished early" (*Persuasion*, 37). In the course of the story, however, she reverses the experience of the fading heroine by regaining her "looks" (in the eyes, at least, of those characters who notice and comment on them); what's more, Anne is represented as a heroine whose gaze is not just lucid but empowering and whose subjective experience of her own bodily feelings removes her entirely from the ranks of the objectified heroines of sensibility.

In arguing that Anne's gaze, as well as her visibility within the text, are sources of unprecedented power for the heroine, I am building on the conclusions of Paul Morrison's elegant and persuasive reading of *Northanger Abbey*, the posthumous novel published simultaneously with *Persuasion*. Moving beyond the frame of reference Claudia Johnson uses—the realm of sentimental fiction—to view the Jane Austen heroine from a Foucauldian perspective as the object of panoptic surveillance, Morrison convincingly shows that Catherine Moreland—the heroine whose reading (in)ability has so often been the focus of critical comment—exists in her text as an object to be read by the patriarchal characters who surround her, as well as by the extradiegetic audience. Morrison focuses on Catherine's positioning within "an openness that encloses, a visibility that incarcerates: the oxymorons of panoptic power" under which "visibility or, better, legibility is a gender-specific trap" (12, 14). Without disputing Morrison's point about the ways *Northanger Abbey*'s heroine is denied access to power and to knowledge, being herself the thing to be seen and be known, I argue that *Persuasion* places its heroine in a distinctly different relation to the act of seeing (and of being seen). From a narratological perspective, the crucial difference between the two novels is that *Northanger Abbey* is less exclusively focalized through the heroine than is *Persuasion*. By making Anne the focal character, Austen's text grants her the power to read others' looks, a power that this text—as if engaged in a dispute with *Northanger Abbey*—genders as specifically feminine.

In *Persuasion*, looking at others is the most reliable means available to characters for comprehending one another's value and meaning, but not everybody can do it well. Looking at physical detail to read interior significance is constructed in this novel as a distinctly feminine thing to do. As the focal character, Anne looks often, and with accuracy, at others: what she deduces from people's "looks" is usually borne out by the plot. By contrast, the men in the novel who are preoccupied with looks and looking—Sir Walter Elliot and his heir, Mr. William Walter Elliot—look to objectify, to fix the objects of their gaze with a value strictly commensurate with appearances. The text contrasts these two Walter Elliots with other men— particularly Wentworth and Admiral Croft—who do not, without prompting, even see the body when they look at another person, men whose masculine worthiness is continually endorsed by the story. If the Walter Elliots' look objectifies the body and the naval men's look ignores it, the heroine's look comprehends both interior and exterior experience, both the body she sees and the significances she reads in its expressions. Anne's capacity to look, so crucial to the narrative structure, is part of the text's construction of femininity.

Sir Walter Elliot, with his mirror-lined dressing room and his unambiguous vanity ("the beginning and the end of [his character]," 36), is, of course, the figure most obsessed with physical appearances. His persistent comments on people's looks become predictable, even parodic ("How is Mary looking?" is, for instance, the first question he asks about an absent daughter [155]). But they serve a wider purpose than caricature: they are a window in the text opening onto physical characteristics that don't typically make their way into Austen's descriptions. Thanks to Sir Walter's remarks (rendered either in dialogue or in free indirect discourse), we know that Mary's nose was red the last time he saw her; that Mrs. Clay has an awkward wrist, a projecting tooth, and freckles; that Lady Russell is developing crow's-feet around her eyes; and that Mr. Elliot is "very much under-hung" (his lower jaw juts forward). Caught in Sir Walter's look, Austen's characters take on a more vivid physicality than her narrators ordinarily give them.

The narrator (who may or may not be using free indirect discourse to echo Anne's opinion of her father) calls Sir Walter's obsession with looks into question in terms of gender: "Few women could think more of their personal appearance than he did" (36). In other words, Sir Walter's concern for looks and looking breaks the stereotype dictating that women are more vain than men, but the narrator's remark also implies that the character's relation to looking has feminine connotations. Sir Walter occupies a stereotypically feminine viewing position, too, in the evaluative way that he looks at men to judge their relative (sexual) attractiveness. He likes Col. Wallis for being "not an ill-looking man" (153), approves Mr. Elliot as being "better to look at than most men" (154), and finally reconciles himself to having Wentworth as a son-in-law after he "saw him repeatedly by daylight and eyed him well" (250). Of course, Sir Walter looks at women, too; his complaint that on the streets of Bath one handsome woman "would be followed by thirty, or five-and-thirty frights" (155) reveals, though, that he looks always to objectify, always to evaluate the body's surface.

Admiral Croft—Sir Walter's foil in so many respects, in terms of class as well as gender—bears an opposite relation to looking. The contrast between them, significant because the more masculine self-made man succeeds in handling the responsibilities the landed nobleman had abrogated, becomes obvious when the admiral confesses to Anne that he has removed most of the "looking glasses" from the master dressing room at Kellynch

(142–43). The admiral has no interest in looking at himself, nor is he troubled by the ravages of sea life that Sir Walter perceives in all naval men's complexions. A less obvious contrast, though, is the difference between the ways the two men look at others. Whereas Sir Walter's look lights on the body—on skin, on bone structure, on teeth—Admiral Croft does not distinguish physical features. He mentions, quite unself-consciously, that he can see no difference between Louisa and Henrietta Musgrove; not only does he not look for evaluative purposes, he evidently does not perceive bodies at all. In only one scene is the admiral represented as looking concertedly at anything: Anne comes on him peering into a shop window at an unrealistically executed painting of a boat. The scene comes on the heels of a passage explaining that Anne "saw [the Crofts] wherever she went" in Bath and that "she always watched them" for the signs of their happy union (179). This time she "might have passed [the admiral] unseen," as his gaze is wholly absorbed in, as he puts it, "staring at a picture." He is interested in the inaccurate representation of an object; his absorption in that spectacle is quickly juxtaposed with his utter lack of interest in people's looks. He draws Anne's attention to various naval acquaintances who pass, but never remarks on their appearances. "If you look across the street, you will see Admiral Brand coming down and his brother. Shabby fellows, both of them! I am glad they are not on this side of the way. . . . They played me a pitiful trick once" (180). Their shabbiness, in other words, is a factor of their behavior, not their dress. As the male partner in the novel's one solidly "attached and happy" marriage (88), Admiral Croft embodies a masculine propensity for *not* looking at the body or its ornaments.

This textual pattern may account for Wentworth's failing to recognize Anne's physical attractiveness until the moment at Lyme when he sees Mr. Elliot's admiring glance at her. Having judged Anne's looks to be unpleasantly "altered" on first seeing her again, Wentworth—true to the text's standard for masculine form—evidently never looks at her again until that moment. When Elliot, as yet unacquainted with his cousin Anne, passes her on the steps to the beach, "Anne's face caught his eye, and he looked at her with a degree of earnest admiration, which she could not be insensible of. . . . It was evident that the gentleman, (completely a gentleman in manner) admired her exceedingly. Captain Wentworth looked round at her instantly in a way which shewed his noticing of it. He gave her a momentary glance,—a glance of brightness, which seemed to say, 'That man is struck with you,—and even I, at this moment, see something like Anne Elliot again' " (124–25). Though the narrator's gratuitous insistence on Elliot's degree of gentlemanliness hints that the frank look he casts on Anne might not be appropriate to his class status, it is not until much later that Anne will conclude from his treatment of Mrs. Smith (and of Anne's own family) that Elliot is "a disingenuous, artificial, worldly man, who has never had any better principle to guide him than selfishness" (214). Anne never makes the connection explicit, but the words she applies to her would-be suitor are an apt summary of her own father's characteristics. The man who makes it his business to look evaluatively at others' bodies is—in *Persuasion*—not a man to be respected. Wentworth—who proves himself eminently respectable in the pursuit of his career, in his willingness to honor any implicit promise he has made to marry Louisa Musgrove, and in his having been the one among Captain Benwick's friends who had the fortitude to tell him about his fiancée's death (to cite just a few examples of his qualifications to be the hero, the masculine ideal, of the book)—cannot make an object of Anne by looking at her body directly. The text places Wentworth in the tricky position of having to be distinguished from the men who look solely to objectify and evaluate, at the same time having to learn to notice and to admire the heroine's body. To come to his proper end, the hero must take his first cue from the look of a less masculine man.

But to associate looking in *Persuasion* only with such objectionable characters as the Walter Elliots would relegate it too hastily to the negative side of a moral equation where behaviors are simply admirable or not for all characters. Refusing to rest with so binary a structure of values, the novel carefully constructs differences of gender and class that make such a conclusion inappropriate. The heroine's earnest absorption in looking (and reading looks) suggests the value of looking from a feminine perspective that does not stop with the evaluation of appearances but goes beyond the surface to read the body's significances. If looking is the female focal character's only source of power and control, it is—within the realm of narrative discourse—a crucially important one. In this novel the feminine look neither ignores the body nor objectifies it but sees surface and significance as integrally related. Anne notes "the look, with which 'Thank God!' was uttered by Captain Wentworth" when Louisa is declared out of danger (132); she sees that Mr. Elliot "looked completely astonished" to recognize her from their encounter at Lyme and that "he was quite as good-looking as he had appeared" there (156); she notices, on first seeing Wentworth in Bath, that "he looked quite red" (185), "looked very well," and "had even a momentary look of his own arch significance" (186); at Bath, "she saw that

[Wentworth] saw Elizabeth, that Elizabeth saw him . . . and she had the pain of seeing her sister turn away" (186). The evening at the concert is—for Anne—an orgy of looking, as she tries repeatedly both to see Wentworth and to catch his eye. When Mrs. Smith teases her about how little she noticed at the concert, Anne says, " 'I ought to have looked about me more,' . . . conscious while she spoke, that there had in fact been no want of looking about; that the object only had been deficient" (201). Her "object" is always Wentworth, but she looks at him for purposes beyond objectification: she looks to communicate and to understand.

The novel attributes the power of feminine looking to women characters other than Anne, but they—as in one hilarious moment of feminine looking run amok—are often too preoccupied to exercise that power. Indeed, the heroine's one blunder of perception occurs in a scene where she herself is too absorbed in watching another woman's gaze to understand what is happening. In the scene I have in mind, Lady Russell seems to Anne to be staring across the street at Captain Wentworth (when in fact she is only looking at window curtains): "She looked instinctively at Lady Russell; but not from any mad idea of her recognizing [Wentworth] so soon as she did herself. No, it was not to be supposed that Lady Russell would perceive him till they were nearly opposite. She looked at her however, from time to time, anxiously; and when the moment approached which must point him out, though not daring to look again (for her own countenance she knew was unfit to be seen), she was yet perfectly conscious of Lady Russell's eyes being turned exactly in the direction for him, of her being in short intently observing him" (188). Chagrined to realize that Lady Russell's object was only window curtains, Anne regrets that her own obsessive looking at Lady Russell's look has caused Anne to lose "the right moment for seeing whether [Wentworth] saw them" (189). Here, in her preoccupation with her own gaze and that of Lady Russell, Anne misses a chance to read Wentworth's.

The lost opportunity is significant, because looking in order to interpret others' looks functions as a feminine form of language in *Persuasion*, an alternative to the explicit verbal discourse that might sometimes simplify communication but would often abrogate propriety. From the feminine perspective the text constructs, bodies are not merely objects but are signs to be read. Anne reads the looks of other characters continually, deducing their motives and reactions from their expressions, as when she looks at Wentworth's face after her sister Mary has audibly remarked on his evident satisfaction at having been invited to Camden Place: "Anne caught his eye, saw his cheeks glow, and his mouth form itself into a momentary expression of contempt, and turned away, that she might neither see nor hear more to vex her" (231). Mary should not have spoken, Anne cannot verbally rebuke her, and Wentworth's contempt can be registered only visually, but Anne understands the scene. For her, the look is a means of communication more proper than words, perhaps more effective.

That communication by looks is a feminine provenance in the novel becomes clear in the revised ending. As Anne and Captain Harville conduct their famous debate about the differences between the sexes, Anne continually watches Wentworth, seated nearby at a writing desk. She catches "one quick, conscious look" (235) from him; she is aware of his writing during her dialogue with Harville but is surprised that Wentworth leaves the room with "not a word, nor a look. He had passed out of the room without a look!" (239). The look comes in the next instant, when he returns to hand her his letter, "with eyes of glowing entreaty fixed on her for a moment" (239). Anne has long ago interpreted his looks at her to mean his attachment is renewed: the language of Wentworth's letter does not communicate any new information to Anne, only confirming what she has already observed.

Wentworth, by contrast, does not have Anne's access to the language of looking: his letter admits he would not have "waited even these ten days, could I have read your feelings, as I think you must have penetrated mine" (240). The feminine look, then, has the power to penetrate male desire; the masculine character must resort to words to find out what he needs to know about the woman's desire. This revision contrasts starkly with the moment in the canceled chapter when Anne and Frederick come to their understanding through a mutually expressive look: "[He] looked with an expression which had something more than penetration in it—something softer. Her countenance did not discourage. It was a silent but a very powerful dialogue; on his side supplication, on hers acceptance" (259). The balanced syntax of that last sentence assigns equal powers of visual communication to him and to her; the revised version shifts the balance of the power of reading looks to the feminine side. Even the sexual dynamic between them is altered in the revision: in the original version, the man looks with "more than penetration"; in the revision, it is the woman whose look has penetrated him. Whereas the canceled chapter's reference to a "silent but very powerful dialogue" emphasizes the communicative nature of looks throughout the text, the revision more firmly assigns a feminine gender to the power of interpreting the body's signs.[6]

Looking, then, connotes a certain kind of power in *Persuasion*, but the limits of that power become clear when characters who look are more strongly marked by their class status than their gender. In the few instances where persons outside the elite class are represented in the novel, they are significantly depicted as looking at their social superiors but as being themselves invisible within the text. The "workmen and boatmen" who observe Louisa's accident at Lyme have a voice that surfaces briefly within the free indirect discourse, but they have no individualized bodies or faces: "Many were collected near them, to be useful if wanted, at any rate, to enjoy the sight of a dead young lady, nay, two dead young ladies, for it proved twice as fine as the first report. To some of the best-looking of these good people Henrietta was consigned" (131). Someone among the central characters looks long enough at the workmen to judge the "best-looking," but the lower-class characters are not even visually differentiated enough to be counted: "some" of them come to Henrietta's aid. The working-class figures can look but cannot be seen: within this novel's scheme of representation they have no bodies and therefore no access to the kind of power Anne comes to hold.

This valence of class persists when the worker who looks across class lines is female, even when her look is a penetrating one. Visiting Mrs. Smith, Anne has crossed the path of Nurse Rooke, whom she does not know. Mrs. Smith asks Anne if she had observed the woman who had opened the door on the previous day, and Anne replies: "No. Was not it Mrs. Speed, as usual, or the maid? I observed no one in particular" (204). The housekeeper, the maid, the nurse are interchangeable for Anne: being outside her class, they have no distinguishing physical features. As with the boatmen, however, the nurse is capable of "looking up": Mrs. Smith explains that Nurse Rook "had a great curiosity to see you, and was delighted to be in the way to let you in" (204). These moments of looking (or not looking) across class lines bring forward further details about the limits of the feminine language of looks in *Persuasion*: workers, like elite women, have license to look, but unlike the heroine, they themselves do not become the object of either an intra- or an extradiegetic gaze within the text. Of course, nineteenth-century femininity is constructed exclusively along class lines (in the sense, for instance, that middle-class women's bodies were supposed to suffer a physical delicacy from which female factory workers and servants were assumed somehow to be immune); therefore, if looking and receiving looks is a feminine activity, it would be presented as inaccessible to any person not of the middle class, regardless of that person's sex. Significantly, this instance of class distinction implies that being objectified within a text—having a body that becomes visible through the narration—is a sign of empowerment in Austen's novel, to take "empowerment" in a very different sense from that which Morrison uses in his reading of *Northanger Abbey*. The privileged women (who have bodies in this text) have far more access to power in *Persuasion*'s world than the working-class characters whose bodies never take shape in the narrative discourse. This pattern reverses the film studies–based assumption that being the object of the gaze is a sign of oppression, just as it complicates the notion of legibility within a panoptic economy of power. In *Persuasion*, characters whose subjectivity matters are also figures whose bodies become objects of the narrative gaze.

The life of the body in *Persuasion* is perceptible only from a subject position within the elite class, then, and in this text the body exists only inside that class. Even though Anne, as the focal character, cannot distinguish the bodies of characters outside her own class, she is living a vividly physical existence; her participation in the feminine language of looks places her repeatedly in the position of intense consciousness of others' bodies and of her own. Introduced into the novel as the "faded" heroine whose own body has lost its conventional charms, Anne at first bears an uncomfortable relation to the physicality that marks her in the text's economy as both feminine and middle-class. Ultimately, though, Anne's enjoyment of visceral experience returns, along with her bloom, to make *Persuasion* end as a celebration of life in the female body.

As Judith Van Sickle Johnson has documented in detail, the heroine's emotional experience is the central subject matter of *Persuasion*; Anne's physical desire—frustrated and finally gratified—is the motor that drives the narrative's movement to its happy-ending closure in her sexual union with Wentworth. Johnson asserts that "although the rekindling of romantic sensibilities causes Anne a good deal of discomfort and agitation, she is nonetheless comfortable with discomfort; she delights in the sharp, physical sensations of her own passionate nature" (44). I think this rendition somewhat romanticizes the text's account of the heroine's physical experience. Although I can see how a reader might delight in what Johnson calls "this new excitement of physical contact, this arousing consciousness of growing intimacy, that lends *Persuasion* its 'peculiar beauty' " (44), I do not think the text attributes this pleasure to the heroine until her marriage plot has passed its climax and reached its resolution. Anne's emotional experience is intense but often painful; her situation as focal character means she is subject to a full range of sensations that she is obliged—as the novel's central consciousness—to register. The result is an almost violent narrative impulse against the heroine's body, inevitable within the novel's structure of discourse.

As I have mentioned above, Anne argues for the "tenderness" of women's emotions in her debate with Harville, and the language associated with Anne's feelings throughout the novel suggests that "tenderness" should be understood here in its most literal, physical sense. "Pain," "sensation," and "agitation"—words for conditions of bodily distress—form the lexicon of emotion in the narrator's commentary on Anne's encounters with Wentworth. The narrative renditions of their early scenes together especially stress this vocabulary: when Wentworth removes her troublesome nephew's hands from around her neck, Anne's "sensations on the discovery made her perfectly speechless. . . . [The gesture] produced such a confusion of varying, but very painful agitation, as she could not recover from" before leaving the room (103). Wentworth's first appearance brings "agitation" and "deep mortification" to Anne's body, so drastically altered (according to his remark so thoughtlessly reported to Anne by her sister) after eight years (85). Listening unseen to Wentworth's conversation with Louisa, Anne hears "a great deal of very painful import . . . which must give her extreme agitation" (111); wondering at Wentworth's having placed her in a carriage to save her from further fatigue, she suffers "emotions so compounded of pleasure and pain, that she knew not which prevailed" (113). Even as she grows convinced that Wentworth still loves her, Anne's physical reaction is mixed: "It was agitation, pain, pleasure, a something between delight and misery" (185). Whatever it was, the narrator never calls it "enjoyment."

The canceled chapter ends with an implication that the heroine's physical discomfort is inevitable even in the happiest circumstances. After reaching her understanding with Wentworth, Anne "was almost bewildered—almost too happy in looking back. It was necessary to sit up half the night, and lie awake the remainder, to comprehend with composure her present state, and pay for the overplus of bliss by headache and fatigue" (263–64). The revised ending removes that extremity of pain but subjects Anne to "fresh agitation" and "full sensation" on her receiving Wentworth's letter (246). Love quite literally hurts in *Persuasion*, and if the female body is the vehicle and object of the empowering language of looking, it is also the site of much discomfort.

To be sure, Anne's physical discomforts usually result from what she must—as focal character—see or overhear by being present in situations that do not directly involve her. The most striking instance would be her overhearing Wentworth's conversation with Louisa during their walk in the country: if Anne, the central consciousness, did not witness this upsetting scene, it would have to be absent from the narration. Similar painful instances of Anne's requisite presence in scenes she might prefer to avoid include her weeping as she plays the piano to accompany the others' dancing, her discomposure during the moments at Camden Place when her family treats Wentworth disparagingly, and her observations of Wentworth's grief over Louisa's accident. Critics have pointed to the lack of privacy in Austen's world as representing the lived experience of early-nineteenth-century, middle-class women, which of course it does. Speaking strictly historically, one could surmise that a woman of Anne Elliot's class and marital status would have had very little opportunity for solitude or for choosing whether to be present at social and family events. From a narratological point of view, however, the lack of privacy of Austen's heroines is more significantly a direct result of the novelist's choice of narrative perspective. If all information is to be conveyed to the narratee through the filter of Anne's perceptions, then the heroine must perforce be present at every significant scene. For Anne, whose observations lead so often and so directly to "painful agitation," her placement as the focal character means her body is subject to a continual emotional battering, the inevitable outcome of her narrative function. Throughout much of *Persuasion*, the heroine's body must necessarily be a body in pain.

That pain is gradually allayed, however, as the more positive sensations of the revised last chapters indicate. Though in many respects Anne Elliot's character seems fully formed at the beginning of the novel (setting her apart from Austen's other heroines, with the possible exceptions of Elinor Dashwood and Fanny Price), her relation to the body changes and improves. Other characters continually note the alteration in Anne's appearance as she recovers her lost bloom; her body as visual object changes more than her values and perceptions, the locations of change in heroines like Emma Woodhouse, Elizabeth Bennet, and Catherine Morland. But Anne does experience a subjective change in her relation to the bodies of other women, particularly the maternal body of Mrs. Musgrove. In early scenes, Mrs. Musgrove is presented explicitly in terms of her excessive fleshiness, and the narrative reflects both Anne's consciousness of Mrs. Musgrove's bulk and her distaste for it. In the early scene where Wentworth commiserates with Mrs. Musgrove over the loss of her son, "a thick-headed, unfeeling, unprofitable Dick Musgrove, who had never done any thing to entitle himself to more than the abbreviation of his name, living or dead" (77), Anne is highly conscious of the fact that her own body is in close proximity with Wentworth's, being "divided only by Mrs. Musgrove. It was no insignificant barrier indeed. Mrs. Musgrove was of a comfortable substantial size, infinitely more fitted by nature to express good cheer and good humour, than tenderness and sentiment; and while the agitations of Anne's slender form, and pensive face, may be considered as very completely screened, Captain Wentworth should be allowed some credit for the self-command with which he attended to her large fat sighings over the destiny of a son, whom alive nobody had cared for" (92). This matrophobic moment—where Mrs. Musgrove's fleshy body and motherly grief are so satirically juxtaposed with "the agitations of Anne's slender form"—has traditionally been read as an instance of Austen's own "regulated hatred," but I would attribute the perception, like the majority of narrative observations in the novel, to Anne herself. As the focal character, as the filter for all visual information in the novel, Anne is surely the one to whom it would occur that Frederick ought to be given "credit" for seeming to sympathize. The passage attributes its revulsion from Mrs. Musgrove's "large bulky figure" (92) partly to the simple fact that its flesh forms a barrier here between Anne's body and the male body she desires, which is, on a symbolic level, a fitting emblem for the pseudomaternal interference of Lady Russell in Anne's original engagement to him. But the passage also suggests that "tenderness" is the exclusive right of the slender, virginal, relatively youthful female body, inappropriate to the body of the sexually experienced mother.

Anne's matrophobic reaction to Mrs. Musgrove, so vivid in this passage, disappears later in the text. After Louisa's injury, Mrs. Musgrove is lightly satirized for her preoccupation with young people's danger of being bumped on the head, but the tenderness of her concern for her daughter is treated with perfect seriousness. The shift in narrative attitude toward the emotional mother's body indicates a development in Anne's own increasing comfort with female bodily experience, suggesting that maternity, tenderness, and physicality can come together in Anne's own experience of marriage after the novel's end.

Jane Gallop has suggested that the impulse in Western culture toward violence against the mother is a result of the ideological separation of the mental from the physical, that is, the consequence of splitting off the "realm of culture, history, politics from the realm of love and the body" (2). Her argument draws on the poststructuralist assumption that all the binary divisions of patriarchy—public/private, male/female, thought/emotion—must lead to aggression against the less empowered term in each pairing. The narrative perspective of *Persuasion* both demonstrates that aggression, in its tendency to subject the heroine's body to pain, and opens it up for inspection. Anne Elliot's access to power through the feminine language of looking lets her blur the oppositions of the textual world in which she is placed by making mind and body functions of the same act—looking and reading looks—and by succeeding through that act in bringing together the interior and exterior significance of the people who come under her gaze. In her ultimate reconciliation with the life of the body, Anne triumphs over the text's violence against her, setting a pattern for the feminist heroine who no longer needs to fade and die or to provide a spectacle of sensibility. The text's sensations are the heroine's own; in the end, her gaze is represented as entirely integrated with the life of her body.

NOTES

1. See Julia Prewitt Brown's critique of narrow feminist readings of Austen, and note the pitfalls in her own feminist-historicist criticism that treats characters as if they were "real people" whose marital fate depends on their situation in history (1990).

2. However, see Kathy Mezei's discussion in this volume of free indirect discourse, "Who Is Speaking Here?"

3. As Mary Lascelles noted (204–5) and Orange reminds us (66), the narrative does afford two brief glimpses into Wentworth's perspective on Anne. Whereas Lascelles regarded these moments as lapses, the narratologist might see them as reminders of how *relatively* consistent the focalization is in this text, as compared with *Sense and Sensibility* or *Emma*, for instance.

4. I am using "sensational" in the sense recently introduced into critical discourse by D. A. Miller and Ann Cvetkovich, among others. Although their usage of the term applies to the late-Victorian genre of sensation novels, the term's focus on the link between text and body makes its appropriation here irresistible.

5. I am using these terms in the sense originated by Gérard Genette; see Prince for brief and lucid definitions.

6. John McGowan has argued that "passion is . . . the most difficult thing to know in Austen's novels. It remains hidden deep within the self, inaccessible to sight, and resistant to verbal or social expression" (6). While this holds true for *Emma*, the subject of McGowan's analysis, *Persuasion* suggests a move on Austen's part toward assigning more power to the heroine who can see and read the hero's passion.

Austen, Jane. *Persuasion*. Ed. D. W. Harding. Harmondsworth: Penguin, 1976.

Berger, John. *Ways of Seeing*. London: B.B.C. and Penguin, 1972.

Brown, Julia Prewitt. "The Feminist Depreciation of Austen: A Polemical Reading."
Novel 23.3 (1990): 303–13.

Cohn, Dorrit. *Transparent Minds*. Princeton: Princeton University Press, 1978.

Cvetkovich, Ann. "Ghostlier Determinations: The Economy of Sensation and *The
Woman in White*." *Novel* 23.1 (1989): 24–43.

Dussinger, John. "The Language of 'Real Feeling': Internal Speech in the Jane
Austen Novel." *The Idea of the Novel in the Eighteenth Century*. Ed. Robert W.
Uphaus. East Lansing, MI: Colleagues Press, 1988. 97–115.

Flavin, Louise. "Austen's *Persuasion*." *Explicator* 47.4 (1989): 20–23.

Gallop, Jane. *Thinking through the Body*. New York: Columbia University Press, 1988.

Gamman, Lorraine, and Margaret Marshment, eds. *The Female Gaze: Women as
Viewers of Popular Culture*. Seattle: Real Comet Press, 1989.

Genette, Gérard. *Narrative Discourse: An Essay in Method*. Trans. Jane E. Lewin.
Ithaca: Cornell University Press, 1980.

Johnson, Claudia. "A 'Sweet Face as White as Death': Jane Austen and the Politics of
Female Sensibility." *Novel* 22.2 (1989): 159–74.

Johnson, Judith Van Sickle. "The Bodily Frame: Learning Romance in *Persuasion*."
Nineteenth-Century Literature 38.1 (1983): 43–61.

Lascelles, Mary. *Jane Austen and Her Art*. London: Oxford University Press, 1939.

McGowan, John P. "Knowledge/Power and Jane Austen's Radicalism." *Mosaic* 18.3
(1985): 1–15.

Miller, D. A. *The Novel and the Police*. Berkeley: University of California Press, 1988.

Miller, Nancy K. *The Heroine's Text: Readings in the French and English Novel, 1722–1782*.
New York: Columbia University Press, 1980.

Morrison, Paul. "Enclosed in Openness: *Northanger Abbey* and the Domestic
Carceral." *Texas Studies in Literature and Language* 33.1 (1991): 1–23.

Orange, Michael. "Aspects of Narration in *Persuasion*." *Sydney Studies in English* 15
(1989–90): 63–71.

Prince, Gerald. *A Dictionary of Narratology*. Lincoln: University of Nebraska Press,
1987.

Stout, Janis P. "Jane Austen's Proposal Scenes and the Limitations of Language."
Studies in the Novel 14.4 (1982): 316–26.

discourse, gender, and gossip

Some Reflections on Bakhtin and Emma

christine | roulston

In recent years, the growing interest generated by Bakhtin's writing in the field of literary criticism and, in particular, in the area of feminist literary criticism reflects the broad scope of his theoretical appeal.[1] For those interested in a form of critique that incorporates the ideological with the linguistic, the historical with the narratological, Bakhtin's work seems to provide the ideal base from which to proceed. As Nancy Glazener has argued, for feminist critics in particular, "[Bakhtin's] assertion that literature represents a struggle among socio-ideological languages unsettles the patriarchal myth that there could be a language of truth transcending relations of power and desire" (109). Bakhtin's emphasis on the fact that any linguistic act necessarily belongs to a particular context and is therefore always ideologically encoded opens up a space for inserting gender difference as a crucial ideological category. Bakhtin's work, however, does not itself address the question of gender as a possible site for ideological struggle, coming from a Marxist tradition that privileges class difference as the place of resistance and conflict.

By analyzing a specific passage from Bakhtin in relation to Austen's novel *Emma*, I will explore in what ways the relationship between gender difference and class difference is problematized by mutual suppression and exclusion rather than operating as an interactive, dialogic encounter. While the categories of class and gender can both be read as ways of constructing the subject from a particular ideological perspective, such a perspective also leads to an essentializing of the category that is not being addressed. Therefore, although Bakhtin represses the potential for reading gender difference as a politicizing discourse of resistance that can affect narrative structures, Austen privileges gendered conflict in her narrative but never addresses the problem of class in relation to gender, even though it is inevitably inscribed in her text. Austen assumes and essentializes class difference, whereas Bakhtin silences and erases gender difference as a possible way of analyzing conflictual structures in the novel. By reading Austen by means of Bakhtin and vice versa, I will try to establish a dialectical relationship between these two kinds of writing, exploring the ways in which each text respectively constructs its notion of difference and examining what it privileges in terms of narrative conflict.

In his survey of the shift and development from epic to novelistic discourse in "Discourse in the Novel," Bakhtin analyzes the role and effect of the sentimental novel.

> The essential aspects of Sentimental style are determined precisely by [this] opposition to a high heroizing pathos, a pathos that gives rise to abstract types. The finely detailed descriptions, the very deliberateness with which petty secondary everyday details are foregrounded, the tendency of the representation to present itself as an unmediated impression deriving from the object itself and finally a pathos occasioned by helplessness and weakness rather than by heroic strength, the deliberate narrowing-down of the conceptual horizon and the arena of a man's experience to his most immediate little micro-world (to his very own room)—all this is accounted for by the polemical opposition to a literary style in the process of being rejected. (*Dialogic Imagination*, 397–98)

This passage reveals a dialectical movement in Bakhtin's critique of the sentimental novel. He begins his analysis in praise of the "sentimental style," reading it as an effective dialogizing force, which distinguishes itself from the abstracting effects of heroic epic. What he specifically valorizes is the attention to detail, the everyday, the mundane, because this kind of representation possesses a singular mimetic force. This realist effect is achieved, in Bakhtin's own words, by a "narrowing-down . . . to a micro-world," a concentration on the emotional, private, and domestic realms. The shift from the epic to the sentimental therefore involves a shift from the public to the private, from the outside to the inside, from the countryside to the home and, as Bakhtin emphasizes, a shift "to [man's] very own room." According to Bakhtin, such mimetic representation requires a shrinkage or narrowing-down of both space and time.[2] Despite his praise of the sentimental novel's "realism," Bakhtin nevertheless reads its raison d'être *only* as an opposition to an earlier literary moment, which itself then needs to be overcome. He claims that "all this is accounted for by the polemical opposition to a literary style in the process of being rejected."

His argument continues to shift in this direction in the second half of his critique, where he argues: "In place of one conventionality, however, Sentimentalism creates another—and one similarly abstract, serving to draw attention away from other aspects of reality. A discourse made respectable by Sentimental pathos, one that attempts to replace the brute discourse of life, inevitably ends up in the same hopeless dialogic conflict with the actual heteroglossia of life" (*Dialogic Imagination*, 398). In these lines, Bakhtin is moving beyond his own earlier argument on the sentimental novel. The very thing that made it dialogic now threatens to make it monologic; the movement toward privatization cuts it off from "other aspects of reality," it "attempts to displace the brute discourse of life." The notion of the real, therefore, has shifted away from the home back into the public square, and the sentimental novel is now being read as that which evades reality rather than as a discourse that "represents" it.

Arguably, what is implicit in Bakhtin's critique of the sentimental novel is a gendered opposition: in talking about the shift in perspective from the open, external space of heroic epic to the enclosed, circumscribed space of the sentimental novel (such as "[man's] very own room") and then describing the effects of such a shift as being somehow inadequate, Bakhtin is skirting the issue of how that inner space is occupied. The domestic realm of the sentimental novel, while occupied by both men and women, is nevertheless constructed in terms of a feminine ideology, dominated as it is by emotion rather than action. It is an imaginative space in which the archetypal qualities of femininity begin to be explored and which the male subject enters by moving from the outside to the inside. It is this gendered occupation of both figurative and physical space that, in turn, polarizes the distinction between the public and the private realms in a gendered way.[3]

Therefore, Bakhtin's critique suggests a reluctance to have the private— and by implication the feminine—realms become a referent for the representation of the real. Bakhtin's noticeable omission of any reference to gendered subjectivity is striking when we consider both his spatial structuring of different types of discourse and the fact that the sentimental novel is constructed precisely out of gendered power struggles. Bakhtin's silence on this point can be interpreted as an essentializing gesture, since by failing to address the very means by which conflict is articulated in the sentimental novel, he is justified in dismissing it as nonconflictual and as not engaging with the "real." The setting up of his argument in this oppositional manner allows Bakhtin effectively to close off the very space he accuses the sentimental novel of eliding, enabling him to make "sentimental style" appear to be a discourse that is both unexamined and monologic. He is then free, in turn, to valorize a more public kind of discourse that engages with the new reality he is constructing, namely, "the brute discourse of life."

As a theorist of the relations among time, space, and discourse, Bakhtin values the public realm—in *Rabelais and His World*, he argues that the value of carnival depends on its public quality and the open visibility of its celebration of transgression and reversal.[4] Indeed, the notion of class itself is dependent on the recognition of a group of people functioning as a politicized community and sharing the same socioeconomic interests. Class is therefore a public, not a private, concept. As V. N. Volosinov argues in *Marxism and the Philosophy of Language*, language becomes the site through which the class struggle is articulated: "Class does not coincide with the sign community, i.e., with the community which is the totality of users of the same set of signs for ideological communication. Thus various different classes will use one and the same language. As a result, differently oriented accents intersect in every ideological sign. Sign becomes an arena of the class struggle" (23).[5]

However, it can be argued that language or sign can also function as an arena for the gender struggle, in as far as feminine and masculine subjects also use the same language, but it becomes marked in different ways, which is precisely what the sentimental novel emphasizes in its production of gendered discourse. Therefore, by setting up an absolute opposition between the private and the public realms in his discussion of the sentimental novel, Bakhtin is foreclosing the possibility of making the private signify in a politicized or public way. Bakhtin's argument implies that the struggle for power which takes place between genders *in language* is still not a political struggle—gender cannot function in the same way as class.

Austen's novel *Emma* effectively engages Bakhtin's reading of the sentimental novel, for Austen places the struggle between genders at the forefront, thus continuing the sentimental legacy; however, her narrative equally points to the difficulties involved in trying to resolve conflicts of class by means of gender and vice versa, as Richardson attempts to do in *Pamela*, for example. In this sense, *Emma* is not being read against Bakhtin but as an attempt to understand what enables him to silence the question of gender difference when it is so radically implicated in issues of class. In Austen, class and gender are no longer strictly oppositional—*Pamela*'s story of a servant girl who converts the landed gentry through her feminine virtue and her writing is no longer viable. Instead, in *Emma*, we are confronted with a strong dialogic narrative of competing discourses involving complex aspects of class and gender, a narrative that, in terms of structure, provides us with a novel that fits into Bakhtin's conception of novelistic discourse, containing multiple voices which engage and confront one another.

Following the tradition of the sentimental novel, Austen uses the private to supersede the public, putting social and domestic relations at the center and political history at the margins. However, private life in Austen is not dependent on the sentimental model of isolation and seclusion;[6] instead, it is intimately bound, to quote Raymond Williams, "to a direct preoccupation with estates, incomes and social positions, which are seen as indispensable elements of all the relationships that are projected and formed" (113). The private is therefore also very public and definable through decorum as much as through sentiment. The marriage contract, in turn, confirms the relationship between public and private, legitimating private passion by turning it into public duty and thereby also regulating and defining socioeconomic relations. It is therefore by controlling and appropriating the institution of marriage that Emma will attempt to define her social role, as a means of acceding to the public realm.

For Austen as for Bakhtin, the question of how communication operates is central to an understanding of social relations. In contrast to Bakhtin's school of thought, however, the explicit tension in Austen's text is not centered around class difference but emerges rather as a tension between gendered forms of representation. In *Emma*, language is explicitly gendered—female speech is called "gossip," and male speech, "conversation."[7] At the close of the novel, after one of the many weddings that take place, Mr. Knightley informs Emma that "this is all that I can relate of the how, where, and when—your friend Harriet will make a much longer history when you see her.—She will give you all the minute particulars, which only woman's language can make interesting.—In our communications, we deal only in the great" (453). This reading of gendered speech functions as a reflexive statement on the narrative structure of the novel from the point of view of its male protagonist, whose role is to maintain distinctions between truth and fiction and between conversation and gossip. However, Mr. Knightley is also participating in a narrative that is being repeatedly transgressed by a kind of linguistic cross-dressing, where men talk like women and vice versa. It is precisely this process that engenders the dialogic structure of the novel, in which language can never limit itself to simply one voice.

Emma is presented to the reader as an inverted world that has to be put back in its proper place. The opening scenes introduce the reader to Emma and her father in an inverse father-daughter relationship. In a pointed parody of the powerful father figure present in the eighteenth-century sentimental novel, Mr. Woodhouse has the distinctive characteristic of gossiping like a woman and never being listened to, whereas Emma possesses the apparent authority of a masculine member of the household.[8] The legitimating power relationship of father to daughter is therefore absent and eventually threatens the social stability of the whole community. Mr. Woodhouse's role as a father is simultaneously respected and ignored; he is described initially as a property owner, where Emma has a place as a possession, which suggests the standard patriarchal right of ownership: "From his fortune, his house and his daughter, he could command the visits of his own little circle, in as great measure as he liked" (51). The phrase "his own little circle," however, immediately weakens the framework of this economic metaphor, implying a movement inward, a turning away from the public sphere toward the realm of the private. One of the most striking aspects of this father-daughter relationship is Emma's intense awareness of its limitless possibilities for herself as acting subject. She tells Harriet, " 'I believe few married women are half as much mistress of their husband's house as I am of Hartfield; and never, never could I expect to be so truly beloved and important, so always first and always right in any man's eyes as I am in my father's' " (109). Emma's narcissism and sense of self therefore depend on a weakened construction of the masculine other, which in turn allows her a maximum sphere of influence. By being "always first and always right," Emma is essentially in a relation of priority vis-à-vis her father and therefore generates, rather than being determined by, narrative action. Her strategies of behavior are therefore all centered around the issue of narrative control, and it is through these that the problematic relationship between class and gender is exposed.

Emma uses her authority for the singular purpose of organizing the narratives of other female figures, which in turn enables her to become a master narrator and to avoid engaging with the question of her own gendered subjectivity. She repeatedly displays a strong resistance to her own personal narrative, which would force her back into the private sphere, and instead places other women where she claims she does not want to be. She tells her father: " 'I promise you to make [no matches] for myself, papa; but I must, indeed, for other people. It is the greatest amusement in the world' " (43). If matchmaking is a game for Emma, then it has clear parallels with the construction of domestic narrative itself and hence with the indirect authorial voice of the novel, which uses matchmaking and matrimony as its principal organizing models.[9] However, it is precisely by pointing to the dangers involved in treating matchmaking as an amusement and a diversion and by pointing to the moral complications of being seduced by the romance structure that the moral and the ethical frameworks of the novel are established. Emma's education consists precisely in learning how to separate the fantasies of fiction from the realities of marriage and finally to privilege the latter, so that in many ways her experience can be read as a critique of the "Pamela" phenomenon, which uses a romance structure to work through the question of feminine virtue.

Emma's paradoxical situation is marked by her occupying a masculine subject position within her community while remaining entirely contained by the discourse of romance, thereby failing to establish a space of resistance. But as readers we may question whether resistance is even possible for Emma and whether Austen herself sees it as desirable, given the social and political status of her heroine's discourse.[10] At the beginning of the narrative, for example, Mr. Knightley argues that "[Emma] always declares she will never marry, which, of course, means just nothing at all" (69). By making such a claim, he is denying the very thing that Emma asserts throughout the novel and thereby potentially invalidating her self-representation.[11] While Emma's denial must necessarily mean "nothing at all" if the narrative and social structures embodied by Mr. Knightley are to be sustained, does this also imply that all Emma's statements become equally emptied of meaning? Are they all merely instances of female gossip that are eventually rectified by the marriage contract at the end of the novel? The extent to which Emma's discourse can be valorized or legitimized provides the most challenging act of reading in the novel, because it is through Emma in particular that the struggle for competing modes of representation is articulated.[12]

One way into Emma's discourse is to examine how she comes to be such a powerful misreader and so blinded to the social relations that define her community. Emma's misreadings, in fact, are closely related to her problematic relationship to her own gender and the structuring of her own identity. She posits the act of matchmaking as a way of fostering a kind of gender solidarity, but in the process she mistakes the discourse of desire and romance for that of feminism, confusing competing modes of discursive authority. Her efforts to understand other female figures by controlling their narratives will only degenerate into a series of misreadings and mismatches—she will end up gossiping "like a woman" in the very attempt to be an accurate reader of others' desires, in the manner of Mr. Knightley.

Once Emma's long-time governess leaves her to get married, Emma chooses as a friend a young, attractive orphan, Harriet Smith, to whom she becomes a mentor. We are told that "*she* would notice her; she would improve her; she would detach her from her bad acquaintance, and introduce her into good society; she would inform her opinion and her manners" (54). In these lines, the pronoun *she* objectifies and controls the pronoun *her*, in a strictly dichotomized subject-object relation. Emma, in other words, is reading Harriet in the terms in which Mr. Knightley effectively, if implicitly, reads Emma. But the explicitness of Emma's desire to control and to educate Harriet reveals, in turn, that her mentorship is nothing more than a parodic inversion of the "real" education that is taking place, that of Emma by Mr. Knightley. Emma uses Harriet in an attempt to construct a romance narrative under her direction, but such a narrative repeatedly exceeds the boundaries within which Emma seeks to confine it. Emma's dual roles of master narrator and educator, as defined by Mr. Knightley, are, finally, profoundly incompatible. The fact that she is a more accomplished teller of tales than a teacher of facts and experience is revealing in itself, since by adopting the role of mentor in relation to Harriet, Emma is usurping a conventionally masculine domain. If Emma were an effective teacher, she would not require Mr. Knightley's mentorship. By placing Emma in both a conflictual and a parodic relation to Mr. Knightley, Austen seems to be emphasizing precisely what Bakhtin implies in his analysis of the sentimental novel; that the feminine, whether in terms of subject position or as discursive practice, cannot be an adequate model for the representation of the real. In this sense, Emma is able only to parody or to imitate Mr. Knightley's roles; she can never construct a separate and autonomous subject position, in spite of her self-prescription as "always first and always right" (109). As Mr. Knightley's equal in every respect except those of gender and age, Emma nevertheless will have no real claim to legitimacy until she becomes Mrs. Knightley and agrees to adopt his model of experience along with his name.[13]

Yet the struggle for who has the right to speak on gender difference remains highly controversial within the narrative structure of the novel. While the conflict is centered around Emma and Mr. Knightley, it is also paralleled by Harriet Smith and Robert Martin, whose narratives function as a distorted mirror image of the main plot. It is Emma's success in turning Harriet away from Robert Martin and toward Mr. Elton that triggers the antagonism between herself and Mr. Knightley. The new alignment of loyalties is therefore Mr. Knightley and Robert Martin against Emma and

Harriet, which on the surface appears to point to a privileging of gender identity over class solidarity. In each case, however, the realignment requires more careful scrutiny, for it indicates that issues of gender and class cannot be articulated independently of one another. Although Mr. Knightley's and Robert Martin's class difference is absolute, they nevertheless communicate more successfully than Emma and Harriet ever do. This is made strikingly apparent when the narrative voice implicitly draws the two male voices together by using the same adjectives to describe their respective marriage proposals. Robert Martin's letter to Harriet is interpreted by Emma in the following way: "The style of the letter was much above her expectation. There were not merely no grammatical errors, but as a composition it would not have disgraced a *gentleman*; the language, though *plain*, was strong and *unaffected*, and the sentiments it conveyed very much to the credit of the writer" (77; emphasis added). What Emma is incapable of reading in terms of social relations, she cannot misread in terms of the written text. She cannot deny the quality of the letter, although she momentarily questions its authorship and thinks it may have been written by Mr. Martin's sisters. Mr. Knightley's own proposal, which takes place at the end of the novel, is described as follows: "The subject followed; it was in *plain, unaffected, gentleman*-like English, such as Mr Knightley used even to the woman he was in love with" (432; emphasis added). Unlike Harriet and Emma, who cannot agree whether a letter is well-written (Harriet is in awe of Mr. Elton's literary skill and less impressed by Robert Martin's directness), Mr. Knightley and Robert Martin always already inhabit the same language. It is clear that this solidarity of discourse reflects a further consensus in interpretation, namely, a correspondence of linguistic and moral practices within clearly defined social and class boundaries. Emma and Harriet, on the other hand, who claim a greater intimacy, lack a mutual ground of communication. In fact, the new social contract that Emma attempts to establish with Harriet ultimately fails, as Emma misreads the question of class difference by privileging fictional and imagined models of desire.

Emma's relationship to Harriet becomes parodic, precisely because Emma can never resolve the emerging contradictions between her privileged class and her underprivileged gender that, in turn, produce misreadings and double standards. Emma repeatedly places Harriet in positions that she herself seeks to avoid, first in relation to Mr. Elton and then in relation to Frank Churchill, where she literally substitutes Harriet for herself, saying: "Dear Harriet!—I would not change you for the clearest-headed, longest-sighted, best-judging female breathing. Oh! the coldness of a Jane Fairfax!—Harriet is worth a hundred such.—And for a wife—a sensible man's wife—it is invaluable. I mention no names; but happy the man who changes Emma for Harriet" (272). In this nominal substitution, Emma objectifies Jane and Harriet by placing them within an interchangeable narrative, enabling Emma herself to maintain the authority of narrating subject. It is only once Harriet finally reveals her desire independently of Emma, in the form of her attraction to Mr. Knightley, that Emma herself is silenced. At this point, Emma loses the material power of her social status as a way of controlling Harriet and finds herself competing at the level of desire—for the same love object. This reversal of their power relationship, however, is short-lived, for it is precisely at this moment of speechlessness that Emma becomes determined to displace Harriet altogether: "It darted through her, with the speed of an arrow, that Mr Knightley must marry no one but herself" (398). Emma therefore enters the very narrative of marriage she had constructed for Harriet, occupying the proper place at the center, a place that the novel itself has reserved for Emma from its title page on. She is transformed from narrator to narrated heroine as she enters the ideological imperative dictated by the novel's indirect authorial voice. This imperative, in turn, requires a model of rivalry that positions one female subject against another; identifying with her class in a final gesture of closure, Emma will triumph over Harriet, and everything will return to its proper place and be determined according to hierarchized social patterns.[14]

Emma's desire cannot, however, be read exclusively as succumbing to a latent and preinscribed social narrative; her privileging of a certain female autonomy is too strong to be ignored. The contradiction resides in the fact that this desire for autonomy remains circumscribed within a patriarchal vision of gender difference. Mr. Knightley remains the final embodiment of truth and is both a product and a supporter of the class system. He occupies a subject position that enables him to read the social and economic implications of class difference much more accurately than Emma can read desire. For example, when Emma is putting forth Mr. Elton as a possibility for Harriet, Mr. Knightley replies: "[Mr. Elton] knows the value of a good income as well as anybody. Elton may talk sentimentally, but he will act rationally" (92).[15] In spite of her narrative authority in relation to other female figures, Emma cannot embody a fully patriarchal discourse— in as far as such a discourse both represents and dictates socioeconomic concerns—because she fails to negotiate the intersection between the public and the private. She cannot read economics as a value system in itself, without interpreting it through the category of desire.

Part of Emma's dilemma as a female subject is that class solidarity is far more appealing than gender solidarity as a way of experiencing social relations.[16] Female models in this novel are disempowering figures overall, so that Emma's readings of other women are generally filtered through a structure of opposition and comparison rather than one of identification. This is certainly true of Harriet, but a more ambiguous case concerns Emma's relationship to Jane Fairfax, Emma's only female intellectual equal. Even more so than Harriet, Jane Fairfax becomes Emma's specular other.[17] As a female figure equal to Emma and yet without the latter's social and economic privileges, Jane Fairfax becomes the only character to dialogize successfully the relationship between the public and the private in the novel. She speaks only once at any length, when she is forced by Mrs. Elton into discussing her future prospects: "When I am quite determined as to the time, I am not at all afraid of being long unemployed.—There are . . . [o]ffices for the sale—not quite of human flesh—but of human intellect. . . . I was not thinking of the slave trade . . . governess trade, I assure you, was all that I had in view, widely different certainly as to the guilt of those who carry it on; but as to the greater misery of the victims, I do not know where it lies" (300). In these lines, Jane is speaking in a way that Emma never could, in the sense that she is forcing the discourse of the public sphere— or, to quote Bakhtin, "the brute discourse of life"—into the domestic realm of the living room. The historical reality of the slave trade and the exploitation of women are brought together as a way of dialogizing the private by means of the public. The result of this is a powerful sense of transgression for both Jane's audience and for the reader, as a distinctly politicized context has been forged.

Apart from this outburst, however, Jane Fairfax remains otherwise bound and silenced by her social and gendered positions. In fact, because of her coldness and reserve, she is ultimately rejected as a model for femininity by Emma, by Mr. Knightley, and implicitly by the narrator.[18] Such a rejection is based on explicitly social criteria, in that Jane's coldness reflects an unwillingness to engage in social relations, which functions as a breach of the social contract.[19] When she does speak, her speech is as disruptive as her silence. Jane Fairfax fundamentally challenges the model of an ideal femininity whereby the female becomes the figure who can ensure that social relations are sustained and communication is not entirely ruptured or blocked. In this sense, Emma is a more accurate embodiment of femininity than Jane, for she is first and foremost a communicator, whereas Jane is bound by the silencing effect of her disempowered condition. This, in turn, binds the notion of an ideal femininity with the ideal class that is being repeatedly valorized in the novel—the landed gentry. Jane remains an ambiguous figure, with whom Emma never becomes intimate, perhaps because she represents the hidden other of the female state, an otherness that Emma can reflect on: "The contrast between Mrs Churchill's importance in the world and Jane Fairfax's, struck her; one was every thing, the other nothing—and she sat musing on the difference of woman's destiny" (376). But this otherness is one with which she does not allow herself to identify. Her insertion of Mrs. Churchill rather than herself as a point of comparison enables her to maintain the objective distancing of the third-person narrative and thereby to avoid engaging directly with any dialectic of oppression.

Emma finally remains caught between a desire to identify with representations of the feminine that depend on structures of oppression and a desire to produce an alternative vision. The ideological ideal underscoring the narrative leads its protagonist to establish a relationship to her own gender based on hierarchy rather than on community. The final determinant is the organization of class, and the social model privileged by the novel is a familial one that corrects the waywardness of romance and puts everyone back in their proper place. The institution of marriage therefore functions as an absolute referent or signified that underpins the teleology of the narrative. However, although such a structure could be said to provide the necessary stabilizing ethos of the text, it is counterbalanced by examples of the potentially disempowering effects of marriage.

In terms of the convention of romance, marriage marks the end of the narrative and closes the text. In *Emma*, however, marriage becomes a potential form of closure at the *beginning* of the narrative: "Sorrow came—a gentle sorrow—but not at all in the shape of any disagreeable consciousness.—Miss Taylor married. It was Miss Taylor's loss which first brought grief" (37). Although marriage, as a celebration of procreation and generation, is a socially favorable event, it is described here from the perspective of loss rather than of fulfillment. The cost of creating a new family involves the disruption of a prior community, namely, that of Emma's household, which is primarily a feminine community, Mr. Woodhouse occupying the role of the mother rather than that of the patriarch. Miss Taylor's marriage and consequent absence threaten to close Emma's personal narrative, which is why Harriet is brought into Hartfield, but the text goes on to mark this as an inadequate substitution. What Emma and the reader come to learn is that it is Mr. Knightley rather than Harriet who should be replacing Miss Taylor. In other words, the construction of a female society is presented as a possibility only in terms of a transitional, rather than an absolute, alternative.

Such a reading points to a further collusion with Bakhtin's critique of the sentimental novel as a mimetic construction that is centered too emphatically on the private, domestic realms. Austen has internalized and transformed Richardson's privileging of the feminine as the new locus of experience and his positing of female values as a potential alternative to aristocratic ones. As Nancy Armstrong has pointed out, by Austen's time, the transition from the virtuous to the domestic woman has already taken place and "social relations appear to be virtually the same thing as domestic relations" (135). If anything, the relationship constructed by Austen between Emma and Harriet functions as a pointed reminder of the perceived inadequacy of purely female social relations. Emma and Harriet's failed friendship can be read as an implicit critique of both Clarissa's intimate relationship with Anna Howe and of Pamela's successful accession to a higher socioeconomic class. Emma's eventual reunion with Mr. Knightley, on the other hand, will stabilize social relations by subordinating the specificity of female friendship to a privileged social and gendered hierarchy.

As suggested earlier, this does not mean that Austen views marriage uncritically. In fact, the most powerful critique of marriage in the novel emerges simultaneously from its most complete family portrait, that of Emma's sister, Isabella, and her husband, Mr. John Knightley. Isabella is described as the most contented and fulfilled female figure in the novel, with a distinct emphasis on her feminine qualities: "Mrs John Knightley was a pretty, elegant little woman, of gentle, quiet manners, and a disposition remarkably amiable and affectionate; wrapt up in her family; a devoted wife, a doating mother. . . . She was not a woman of strong understanding or any quickness" (116). Isabella, like Harriet, is determined by her exclusive femininity, which implicitly elides the intellectual sphere. Her circumscribed female world is presented ambivalently in the narrative, since its narrow parameters contain her within a limited realm of understanding. It is Emma, as an intellectual subject, who expands this private, feminine space to reveal its inconsistencies and to expose the mildly abusive role of the husband: "He was not a great favourite with his fair sister-in-law. Nothing wrong in him escaped her. She was quick in feeling the little injuries to Isabella, which Isabella never felt herself" (116).

Emma's ability to suffer in the place of her sister ironically anticipates another occasion, where Emma rejects identification with the feminine and inflicts the injury herself. This is the episode of the picnic on Box Hill, where Emma publicly insults and humiliates the elderly Miss Bates. Miss Bates is another example of weak-minded and yet nurturing femininity, but unlike Isabella, she is extremely poor and not supported by a family structure. Emma's mistreatment of Miss Bates, although it occurs only once, is a slightly more extreme version of John Knightley's mistreatment of his wife,[20] in its disregard of social decorum.[21] In each case, a form of social transgression is taking place, yet they are responded to in radically different ways. Emma's transgression becomes a painful part of her education, and from it an implicit contract is established between herself and Mr. Knightley never to repeat the offense. Mr. Knightley responds to the public nature of the insult and to the social inequality of the participants involved. Emma's transgression, in other words, is socially monitored and eventually remedied. Mr. John Knightley's offense, however, remains confined within the realm of Emma's consciousness. It is never vocalized and therefore cannot be resolved by means of a contractual obligation. Unlike Emma, therefore, Mr. John Knightley is not made socially responsible for his behavior, which differs only in terms of its private, domestic quality.

This absence of censorship with regard to Mr. John Knightley is made possible primarily because Mr. Knightley himself does not perceive his brother's behavior as problematic, and within the structure of the narrative, Mr. Knightley is the figure responsible for vocalizing social transgressions. Mr. Knightley's silence on this issue tacitly implies that silence is the appropriate reaction. In fact, because Mr. Knightley's lack of insight with regard to his brother is not foregrounded by the narrative and brought to the reader's attention, it is not immediately apparent that he is interpreting Emma's behavior differently from his brother's, which is not being interpreted at all. For Mr. Knightley, therefore, the fact that Emma can insult Miss Bates in public is implicitly a more serious transgression than Mr. John Knightley insulting his wife in private. As a woman, Emma is responsible for setting the standard for harmonious social relations, whereas Mr. John Knightley is free to set his own standards with his wife. The feminine, in other words, becomes the locus for ensuring that public decorum is maintained, while also remaining subject to private suffering.

What, therefore, is the kind of feminine model that Austen is valorizing in *Emma*, and why is Emma herself implicitly presented as the ideal female figure in the text? Austen's protagonist helps to transform the eighteenth-century sentimental tradition, in the sense that Emma is *not* an already perfect heroine, whose material identity must be protected from violation. Austen's narrative articulates a historical shift away from the concrete materiality of the body to the more fluid immateriality of social relations, where ideal femininity is definable through its ability to communicate rather than through its innate virtue. This helps to explain why Emma is a more appropriate heroine than Jane Fairfax, whose capacity for private suffering reflects a nostalgia for an earlier literary paradigm. Emma's subjectivity cannot be adequately described by means of the discourse of virtue because there is more than her private self involved. As we have seen, the fault for which Emma is the most severely chastised is essentially a failure in public relations, a momentary inability to respect social decorum. She is not chastised in the same way for her poor treatment of Harriet, which takes place primarily behind closed doors but the effect of which is certainly visible to Mr. Knightley (393). Emma's "value," if not her "virtue," lies in her ability to place her private self at the disposal of the public world of communication. It is precisely Emma's openness—her transparent subjectivity and her continuing correspondence with the social world—that makes her the ideal heroine, creating an open dialogue between the private and the public self. This new feminine model is less static and yet potentially more conservative than its eighteenth-century counterpart, because it is fully answerable to the existing social order. The private discourse of virtue, on the other hand, could generate a more explicit discourse of resistance to that order by its withdrawal from social relations.[22]

For Austen, however, the latter model is inadequate. The text of *Emma*, in particular, reveals that language as social communication possesses a socially transformative power precisely because it does not have an absolutely referential and monologic relationship to external reality. Nor does language, for Austen, always embody or represent the truth, as is stated toward the end of the novel: "Seldom, very seldom, does complete truth belong to any human disclosure; seldom can it happen that something is not a little disguised, or a little mistaken" (418–19). As "human disclosure," language is subject to human error, and therefore it simultaneously fills and widens the gap between subjectivity and reality. And if language is what mediates the relationship between the subjective and the real, it is also what transforms it. Austen makes use of this transformative capacity of language as a way of exploring and monitoring social relations.

In *Emma*, the language in question is the language attributed to the feminine: the private discourse of gossip, whose primary characteristic is that it generates misreadings through an endless process of circulation. It is these misreadings, in turn, that sustain social relations and ultimately have a transformative effect on the agents of communication themselves. Therefore, although Mr. Knightley is the one who reads social relations accurately, it is the indeterminate discourse of gossip, embodied by Emma, that is privileged in the novel, as far as the narrative structure is concerned. Gossip, unlike rational discourse, can transform social relations because it has the capacity to generate narratives. In one sense, for Austen, the truth of language as a social act is that it always functions as gossip, inevitably engaging in misrepresentation. This, in turn, makes it both productive and in need of being controlled and contained, for gossip ultimately cannot claim the same status as truth.[23] Gossip is also a discourse of participation which involves the whole community and which directly or indirectly affects the individuals within it. At some level, therefore, gossip is always responding and being responded to, which is why it has such close affinities with Bakhtin's analysis of social communication. In his essay on "The Problem of Speech Genres," Bakhtin writes: "The very boundaries of the utterance are determined by a change of speech subjects. Utterances are not indifferent to one another, and are not self-sufficient; they are aware of and mutually reflect one another. These mutual reflections determine their character. Each utterance is filled with echoes and reverberations of other utterances to which it is related by the communality of the sphere of speech communications" (*Speech Genres*, 91). For Bakhtin and for Austen, language is not static and strictly representational but rather always in process and conditioned by previous utterances.

Yet gossip both colludes with and differs from Bakhtin's theory in the sense that it is a strictly private genre. In her book on gossip, Patricia Meyer Spacks describes its function in the following way: "[Gossip] provides a mode of power, of undermining public rigidities and asserting private integrity, of discovering means of agency for women, those private citizens deprived of public function. It provides also often the substance and the means of narrative" (170). In Austen, the empowering aspect of the discourse of gossip for women remains ambivalent, but it is nevertheless the means by which both male and female subjectivities are constructed. Because gossip is a private genre that nevertheless is circulated in a public manner (everyone speaking "privately" about everyone else), the self-knowledge that emerges is both social and personal. Therefore, although gossip brings about the subject's knowledge of her or his own desire, this desire itself has also been defined by the process of gossiping. In this sense, gossip functions as a form of social control, where the individual discovers not only the act of desiring but also learns who to desire.[24]

Nevertheless, the radical aspect of gossip is that it momentarily undoes social and gendered hierarchies by implicating everyone within the speech community. Even Mr. Knightley, who in many ways positions himself as the absolute referent in the text and who repeatedly corrects misreadings rather than producing them, becomes entangled in the social relations brought about by gossip. In his case, however, gossip unfolds as a form of narrative strategy rather than as dialogue. Mr. Knightley does not engage in gossip in order to produce alternative narratives, in the way that Emma does, but he nevertheless becomes subject to its effects. This, in turn, leads to a destabilizing of his position as guarantor of social values. It is in his apparently unified and self-confirming roles of mentor/father and lover that slippages occur and contradictions come into being. To begin with, his entire relationship to Emma is familial rather than erotic, and as in *Mansfield Park*, it is the familial connection that is ultimately valorized.[25] One of Mr. Knightley's functions is the suppression of the erotic, which in this narrative is synonymous with gossip, in as far as the latter puts into play the circulation of desire. As Emma's mentor, he must also teach her to put the erotic in its place. But his position becomes self-contradictory once he is transformed into a desiring subject.

It is during a ball organized by the inhabitants of Highbury that an ambiguous relationship between the familial role of father and the erotic one of lover is foregrounded. During the evening, Emma notices that Mr. Knightley has placed himself among the nondancers, the "husbands, and fathers, and whist-players" (323), and yet it is precisely when Mr. Knightley is establishing himself as a "father" that he slips into an erotic role, for we are told that "he could not have appeared to greater advantage perhaps any where, than where he had placed himself. His tall, firm, upright figure, among the bulky forms and stooping shoulders of the elderly men, was such as Emma felt must draw every body's eyes" (323). Mr. Knightley is therefore put out of place by the erotic quality of Emma's gaze, which forces him from the position of father to that of lover. As an ironic extension of that gaze, Mr. Knightley then takes up the role of gallant knight and saves Harriet from the insults of Mr. Elton by asking her to dance. His physical displacement from the husbands and fathers to the dancers frames him within an erotic context, drawing him into the circulating narratives of desire, since Harriet falls in love with him and this eventually leads to Emma's realization of her own attraction. The circular motion of the ballroom dance, whose public performance simultaneously masks and reveals private instances of desire, sensuously plays out the sexual dynamics that the circulation of gossip produces at the discursive level. Once Mr. Knightley has left the fathers behind, he becomes inevitably implicated in the effects of the sexual play he has been trying to control.

Nor does Mr. Knightley himself entirely avoid being affected by the sexual tension brought about by gossip, which occurs, in fact, as soon as his own gendered position is challenged. If Mr. Knightley does not appear threatened by female speech, he becomes very threatened by a male speech that is not based on the same model as his own, such as Frank Churchill's. Although circumscribed within the parameters of rational argument, Mr. Knightley's discourse is no longer "plain and unaffected" when he discusses his only rival. What he criticizes in Frank Churchill is ostensibly his failure to do his duty toward his father: "There is one thing, Emma, which a man can always do, if he chuses, and that is, his duty. . . . If he would say so to [his mother] at once, in the tone of decision becoming a man, there would be no opposition made to his going" (164), followed by, "I can allow for the fears of the child, but not of the man" (165). Mr. Knightley, in effect, is threatened by a vision of masculinity that differs from his own while remaining evidently appealing and seductive. His representation of Frank Churchill reveals a repeated attempt to effeminize him and to cancel out his masculinity. He describes Frank's handwriting as follows: "I do not admire it. . . . It is too small—wants strength. It is like a woman's writing" (297). Mr. Knightley's essentializing of gender difference to illustrate the negative side of this binary opposition reveals his firmly gendered reading of social relations. As soon as the gendered element ceases to occupy its proper place, it can be used as a critique of improper subjecthood.

Frank Churchill, as a male participating in gossip and the telling of stories, threatens Mr. Knightley's rigid concept of the patriarchal role, his desire for Emma, and his position within the community. Although Frank Churchill is the outsider, he forces Mr. Knightley onto the margins of the circles of intrigue, as is revealed in the word game proposed by Frank and played by Jane, Emma, and himself, as Mr. Knightley looks on: "Frank was next to Emma, Jane opposite to them—and Mr Knightley so placed as to see them all; and it was his object to see as much as he could, with as little apparent observation" (344). The scene is filtered through Mr. Knightley's ostensibly omniscient gaze, but the knowledge it reveals depends on his entering into the semiotics of gossip. His position as observer implicates him in the circulation of private information, embodied by the letters themselves, which represent the ludic enactment of the principal narrative strategy of the novel. Neither fully on the outside nor on the inside, both excluded and yet implicated, Mr. Knightley observes and yet is barred from action. Austen does not allow any of her characters absolute access to full narrative authority.

Therefore, as a private, pervasive language, capable of challenging rational apprehensions of the world, gossip does seem to be a discourse that can effect social change. Such a reading of the discourse of gossip echoes Spacks's analysis, which sees gossip as both radical and empowering: a private, feminine genre that can influence and transform social relations. However, such transformation in *Emma* is momentary rather than permanent. Within the structure of the novel, gossip eventually serves to put everyone back in their proper place and their proper class. The self-knowledge that gossip brings with it is a knowledge of desire which momentarily disrupts but which finally confirms a social structure based on hierarchies: Emma learns that she desires Mr. Knightley, and Harriet learns that she must not desire him. As a social discourse, gossip can be effective only if it eventually gives way to knowledge, and that knowledge is the knowledge of property and propriety. By the end of the novel, Emma has learned what Mr. Knightley already knows, and her education is essentially complete.[26]

Nevertheless, the close of the narrative is marked by a potential discourse of resistance. If social and gendered hierarchies have been restored, Mr. Knightley is also the only character who is out of place and out of context at the end of the novel. He moves from Donwell Abbey to Hartfield in response to the fact that Emma's father is too frail to be relocated.[27] However, Mr. Knightley's move is perhaps less a moving out of context than a final legitimation of his desired context in Emma's home. In many ways, his entire life narrative has taken place at Hartfield: he has watched Emma grow up, he keeps charge of Mr. Woodhouse's property, and he is related to the family by his younger brother's marriage to Isabella, Emma's sister. Emma therefore remains the central narrative force—the novel opens and closes in her home—even as Mr. Knightley's presence works as a social corrective.

Emma's acceptance of the marriage proposal also contains a certain ambiguity: "What did she say?—Just what she ought, of course. A lady always does—she said enough to show there need not be despair—and to invite him to say more himself" (418). In these lines Emma seems to move from a position of independence to one of submission—she finally speaks like a lady, her discourse is no longer conflictual, she says "what she ought." The very prescriptive quality of the description, however, removes Emma from her own language. In a novel filled with direct speech, that this acceptance is in reported speech and that Emma, as speaking subject, is not fully present somewhat ironize her position. While marriage determines the teleology of the novel, it is also dramatized in an ambivalent way throughout the narrative.

From within the boundaries of the private sphere, Austen therefore offers a sharp critical analysis of how gendered language is produced and how it can disrupt gendered subject positions and social hierarchies. The circulation of gossip repeatedly prevents the establishment of a fixed and stable monologic discourse, keeping the languages in the novel fluid and dialogic. At the same time, however, it can be argued that the limit of Austen's private sphere is the barrier of class itself; while she can dramatize the interdependence of masculine and feminine modes of speech and explore the female subject's struggle for meaning and identity, she does not go as far as to suggest that class structures need to be disrupted for female emancipation to be realized.

In one sense, such a reading confirms Bakhtin's critique of the private realm as a nonpolitical space and one that fails to confront "the brute discourse of life" and hence to transform social relations. However, Bakhtin's glossing over of the private merely perpetuates the private/public dichotomy, maintaining the privileged position of the latter without questioning its positionality. Austen's adherence to the class system on the one hand and her critique of gender relations on the other reveals instead a complex interplay between female subjectivity and patriarchal power. Indeed, what is repeatedly exposed in Austen's novel is how the female subject can have access to an economic base only through the institution of marriage. This, in turn, necessarily ties her to male structures of class over and above a potential female solidarity. From this perspective, female subjects remain isolated from one another and cannot speak as a unified voice or as a class. Emma, Jane, and Harriet have even less in common after their respective marriages except for the binding experience of matrimony, which ensures their individual survival.

The paradox of the female subject position in *Emma* is further complicated by Austen's ambivalent reading of marriage itself, as both absolutely necessary and yet rarely described in wholly positive terms. On the one hand, she articulates a conservative position in rejecting the tradition of female friendship which prevailed in the eighteenth-century sentimental novel and which denoted a certain female solidarity. On the other hand, she creates a more complex social role for the feminine, one that produces a new form of "public" engagement. Emma's struggle for autonomy becomes a struggle for her social identity, her public as well as her private self. She cannot make use of the eighteenth-century model of self-isolation, nor can she evade the class structure that defines her socially. These issues, however, require a mode of analysis that can read the issue of class through that of gender and vice versa. Bakhtin's work offers the critical tools for reading the ideological dimensions of all forms of discourse and hence locating the intersection between the political and the literary. By being brought into dialogue with the question of gender difference, a Bakhtinian analysis can contribute in valuable ways to understanding the dialogical process taking place at the intersection between the private and the public realms, without negating either term.

Who, finally, can claim the last word in *Emma*? Austen has set up a distinctly gendered discourse as a way of examining the private and public spheres by opposing gossip to rational speech, revealing that they are interdependent. The narrative of *Emma* also dramatizes the contradictions built into any attempt to create a dialogic relationship between class and gender. Yet we cannot but question whether Austen is using gender-based discourse as a form of social critique or as a means of confirming the *status quo*. On the one hand, Austen helps to reveal why Bakhtin felt justified in claiming that the private realm of the domestic novel could not adequately engage with the external world. On the other hand, Austen also points to the fact that this lack of engagement between the public and the private is not based on natural oppositions but is ideologically motivated.

The examination of gendered speech positions is therefore fundamentally tied to the question of class difference, for what *Emma* reveals is that there is no unified way of speaking as a woman. In this sense, the discourse of gossip becomes a deceptive and self-deceiving attempt at female intimacy and community. In fact, through the character of Emma, Austen has managed to explore the fundamental paradox of the relationship between female subjectivity and power. Emma is a character who simultaneously defends and denies the place of the woman; she actively resists male appropriation, and yet she occupies an entirely masculine subject position in relation to her own gender. Her struggle is personal rather than communal, which is why it fails as a politicizing discourse. For Emma's discourse to become political, however, she would have to understand the experience of disempowerment, as Jane Fairfax does. Finally, she would have to relinquish the very privileges of class that sustain her autonomy to begin with. What Austen does explore in *Emma* is a gender-based struggle for the appropriation of meaning, but she does not go so far as to acknowledge that class structures must change for the position of women to change. Bakhtin, on the other hand, implicitly criticizes the "sentimental novel" for not dealing with "the real," because he resists the need to read the organization of gender as a means of dialogizing private space. The meeting between Austen and Bakhtin, therefore, opens up a space for reading class and gender as being necessarily and inevitably implicated in each other in what Bakhtin calls "novelistic discourse."

NOTES

1. Of interest are more recent articles such as Nancy Glazener, "Dialogic Subversion: Bakhtin, the Novel, and Gertrude Stein," and Wayne C. Booth, "Freedom of Interpretation: Bakhtin and the Challenge of Feminist Criticism."

2. This interpretation parallels Ian Watt's interpretation in *The Rise of the Novel*, where realism is defined as writing which rejects the notion of universals and which concentrates on "the detailed presentation of [the characters'] environment" (18). For Bakhtin, however, this kind of definition is only partially satisfactory.

3. For a convincing analysis of the relationship between "inside" and "outside" in Jane Austen's time, namely, at the beginning of the Industrial Revolution, see Raymond Williams, *The Country and the City*, 108–19.

4. See, in particular, Mikhail Bakhtin, *Rabelais and His World*, chap. 2, "The Language of the Marketplace in Rabelais," 145–95, and chap. 3, "Popular-Festive Forms and Images in Rabelais," 196–277.

5. For my purposes here, the works of Bakhtin and Volosinov are being referred to interdependently as belonging to the same corpus and school of thought. For further detail on this issue, see Tzvetan Todorov, *Mikhail Bakhtin: The Dialogic Principle*, xi, 4–13.

6. Within the Richardsonian tradition of the sentimental novel, the moral and physical isolation of the heroine is of paramount importance, even though their narratives are also determined by economic factors, as Christopher Hill argues in "Clarissa Harlowe and Her Times."

7. I am using descriptions of Mr. Woodhouse and Miss Bates for my definitions of gendered language in Austen's text. Mr. Woodhouse is described as rejecting male language in the following way: "To be sitting long after dinner, was a confinement that he could not endure. Neither wine nor *conversation* was any thing to him; and gladly did he move to those with whom he was always comfortable" (142; emphasis added). Miss Bates, on the other hand, is the embodiment of female language: "She was a great talker upon little matters . . . full of trivial communications and harmless *gossip*" (52; emphasis added). Both represent a parodic version of the more complex gendered language patterns that take place between Emma and Mr. Knightley.

8. For example, the fathers in Richardson's *Clarissa* and in Rousseau's *La nouvelle Héloïse* both function as models of absolute power and unquestioned authority.

9. In "'The Tittle-Tattle of Highbury': Gossip and the Free Indirect Style in *Emma*," Finch and Bowen argue that a corresponding structure is established between the free indirect style of the novel's unlocatable narrative voice and Emma's present authorial voice, which eventually has to submit to the novel's ideological imperative: "*Emma*'s agenda is clear: the heroine must renounce her manipulative tendencies so that the novel itself can realize its own manipulations. What the novel has articulated as publicly and politically imperative must become Emma's private imperative as well" (11). See also in this volume Kathy Mezei's analysis of free indirect discourse as a site for control of the text.

10. In *Jane Austen and the War of Ideas*, Marilyn Butler argues for the reactionary quality of all the novels written in Austen's time, as a reaction to the sentimental tradition: "Almost every novelist of Jane Austen's day is in some degree or other in the most literal sense a reactionary. To understand the nature of the reaction, it is necessary to turn the perspective of a nervous era upon its sentimental inheritance" (8).

11. Emma, on the other hand, argues that Mr. Knightley *must* never marry (233), which points to the different ontological status of these unconscious revelations of desire; although Emma offers an imperative command that could be denied by the addressee, Mr. Knightley negates the possibility of a response by denying Emma's ontological self in order to affirm his desire.

12. David Lodge makes this point in *After Bakhtin*: "There is, to my knowledge, no precedent for such a novel before *Emma*—that is, a novel in which the authorial narrator mediates virtually all the action through the consciousness of an unreliable focalizing character" (128). Marilyn Butler also argues that "Emma's train of thought is given in full; it is the medium of the narrative . . . and the whole essence of the presentation is that it is unreliable" (250). And Julia Prewitt Brown calls Emma "a reservoir of indeterminacy" in "Civilization and the Contentment of Emma," 91. The unstable quality of Emma's narration is arguably a sign of her modernity as a gendered subject, articulating an absence of complete correspondence between subjecthood and narrating voice, which is not a problem, for example, in the sentimental tradition.

13. In "*Emma* and the Legend of Jane Austen," Lionel Trilling speaks about the problem of the full representability of the feminine and reads Emma as an exception to this: "Women in fiction only rarely have the peculiar reality of the moral life that self-love bestows. Most commonly they exist in a moonlike way, shining by the reflected moral light of men. They are "convincing" or "real" and sometimes "delightful," but they seldom exist as men exist—as genuine moral destinies. . . . It is only on the rare occasions when a female character like Emma confronts us that the difference makes us aware of the usual practice" (154). While Emma's moral destiny is fully realized in the novel, Trilling elides the fact that it is only realized through Mr. Knightley, as a complement to his moral completeness, of which Emma is initially a parody.

14. In relation to the reorganization of desire according to social and economic imper-

atives, Finch and Bowen argue that "the very stuff of Austen's comedic vision always involves such a moment of supreme ideological triumph when political constructions are naturalized and therefore rendered invisible as such: . . . the economic imperative is brought to bear on the very structure of desire" (2). It is this essentializing process that prevents the possibility of an alternative vision of social relations.

15. See Mark Schorer, "The Humiliation of Emma Woodhouse," 98–111, for an insightful analysis of the repeated use of economic metaphors to articulate forms of desire. With economics inscribed into the very fabric of the language, it is necessary to be able to recognize it as a determining factor of social relations, which is how Mr. Knightley achieves greater accuracy than Emma.

16. In *Jane Austen: Women, Politics, and the Novel*, Claudia L. Johnson argues that it is precisely the embodiment of female authority which distinguishes Emma and that this cannot be achieved without the privileged social background: "Emma is a world apart from conservative fiction in accepting a hierarchical social structure not because it is a sacred dictate of patriarchy—*Mansfield Park* had spoiled this—but rather because within its parameters class can actually supercede sex" (127). Although this analysis of Emma's position is accurate, it does not take into account the necessarily problematic relations that Emma establishes with her own gender as a result of her authority.

17. Wayne C. Booth, "Control of Distance in Jane Austen's *Emma*," 200, and Schorer (107) both point to the fact that Jane Fairfax poses a serious threat to Emma's supremacy in the narrative.

18. Marilyn Butler argues for the importance of openness as the ideal model for the individual in Austen's work: "All forms of inwardness and secrecy tend to be anti-social. There is a moral obligation to live outside the self, in honest communication with others" (258).

19. The fact that Jane is materially silenced on account of her secret engagement to Frank Churchill does not absolve her but serves to confirm her "essential" nature.

20. John Knightley also lacks respect for Emma's father (116–17), who, in terms of discourse, is implicitly linked with Miss Bates, which, in turn, sets up a paradoxical structural and psychological affinity between Emma and her brother-in-law.

21. The episode between Miss Bates and Emma takes place as follows: " 'Oh! very well,' exclaimed Miss Bates, 'then I need not be uneasy. Three things very dull indeed. That will just do for me, you know. I shall be sure to say three dull things as soon as ever I open my mouth, shan't I?'—(looking round with the most good-humoured dependence on every body's assent)—'Do not you all think I shall?' Emma could not resist. 'Ah! ma'am, but there may be a difficulty. Pardon me—but you will be limited as to number—only three at once' " (364).

22. This is not to say that the female strategies of resistance employed in the sentimental novel are not also highly problematic. For example, both Pamela and Clarissa eventually capitulate to different forms of patriarchy because there is no alternative social structure available, and the nature of their resistance means that they have been isolated from the beginning.

23. Finch and Bowen argue that the narrative function of gossip is ultimately to confirm rather than to undermine the social agenda, in that it ends up coinciding with the narrative voice of the novel: "And just as gossip *in* the novel is distributed among certain members of the Highbury community, so the narrative authority *of* the novel—by being located nowhere in particular—manages to be everywhere at once" (6). Jan Gordon, on the other hand, suggests that "gossip is a kind of mass epic with its own storytellers in Jane Austen, but one which is invariably threatening to other kinds of stories being narrated," in "A-filiative Families and Subversive Reproduction: Gossip in Jane Austen," 7. These opposing interpretations reveal the complex ways in which gossip operates in *Emma*, for neither the conservative nor the radical aspect can be completely negated, as I try to show.

24. Finch and Bowen suggest that gossip "exercises mild disciplinary control over its members" (7), creating a consensual set of values that are then circulated and internalized. This is, indeed, a convincing reading, but it discounts the disruptive effect of gossip at the moment of utterance, the way in which it forces individuals to question their points of reference, even if the final narrative structure is one of recuperation. .

25. See Glenda A. Hudson, *Sibling Love and Incest in Jane Austen's Fiction*, who argues that sibling relations form a recurring model for Austen's representation of sexual desire. For an analysis of *Emma*, see pp. 50–55.

26. Finch and Bowen argue that the function of gossip is recuperative rather than innovative in that it reveals narratives that are, in fact, already known: "At the level of the novel's *plot*, gossip frankly reveals the subject's 'secrets,' which, upon revelation, turn out to be universally known, overdetermined, and—as Mr. Knightley likes his neighbours to be—public and open" (12).

27. Claudia L. Johnson also notes that this is a radical form of displacement: "In moving to Hartfield, Knightley is sharing *her* home, and in placing himself within her domain, Knightley gives his blessing to her rule" (143).

WORKS CITED

Armstrong, Nancy. *Desire and Domestic Fiction*. Oxford: Oxford University Press, 1987.

Austen, Jane. *Emma*. Harmondsworth: Penguin, 1966.

——. *Mansfield Park*. Harmondsworth: Penguin, 1966.

Bakhtin, Mikhail. *The Dialogic Imagination*. Trans. Caryl Emerson and Michael Holquist. Austin: University of Texas Press, 1981.

——. *Rabelais and His World*. Trans. Hélène Iswolsky. Bloomington: Indiana University Press, 1984.

——. *Speech Genres and Other Late Essays*. Trans. Vern W. McGee. Austin: University of Texas Press, 1986.

Booth, Wayne C. "Control of Distance in Jane Austen's *Emma*." *Jane Austen: "Emma."* Ed. David Lodge. London: Macmillan, 1968. 195–216.

——. "Freedom of Interpretation: Bakhtin and the Challenge of Feminist Criticism."

Bakhtin: Essays and Dialogues on His Work. Ed. Gary Saul Morson. Chicago: University of Chicago Press, 1986. 145–176.

Brown, Julia Prewitt. "Civilization and the Contentment of *Emma.*" *Jane Austen.* Ed. Harold Bloom. New York: Chelsea House, 1986. 87–107.

Butler, Marilyn. *Jane Austen and the War of Ideas.* Oxford: Clarendon, 1975.

Finch, Casey, and Peter Bowen. " 'The Tittle-Tattle of Highbury': Gossip and the Free Indirect Style in *Emma.*" *Representations* 31 (1990): 1–18.

Glazener, Nancy. "Dialogic Subversion: Bakhtin, the Novel, and Gertrude Stein." *Bakhtin and Cultural Theory.* Ed. Ken Hirschkop and David Shepherd. Manchester: Manchester University Press, 1989. 109–29.

Gordon, Jan B. "A-filiative Families and Subversive Reproduction: Gossip in Jane Austen." *Genre* 21 (1988): 5–46.

Hill, Christopher. "Clarissa Harlowe and Her Times." *Puritanism and Revolution.* Bath: Pitman, 1958. 367–94.

Hudson, Glenda A. *Sibling Love and Incest in Jane Austen's Fiction.* London: Macmillan, 1992.

Johnson, Claudia L. *Jane Austen: Women, Politics, and the Novel.* Chicago: University of Chicago Press, 1988.

Lodge, David. *After Bakhtin.* London: Routledge, 1990.

Richardson, Samuel. *Clarissa.* Harmondsworth: Viking, 1985.

——. *Pamela.* Harmondsworth: Penguin, 1980.

Rousseau, Jean-Jacques. *La nouvelle Héloïse.* Paris: Garnier-Flammarion, 1967.

Schorer, Mark. "The Humiliation of Emma Woodhouse." *Jane Austen.* Ed. Ian Watt. Englewood Cliffs, N.J.: Prentice-Hall, 1963. 98–111.

Spacks, Patricia Meyer. *Gossip.* Chicago: University of Chicago Press, 1986.

Todorov, Tzvetan. *Mikhail Bakhtin: The Dialogic Principle.* Trans. Wlad Godzich. Minneapolis: University of Minnesota Press, 1984.

Trilling, Lionel. "*Emma* and the Legend of Jane Austen." *Jane Austen: "Emma".* Ed. David Lodge. London: Macmillan, 1968. 148–169.

Volosinov, V. N. *Marxism and the Philosophy of Language.* Trans. Ladislav Matejka and I. R. Titunik. Cambridge: Harvard University Press, 1986.

Watt, Ian. *The Rise of the Novel.* London: Hogarth, 1957.

Williams, Raymond. *The Country and the City.* London: Hogarth, 1957.

who is speaking here?

Free Indirect Discourse, Gender, and

Authority in Emma, Howards End,

and Mrs. Dalloway

kathy | mezei

ane Austen said of Emma, "I am going to take a heroine whom no one but myself will much like" (Austen-Leigh, 157). E. M. Forster said of Margaret and Helen in *Howards End* that "occasionally the swish of the skirts . . . irritate[s]" (Furbank, 1:190). Virginia Woolf said of Mrs. Dalloway: "The doubtful point is the character of Mrs. Dalloway. It may be too stiff, too glittering and tinsely" (*Writer's Diary*, 61). Uttering these reservations in private about the representation and reception of their "heroines," Austen, Forster, and Woolf signal their/our problem with "who is speaking here." For how *do* Emma, Margaret, and Clarissa Dalloway emerge from the text? How can we describe the shifting, viscous relations between author, implied author, narrator, and these heroine-focalizers? Who speaks for whom? And what role does the construction of gender in narrators, focalizers, and characters play in our understanding of the novels' unfolding? While our dilemma as readers is to untangle our response to the polyphony of voices calling to us, surely some of our delight and pleasure stems from this confusion of voices, this confusion of gender.

In *Emma, Howards End*, and *Mrs. Dalloway*, we discover that a struggle is being waged between narrators and character-focalizers for control of the word, the text, and the reader's sympathy, a struggle paradigmatic of the conflict between conventional gender roles and of the resistance to traditional narrative authority in which a masterly male subject speaks for and over the female object of his gaze.

The site for this textual battle between author, narrator, and character-focalizer and between fixed and fluctuating gender roles is the narrative device "free indirect discourse" (hereafter FID). The undecidability inherent in the structure of FID makes it an appropriate space for the complicated interchange between author, narrator, character-focalizer, and reader. Its structural indeterminacy shelters and accentuates forms of gender indeterminacy. Its indeterminacy of voice undoes any rigid "between-ess" or categoric polarization of author, narrator, and character; as a rhetorical figure it mediates between, through, and across voices seeking to be heard. That FID—a narrative device, a type of discourse—has provoked ideological controversy is evident in the charged descriptions with which theorists express their anxiety about the narrator's control over characters' discourse or, conversely, the characters' intrusion into the narrator's speech. Following is a list of these colorful descriptors of FID: contamination (Hough; McHale; Stanzel); interference (Bal; Volosinov); intervention, colored (Hough); infiltration, tainting (McHale); slipping (Schuelke; McHale); concealing (Bakhtin); illegitimate intrusions by the narrator (Pascal); ironic distance (Hernandi); ambiguity (Cohn); borrowing (Fludernik).

From Adolph Tobler's earliest sighting of FID in 1887, there has been disagreement over its nature, definition, and function, a pragmatic reflection of its structural and semantic indeterminacy. Even the *name* of this type of discourse has been unresolved: colored narrative (Hough); erlebte rede (Etienne Lorck); style indirect libre (Charles Bally; Marguerite Lips); free indirect speech (Pascal); free indirect style (Dillon and Kirchhoff); narrated monologue (Cohn); represented speech (Jespersen; Banfield); substitutionary narration (Hernandi); quasi-direct discourse (Volosinov); pseudo-objective discourse (Bakhtin).[1] The debate over naming reflects a further taxonomic controversy over whether FID is a linguistic phenomenon best defined by linguistic features such as tense, person, and relation to direct and indirect discourse and interior monologue or whether it is a literary phenomenon marked by the context of its utterance, the narrative instance (Genette), and its relation to diegesis and mimesis. In her comprehensive study of FID, *The Fictions of Language and the Language of Fiction*, Monika Fludernik also draws attention to the importance of the "contextual flavour of speech and thought representation" for FID (5).

I have settled on the term FID because its incorporation of free/indirect/discourse opens up an array of interpretive possibilities. To ground our discussion, I propose a definition that combines suggestions made by Anne Neumann and Brian McHale. Neumann defines FID as "that mode of indirectly reported speech or thought which quotes what we feel could be at least some of the words of a character's actual utterance or thought, but which offers those words interwoven with the narrator's language (though not syntactically subordinated to it) without explicitly attributing them to the character in question" (366). And according to McHale, "the basic grammatical characteristics of FID [are] absence of reporting verb of saying/thinking, backshift of tenses, conversion of personal and possessive pronouns" (264).

Now let us turn briefly to the possibilities implied by the three elements of "free indirect discourse." The term and concept "*free*" is significant because, as Paul Hernandi said, "FID does not reduce the most important part of the communication [what characters said] to the status of a secondary clause introduced by "that," a lifeless subordinating conjunction" (36). "Leaving out the reporting verb," Volosinov remarked, "puts responsibility onto the character; it also means the author takes the characters' utterances seriously" (150). "Free" indicates that the narrator has delegated a certain authority and equality to the character and has *deliberately* repressed overt markers of his or her control. Imagine FID as an expression of the character's bid for freedom from the controlling narrator rather like the gingerbread man gleefully escaping from his creator. Unfortunately, both the character and the gingerbread man are inevitably gobbled up, if not by their creator, then by the wily fox, another character, or the waiting reader.

"Indirect" is significant because it implies the indeterminacy of this discourse, an "indirect" discourse into which the reader must insert him/herself and try to determine the positions of narrator and character-focalizer. It points to that which is not fixed or determined or directed, privileging subtlety and uncertainty.

"Discourse" is significant because it embraces both form and content, both speech and writing; it includes monologue, conversation, dialogue, dialect; it is the very substance of narrative. "It is the sort of talk that novelistic environments make possible" (Bakhtin, 427), and we need to remember that the utterances that constitute discourse are shaped by ideological and institutional contexts and by interpretive communities.

Whereas direct discourse and even indirect discourse are contextualized by a narrator through a reporting verb, in FID an ambiguous relation operates between narrator and character-focalizer through what Bakhtin described as double-voiced discourse; the hierarchy in which a narrator "controls" the discourse of the character-focalizer is disrupted. Because FID is a "zone . . . [where] a dialogue is played out between the author and his character" (Bakhtin, 320), FID can set up two quite contrary positions: narratorial irony toward and distance from the character-focalizer, as in *Madame Bovary*, or narratorial empathy toward the character(s), which results in a more engaged reader response, as in *Mrs. Dalloway*. "The narrator, though preserving the authorial mode . . . places himself . . . directly into the experiential field of the character, and adapts the latter's perspective in regard to both time and place" (Pascal, 9).[2]

However, the question of empathy can be viewed from quite the opposite perspective: George Dillon and Frederick Kirchhoff argue that Bronzwaer in *Tense in the Novel* is wrong in assuming that the "apparent merging of points of view . . . expresses the narrator's empathy or identification with his character" (438).

> FIS [FID] is more often a strategy through which the narrator appears to withdraw from the scene and thus present the illusion of a character's acting out his mental state in an immediate relationship with the reader. Paradoxically, FIS, in which the possibilities of confusing a narrator with his character are greatest, is also the mode through which the character *seems* freest from the mediating agency of the narrator. And while it is true that this immediacy generally encourages the reader's empathetic—or at least sympathetic—response to the character, this is no guarantee that the narrator himself experiences a similar response. (438–39)

These definitional indeterminacies simply reinforce FID's necessary malleability. But in investigating the relationship between character and narrator, we rub against the confusion between (implied) author and narrator. Bakhtin and Volosinov, for example, speak of the interplay of *author* and character, whereas other critics (Hough, Banfield) refer to the *narrator* in interaction with the character and ignore the author. Although critics have indiscriminately interchanged author and narrator in their analyses of FID (see Bakhtin, 320), I think it important to remember that in a fictional text, there lives an author as well as an implied author who may or may not be the narrator; a narrator; and, if it is a heterodiegetic text, one or more character-focalizers, along with characters who are not focalizers. As I will show later, Austen, Forster, and Woolf deliberately "construct" narrators with distinctive voices and functions, functions that go beyond those of an implied author. For all three, but particularly for Woolf and Forster, the narrator mediates between an author who may possess radical and contro-

versial views (on sex, class, gender, propriety) and a potentially conservative and disapproving audience. The narrator shelters the author from the
implied criticism of readers, deflecting attention away from the author
toward him/herself; much of this deflection occurs in instances of FID.

Then, too, as Genette reminds us (*Narrative Discourse Revisited*, 65), one
must distinguish between FID and focalization, FID being an instance of
reported discourse, an utterance, whereas focalization is a representation
of a character's perspective, of what that character sees. We should recognize, however, that FID is frequently the mode by which a narrator focalizes through a character, appropriating that character's words to make the
reader see through his/her eyes. Focalization and effacement are effective
narrative strategies for asserting control, because the narrator can choose
his/her focalizer and can choose to be either present or *apparently* absent
from the narration.

As well, different forms of discourse that reflect diverse perspectives
and positions of authority are enacted within FID. Vying for authority and
control in what Henry Gates Jr. calls the "bi-vocality of free indirect discourse" (144–45) are speaking and writing. Consequently, FID becomes a
site for the struggle for control not only between the authority of the
narrator and the independence-seeking character and between representations of dominator and dominated (white and black voices), heterosexual
and homosexual, men and women, but also between speech (orality, dialect) and formal writing and across demarcated gender boundaries.[3] And,
although FID plays upon binary oppositions, it also blurs and elides them
so that FID is not merely an oppositional site of binary polarization but also
a place and moment in which uncertainty is validated and in which oppositions are foregrounded and transgressed.

Despite some evidence otherwise (McHale), FID occurs primarily in
prose fiction and is a distinctive marker of the development of the fiction
of realism in heterodiegetic forms of narration.[4] As Bakhtin explained,
"Pseudo-objective narration is generally characteristic of novel style, since
it is one of the manifold forms for concealing another's speech in hybrid
constructions" (305). In fact, FID can be seen as so essential to the fictional
mode that its occurrences may serve as a *mise en abîme* of the entire text (see
Rimmon-Kenan, 115).[5]

In Austen, Forster, and Woolf, the ambiguous gender roles and relations of
narrators and characters and the shifting of agency between narrator and

focalizer, embedded in FID, serve as a mise en abîme of the novels' inquiry into the societal models of male and female positions: "When the constructed status of gender is theorized as radically independent of sex, gender itself becomes a free-floating artifice, with the consequence that *man* and *masculine* might just as easily signify a female body as a male one, and *woman* and *feminine* a male body as easily as a female one" (Butler, 6). Although a narrator may exhibit gender-marked features of discourse, gender in narrators, unlike in characters and focalizers, is rarely embodied and remains discourse-based. In the context of FID, Judith Butler's question in *Gender Trouble*, "What political possibilities are the consequence of a radical critique of the categories of identity?" (xi) can be rephrased as, What textual possibilities are the consequence of a radical critique of the categories of identity? When a male author focalizes through a female character (E. M. Forster through Margaret in *Howards End*, Flaubert through Emma in *Madame Bovary*), the contradictory activity of taking up gender positions and blurring gender roles mirrors the shadowboxing between narrator and focalizer and is frequently located within the appropriately indeterminate space of FID. If narrators are constructed as male, as they seem to be in *Madame Bovary* and *Howards End*, do they speak out authoritatively or ironically, thereby reducing the female focalizer to an object of the male narratorial gaze? Is it possible for these female focalizers to become genuine speaking subjects and attain agency despite their narrators? Or, by subscribing to FID's indeterminacy, is the narrator representing the slippage between the author's possibly ambivalent sexuality and society's concept of appropriate sexual behavior?[6] Because of its own indeterminate form, FID offers a coded structure within the text to reveal authors' discomfort with conventional gender roles and forms of gender polarization.

FID is "an utterance, which as such no one (not one) could have uttered" (Ginsburg, 136), an utterance that with its indeterminacy, doubleness, and ambiguity sets up a site in which gender relations or tensions are enacted at the level of both story and discourse. The "other story" (Hite), the muted marginalized story, finds a way to voice itself. While the muted voice might be repressed or repudiated by the narratorial voice or by the collective, choral voice of gossip, it might also infiltrate and subvert these authoritative voices. A character who dares to defy the narrator's authority by speaking other, like Austen's Emma or Flaubert's Emma, may be rapidly contextualized or ironized by the narrator (all forms of control) and thus silenced, or (s)he may be allowed through the indeterminacy of the structure of FID to persist as a subversive other voice. She may even "contaminate" the narrator's discourse, resulting in a fertile hybridization.

The indeterminacy and instability of FID puts the onus on the reader, who has to decide where in all this the author stands. The author, of course, may wish to leave the threads of ambiguity dangling.

A HEROINE WHOM NO ONE BUT MYSELF WILL MUCH LIKE

Quentin Bell reports an argument between him and David Garnett in which Garnett insisted that Emma was a cold-hearted snob. When Bell pointed out that she was kind to her tiresome old father, Garnett retorted, "We've only got Jane Austen's word for it" (14).[7]

"We have only Jane Austen's word for it" is a felicitous way to describe the operation of FID. Ian Watt's observation in his 1957 *Rise of the Novel* that Austen combined the "realism of presentation and realism of assessment, of the internal and of the external approaches to character" (338) is an early if unformulated recognition of Austen's efficacious use of FID (Cohn, 108).[8] In *Emma* we have a female author and a narrator whose gender is undisclosed and whom Graham Hough describes as at times "talking on behalf of society or Dr. Johnson or God" or at times "as an individual woman, shrewd, sensible, sometimes tart and frequently amused" (209).[9] Describing the narrator ("the linguistic subject, a function, not a person"), Mieke Bal reminds us that "the narrator of *Emma* is not Jane Austen. . . . In order to keep this distinction in mind, I shall refer to the narrator as *it*" (119). Bal is right to caution us against same-sex assumptions; the gender of the narrator in *Emma* remains ambiguous, fluctuating, and the reader must assign gendered pronouns according to his/her interpretation.[10] Unlike Emma, "the authorial narrator located outside the story is not imagined as a full bodily presence" (Schabert, 312).

The narrator does have a tendency to resemble Mr. Knightley in (his) discourse and views of Emma.[11] Therefore, the reader falls under the sway of a narrator with pronounced opinions who has allied her/himself with an authoritative, masterly male protagonist and who judges Emma and observes her with irony. As the novel opens, the narrator's irony immediately manifests itself: "Emma Woodhouse, handsome, clever, and rich, with a comfortable home and happy disposition, seemed to unite some of the best blessings of existence; and had lived nearly twenty-one years in the world with very little to distress or vex her" (37). In this way, we are forewarned that things will arise to distress or vex Emma, and we cheerfully anticipate that they will form the source of the novel's plot. The narrator has already woven the reader into her/his web. Since the novel revolves around plotting (of marriages), Emma plots the marriage of Harriet Smith to Mr. Elton ("'I promise you to make none [matches] for myself, papa; but I must, indeed, for other people. . . . Only for Mr Elton . . . I must look about for a wife for him'" [43–44]); the neighbors plot Emma's marriage to Frank Churchill ("There were wishes at Randalls respecting Emma's destiny" [69]); Frank Churchill plots to disguise his secret engagement to Jane Fairfax by paying suit to Emma; and the narrator "plots" Emma's marriage to Mr. Knightley. Gossip and misreading further entangle these interwoven plots.

Because the narrator focalizes extensively through Emma, the reader, thus privy to Emma's thoughts and doubts, is given every opportunity to be sympathetic to Emma, particularly as the novel progresses and Emma's *blunders* increase.[12] Our readerly response to instances of FID is markedly different from our response to Emma speaking assertively in direct discourse and falling into one trap or plot after another.[13] When Emma speaks directly we experience either delight at her openness, amusement at her misreadings, or sly satisfaction at her comeuppance, but Emma speaking through FID is another matter. For example, here is Emma after Mr. Elton's unwelcome marriage proposal and the obvious failure of her plot to marry Harriet and Mr. Elton. She is at last alone: "The hair was curled, and the maid sent away, and Emma sat down to think and be miserable.—*It was a wretched business indeed!—Such an overthrow of every thing she had been wishing for! Such a development of every thing most unwelcome!—Such a blow for Harriet!*" (153; the "narrator's language" is in roman, Emma's "actual utterance or thought" is in italic script, and note that at times the two voices are not easily distinguishable). The narrator draws us into the immediacy of Emma's thought processes and into her characteristic language and idiom; dialogism ensues between the narrator and Emma, between propriety and resistance, convention and mischief-making, with FID becoming a site of resistance where Emma voices her own unconventional thoughts. FID, however, serves to blur the distinction between the two. By carefully positioning the narrative instance and by deliberately effacing herself—as she does in the passage above—and thus permitting an other and different voice to emerge, the narrator may be more complicit in Emma's resistance than is immediately apparent.[14] Or, to put it another way, the author, Austen, in manipulating the narrator's timely absence, is at work encouraging us into an "empathetic response" to her heroine. Emma's heartfelt shock and regret at the consequences of her plotting, presented through

FID—"It was a wretched business indeed!"—elicits our sympathy. Because we enter into Emma's intimate thoughts, the reader may even feel a tinge of regret that Emma was not able to overwrite the conventional marriage plot and marry off the "ill-born" Harriet to Mr. Elton.

For further evidence of how the narrator has rendered Emma sympathetic, look at the scene in which Emma reluctantly visits the enviable, perfect, passive Jane Fairfax, and notice how the focalization and FID interact to influence the reader: "Emma was obliged to play; and the thanks and praise which necessarily followed appeared to her an affectation of candour, an air of greatness, meaning only to shew off in higher style her own very superior performance. *She was, besides, which was the worst of all, so cold, so cautious! There was no getting at her real opinion.* Wrapt up in a cloak of politeness, she seemed determined to hazard nothing. *She was disgustingly, was suspiciously reserved.* . . . Emma *could not forgive her*" (182–83; emphasis added to denote Emma's language). "Disgustingly," "suspiciously," "could not forgive her" are Emma's words; the narrator is primarily present structurally in her organization of the context for Emma's ruminations. Although a few pages earlier the narrator had sympathetically narrated Jane's sad history, here Emma's words—critical, negative, human words—seduce the reader. We may feel that we should like Jane, but we cannot. Emma has convinced us. Moreover, Austen has apparently encouraged Emma to resist the narrator's own discourse and authority.

As Emma is improved and reproved, gaining our and the narrator's approval, the ironic distance between the narrator and Emma lessens, and the narrator looks over Emma's shoulder, nodding as it were. Yet because Emma in the earlier part of novel reenacts what Austen herself does—the construction of marriage plots—how seriously should we take the narrator's critique of Emma's plotting and blunders? Or does the narrator mediate with an ironic, masterly (Knightley) voice, the voice of social approbation, between a rebellious, mischievous author and a rebellious, mischievous heroine and by (her) very presence deflect the reader from rejecting the author's encoded critique of propriety and marriage rituals?[15] By her gradual approval of Emma, the narrator opens the way for the reader's favorable reception of this heroine. As the tangle of relationships is sorted out and Mr. Knightley proposes, the narrator, through an instance of FID, reveals Emma's thoughts: "Serious she was, very serious in her thankfulness, and in her resolutions; and yet there was no preventing a laugh, sometimes in the very midst of them. *She must laugh at such a close! Such an end of the doleful disappointment of five weeks back! Such a heart—such a Harriet!*

Now there would be pleasure in her returning.—*Every thing would be a pleasure. It would be a great pleasure to know Robert Martin*" (456). To use the narrator's own words, the narrator "seems" to give her approbation to Emma. By the end of the novel, the distinction between the narrator's voice and Emma's is less marked. The reader, by way of the filter of the narrator, is amused by Emma's exuberance and experiences palpable relief in the narrator's successful resolution of the marriage plot to Emma's advantage. Through the ambivalence and doubleness of FID, Austen can mute the masterly narratorial voice and project Emma's own increasingly engaging persona.

One of the characteristics of FID, as discussed earlier, is its slippage between narrator and the character-focalizer. Because of this slippage, the reader has been deliberately destabilized, swaying between the narrator's authoritative and slightly amused, slightly reproving voice and Emma's wit, courage, and rebellion. This destabilization of the reader through the indeterminacy created by FID is important, for it cleverly unsettles the reader's expectations of both the plot and of Emma, paradoxically creating a reader more open to changes, shifts, and twists. The narrator has "refracted" (Bakhtin) her discourse through Emma, in this way diffusing the authority of the monologic authorial voice, permitting a voice of resistance to the marriage plot, to restrictive social codes and conventions, and to the constrained lives of women.

The irony of the closing, in which the narrator has the last word, lies in its patness: "But, in spite of these deficiencies, the wishes, the hopes, the confidence, the predictions of the small band of true friends who witnessed the ceremony, were fully answered in the perfect happiness of the union" (465). The parody of a romance ending absolves the reader from feeling that Emma has capitulated either to a marriage plot or to the narrator's authority. As Alison Booth wrote in *Famous Last Words*, "the premature closure of the female quest plot, and the predominance of the romance plots leading either to marriage or death, does not close the play of the *discourse* along with the *story*." Booth continues on to explain that how "the novel ends often exposes the difference between the narrative 'expression' and its 'content,' and either or both . . . may serve to undermine social and literary convention. The woman's story and the design of the text itself may find ways to contradict the last words that ostensibly control the meaning of the ensuing silence" (2, 3). For Austen, the progenitor of FID, it seems that FID, along with irony, becomes an effective space in which questions of gender, authority, and propriety can be subtly interrogated.[16]

In *Howards End*, E. M. Forster employs a noticeably intrusive narrator, and as in *Emma*, the interplay between narrator and character complicates our reading.[17] *Howards End* was published in 1910, the year pinpointed by Virginia Woolf to mark the changing shape of the English novel: "In or about December, 1910, human character changed" ("Mr. Bennett and Mrs. Brown," *Collected Essays*, 320). Forster tries if not to revolutionize the shape of the novel, at least to concern himself with certain radical issues— the condition of women, the English class system, and the effects of a powerful bourgeoisie and commerce on the life of the mind and the spirit. He also sets his narrator to focalize through Margaret: narratorial cross-dressing. Margaret is the elder and more conventional of the two sisters in the novel, and P. N. Furbank, Forster's biographer, claims that "of course, in many important ways, Margaret was Forster himself; her views are certainly his" (1:173). In 1958, either disillusioned with his younger self or disinterested in heterosexual love, Forster wrote in his commonplace book: "Have only just discovered why I don't care for it; not a single character in it for whom I care . . . occasionally the swish of the skirts and the non-sexual embraces irritate" (Furbank, 1:190).[18] However, in a 1955 interview he had said, "There are some [characters] I like thinking about . . . Margaret Schlegel . . . whose fortunes I have been interested to follow" ("E. M. Forster," 33). Forster's ambivalence toward Margaret, an ambivalence that may have its roots in Forster's homosexuality, expresses itself in the novel through the conflictual relation between the narrator and Margaret as focalizer, for on occasion the narrator seems to mock or undermine Margaret. It is also possible that, by his offhand tone, the narrator is attempting to impress the reader with his knowledge of women's affairs.

By simultaneously foregrounding and undermining Margaret, Forster could be projecting his own uncertainty about socially constructed gender roles. Focalizing through Margaret allows Forster to empathize with the emancipated new woman, the feminine, and the artistic, while reproving her through the narrator allows him to view her through the eyes of "society." The narrator, here as in Austen, seems to mediate between the reader and an author who may be encoding his sexual in-betweenness and his radical social vision within the novel's narrative structure.

The novel's beginning (not unlike *Emma*'s) leads the reader into several perplexities concerning the relation between narrator and character. Here, as in *Emma* and *Mrs. Dalloway*, the narrator, in contrast to the characters whose speech "he" reports, is not embodied. Thus there are no physical markers of gender, which is indicated only by linguistic and semantic features of discourse:

> One may as well begin with Helen's letters to her sister.
> *Howards End,*
> *Tuesday.*
> *Dearest Meg,*
> *It isn't going to be what we expected. It is old and little, and altogether delightful—red brick.* (5; emphasis in original)

What is the effect of the opening "one"? Is it a collective "we" that bonds the reader to the narrator and author, or does it serve to distinguish and differentiate the impersonal and powerful narrator—the narrator who chooses somewhat arbitrarily ("may as well") to begin with Helen's letters to her sister, Margaret? The narrator has asserted "his" presence, but the first voice heard after the intrusive narrator's opening is Helen's; her letter serves as direct discourse, contextualized and situated by the narrator. Meg is the implied addressee/narratee. The character's—Helen's—voice continues unmediated: "It isn't going to be what we expected." Although Helen seems to be referring to Howards End, this sentence foreshadows (similar to the foreshadowing implied by Austen's "seems" in the opening of *Emma*) that the narrative will not be what we expected. Later in the letter the narrator intrudes by replacing Helen's description of what she wore for dinner with the word "omission": "I am going to wear [omission]. Last night Mrs Wilcox wore an [omission], and Evie [omission]" (6). This erasure of Helen's words ensures that even in Helen's own direct discourse—her letter—the narrator's presence is felt: either what she wears is not important, or the male narrator feels unqualified to describe the outfit; in any case this insertion reminds us of the presence of a controlling narrator and breaks the illusion of the autonomy of the letter and Helen's speaking.

Unlike Austen's (and Woolf's) narrators, whose gender is indeterminate and shifting, Forster's narrator presents as male. The narrator's reluctance to discuss women's dress is one piece of evidence; another, via syntax and prenomial reference, has been pointed to by Barbara Rosecrance and occurs when the narrator muses: "Pity, if one may generalize, is at the bottom of woman. When men like us, it is for our better qualities, and however tender their liking, we dare not be unworthy of it, or they will quietly let us go. But unworthiness stimulates woman. It brings out her deeper nature, for good or for evil" (227).[19] In contrast to Austen (and Woolf), Forster's gender indeterminacy is located less within the narrative voice than in the narrator's interaction with Margaret as focalizer. The narrator, like Emma Woodhouse's narrator, both focalizes through Margaret and sustains a fractious dialogic relationship with her, asserting his superiority and control. "To Margaret—and I hope that it will not set the reader against her—the station of King's Cross had always suggested Infinity. Its very situation—withdrawn a little behind the facile splendours of St Pancras—implied a comment on the materialism of life. . . . If you think this ridiculous, remember that it is not Margaret who is telling you about it" (13). Whether the contemporary reader finds this narratorial intervention pompous and annoying, playfully self-reflexive, or perhaps ironic, we wonder why the narrator disassociates himself from Margaret in such a manner. Forster could simply be drawing attention to the novel's narrativity, representing the typical superior male attitude to females who attempt to philosophize, or, in the guise of a narrator, revealing his indeterminacy about gender and gender roles, as it is Margaret who is thinking deep thoughts, not the (male) narrator.

Whatever the interpretation, most readers gladly shift away from such an intrusive narrator to gravitate to Margaret's focalization, with which we can more readily identify and sympathize. In *Howards End*, the evolution and the effect of focalization differs from that of *Emma*, for although she accommodates herself to the Wilcoxes in the way Emma bows to social conventions, Margaret does not, like Emma, move closer to the narrator's (self-righteous) perspective. To the contrary, the narrator shifts toward Margaret's vision, adapting her perspective and her rationalizations. In tone, Forster's narrator also contrasts with Austen's gently ironic narrator, adopting a diffident, mocking tone intermingled with solemn philosophizing: "It will be generally admitted that Beethoven's Fifth Symphony is the most sublime noise that has ever penetrated into the ear of man. All sorts and conditions are satisfied by it. Whether you are like Mrs Munt, and tap surreptitiously when the tunes come—of course, not so as to disturb the others—or like Helen, who can see heroes and shipwrecks in the music's flood . . ." (31). However, Forster was aware of the conflict between the autonomy and credibility of characters and the temptation to control them by the (implied) author or narrator:

> This power to expand and contract perception (of which the shifting viewpoint is a symptom), this right to intermittent knowledge—I find it one of the great advantages of the novel-form . . . we can enter into people's minds occasionally but not always, because our own minds get tired; . . . novelists . . . have behaved like this to the people in their books;

played fast and loose with them, and I cannot see why they should be censured.

> They must be censured if we catch them at it . . . to take your reader into your confidence about the universe is a different thing. It is not dangerous for a novelist to draw back from his characters . . . and to generalize about the conditions under which he thinks life is carried on. It is confidences about the individual people that do harm, and beckon the reader away from the people to an examination of the novelist's mind. (*Aspects of the Novel*, 83, 84)

Forster was able to undermine the authoritative voice—represented by the Wilcoxes, who on the surface are so adept at organizing baggage, business, houses, and people—by deflecting it into a dialogic relationship between an evasive and variable narrator and a thoughtful female focalizer. Episodes of FID, particularly toward the close of the novel, reflect the novel's and the narrator's indeterminacy—can one connect with anyone? Who is telling this story? What role does gender play?

Near the close of the novel, Helen and Margaret spend the night together at Howards End.

> The peace of the country was entering into her. It has no commerce with memory, and little with hope. Least of all is it concerned with the hopes of the next five minutes. It is the peace of the present, which passes understanding. Its murmur came "now," and "now" once more as they trod the gravel, and "now" as the moonlight fell upon their father's sword. They passed upstairs, kissed, and amidst the endless iterations fell asleep. The house had enshadowed the tree at first, but as the moon rose higher the two disentangled, and were clear for a few moments at midnight. Margaret awoke and looked into the garden. *How incomprehensible that Leonard Bast should have won her this night of peace! Was he also part of Mrs. Wilcox's mind?* (293–94; narrator's language in roman, Margaret's in italic)

This passage is an extraordinary mise en abîme, as narrator and focalizer "disentangle" and then tangle again, forcing the reader continually to (re)locate herself. The narrator's discourse dominates—philosophical, superior, reflective; his observations are rendered in the present tense, sometimes in the gnomic present: "It has no commerce with memory." Although we step outside Margaret with the narrator, who parades his greater omniscience, we remain within her sphere of perception and values. Then, as Margaret awakes and looks into the garden, we enter into her focalization and discourse, and the last two sentences are uttered in her discourse. We even have direct evidence that these are her actual words, since on the previous page she spoke about Mrs. Wilcox: "I feel that you and I and Henry are only fragments of that *woman's mind*" (292; emphasis added).

The slippage of voice between narrator and Margaret represents the indeterminacy cast by the novel's ineluctable movement to an uncertain ending in which "connections" remain tenuous and fragile and forays into gender roles and sexual conduct remain, understandably, unresolved. For Forster, like Austen, also used instances of FID to query gender roles and expectations: What is womanly? What is manly? Through FID, the narrator alternates between Margaret's and Mr. Wilcox's views on appropriate gender roles and sexuality. Mr. Wilcox, on realizing that Margaret will refuse to fuss about his affair with Jacky Bast, thinks, "Against the tide of his sin flowed the feeling that she was not altogether womanly. Her eyes gazed too straight; they had read books that are suitable for men only" (228). The mode of speech—"too straight," "suitable for men only"—is Mr. Wilcox's, mediated by the narrator.

Margaret's thoughts are more complicated, and as Furbank has suggested, possibly reflect Forster's own ideas: "She tried to translate his temptation into her own language, and her brain reeled. Men must be different, even to want to yield to such a temptation. . . . Are the sexes really races, each with its own code of morality, and their mutual love a mere device of Nature to keep things going?" (224). And, "She knew that Henry was not so much confessing his soul as pointing out the gulf between the male soul and the female, and she did not desire to hear him on this point" (229). Although Forster mocks conventional expressions of gender polarization, he offers no simple resolution to the problem of gender, only a space of inquiry opened for the reader. The narrator, then, tactfully concedes to Margaret's wish, we are spared Henry's views even through FID, and we move on.

Forster, in marrying Margaret to Mr. Wilcox, both acquiesces to the marriage plot and undermines it. Like Emma, Margaret marries an older man, a pillar of English social values and customs, but Margaret exerts control within the marriage to an even greater extent than Emma. Through this "connection"—marriage—Forster both exposes the hollowness of the Wilcoxian vision and refuses to discard it entirely. Forster and Austen encode uncertainties about the desirability of strong and independent female figures in the fluctuating absence/presence of their narrators, for Emma and Margaret are alternately admired and then chastised by their narrators and are alternately given the power to speak freely and intelligently and then reprimanded for their frank modes of discourse.

In *Emma* the narrator intruded to speak on behalf of the author and to guide the reader, with tempered commentary and/or irony, toward a greater respect (through FID) for Emma's voice and vision. In *Howards End*, the narrator has simultaneously drawn attention to himself and set up an ambivalent reception to his presence for the reader. Significantly, in both novels, the male and/or controlling voice is subdued, and credence and power shift to the female focalizer.

her subversive stance is hidden by the other voices.

TOO GLITTERING AND TINSELY

In *Mrs. Dalloway* (1925), by employing a polyphony of voices, Virginia Woolf paradoxically effaces the narrator, who is seemingly diminished by the presence of so many other (internalized) voices, yet she also enormously augments the narrator's structural role as he/she weaves from one voice to the next in a display of virtuosity. In contrast to *Emma* and *Howards End*, Woolf in *Mrs. Dalloway* tackles the marriage plot by writing backward and beyond the ending; Mrs. Dalloway is middle-aged and already married—an unlikely heroine. Woolf's radical narrative perspective reflects her radical perspective on the lives of women.

Woolf's narrative strategy, particularly from *Jacob's Room* (1922) to *Between the Acts* (1941), was to decenter the subject and to diffuse the monologic patriarchal voice through multiple focalizers and FID.[20] As she wrote in her diary when she began *Between the Acts*: " 'I' rejected: 'We' substituted: to whom at the end there shall be an invocation? 'We' . . . the composed of many different things. . . . we all life, all art, all waifs and strays—a rambling capricious but somehow unified whole—the present state of my mind?" (*Writer's Diary*, 289–90).

Woolf was well aware of the psychological effect of focalization and of the power of the controlling narrator who manipulates focalization. In *To the Lighthouse* (1927), Mr. Ramsay, focalized through his wife, Mrs. Ramsay, through the painter Lily Briscoe, or through the other marginalized voices —his children, Cam and James—is a pitiable caricature of male authority. Had he been primarily self-focalized or focalized through his young disciple, Charles Tansley, the story would have been different. Woolf wanted to tell not the master narrative but "the other story," of the effect of an egocentric and powerful father and husband on his family. Mr. Ramsay's heroic quest to reach beyond "P" to "R" in his philosophic inquiries, though certainly important to the story, is only part of the story.

In *To the Lighthouse*, an entire section, "Time Passes," is given over to the narratorial voice, with the consequence that the reader is sharply reminded of the difference between a present, speaking narrator and an absent or effaced narrator and is thus alerted to the agility and hidden power of the narrator in "The Window" and "The Lighthouse" sections. Evidently, Woolf realized that FID was an effective device to disrupt distinctions between narrator and character and a strategic site within which to locate the apparent effacement of the narrator. While closing *To the Lighthouse*, she wrote:

> It is proved, I think, that what I have to say is to be said in this manner. As usual, side stories are sprouting in great variety as I wind this up: a book of characters; the whole string being pulled out from some simple sentence. . . . I think I can spin out all their entrails this way; but it is hopelessly undramatic. It is all in oratio obliqua. Not quite all; for I have a few direct sentences. . . . This is the greatest stretch I've put my method to, and I think it holds. By this I mean that I have been dredging up more feelings and characters. . . . I'm haunted by that damned criticism of Janet Case's "it's all dressing . . . technique." (*Writer's Diary*, 99–101)

Woolf needed the "technique"—the "dressing"—to transmit feelings and characters in what she felt was a more realistic method than Arnold Bennett's, whose practice she had criticized in her 1924 essay "Mr. Bennett and Mrs. Brown." In *Mrs. Dalloway* she seems to have worked out a technical response (she calls it her "tunnelling process") to Mr. Bennett's unsatisfactory realism by doing away with the concept of a central authoritative voice normally located in a narrator (as in *Emma* or *Howards End*).[21] *Mrs. Dalloway*'s narrator promiscuously focalizes through Clarissa, Peter Walsh, Miss Kilman, Elizabeth, Septimus, and Rezia, dipping into their discourse and thoughts through FID.

A technical tour de force, much examined by critics, opens the novel and, like the openings of *Emma* and *Howards End*, directs the reader:

> Mrs Dalloway said she *would buy the flowers herself.*
>
> *For Lucy has her work cut out for her. The doors would be taken off their hinges; Rumpelmayer's men were coming.* And then, thought Clarissa Dalloway, what a morning—fresh as if issued to children on a beach.
>
> *What a lark! What a plunge!* For so it had always seemed to her when, with a little squeak of the hinges, which she could hear now, she had burst open the French windows and plunged at Bourton into the open air. *How fresh; how calm, stiller than this of course, the air was in the early morning;*

like the flap of a wave; the kiss of a wave; chill and sharp and yet (for a girl of eighteen as she then was) *solemn*, feeling as she did, standing there at the open window, that *something awful was about to happen.* (5; narrator's language in roman, Clarissa's language in italic)[22]

Mrs. Dalloway usurps the narrator's role by the second sentence, relinquishes it in the fourth, reclaims it in the fifth. By the sixth sentence, through FID, the narrator begins to summarize and contextualize "events" and initiate the novel's plot. Here again an instance of FID serves as a mise en abîme of the novel's story and discourse. Is Woolf then wresting control not only from her narrator but also from the concept of the kind of primary focalizer we met in *Emma* and *Howards End* in order to undermine narrative authority, particularly as it represents (mimics) patriarchal authority? Indeed, as if to emphasize this decentering, the narrator will focalize through several characters, male and female, all within a small space—one sentence, one paragraph—and by these techniques of focalization and FID break down the sentence, sequence, and the conventional hierarchy of gender and patriarchy. Yet, the reader cannot help but be conscious of the virtuosity and control of this narrator who so adroitly maneuvers through the novel. Like Orlando, the narrator switches gender or, more accurate, dons the mask of male discourse, only to shed it for the mask of female discourse. Unlike Austen's fluctuating narrator, who if Graham Hough is correct, at times talks on behalf of male authority, at times as an "individual woman" (Hough, 209), the gender of Woolf's narrator is more indeterminate and layered.

For example, let us look at the "Proportion Speech" (*Mrs. Dalloway*, 110–13) associated with the persona of the physician, Sir William Bradshaw, who worships the Goddess of Divine Proportion and represents Convention so powerfully that Septimus Smith can resist only by killing himself:

> But Proportion has a sister, less smiling, more formidable, a Goddess even now engaged—in the heat and sands of India, the mud and swamp of Africa, the purlieus of London, wherever, in short, the climate or the devil tempts men to fall from the true belief which is her own—is even now engaged in . . . setting up . . . her own stern countenance. Conversion is her name and she feasts on the wills of the weakly. . . . But conversion, fastidious Goddess, loves blood better than brick, and feasts most subtly on the human will. For example, Lady Bradshaw. Fifteen years ago she had gone under. It was nothing you could put your

finger on; there had been no scene, no snap; only the slow sinking, water-logged, of her will into his. (110–11)

Within the narrative flow of the novel, the Proportion passage is jarring; readers balk at its incongruity, but there it is, mimicking the voice of male authority, the singular occurrence of an obtrusive narratorial voice. In its narratological incongruity, this passage reminds us of the "Time Passes" section in *To the Lighthouse*. For a moment, we seem to step out of the consciousness and discourse of the characters to encounter the narratorial voice, who speaks here for a few passages without continually dissolving into discourses of the others, which has been the novel's narrative pattern. In its authority, in its use of capitals ("Proportion"), this particular discourse mimics the language of patriarchy, an ironic variation of the concept of FID. However, the features of this passage, with its hyperbolic language of empire and power brokering (the colonies, such as India and Africa; factories; and parliaments) and its stockpiling of parallel phrases to the point of extravagance ("in the heat and sands of India, the mud and swamp of Africa, the purlieus of London") are abruptly undercut by the terse phrase "wherever, in short, the climate or the devil tempts men to fall from the true belief which is her own." This creates an ironic space for the reader rather like that constructed by Austen's narrator. Although in this passage we do not encounter indeterminacies of FID in which the narrator performs a sleight of hand in switching between speakers, there is nevertheless a double-voiced discourse. While the narrator, it is true, seems to speak to us directly, Woolf, in employing features of exaggeration such as capitalization, proliferation of phrases, and the heightened language of empire in an exaggerated manner, makes us aware of a submerged and ironic voice. Nor can we determine the speaker's gender, only that there is a parody of male discourse and empathy for Lady Bradshaw's plight. This contrasts with other occurrences of FID in which the narrator (female? indeterminate?) sympathetically enters into the consciousness and language of, for example, Septimus Smith or Peter Walsh. Here is Peter in Regent's Park: "This susceptibility to impressions had been his undoing, no doubt. Still at his age he had, like a boy or a girl even, these alternations of mood; good days, bad days, . . . After India of course one fell in love with every woman one met" (79). The narrator has set Peter to walk in Regent's Park but then steps aside while he muses in his own words. The strategy is different here from the Proportion passage, for we are less conscious of a narratorial presence and more conscious of the other voice (Peter) speaking.

Let us also take the "match burning in a crocus" passage, in which an empathetic if coded evocation of women's love and female orgasm is offered through FID: "She [Clarissa] could not resist sometimes yielding to the charm of a woman, not a girl, of a woman confessing. . . . She did undoubtedly then feel what men felt . . . one yielded to its expansion, and rushed to farthest verge and there quivered and felt the world come closer, swollen with some astonishing significance, some pressure of rapture, which split its thin skin and gushed and poured over with an extraordinary alleviation over the cracks and sores" (36). Is the description of orgasm the narrator's or Clarissa's? Its agency seems indeterminate and is perhaps not important to pin down; nevertheless, the extreme empathy with which this experience is evoked (in contrast to the mocking tone of the Proportion passage) suggests a shared and intense intimacy between the narrator and Clarissa.

Ambiguity of gender goes hand in hand with the apparent blurring of narrator into character, and Woolf goes much further than either Austen or Forster in her attempt to diffuse the unitary authorial voice by attributing discourse to many different voices and undermining distinctions between them or between narrator and focalizers.[23] FID is, after all, "a structure of undecidability, transgress[ing] and violat[ing] binary oppositions" (Ginsburg, 133).[24] Nevertheless, the narrator is always present and in control since it is s/he who contextualizes the instances of FID and orchestrates the movement from one voice into another.[25]

Woolf had her doubts about Mrs. Dalloway, calling her "tinsely": "[her character] may be too stiff, too glittering and tinsely" (*Writer's Diary*, 61).[26] She then goes on to say, "But then I can bring innumerable other characters to her support" (61) and, most pertinently, "Then I invented her memories" (79), both strategies being instigated through instances of FID. I suspect Forster's doubts about Margaret had to do with her sex, her potentially insufferable rightness, and his own sexual ambivalence, whereas Woolf worried about spinning an entire novel around the slight figure of a society lady. In the opening passage quoted above, Clarissa's memories of Bourton (and of Peter and Sally and of lost love) are recalled through FID, revealing information about Clarissa herself in an oblique manner: "For so it has always seemed to her . . . she had burst open the French windows and plunged at Bourton into the open air [narrator's language]. How fresh, how calm, stiller than this of course [Clarissa's language]" (5).[27]

As Clarissa Dalloway sets out on her walk to buy flowers for her party, she is watched (focalized) by others. A neighbor, Scrope Purvis, observes her through FID: "A charming woman, Scrope Purvis thought her (knowing her as one does know people who live next door to one in Westminster); a touch of the bird about her" (6). He never appears again in the novel, but his words (and gaze) form part of the polyvocal discourse that creates "Clarissa" and comes to her support. Like Jacob, Clarissa is known (and not known) by the fragmentary observations of others as much as by her own thoughts and words. It is as if the narrator absents him/herself from the controlling and authoritative commentary found in Austen and substitutes a shifting focalization. Instead of the narrator delivering impressions of Clarissa, we receive the "support of innumerable other characters" (*Writer's Diary*, 61) In this way, Woolf undermines both the masterly authoritative narrator and the concept of a narrator located in a fixed gender role, for this narrator adroitly adopts Septimus Smith's troubled vision and voice as readily as s/he does Peter Walsh's, Miss Kilman's, and Sir William Bradshaw's. One might almost say that through the varied use of FID, the core of Clarissa, Mrs. Dalloway, is constructed.

By observing how the narrator withdrew discreetly in *Emma*, wavered uncertainly in *Howards End*, or seemed to efface herself in *Mrs. Dalloway* in the space of FID, we encounter authors who wish to veil or unveil "who is speaking here." FID provides an ideal site within which to query authority and speaking, question traditional gender roles, and explore indeterminacies of gender.

NOTES

1. Brian McHale, "Free Indirect Discourse: A Survey of Recent Accounts," outlines the origins and evolution of the concept of FID. See also Roy Pascal, *The Dual Voice*.

2. "From a strictly grammatical point of view, it is the author's speech, whereas according to the sense of it, it is the character's speech" (Volosinov, 145). "One mind is responsible for the form and another for the content of a statement" (Hernandi, 36–37).

3. Gates describes how the quest of the black speaking subject to find his/her own voice is often manifested as a double-voiced narrative strategy within FID. See, in particular, "Zora Neale Hurston and the Speakerly Text": "As the protagonist approaches self-consciousness, however, not only does the text use free indirect discourse to represent her development, but the diction of the black characters' discourse comes to inform the diction of the voice of narrative commentary such that, in several passages, it is extraordinarily difficult to distinguish the narrator's voice from the protagonist's" (191).

4. In conversation, contributor Melba Cuddy-Keane pointed out that FID may be a frequent rhetorical strategy in nonfiction prose by women (i.e. Doris Lessing's "My Father"), and contributor Janet Giltrow mentioned that it is also a feature of modern travel narratives (i.e. Bruce Chatwin's *The Songlines*).

5. Rimmon-Kenan pushes the significance of FID even further, claiming: "It . . . gains the status of a miniature reflection of the nature of all texts and all language. For language, as Derrida has repeatedly argued . . . always 'quotes' other language, constituting itself on linguistic iterability and cultural *clichés* whose direct utterers are nowhere present. From this point of view, *all language becomes—in operation if not in grammatical form—a kind of free indirect discourse*" (115; emphasis added).

6. Slipping "refers to a move or a 'slip' from one mode of representation to another within the same sentence" (McKenzie, 156). This slippage or indeterminacy is characteristic of FID and complex texts. Narrators may establish "a point of view differentiated from one sequence to another" (Dillon and Kirchhoff, 433). Moreover, there is no consistent set of linguistic markers to determine FID, which can, at times, easily slip into direct or indirect discourse (433).

7. I am very grateful to Quentin Bell for directing me to the source of this wonderful interchange; see "The Exquisite Jane Austen."

8. Cohn claims that Austen was the "first extensive practitioner" of FID or narrated monologue (108).

9. For a discussion of FID in Austen, see Hough, Flavin, Neumann, and Finch and Bowen.

10. In her article "The Authorial Mind and the Question of Gender," Ina Schabert examines the dilemma of the gender of the narrator, who was "usually represented as existing outside the sphere where gender differences hold" (312). Schabert points out that there is a range of narratorial gender distinctions, which include androgynous and cross-gender narration, and in allocating gender to a narrator, critics need to do justice to this range and avoid essentialist assumptions.

11. The reasonable voice of Mr. Knightley, allied as it is with the narrator, further manipulates the reader to view Emma critically. See John Hagan, "The Closure of *Emma*."

12. Louise Flavin takes the opposite view, claiming that Austen undermines Emma through FID: "In Austen's novels it reinforces the reader's sense that a character is in some way untrustworthy" (55). See also Helen Dry's study of "narrated monologue constructions" and factives to represent Emma's point of view.

13. The narrator's decision to report certain of Emma's speeches and to omit others is worth noting. Both the Miss Bates scene and the marriage proposal scene are well known. When, during a parlor game, Miss Bates is requested to say "three dull things," Emma cannot resist interjecting, "But there may be a difficulty . . . you will be limited as to number—only three at once" (364). After being reprimanded by Mr. Knightley, Emma expresses her remorse in FID: "How could she have been so brutal, so cruel to Miss Bates!" (369). And when Mr. Knightley proposes, the narrator reports to us that Emma "spoke then, on being so entreated.—What did she say?—Just what she ought, of course. A lady always does" (418). Since this is a strategic moment in the romance plot, perhaps the narrator's dispensing of Emma's direct discourse here reveals her (and Austen's) impatience with the predictability of the marriage plot ending.

14. Remember Anne Elliot in *Persuasion*, book 2, chap. 5 remarking that: "Men have

had every advantage of us telling their own story" (185). Through FID, Austen has found a way to insert the other story, the story of the other.

15. In "Sense and Reticence: Jane Austen's 'Indirections'" in *Fictions of Authority*, Susan Lanser argues that FID in Austen serves as a form of indirection, a way of suggesting "a narrative stance whose attribution cannot be verified" (74), particularly when the narrator utters maxims or generalizations. She claims that Austen's use of FID reveals the equivocality of her art in that her practices have "helped to construct female narrative authority as indirection and ambiguity" (80).

16. Austen's irony is another mode of resistance, and the relation between her use of irony and FID would be an interesting study.

17. In *Forster's Narrative Vision*, Barbara Rosecrance describes this narrator as the "most intensely personal of all Forster's narrators" (113), who "goes further in self-dramatization, in manipulation of the reader, in the frequency and length of intervention than in any other Forster novel" (131).

18. Scott R. Nelson, "Narrative Inversion: The Textual Construction of Homosexuality in E. M. Forster's Novels," discusses how Forster as a homosexual confronts his sexuality in the structure of the text.

19. Rosecrance comments that "uniquely in this novel, Forster's narrator indicates his gender . . . speculating on the difference between male and female friendships" (131–32). See, however, Kinley E. Roby's contrary claim in "Irony and the Narrative Voice in *Howards End*" that this same passage indicates that the narrator is a woman. I think Roby misreads the syntax of this passage, but he is right to point out the indeterminacy of the narrative voice and that its role is essentially ironic.

20. *Jacob's Room* is another instance of narratorial cross-dressing, though a muted instance in that Woolf spends very little time focalizing through Jacob; Jacob is constructed through others' impressions of him, a device Woolf fine-tunes in *Mrs. Dalloway* for her construction of Clarissa Dalloway. For detailed discussions of these narrative effects in *Jacob's Room* and *Mrs. Dalloway*, see Denise Delorey and Patricia Matson, and for an investigation of the breakdown of the patriarchal voice in Woolf's first novel, *The Voyage Out*, see Susan Stanford Friedman, all in this volume.

21. In *Between the Acts* (1941), Woolf attempts an even more radical strategy—what she describes as anonymity: "Anonymity was a great possession. It gave the early writing an impersonality, a generality. . . . It allowed us to know nothing of the writer: and so to concentrate upon his song. . . . But at some point there comes a break when anonymity withdraws. Does it come when the playwright had absorbed the contribution of the audience; and can return to them their own general life individualised in single and separate figures? . . . The playwright is replaced by the man who writes a book. The audience is replaced by the reader. Anon is dead" (Silver, 397–98).

22. With reference to the indeterminacy of Woolf's FID, especially with regard to the opening passage cited above, Seymour Chatman makes a pertinent point: "By establishing the indirect report [indirect tagged speech], Virginia Woolf prepares the way for indirect free statements which are indifferently attributable to either

narrator or character" (254). Although Chatman uses this example to show how "narrator and character are so close, in such sympathy, that it doesn't matter to whom the statement is attributed" (254), it seems to me that Woolf's indifference is deliberate. Interestingly, Wayne Booth in his *Rhetoric of Fiction* is rather aggrieved by this ambiguity, quoting David Daiches in relation to *To the Lighthouse* to support his complaint that the distinction between the thought processes of author and characters was not clear enough (373 n. 27).

23. See Pamela Caughie's discussion of the narrator-character boundaries in which she points out that what is "striking about [Woolf's] narrators is just how obtrusive they are," which has the effect of disturbing our "habitual relations to the narrative" (64). She goes on to comment that "blurring distinctions between characters and between characters and narrator, Woolf makes the source of a thought doubtful, thereby inhibiting our tendency to seek the author's view in the characters or narrator" (75).

24. As Suzanne Ferguson points out, "The disappearance of the author has been such an article of faith . . . that . . . readers and teachers have gone about analysis of a number of third-person impressionist works just as if the author had in fact withdrawn, when actually his presence is quite palpable and might even be seen to give impressionist works one of their characteristic qualities, i.e., that of a 'multiple vision': simultaneous perspectives" (231).

25. See Stefan Oltean, "Textual Functions of Free Indirect Discourse in the Novel *Mrs. Dalloway* by Virginia Woolf," where he argues that "FID in *Mrs. Dalloway*, as a mode of duality, plurality and equivocation of the enunciative rather than the denotative positionality, sustains a type of psychological realism consisting in the representation of the manner in which existence is reflected in several centers-of-consciousness concomitantly engaged in a continuous *dialogue* with the narrator and situated under the control of the latter" (547).

26. See also her comments that [Lytton] "thinks she is disagreeable and limited, but that I alternately laugh at her and cover her, very remarkably, with myself" (*Writer's Diary*, 78).

27. The use of "of course" is an example of a linguistic marker indicating social positioning and attitudes, one that is meant to draw the reader into the upper middle-class world of the Dalloways. Woolf captures, mimics, and mocks this discourse as she does the pretensions of this class, but she is also careful to represent it. See Janet Giltrow's discussion of the "ironies of politeness" for a careful analysis of the construction and effects of this kind of discourse.

WORKS CITED

Austen-Leigh, James Edward. *Memoir of Jane Austen*. London: Oxford University Press, 1926.

Austen, Jane. *Emma*. 1816. Harmondsworth: Penguin, 1985.

——. *Persuasion*. 1818. Boston: Houghton Mifflin, 1965.

Bakhtin, M. M. *The Dialogic Imagination: Four Essays*. Trans. Caryl Emerson and Michael Holquist. Austin: University of Texas Press, 1981.

Bal, Mieke. *Narratology: Introduction of the Theory of Narrative*. Trans. Christine van
  Boheemen. Toronto: University of Toronto Press, 1985.

Banfield, Ann. "Narrative Style and the Grammar of Direct and Indirect Speech."
  Foundations of Language 10.1 (May 1973): 1–39.

———. *Unspeakable Sentences: Narration and Representation in the Language of Fiction*.
  Boston: Routledge and Kegan Paul, 1982.

Bell, Quentin. "The Exquisite Jane Austen." *Books and Bookmen* 24.3 (December
  1978): 13–25.

Booth, Alison, ed. *Famous Last Words: Changes in Gender and Narrative Closure*.
  Charlottesville: University Press of Virginia, 1993.

Booth, Wayne C. *The Rhetoric of Fiction*. Chicago: University of Chicago Press, 1968.

Bronzwaer, W. J. M. *Tense in the Novel: An Investigation of Some Potentialities of Linguistic
  Criticism*. Groningen: Wolters-Noordhoff, 1970.

Butler, Judith. *Gender Trouble: Feminism and the Subversion of Identity*. New York:
  Routledge, Chapman, and Hall, 1990.

Caughie, Pamela. *Virginia Woolf and Postmodernism: Literature in Quest and Question of
  Itself*. Urbana: University of Illinois Press, 1991.

Chatman, Seymour. "The Structure of Narrative Transmission." In *Style and Structure
  in Literature: Essays in the New Stylistics*. Ed. Roger Fowler. Oxford: Basil Blackwell,
  1975. 213–57.

Cohn, Dorrit. *Transparent Minds: Narrative Modes for Presenting Consciousness in Fiction*.
  Princeton: Princeton University Press, 1978.

Dillon, George L., and Frederick Kirchhoff. "On the Form and Function of Free
  Indirect Speech." *PTL* 1 (1976): 431–40.

Dry, Helen. "Syntax and Point of View in *Emma*." *Studies in Romanticism* 16.1 (Winter
  1977): 87–99.

"E. M. Forster." *Writers at Work. The "Paris Review" Interviews*. Ed. and with an
  introduction by Malcolm Cowley. 1959. London: Viking.

Ferguson, Suzanne. "The Face in the Mirror: Authorial Presence in the Multiple
  Vision of Third-Person Impressionist Narrative." *Criticism* 21.3 (1979): 230–50.

Finch, Casey, and Peter Bowen. " 'The Tittle-Tattle of Highbury': Gossip and the
  Free Indirect Style in *Emma*." *Representations* 31 (Summer 1990): 1–18.

Flavin, Louise. "Free Indirect Discourse and the Clever Heroine of *Emma*."
  Persuasion 13 (December 1991): 50–57.

Fludernik, Monika. *The Fictions of Language and the Language of Fictions: The Linguistic
  Representation of Speech and Consciousness*. London: Routledge, 1993.

Forster, E. M. *Aspects of the Novel*. 1927. London: Penguin, 1977.

———. *Howards End*. 1910. Harmondsworth: Penguin, 1970.

Furbank, P. N. *E. M. Forster: A Life*. 2 vols. New York: Harcourt, Brace, Jovanovich,
  1977–78.

Gates, Henry Louis, Jr. "Color Me Zora: Alice Walker's (Re)Writing of the Speaking
  Text." In *Intertextuality and Contemporary American Fiction*. Ed. Patrick O'Donnell
  and Robert Con Davis. Baltimore: Johns Hopkins University Press, 1989. 144–67.

———. "Zora Neale Hurston and the Speakerly Text." *The Signifying Monkey: A Theory of*

Afro-American Literary Criticism. New York: Oxford University Press, 1988. 170–216.

Genette, Gérard. *Narrative Discourse Revisited*. Trans. Jane E. Lewin. Ithaca: Cornell University Press, 1988.

Ginsburg, Michal Peled. "Free Indirect Discourse: A Reconsideration." *Language and Style* 15.2 (1982): 133–49.

Hagan, John. "The Closure of Emma." *Studies in English Literature, 1500–1900* 15.4 (1975): 545–61.

Hernandi, Paul. "Dual Perspective: Free Indirect Discourse and Related Techniques." *Comparative Literature* 42 (1972): 32–43.

Hite, Molly. *The Other Side of the Story: Structures and Strategies of Contemporary Feminist Narrative*. Ithaca: Cornell University Press, 1989.

Hough, Graham. "Narrative and Dialogue in Jane Austen." *Critical Quarterly* 12.3 (1970): 201–29.

Jespersen, Otto. *The Philosophy of Grammar*. New York: W. W. Norton, 1965.

Lanser, Susan S. *Fictions of Authority: Women Writers and Narrative Voice*. Ithaca: Cornell University Press, 1992.

McHale, Brian. "Free Indirect Discourse: A Survey of Recent Accounts." *PTL* 3 (1978): 249–87.

McKenzie, Malcolm. "Free Indirect Speech in a Fettered Insecure Society." *Literature and Communication* 7.2 (1987): 153–59.

Nelson, Scott R. "Narrative Inversion: The Textual Construction of Homosexuality in E. M. Forster's Novels." *Style* 26.2 (Summer 1992): 310–26.

Neumann, Anne Waldron. "Characterization and Comment in *Pride and Prejudice*: Free Indirect Discourse and 'Double-voiced' Verbs of Speaking, Thinking, and Feeling." *Style* 20 (1986): 364–94.

Oltean, Stefan. "Textual Functions of Free Indirect Discourse in the Novel *Mrs. Dalloway* by Virginia Woolf." *Revue Romaine de Linguistique* 26 (November–December 1981): 533–47.

Pascal, Roy. *The Dual Voice: Free Indirect Speech and Its Functioning in the Nineteenth-Century Novel*. Manchester: Manchester University Press, 1977.

Rimmon-Kenan, Shlomith. *Narrative Fiction: Contemporary Poetics*. London: Methuen, 1983.

Roby, Kinley E. "Irony and the Narrative Voice in *Howards End*." *The Journal of Narrative Technique* 2.2 (1972): 116–24.

Rosecrance, Barbara. *Forster's Narrative Vision*. Ithaca: Cornell University Press, 1982.

Schabert, Ina. "The Authorial Mind and the Question of Gender." *Telling Stories: Studies in Honour of Ulrich Broic on the Occasion of His 60th Birthday*. Ed. Elmar Lehmann and Bernd Lenz. Amsterdam: Grüner, 1992. 312–29.

Schuelke, Gertrude. " 'Slipping' in Indirect Discourse." *American Speech* 33.2 (1958): 90–98.

Silver, Brenda. " 'Anon' and 'The Reader': Virginia Woolf's Last Essays." *Twentieth-Century Literature* 25.3/5 (Fall/Winter 1979): 356–441.

Stanzel, F. K. *A Theory of Narrative*. Cambridge: Cambridge University Press, 1986.

Tobler, Adolph. "Vermischte Beiträge zur französichen Grammatik." *Zeitschrift für Romanische Philologie* 24 (1887): 433–61.

Volosinov, V. N. *Marxism and the Philosophy of Language.* Trans Ladislav Matejka and I. R. Titunik. New York: Seminar, 1973.

Watt, Ian. *The Rise of the Novel: Studies in Defoe, Richardson, and Fielding.* Hammondsworth: Pelican, 1974.

Woolf, Virginia. *Between the Acts.* 1941. Harmondsworth: Penguin, 1976.

——. *Collected Essays.* Vol. 1. London: Chatto and Windus, 1966.

——. *Mrs. Dalloway.* 1925. Harmondsworth: Penguin, 1969.

——. *To the Lighthouse.* 1927. Harmondsworth: Penguin, 1972.

——. *A Writer's Diary.* Ed. Leonard Woolf. London: Hogarth, 1969.

parsing the female sentence

The Paradox of Containment in

Virginia Woolf's Narratives

denise | delorey

ike her experimental contemporaries James Joyce and
D. H. Lawrence, Virginia Woolf saw art as the material with which she
might help remake the world. Indeed, her radical secular faith in Art led her
to suggest in *Three Guineas* that it was the very enterprise that could displace
war.[1] But Woolf's is an explicitly gendered, frankly political "solution" to
the aesthetic challenges of that multifarious early-twentieth-century moment we have retrospectively come to call modernism. Her feminist aesthetic, with its unabashedly antimasculinist, pacifist ideological underpin-
nings, is set out most clearly in her famous works *A Room of One's Own* and
Three Guineas.

As a writer situated productively between an almost religious devotion
to form and a passionate instinct for deconstruction, Woolf's work illustrates some of the ways in which a gendered point of view informs and
reforms "universal" narratological categories and how, in turn, such categories can help illuminate her "difficult" narratives. Woolf's modernist
aesthetic was shaped by an ongoing conversation not simply between tradition and innovation but, more specific, between her modern narrative
poetics and her feminist politics as well. So it is within the context of a
broader, and more current, version of that conversation—between the
"feminist" and the "narratology" in feminist narratology—that I read the
three novels in which Virginia Woolf came into her own as a novelist.
Woolf's vision of a newly formed modern novel relies on the voice of the
female novelist. How that voice might sound and what it would speak of
intersect in Woolf's postulation in *A Room of One's Own* of a "female sen-

tence." Equipped with this "perfectly natural, shapely" sentence suited to their own use, Woolf suggests, women might build whole new forms of "novels" (the quotation marks signify her dissatisfaction with that term). "No doubt," she continues, "we shall find her knocking that into shape for herself when she has the free use of her limbs; and providing some new vehicle, not necessarily in verse, for the poetry in her" (*Room*, 80). If Woolf's speculations on these forms sound vague, their artistic realizations in her own fiction serve as clear examples of their possibilities.[2]

Beginning with *Jacob's Room*, we can see Woolf's fictional practice moving closer and closer to her vision of a new kind of novel as she writes her way through some of its more venerated traditional romantic modes: the bildungsroman in *Jacob's Room*, the eponymous woman-centered novel in *Mrs. Dalloway*, and the roman à clef in *To the Lighthouse*. While each of these narratives is constructed in response to particular and recognizably modernist formal challenges, Woolf's renovations of the novel form also always entail the grammatical and ideological imperatives of her female sentence. This essay traces a development in Woolf's strategic focus on the parenthetical as a feminist narrative principle.

The *American Heritage Dictionary* defines the parenthetical as "a qualifying or amplifying phrase occurring within a sentence in such a way as to form an interpolation independent of the surrounding syntactical structure. . . . a comment departing from the theme of discourse; digression" and "an interruption of continuity; interval; interlude" (953). Implicit in this structural definition is the devaluation of that which comes between parentheses, that which could be excised without threatening the sense inherent in the "syntactical structure" of discourse. Woolf does not so much redefine that structure as claim the space and embrace the implications of the parenthetical within it. Her parentheses simultaneously deflate the momentous events on which traditional masculinist narratives turned and open up a space for the "moments of being" that had historically been seen as parenthetical to the real workings of the world. Yet, as we shall see, in the process of carving out a narrative space for her provisional female subject(s), Virginia Woolf generates in each of these three novels a slightly different version of the same compelling paradox of containment. From her holistic rendering of the uncontainable subject to her problematic use of the trope of chastity, to her liberating use of parentheses as aperture, her grammatical transformations nevertheless always skirt the reinscription of the forms they surpass. For all her deconstructions, Woolf is at heart a structuralist who fervently believes: "Writing must be formal. The art must be respected" (*Writer's Diary*, 74).

Jacob's Room, first published in 1922, is in part a parodic bildungsroman, describing the education of a young English gentleman Jacob Flanders and culminating, rather extraordinarily, in his death in the First World War. It is also a radical experiment in character building, remarkable for its artistic accomplishment. E. M. Forster's praise is quoted on the cover of the paperback edition: "The coherence of the book is even more amazing than its beauty. In the stream of glittering similes, unfinished sentences, hectic catalogues, unanchored proper names, we seem to be going nowhere. Yet the goal comes, the method and the matter prove to have been one, and looking back from the pathos of the closing sentence we see for a moment the airy drifting atoms piled into a colonnade. . . . A new type of fiction has swum into view."

As Forster also points out, the "method" and "matter," or what we might call "discourse" and "story," are here working in such concert as to be inseparable.[3] Indeed, the form of the bildungsroman becomes the subject of *Jacob's Room*; it is a book about the impossibility of representing Jacob. As the narrator explains it: "One must do the best one can with her report. Anyhow, this was Jacob Flanders, aged nineteen. It is no use trying to sum people up. One must follow hints, not exactly what is said, nor yet entirely what is done" (154). Like the postimpressionist painters she so admires, Woolf has abandoned efforts at comprehensive or realistic representation and is exploring linguistic brushstrokes that would evoke rather than define character. Woolf is a modernist who is skeptical of the notion of "decisive information concerning the subject" (Auerbach, 547). Subjectivity is illusory, and she aims to discern its traces rather than to capture it.

But the rhapsodic quality of the formal innovation of *Jacob's Room* must not be separated from Woolf's feminist/pacifist political viewpoint: both the structure and the thematic concerns of the text function politically. In late September 1922, Woolf wrote in her diary: "I think *Jacob* was a necessary step for me, in working free. . . . There's no doubt in my mind that I have found out how to begin (at 40) to say something in my own voice" (*Writer's Diary*, 53, 57). That female voice tells the story of Jacob's education in a way that predicts the later polemics of *A Room of One's Own* in 1929 and *Three Guineas* in 1938. Her necessarily female narrator's focus on a prewar male British subject, read in the wake of World War I, embodies an antiheroic argument and provides structural irony on at least two levels.

First, rather than a "simple" feminist co-optation or revision of the bildungsroman genre, Woolf's approach to focalization exposes the form itself—with its traditional articulation of a male social subject—as inadequate to modern (and not incidentally, feminine) subjectivity. She uses the form against itself to prove the lie of the "I," that pillar of subjectivity supporting the temple of war or what she would call later, in *A Room of One's Own*, "the straight dark bar" that falls across the page when she tries to read (103). And she conflates the aesthetic impediment of this overbearing subject and its larger political implications. Listen to the tone in Woolf's characterization of that subject which can also serve as an abstract of Jacob's "character" and his narrator's attitude toward it: "Not but what this 'I' was a most respectable 'I'; honest and logical; as hard as a nut, and polished for centuries by good teaching and good feeding. I respect and admire that 'I' from the bottom of my heart. But—here I turned a page or two, looking for something or other—the worst of it is that in the shadow of the letter 'I' all is shapeless as mist" (*Room*, 104).

Second, when all Jacob's education culminates in his death, the narrative reveals the sad incongruity of such careful cultivation of a generation of the best and brightest as cannon fodder. Or, should we say, "canon fodder," since by an additional turn of the screw, Woolf suggests in *Jacob's Room* (and argues convincingly in *Three Guineas*) that an education that teaches romantic myth and even fact as Truth and naturalizes the logic of masculine culture makes war inevitable, sealing the fate of all its Jacobs.

The focalization of the novel typifies Woolf's articulation of gender within a sophisticated web of relationships between narrator, narrated, and narrative to effect a female narrative subjectivity that transcends the traditional (that is, heterosexual) paradigms of reading and writing. In this novel, for instance, what Woolf gives us finally is not Jacob but Jacob's room, a textual space that ultimately signifies its illusive "hero" by his absence or, more precise, by the always shifting impressions of him in the text—here of a solid presence, and there, a vague outline or shadow. Jacob is perhaps most present at the moment when, on the final page of the book, we are left with his friend Bonamy, "standing in the middle of Jacob's room," most keenly aware of his absence: a void punctuated by the image of his distraught mother holding out an empty pair of his old shoes, the very shoes of the British gentlemen he was presumably raised to fill.

"People, like Arnold Bennett," wrote Virginia Woolf, "say I can't create, or didn't in *Jacob's Room*, characters that survive" (*Writer's Diary*, 63). And this, it seems, is exactly the point. For Jacob's room is finally an ironically empty memorial. The reader hardly mourns the passing of this quaint British subject because the narrator has insistently substituted the (impossibly) definitive characterization of Jacob, which would have invited our identification with him, for a constellation of shapes, glimpses, images of "Jacobness" through which we nevertheless come to see him. And while Jacob is never reduced to a caricature, the fictional "touches" that suggest his individuality are always undercut by the conventional, generic qualities of his character, which would have been so familiar to Woolf's readers. We ultimately believe in Jacob primarily as the subject of his narrator's discourse. That is, her subjectivity is paradoxically inscribed in her deconstructive narration of the subject.

Woolf relies heavily for this effect on the affectionately mocking voice(s) of her narrator; and the extent to which we are drawn into her relationship with her subject is central to our own connection with the text. The nuances of this relationship depend on the narrator's sardonic translation of the conventions of the genre played against Jacob's utterly unconscious conventionality. In fact, the unconventional consciousness of the narrator not only competes with but also effectively displaces the conventional subject. The narrator constructs the text by observing and analyzing Jacob's actions, never presuming to enter Jacob's consciousness. But it is important to recognize that the narrator is not simply strategically heterodiegetic but definitively so by virtue of her gender. Indeed, she is the same narrator who is chased by a horrified "Oxbridge" Beadle from his "turf" to the gravel path some seven years later in *A Room of One's Own*: not omniscient, certainly not objective; her only possible stance is outside, peering in, and providing a running commentary in a lively, critical, and often sympathetic voice.

The advantages and limits of this "outsider" position, which is simultaneously perceptual and conceptual, are made clear in a fairly extended scene at the end of chapter 3, which focuses specifically on Jacob at university. A close reading of this scene reveals the central subject of *Jacob's Room*. Woolf invokes the replete atmosphere of a Cambridge quad in the hours after dinner. The young men back in their rooms are first compared to a "hive full of bees, the bees home thick with gold, drowsy, humming, suddenly vocal." "Were they reading?" she wonders. "Certainly, there was a sense of concentration in the air. Behind the grey walls sat so many young men, some *undoubtedly* reading, magazines, shilling shockers, no doubt; legs, perhaps, over the arms of chairs; smoking; sprawling over tables, and writing while their heads went round in a circle as the pen moved—simple young men, these, who would—but there is no need to think of them grown old" (43; emphasis added). Notice how the redundant qualifiers— "undoubtedly," "no doubt," "perhaps"—amplify the satiric effect of the image of the circling heads of these "simple young men." But just as we prepare to relish the extension of her comic vision into their mediocre old ages by the clause "who would," our narrator pulls us up short with her final clause. "There is no need to think of them grown old" because, of course, as we know in retrospect, many of them will not even reach middle age.

This deft tonal modulation between satire, lyricism, and a kind of foreboding continues through this passage and is typical of the book as a whole. Young men "lying in shallow armchairs" read, "holding their books as if they had hold in their hands of something that would see them through" (43). Again, while her tone is never strident, it is always subtly incriminating of this rarefied, self-contained world, so that when Jacob's friend Bonamy is shown reading Keats contentedly one moment and the next "eager and contented no more, but almost fierce," our narrator asks: "Why? Only perhaps that Keats died young—one wants to write poetry too and to love—oh, the brutes! It's damnably difficult. But, after all, not so difficult if on the next staircase, in the large room, there are two, three, five young men all convinced of this—of brutality, that is, and the clear division between right and wrong" (44). When the clock strikes, its tone is "reverent," "muffled." But the "swaddlings and blanketings" of the Cambridge night not only keep the world out but also dim and blur all the young men's attempts to see beyond them; none of their creative imaginings "could show clearly through" them.

As we move in for a closer look inside one of the rooms, the narrator begins by dutifully describing the physical details—sofa, chairs, square table— and then tells us that "the window being open, one could see how they sat—legs issuing here, one there crumpled in a corner of the sofa; and, presumably, for you could not see him, somebody stood by the fender, talking" (44). It is from this fortuitous vantage point (on the gravel, as it were) that the narrator observes a moment between Jacob and his classmate Simeon in which the sounds of their low, modulated voices discussing some allusion to Julian the Apostate empty into a quiet intimacy, described as "a sort of spiritual suppleness, when mind prints upon mind indelibly" (46). The passage is seductive, then gently mocking, as this mood "rose softly and washed over everything, mollifying, kindling, and coating the mind with the luster of pearl" (46). And then, lest we too succumb to the lustre, the narrator concludes with a satiric edge: "But Jacob moved. He murmured good-night. He went out into the court. He buttoned his jacket across his chest. He went back to his rooms, . . . his footsteps rang out, his figure loomed large. Back from the Chapel, back from the Hall, back from the Library, came the sound of his footsteps, as if the old stone echoed with magisterial authority: 'The young man—the young man—the young man—back to his rooms'" (46). Thus Jacob slips, ironically, back from the specific to the generic, from a young man named Jacob to any young Cambridge man, fattened on this spoon-fed, candlelit, *literary* image of his worldly self. More important in terms of this discussion, as the scene comes to a close, we realize that it has been our clever narrator who has energetically asked questions and made the kind of sharp observations that these favored young men remain unawakened to by all their education and acculturation.

Moreover, the narrator's consistent qualifications suggest that her appreciation of the obstacles between her own consciousness and any knowledge of the internal life of her subject is not a cynical excuse for her failure but rather a strategic lack of pretense that invites us into her narrative project. Her writing and our reading illuminate by analogy the fundamental human activities of seeing and of knowing "others." Typically, she sums up this project in the form of an ironic disclaimer, concluding:

> It seems that a profound, impartial, and absolutely just opinion of our fellow-creatures is utterly unknown. Either we are men, or we are women. Either we are cold, or we are sentimental. Either we are young, or growing old. In any case life is but a procession of shadows, and God knows why it is that we embrace them so eagerly, and see them depart with such anguish, being shadows. And why, if this and more than this is true, why are we yet surprised in the window corner by a sudden vision that the young man in the chair is of all things in the world the most real, the most solid, the best known to us—why indeed? For the moment after we know nothing about him.
>
> Such is the manner of our seeing. Such the conditions of our love. (72)

This realization of the inadequacy of categories to make up or contain character is the core of the book: it, and not Jacob, is what we think of long after we've finished reading this short evocation of an abbreviated life. Just as Jacob enters the text in absentia in the inexplicably sad cry of his young brother Archer for "Ja—cob! Ja—cob!" in the opening beach scene, so his absence is remarked by his friend Bonamy's plaintive cry in the final scene, "Jacob! Jacob!" (8, 187). The pair of unanswered cries comprises, like a set of aural parentheses, the inevitably empty space that is the real subject of this text.

Already apparent in this radical departure in characterization is Woolf's insistence on the novel as a constructed space through which the ephemeral traces of life may pass and whose failure finally to contain that life is not a failed biography but a triumphant sign of inscrutable human connections evidenced in the always displacing and never transcendent subject. Woolf's modernist experimentation cannot be separated from her politics. Yet even in this dismantling of the "I," narration is the subject and the means of this female subject's articulation—her right to go to university, her right to write.[4]

Although *Mrs. Dalloway* (1925) predates *A Room of One's Own* by three years or so, it is in many ways the demonstration of the feminist aesthetic outlined in that later work (and amplified in its pacifist sequel, *Three Guineas*). As the title suggests, Mrs. Dalloway is the antiromantic subject of this text, whose first name—Clarissa—is an ironic and complex allusion to her famous literary predecessor, Clarissa Harlowe. The title is also ironic, because "the name designates a fictitious persona, a social mask that disguises the form Clarissa Parry" (Henke, 126). Just as she had in her revisionary undoing of the subject of the bildungsroman in *Jacob's Room*, Woolf exploits her audience's familiarity with Richardson's *Clarissa*, a text that many critics consider the first novel, to acknowledge the literary legacy inherited by *Mrs. Dalloway* and to magnify her heroine's tendentious difference from it.

The expectation of readers trained by romantic novels to anticipate that, against all obstacles put in her way by the plot, the heroine would inevitably become a wife by the end of the narrative, is deflated at the outset. Mrs. Dalloway both is and isn't at the center of the book, and the eponymous title at once suggests the concentration of the narrative on one woman and the broader generic quality of a text that will (as it did in *Jacob's Room*) "build up out of the fleeting and personal the lasting edifice which remains unknown" (*Room*, 97). Characteristically, the personal is explored for its power to point out toward the larger social context. Yet for all the satiric threads that lead away from Clarissa in this subtly complex narrative, the text manages, finally, to be every bit as much Mrs. Dalloway as Richardson's Clarissa is his text. Woolf continues her spatial narrative experiment here, rendering subjectivity in a kind of domestic geography. But when she

DENISE DELOREY

attempts to move beyond the deconstruction of the universal subject to effecting the double consciousness of a particular female subject, the problem of embodiment emerges as a full-blown paradox of containment. It becomes apparent in *Mrs. Dalloway*'s troubling conflation of textuality and sexuality that the principle of artistic integrity gets figured in Woolf's Clarissa, as it had in Richardson's, through the trope of female chastity.

Just as Woolf argues in *A Room of One's Own* that it is "something called integrity" that enables her to write an uncompromised woman's novel, so Clarissa Dalloway's self-containment makes possible her realization of her frail but unmistakable place within the intricate network of human connection that for Woolf constitutes a human subjectivity beyond strictly plotted gender roles. Despite the insistent spatiality of her modernist aesthetic, Woolf believes the shape of the novel is "not made by the relation of stone to stone, but by the relation of human being to human being" (*Room*, 74). Yet her antiromantic project rejects the overdetermined oppositional romantic couple and the limiting mother-child dyads that so frequently structured the nineteenth-century novel. Woman's sensibility has been constrained within those limits by the dutiful conventions of the heterosexual social fiction. Because Woolf wants to extricate woman from her sexual function to show her relationship to the whole of reality, Clarissa is necessarily figured in relation to her husband and daughter, but she seems emotionally unencumbered by intense feelings of identification with either of them. Only when she is released from what Woolf sees as the consumptive passions of marriage and motherhood can woman attain her humanity.

Instead of the marriage that binds the heroine in the romance plot, the fabric of *Mrs. Dalloway*'s life is woven from an intricate system of innumerable, often invisible threads of affiliation. The title character's intuitive sympathy with a total stranger, Septimus Warren Smith, is the profound coupling that structures this text. Clarissa's epiphany regarding this exquisite bond is its consummation. The spaces of two utterly discrete, yet inextricable, lives converge momentarily; and their connection is crystallized in Clarissa's surprisingly intense empathic response to Smith's death. Set off by a party guest's offhand reference to the tragic suicide of one of her husband's patients—significantly, a young man destroyed by the war—Clarissa launches into some two and a half pages of digressive speculation on the causes and conditions of the young veteran's death, a narrative interlude that concludes with her startling realization: "She had escaped. But that young man had killed himself. . . . She felt somehow very like him. . . . She felt glad he had done it; thrown it away while they went on living. The clock was striking. The leaden circles dissolved in the air. But she must go back. She must assemble" (164–65).

Ironically, though, Clarissa can only "assemble" by an act of dissemblance, which perhaps differs from Smith's madness only in degree. And Woolf's narrative interpolation of a parenthetical space representing the deep spiritual alliance between two otherwise unrelated subjects was necessarily complicated by the ideal of an integral self that supplies its own inner light. This state of creative grace is attained through a certain unswerving imaginative fortitude that refuses to be distracted by outside influences from "the thing itself," most especially not by "external authority." For Woolf, genius and "something one calls integrity" are the requirement for and the marks of a Great Novel. Wondering that any book of such an infinitely complex structure can hold together for long, she explains that "what holds them together in these rare instances of survival . . . is something that one calls integrity. . . . What one means by integrity in the case of novelist, is the conviction that he gives one that this is the truth . . . for Nature seems, very oddly, to have provided us with an inner light by which to judge of the novelist's integrity or disintegrity" (*Room*, 75).

"But how," she wonders, "would all this be affected by the sex of the novelist. . . . Would the fact of her sex in any way interfere with the integrity of a woman novelist—that integrity which I take to be the backbone of the writer?" (76). The answer, of course, is yes, at least if she is to write as a woman. The most formidable obstacles to writing as a woman—once we've eliminated the more concrete problems of money and time—are the "perpetual admonitions" of the patriarchal male voice. These verbal assaults by external authority (presumably by internalized authority as well) on the female artist's integrity persistently threaten to divert her mind from its own truth, "alter her values in deference to the opinion of others," and contaminate her novel. Once the female artist engages these voices, described as "now grumbling, now patronising, now domineering, now grieved, now shocked, now angry, now avuncular," she is lost. Indeed, most do succumb; and Woolf imagines "all of the women's novels that lie scattered, like small pock-marked apples in an orchard, about the second-hand book shops of London. It was the flaw in the centre that had rotted them" (77–78).

It is difficult not to read this "violation" as a revision of the fall, in which Eve is the female artist seduced by a chorus of male voices and who is lost whether she merely responds or acquiesces: thus Clarissa Dalloway's profound impenetrability. Like her namesake, this Clarissa equates chastity with identity. And her maiden name "Parry," punning on the verb meaning to deflect a blow or to evade a question, both describes her strategy for and predicts her equivocal success at preserving herself. By opting to marry the Adamically uxorious Richard Dalloway rather than the needy womanizer Peter Walsh, Mrs. Dalloway renounces the dangers of passionate fusion for the sanctuary of companionate marriage. For Mrs. Dalloway cannot abide either of the two choices offered the heroine as action in the world: "Love and religion! Had she ever tried to convert any one herself? Did she not wish everyone merely to be themselves?" (112). Clarissa turns a deaf ear to the voices which would force her from her own private faith or would appropriate her sensibility. Certainly, the audacity of Mrs. Dalloway's "impenetrability" is undeniable. What could be more threatening to the romantic heterosexual myth than love as usurpation of the will, an obliteration of the individual. This description of the fate of Lady Bradshaw indicates the insidious process Clarissa long ago refused: "But conversion, fastidious Goddess, loves blood better than brick and feasts most subtly on the human will. For example, Lady Bradshaw. Fifteen years ago she had gone under. It was nothing you could put your finger on; there had been no scene, no snap; only the slow sinking, water-logged, of her will into his" (90). In a world where everything seems structured to "counsel submission," Clarissa's resistance takes on new layers of political resonance. But we see in Woolf's notion of heroism not only a continuity between sexual and textual politics but also the broader implication of the dynamic of the "personal" marital relation in global politics. When Woolf consistently rejects the "Red Light of Emotion" for the "White Light of Truth," she undercuts traditional romantic myths of femininity, but not without some cost to women.

In *Three Guineas* Woolf counseled that "it should not be difficult to transmute the old ideal of bodily chastity into the new ideal of mental chastity" (82). In *A Room of One's Own* she substitutes a spiritual/aesthetic constancy for bodily integrity; but in *Mrs. Dalloway* the "new" and the "old" ideal blur in the (inevitable?) figure of Clarissa's body. Mrs. Dalloway is no artist, yet she has a room of her own—an isolated attic room, like a nun's cell, in which she preserves not only her privacy but also a chastity which marks an absence of lust (echoing the classic version) and which is strangely described as "a virginity preserved through childbirth" (29). Especially when viewed through the eyes of potential converter Peter Walsh, Clarissa's "hardness"—"She seemed contracted, petrified. She did not move. . . . He felt he was grinding against something physically hard; she was unyielding.

She was like iron, like flint, rigid up the backbone" (58)—suggests that such an act of will threatens to turn a woman to stone. Certainly, Woolf never minimizes what is essentially a self-preservatory gesture: "Like a nun withdrawing, or a child exploring a tower, she went upstairs. . . . There was an emptiness about the heart of life; an attic room. The sheets were clean, tight stretched in a broad white band from side to side. Narrower and narrower would her bed be. . . . She slept badly, she could not dispel a virginity preserved through childbirth which clung to her like a sheet" (29). Or like a shroud, as her bed begins to feel more and more like a coffin. The "blank sheets" that might in another context signify Clarissa's power to maintain her integrity, to write and speak as a woman, are much more ambivalent here. Woolf implicitly invokes Mrs. Dalloway's namesake again: Clarissa Harlowe, too, valued her bodily "integrity" above even her life; indeed, for her the two were synonymous. Woolf articulates the double bind of the social contract for women that Richardson's text had only hinted at; and she makes explicit the fact that marriage, the only means of her survival, always entails a kind of death for the heroine.[5]

Yet her rejection of passionate fusion in favor of broader human affiliations hovers on the verge of a new romantic ideal of chastity for the female artist, an alternative that seems to require a renunciation of her own body. As Mrs. Dalloway ascends to her private place above the verbal trials, seductions of the ear, the heart, the flesh, she enters a parenthetical space that requires her separation from her body and where her value is based on the inviolability of her "text." Like her eighteenth-century foremother, this Clarissa's integrity—marked by her remarkable virginity—integrates the text, and the wholeness of the text is intended to reflect the integrity of its author. Woolf's antiheroine escapes the traditional sentence—as the means of a reiterative restaging and enactment of the endless trial of the female subject. But in her place stands an intentionally unmoved and strangely unmovable woman who figures the paradoxical attempt to transcend the trap of chastity through the trope of chastity. And who leads us to wonder to what fate the integrity of Woolf's female sentence sentences women.

As I hope the previous two discussions have made clear, I am using grammatical terms analogically to extrapolate the effect of Woolf's female sentence on the innovative story grammar of the novel as a whole. Put another way, if we could parse her novels as if they were examples of the (female) sentence, we would typically find Woolf's subject in parentheses. This central tenet of Woolf's radical revisionary strategy is described by Erich

Auerbach in his famous essay "The Brown Stocking." Using a passage from *To the Lighthouse* to exemplify what he describes as a "shift in emphasis" characteristic of modernism, Auerbach argues, "This shift of emphasis expresses something that we might call a transfer of confidence: the great exterior turning points and blows of fate are granted less importance; they are credited with less power of yielding decisive information concerning the subject; on the other hand there is confidence that in any random fragment plucked from the course of a life at any time the totality of its fate is contained and can be portrayed" (547). Auerbach's ambivalence about the modernist project notwithstanding, he characterizes Woolf's aim precisely. But where Auerbach's critique subsumes the sexual politics of the Woolfian aesthetic under a generic modernism, Woolf overtly rejected those old points of "universal" emphasis as "masculinist." For her, this made such "blows of fortune" not merely inadequate subjects for modern fictional life but also a constricted and regressive point of view that amounts in Woolf's estimation, at that point in history, to a threat to human survival.

Consequently, what we might call Woolf's "transformational grammar" does not change the formal definitions but transforms their signification. Parentheses, as marks of punctuation, become in the Woolfian sentence a means of *puncturing* the illusion of the complete sentence—and, by extension, the illusion of a fixed, prefigured, and textual structure and, by extension, an overdetermined social structure. Moreover, her ideas about what subjects are fit for, indeed required by, modern fiction are reflected in her structural use of parentheses. As we saw in *Jacob's Room*, "decisive information concerning the subject" is sacrificed in Woolf's aesthetic to the shifting constellation of factors that intersect momentarily in the text, the illusory traces of a very specific, if always provisional, subjectivity. So that while Woolf uses parentheses to deflate the dramatic events on which traditional masculinist narratives (and history) turned, this strategy is more intricate than a mere reversal of priority. Instead, it amounts to a displacement of the subject that can work both ways. Parentheses can mark simultaneously the brief containment of those evanescent "moments of being," like the darning of stockings, that make up a life, and the opening up of a profound textual space signifying a reality that transcends that life and is ultimately uncontainable. For Woolf such gaps are not flaws but apertures that allow the subject of language to move beyond form to truths which are perhaps unpresentable.

Nowhere in Woolf's fiction is this peculiar space better exemplified than part 2 of *To the Lighthouse*, in the centerpiece called "Time Passes." Here, in a bracketed aside that is never explained or elaborated, we learn that Mrs. Ramsay, until now the apparent subject of the text, has died: "[Mr. Ramsay, stumbling along a passage one dark morning, stretched his arms out, but Mrs. Ramsay having died rather suddenly the night before, his arms, though stretched out, remained empty]" (194). This extraordinary sentence resonates with the ambiguous complexity of Woolf's parentheses as markers in a spatially conceived narrative time; and it is, I would argue, a quintessentially female sentence. The brackets set the sentence apart as different from, but unmistakably within, the text, apparently relegating what would traditionally be considered a crucial moment to the nature of an incidental aside. Are they an attempt to contain Mrs. Ramsay as a force in and on the narrative and make the third part of the text possible? Or, do they, on the contrary, finally open the text to Mrs. Ramsay, perhaps show-ing, as Gayatri Chakravorty Spivak has argued, that Mrs. Ramsay is the text (310–11)?

Consider the complex structure of the sentence as microcosmic of the text. Mr. Ramsay is apparently the subject. But what is the predicate? The clause in which we learn of Mrs. Ramsay's death is dependent, sand-wiched between two independent clauses: the opening, "Mr. Ramsay . . . stretched his arms out," and the closing, "his arms, though stretched out, remained empty." Notice the lack of affect in this rather breathless word-ing. "Stretched out" is repeated twice and the other verbs are intransitive, that is, requiring no direct objects. Thus, we have Mr. Ramsay at the begin-ning and at the end of the sentence, his outstretched arms encompassing Mrs. Ramsay's death, in a kind of cinematically pantomimed parentheses. Yet, even as she is being erased as the intended object of Mr. Ramsay's embrace, even as she escapes that stifling sentence, Mrs. Ramsay is in-scribed within the empty space that remains between her husband's out-stretched arms.

There is a suggestive slippage here that helps elucidate the structure of the novel as an integral whole. For just as the visual image of Mr. Ramsay conjured by this sentence seems to displace its subject and consciously hold an empty space for Mrs. Ramsay, so her death, occurring offstage as it were, is less significant than its effect—her subsequent absence from the house, the family, the text. Moreover, these textual arms trace much more than Mrs. Ramsay as a subject indicated by her profound "presence as absence." The emptiness signifies a space beyond the body, beyond the text, beyond language, which the "arid scimitar" of the masculinist fictional subject simply cannot penetrate.[6]

Virginia Woolf's modernist innovation of the novel in these three works—the radical displacements of the subject enabled and effected by her experimental structures—cannot be separated from her postwar feminist/pacifist politics. First, Woolf places the universal subject in parentheses in *Jacob's Room*; second, she carves out a parenthetical space between subjects, but beyond any individual subjectivity, to represent our connection within an intricate web of human affiliation, through which an implicitly pacifist/feminist subjectivity is provisionally defined; third, she uses parentheses to open up a textual space for the unpresentable truths of human experience. The fictional "I" who narrates Virginia Woolf's novels is thus both the means of inscribing her own specifically female subjectivity and of signaling the end of the imperial subject. Although only a narrative poetics can fully account for the complexity and texture of the deployment of subjectivity within the Woolfian narrative, an implicitly universal narratology cannot articulate the feminine/feminist specificity of Woolf's narrative structures and so misses the point—and the difference—of her modernist aesthetic—and of her female sentence.

NOTES

1. Woolf, *Three Guineas*, 97. Woolf argues that "once we know the truth about war, and the truth about art . . . , we should not believe in war, and we should believe in art."

2. By gendering her new sentence, Woolf had already, in 1928, anticipated the textual/sexual politics that would occupy so many critics in the late 1970s and 1980s. Her insights into sexual difference, while empirically based, already envision notions such as writing the female body. She wrote toward the end of *A Room of One's Own*, "The book has somehow to be adapted to the body, and at a venture one would say that women's books should be shorter, more concentrated" (*Room*, 81).

3. Although I cannot develop the idea here, the richness of this inextricability certainly supports Barbara Herrnstein Smith's argument in "Narrative Versions, Narrative Theories" against the rigidity of Seymour Chatman's two-level distinction—story/discourse.

4. My formulation of the female narrator in this text owes much to Richard Onorato's reading of an earlier version of this essay.

5. The quotation marks around "blank sheets" here signify their reference to a short story by Isak Dinesen called "The Blank Page." An old woman tells the story of a convent outside of which bridal sheets are hung by the nuns after the wedding night and to which pilgrims travel to decipher the stains. The story—a fable about the indirections of female creativity—is about the possible alternative "readings" of a

blank sheet/page. Woolf would have us read Mrs. Dalloway's blank sheets as proof of the failure of male violation and a testament to her personal integrity and, thus, implicitly subversive. But, as my discussion suggests, the renunciatory gesture is a problematic revision in which the understandable, even necessary attempt to escape from the trap of sexual roles (wife, lover, mother) looks dangerously like a reinscription of the denial of female sexuality.

6. It is also worth noting here that in *A Room of One's Own*, Woolf describes the importance to society of woman's role as supporter of man's illusions of his own superiority (anticipating Luce Irigaray): "Women have served all these centuries as looking-glasses possessing the magic and delicious power of reflecting the figure of man at twice its natural size" (35). Later, she ironically describes how the obituary of a Lady Dudley speaks primarily of her husband's idiosyncrasies. These mirror images are reversed in Mrs. Ramsay's "reflected" absence.

WORKS CITED

Auerbach, Eric. "The Brown Stocking." In *Mimesis*. Princeton: Princeton University Press, 1974. 525–53.

Henke, Suzette. "*Mrs. Dalloway*: The Communion of Saints." In *New Feminist Essays on Virginia Woolf*. Ed. Jane Marcus. Lincoln: University of Nebraska Press, 1981. 125–47.

Smith, Barbara Herrnstein. "Narrative Versions, Narrative Theories." In *On Narrative*. Ed. W. J. T. Mitchell. Chicago: University of Chicago Press, 1980. 209–32.

Spivak, Gayatri Chakravorty. "Unmaking and Making in *To the Lighthouse*." In *Women and Language in Literature and Society*. Ed. Sally McConnell-Ginet, Ruth Borker, and Nelly Furman. New York: Praeger, 1980. 310–27.

Woolf, Leonard, ed. *Collected Essays*. Vol. 4. London: Chatto and Windus, 1966.

Woolf, Virginia. *Jacob's Room*. New York: Harvest/Harcourt Brace Jovanovich, 1960.

——. *Mrs. Dalloway*. London: Granada, 1976.

——. *A Room of One's Own*. New York: Harvest/Harcourt Brace Jovanovich, 1957.

——. *Three Guineas*. New York: Harvest/Harcourt Brace Jovanovich, 1966.

——. *To the Lighthouse*. New York: Harvest/Harcourt Brace Jovanovich, 1955.

——. *A Writer's Diary*. London: Triad/Granada, 1978.

spatialization, narrative theory,

and virginia woolf's

the voyage out

susan | stanford friedman

irginia Woolf's first novel, *The Voyage Out* (1915), is founded on a basic contradiction. It simultaneously narrates a failed *Bildung* for its protagonist and inscribes a successful *Bildung* for its author. Rachel Vinrace journeys on her father's ship from a sheltered London existence to Santa Marina, a former British colony in South America. As a conventional marriage plot, the story charts Rachel's development: her "coming out" into society, her courtship, and her engagement. But before she marries, she suddenly becomes ill and dies. Shockingly, life goes on uneventfully among the enclave of British tourists in the final chapters. Warned by ominous resonances early in the journey, we, the readers, may anticipate the end but nonetheless feel cheated out of the narrative resolution that the text insistently leads us to expect by invoking the conventions of the bildungsroman.

Yet, at the same time, this narrative of failure represents an exhilarating victory over the tyranny of conventional plot as Woolf would later call it in her 1923 essay "Modern Fiction" (153–54). As Rachel Blau DuPlessis argues in *Writing Beyond the Ending*, the death of Rachel represents Woolf's first attempt to "write beyond the ending" of the marriage plot (47–53). In relation to ideological scripts of female destiny in the nineteenth-century women's bildungsroman, *The Voyage Out* kills off the traditional life story of upper middle-class British women and thus accomplishes a victory of sorts over the "powerful and unscrupulous tyrant who has him [the writer] in thrall to provide a plot . . . in the accepted style" ("Modern Fiction," 153). This story of liberation is fundamentally at odds with the sad tale of a young life ended before it had hardly begun.

I am interested in the dissonance between these two readings of the novel. They imply, I believe, two different narratives operating relationally and interactively on the reader. This complicates what Peter Brooks calls the narrative desire that governs the plot and gives it its dynamic. In *Reading for the Plot*, Brooks defines narrative as "the play of desire in time" (xiii) and identifies two sites for this play: first, the text itself, wherein desire to order compels the plot's unfolding; and second, the space between text and reader, wherein the reader's desire for plot impels the reading (37–61). Analysis of these narrative desires involves seeing "the text itself as a system of internal energies and tensions, compulsions, resistances, and desires" (xiv). Like Paul Ricoeur in "Narrative Time," Brooks insists on the temporal dimension of narrative, on narrative's essential relation to time. I want to extend Brooks's "dynamics of narrative" by reintroducing the issue of space into a discussion of narrative—by considering narrative, in other words, as the play of desire in space as well as time. This approach will invite a reading of the multiple and dialogic narratives that can be constituted within the text and through the reader's engagement with it. In the case of *The Voyage Out*, the two main narratives clash as different stories of defeat and victory. Part of the reader's pleasure with the text results from this conflict between the desire for conventional narrative closure and the desire for resistance to the implied harmony of such an ending.

I define narrative most simply as the representation of movement within the coordinates of space and time.[1] Here, I adapt M. M. Bakhtin's concept of the chronotope, by which he means the special form in which the "intrinsic connectedness of temporal and spatial relationships" is expressed in literature (84). Invoking Einstein's theory of relativity, Bakhtin argues for the "inseparability of space and time" (84) and resorts repeatedly to spatial tropes in his analysis of various chronotopes. I also want to develop Julia Kristeva's adaptations of Bakhtin's spatial tropes in her two early essays "Word, Dialogue, and Novel" (1966) and "The Bounded Text" (1966–67), both of which are included in the collection *Desire in Language*. Here, in introducing her concept of intertextuality, she advocates a reading practice based in the "spatialization" of the word along vertical and horizontal axes in an intertextual grid. In this essay, I will adapt her spatial tropes to suggest that we can read narrative by interpreting the text's horizontal and vertical narrative movements and intersections. Such interactions are events, I will argue, that take place at every moment in the text in a kind of interdependent interplay of surface and depth. Such moments may appear as juxtapositions, oppositions, conflations, convergences, or mirrorings of narrative coordinates. These moments in turn join to form a fluid "story" of a dynamic text ever in process, ever "narrated" by the reader. *The Voyage Out* will serve as a case in point for a spatialized strategy of reading narrative, especially dissonant texts such as Woolf's first novel.[2]

KRISTEVA'S SPATIALIZATION OF THE WORD

For Kristeva, spatialization—with its attendant graphic tropes of coordinates, axes, trajectory, horizontal, vertical, surface, intersection, linearity, loop, dimension, and so forth—allows for the visualization of the text-in-process, the text as a dynamic "productivity," an "operation" (*Desire*, 36–37). Spatialization does not mean the erasure of time by space, as it does for Joseph Frank, who in his influential essay "Spatial Form in Modern Literature" argues that avant-garde narrative techniques in modern literature created an illusory effect of simultaneity and unity. Rather, for Kristeva, spatialization constitutes the text as a verbal surface or place in which both space and time, synchrony and diachrony, function as coordinates for textual activity. Kristeva's earliest essays pose a critique of the static analysis of structuralism and a call for the identification of textual process. Invoking Bakhtin, Kristeva identifies this process as fundamentally dialogic and intertextual—at the level of word, sentence, and story. Bakhtin, she explains, "considers writing as a reading of the anterior literary corpus and the text as an absorption of and a reply to another text" (*Desire*, 69). "Each word (text)," she notes, "is an intersection of word (texts) where at least one other word (text) can be read.... Any text is constructed as a mosaic of quotations; any text is the absorption and transformation of another" (66). She verbally graphs these intersections by identifying the text's "three dimensions or coordinates" as the writing subject, the addressee, and exterior texts (see Fig. 1). What she calls the horizontal axis can be drawn as a line from writing subject across to the addressee, who is either a character to whom the speech is directed or more generally the reader. This horizontal axis represents the text as a transaction between writer and reader. The vertical axis implies a line starting with the text and moving down to the exterior texts, or contexts, of the text in question. This vertical axis emphasizes the text as a writing in relation with other writings. In other words, a text's dialogic interaction operates along both horizontal and vertical axes, from writing subject to addressee, from text to contexts. What emerges from a text is not "a *point* (a fixed meaning)," but rather a dialogue of writer and reader, text and context (65).[3]

In her early work, Kristeva's insistence on spatialization, which embeds

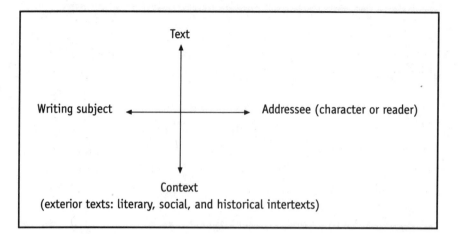

Figure 1. Kristeva's Horizontal and Vertical Coordinates

her critique of pure formalism, is part of her Bakhtinian project to (re)insert the social and historical context as a necessary dimension of a text. Reading, she suggests, should never be merely a "linguistic" process focused on an isolated text. Consequently, she advocates a reading of what she calls the "translinguistic," by which she means the text's dialogue along horizontal and vertical axes with its writer, readers, and context (*Desire*, 69). She coins the term "ideologeme" to identify the point of intersection between the text and its precursor texts. This ideologeme is "materialized" "along the entire length of its [the text's] trajectory, giving it its historical and social coordinates" (36). Reading for the dialogic ideologeme means reading the text "within (the text of) society and history" (37).

SPATIALIZING NARRATIVE

Kristeva's spatialization of the word has potential applications for narrative. I will maintain her insistence on historical and intertextual resonances, but alter her model of a text's vertical and horizontal axes. As an interpretive strategy (not as a narrative typology), I propose two kinds of narrative axes whose intersections are reconstructed by the reader in the interactive process of reading. Bakhtin's notion of the novel's double chronotope is useful: "Even in the segmentation of a modern literary work, we sense the chronotope of the represented world as well as the chronotope of the readers and creators of the work. . . . Before us are two events—the event that is narrated in the work and the event of narration itself (we ourselves participate in the latter, as listeners or readers); these events take place in different times . . . and in different places" (254–55). The totality of the

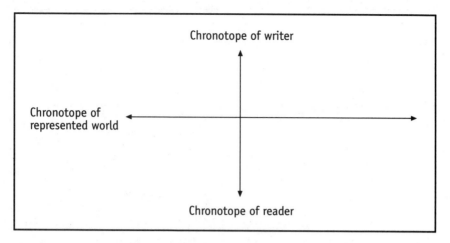

Figure 2. Graphing Bakhtin's Double Chronotopes

work, he concludes, is made up of the interacting chronotopes of the writer, reader, and text. We can graph Bakhtin's two chronotopes along horizontal and vertical narrative axes (see Fig. 2). The horizontal narrative axis involves the linear movement of the characters through the coordinates of textual space and time. The vertical narrative axis involves the space and time that the writer and reader occupy as they inscribe and interpret what Kristeva calls the "subject-in-process" constituted through the "signifying practice" of the text and its dialogues with literary, social, and historical intertexts.

Both axes represent a movement through space and time—the one (horizontal) referring to the movement of characters within their fictional world, the other (vertical) referring to the "motions" of the writer and the reader in relation to each other and to the text's intertexts. Where the horizontal movement exists in finite form within the bounded world of the text, the vertical movement exists fluidly as a writing inscribed by the writer and reconstituted by the reader more or less consciously and to a greater and lesser degree depending on the specific writers and readers. As different functions of narrative, these axes feed off each other symbiotically; neither exists by itself as a fixed entity. I separate them only for strategic purposes, for the insight that such a spatialization provides for interpreting the overdetermined complexities of narrative. A fully spatialized reading of a given narrative text, as narrative, involves an interpretation of the continuous interplay between the horizontal and vertical narrative coordinates. The "plot" of intersection, "narrated" by the reader, is a "story" based on a reading of the different forms that intersection takes through time, that is,

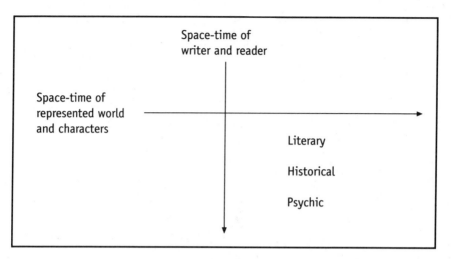

Figure 3. Horizontal and Vertical Axes of Narrative

how the horizontal and vertical narratives converge and separate, echo and oppose, reinforce and undermine each other (see Fig. 3).

Before turning to *The Voyage Out*, let me specify in more detail what I mean by horizontal and vertical narrative coordinates. The horizontal narrative is the sequence of events, whether internal or external, that "happen" according to the ordering principles of the plot and narrative point of view. Setting, character, action, initiating "problem," progression, and closure are its familiar components—the focus of much traditional narratology.[4] The horizontal narrative follows and is constrained by the linearity of language—the sequence of the sentence that moves horizontally in alphabetic scripts is repeated in the horizontal movement of the plot from "beginning" to "end," however the categories of start and finish are customarily understood. Determined in part by historically specific narrative conventions, the forms of the horizontal narrative differ particularly in their handling of chronology, teleology, and narrative point of view: from the "well-made" to the picaresque or "plotless" plot; from the omniscient to the multiple, unreliable, or first-person narrator; from the epistolary to the embedded and complexly framed narratives. But for all forms, reading the horizontal narrative involves interpreting the sequence inscribed in the linearity of sentence and story. In simplest terms, we ask, Who is the story about? What happens? Where? Why? What does it "mean"? *Ulysses* and *Mrs. Dalloway*, for example, plot the movements of their characters through the cities of Dublin and London on a single day in June. Reading the horizontal narrative axis, we focus on the exterior and interior actions and thoughts of Clarissa and Septimus, Stephen, Bloom, and Molly (as well as a host of others). As readers, we may imaginatively inhabit their space and time, to become what Peter Rabinowitz and James Phelan variously call the "narrative audience" that participates in "the mimetic illusion" (Phelan, 5).[5] As with any text, the horizontal narrative is reconstituted in the process of reading. Its attendant meanings are consequently dependent on what Brooks calls the reader's "performance" of the text (37), what Ross Chambers refers to as the "performative force" of the narrative (4–5), and what Phelan identifies as "narrative dynamics." But, in bringing the horizontal narrative to life, the reader (like the writer) nonetheless remains in a different space and time than that of the characters.

The vertical axis of narrative involves reading "down into" the text as we move across it. The vertical does not exist at the level of sequential plot but rather resides within, dependent on the horizontal narrative as the function that adds multiple resonances to the characters' movement through space and time. The palimpsest—a tablet that has been written on many times, with prior layers imperfectly erased—serves as an apt metaphor for the vertical dimension of narrative. Instead of the single textual surface of the horizontal narrative, the vertical narrative has many superimposed surfaces, layered and overwritten like the human psyche. Freud's image of the psyche as the "mystic writing-pad" serves equally well, for with this mechanism, the written impression remains embedded but hidden in the wax beneath the clean plastic slate ("Note"). The point of these tropes is not to suggest a simple equation of the horizontal narrative with consciousness and the vertical narrative with the unconscious. Rather, they suggest that every horizontal narrative has an embedded vertical dimension that is more or less visible and that must be traced by the reader because it has no narrator of its own. Although not yet named as such, the vertical narrative has been the focus of much poststructuralist, feminist, Afro-Americanist, and Marxist narrative theory.[6]

Although interwoven, three distinct strands of the vertical narrative can be usefully separated for purposes of analysis: the literary, the historical, and the psychic (see Fig. 3). Both the literary and historical aspects of the vertical narrative involve reading the horizontal narrative's dialogues with other texts: interpreting, in other words, the various forms of intertextuality that Kristeva introduces in her tropes of spatialization. Whether consciously or unconsciously produced by the writer, these dialogues exist as "the mosaic of quotations" that traverse the text. They are the layered surfaces beneath and within the horizontal narrative, but they are not narrated by it and may seem tangential to it. When consciously intended by the writer, these intertextual resonances establish an indirect communication between writer and reader with the characters and events of the horizontal narrative as points of mediation. Such resonances do not usually exist in the mind of the characters in the space and time of the horizontal narrative. In *Mrs. Dalloway*, for example, it is the reader who "narrates" the story of Septimus as Shakespearean fool, as scapegoat, as sacrificial lamb and Christ figure within the anguished postwar landscape.

The literary aspect of the vertical narrative exists first of all in relation to genre. The writer's and reader's awareness of genre conventions exists as a chronotope, a space-time, within which the specific text is read—for its invocations and revocations, its uses and rescriptions, its repetitions and play. We read, for example, James Joyce's *A Portrait of the Artist as a Young Man* and D. H. Lawrence's *Sons and Lovers* with the grid of the bildungs-roman as stories of development in which Stephen and Paul progressively emerge from their families through plots of vocational and sexual initiation. More broadly, all literary texts exist—however centrally, ambivalently, or marginally—within one or more literary traditions or cultures. Horizontal narratives, consequently, have an indirectly narrated vertical dimension that accomplishes a dialogic engagement with what has been written before. In *The Signifying Monkey*, Henry Louis Gates proposes the term "signifyin(g)" to identify a culturally specific form of intertextuality, a mode tied to the African-American oral and written traditions of speakers and writers self-reflexively and intentionally playing off the discourse of others in the tradition. The epistolary mode of Alice Walker's *The Color Purple*, in which Celie writes letters first to God and then to her sister, not only dialogues with such epistolary inscriptions of rape as Richardson's *Clarissa* but also signifies on the oral frame of Hurston's *Their Eyes Were Watching God*, in which Janie narrates the events of the story to her friend Phoeby, and on the story of incest in Toni Morrison's *The Bluest Eye*. More generally, we recognize that intertextual reference may be highlighted or muted, intentionally or unintentionally present, collaborative or revisionist. But common to all intertextual resonances is a *story* of dialogue narrated by the reader that takes place outside the spatial and temporal coordinates through which the characters of the horizontal narrative move.

The historical aspect of the vertical narrative represents a similar mosaic of quotations, one that refers to the larger social order of the writer, text, and reader. Such a mosaic may involve reference to a specific historical event that the text reconstructs, such as Morrison's retelling in *Beloved*, with key departures, of Margaret Garner's attempt to kill her children when faced with their and her own return to slavery in 1856. Or, more broadly, this historical mosaic may involve what DuPlessis calls "cultural scripts" layered into the horizontal narrative (ix–xi, 1–19). DuPlessis's term acknowledges the part that "story" plays in both ideological and oppositional discourses. These political resonances that traverse the text might include interlocking narratives of race, gender, class, ethnicity, sexuality, religion, and so forth—stories, in other words, that reproduce, subvert, and otherwise engage with the dominant and marginalized cultural scripts of the social order. For Fredric Jameson, such narratives constitute what he calls the "political unconscious," by which he means the "buried and repressed" narrative of class struggle present in trace form on the surface of the text (20). His assertion that narratives of class struggle subsume all other stories is dangerously bounded, but his call for the critic to read the text for signs of its repressed political scripts is useful. In Morrison's *Beloved*, the vertically embedded cultural scripts or textual unconscious include many "stories" of race and gender relations: for example, the master's right to violate slave women; Western theories of black and African inferiority and bestiality; patterns of slave resistance; white women's liminal position between race privilege and gendered alterity. Whether these political and historical narratives are buried in the text or openly scripted, reading this aspect of the vertical narrative allows for an analysis of the text in dialogue with "its historical and social coordinates," as Kristeva advocates (*Desire*, 36).

Reading the psychic aspect of the vertical narrative involves recognizing that a text can be read as a linguistic entity structured like a psyche, with a conscious and an unconscious that interact psychodynamically. Freud's concept of the psyche as perpetually in the process of splitting suggests that nothing is ever lost, only forgotten.[7] Analogically speaking, the text is, like a dream, the result of a negotiation in which the desire to express and the need to repress force a compromise that takes the form of disguised speech. The text, then, can be read as a site of repression and insistent return. Freud's grammar for the dreamwork—the mechanisms of displacement, condensation, nonrational modes of representability, and secondary revision—is useful for decoding disguised expression (*Interpretation of Dreams*, 311–546). These mechanisms are often at work in the enigmatic textual sites that deconstruction unravels to subvert underlying binaries. As Shoshana Felman does in her reading of James's *Turn of the Screw*, textual gaps, silences, knots, and aporias can be read vertically to gain some sort of access to the textual unconscious.

This is also, I would suggest, what Kristeva is doing in her integration of Lacanian psychoanalysis, Bakhtinian dialogics, and Barthesian semiotics in her *Revolution in Poetic Language*.[8] Kristeva flips over Lacan's axiom that the unconscious is structured like a language to suggest that the text is structured like a psyche. Language, she argues, always engages in a dialectical interplay of two modalities, the semiotic and the symbolic. The semiotic—that oral and rhythmic dimension of language that exists prior to and outside a system of signification—harkens back to the pre-oedipal period of the child's desire for the maternal body. The symbolic—that meaning-centered, instrumental aspect of language that exists after the child grasps the principle of signification—reverts back to the oedipal period when (according to Lacan) the child's realization of sexual difference allows for the acquisition of language based on a system of differences governed by the Law of the Father ("Signification of the Phallus").[9] Reading for the interplay of the semiotic and the symbolic—newly and differently constituted in every text—is one form that reading the vertical narrative can take.

A relational reading strategy based on the compositional history of the text—the chronotope of the writer—offers another mechanism for reading the psychic dimension of the vertical narrative. Instead of privileging the "final" text as the "definitive" one, we can read the various versions of a text as an overdetermined palimpsest in which each text forms a distinct, yet interrelated part of a larger composite "text."[10] Freud's concept of dreams in a series as being part of a larger dream-text that can be interpreted is useful (*Interpretation of Dreams*, 369, 563). He suggests that the mechanisms of the dreamwork govern the relation among the dreams and that "the first of these homologous dreams to occur is often the more distorted one and timid, while the succeeding one will be more confident and distinct" (369). Freud's grammar can be adapted to read what gets repressed on the one hand and worked through on the other in a series of drafts preceding a published text. Tracking the various versions of the same story can reveal a process of conscious or self-conscious self-censorship whereby textual revision of the horizontal narrative represses or further disguises certain forbidden elements that remain as part of the vertical narrative. Reading the composite "text" involves reconstructing the "story" of condensation, displacement, and secondary revision from one version to another. In short, earlier versions of a text can be read vertically as the textual unconscious of the horizontal narrative in the published text. For example, H.D.'s Madrigal Cycle, a triptych of three autobiographical novels about her life during the teens, form a composite text in which the last one she wrote (*Bid Me to Live [A Madrigal]*) represses the stories of lesbian desire and illicit motherhood that are fully narrated in the earlier texts, *Paint It To-Day* and *Asphodel*, both of which she ultimately considered to be "drafts" for *Bid Me to Live*.[11]

Conversely, a writer's repeated return to the scene of writing a particular story can be read as a kind of repetition compulsion in which the earliest versions are the most disguised, with each repetition bringing the writer closer to the repressed content that needs to be remembered. Here, I am adapting Freud's notion of analysis as a transference scene in which the analysand repeats the symptoms and dreams produced by repressed material in a process of "working through" that ultimately leads to conscious recollection of what has been forgotten ("Further Recommendations"). This analogy between analytic and novelistic transference is especially cogent in autobiographical narratives, in which the split subject of the writing "I now" and the written-about "I then" perform the different roles of analyst and analysand in a kind of "writing cure." Earlier or later versions of the horizontal narrative, in other words, can, when read together as a composite text, give us access to the psychic dimension of the vertical narrative. Joyce's autobiographical narratives about Stephen D(a)edalus, for example (including "A Portrait of the Artist," *Stephen Hero*, *A Portrait of the Artist as a Young Man*, and *Ulysses*), constitute a composite "text" in which the death of Joyce's mother and the son's remorse remain unnarratable until the final text in the series, present only in trace forms that can be interpreted with Freud's grammar for the dreamwork.[12]

SPATIALIZED NARRATIVE IN *THE VOYAGE OUT*

A "full" reading of narrative axes is not possible in a bounded text because, like the dream in Freud's psychoanalysis, the text's dialogism is unbounded, as is the story of the intersections between the horizontal and vertical coordinates. But the possibilities of spatialized interpretation become evident by focusing on certain moments within the narrative of *The Voyage Out*. Omnisciently narrated in a linear chronology, the horizontal narrative tells the story of Rachel's "voyage out": to South America and the possibilities of adulthood. On board ship, she is awakened by the dazzling Dalloways, surrogate mother and father figures who both enchant and frighten her. Under the tutelage of her Aunt Helen, her dead mother's old friend, Rachel falls in love with Terence Hewet, becomes engaged during an excursion upriver, catches a mysterious tropical fever, and dies before she is married. Subplots abound, usually focused around the issues of

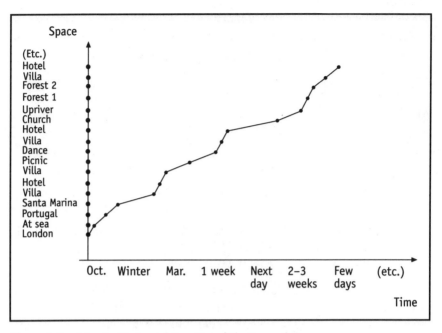

Figure 4. Graphing the Horizontal Narrative of *The Voyage Out*

courtship, marriage, and single life. The text has a rich panoply of characters moving through settings visualized with the sharp care of a Jane Austen or George Eliot novel. While Rachel dominates as the main center of consciousness, the horizontal narrative alternates between intense tableaux focused on Rachel's subjectivity and more diffuse scenes that render the social milieu and forward the action (see Fig. 4).

The rich resonances of this horizontal plot appear vertically as interwoven historical, literary, and psychic "stories" that are sometimes overtly, sometimes covertly "there" in the horizontal narrative but don't become fully "narrated" until they are read (see Fig. 5). I will first sketch in some of the historical and literary narratives before moving on to the even more complex psychic ones. In narrating a journey from London to a former South American colony, *The Voyage Out* invokes cultural narratives of empire, especially the mission of the English to civilize the world by ruling it. Rachel's emergence from the suffocation of Richmond leads her not so much away from London as into its repetition in the British community of Santa Marina. Rachel's voyage out becomes a voyage in—into the heart of the ideological configurations of empire, gender, and class that her story both acts out and resists.

Rachel's conversation on board ship with Richard Dalloway, a former

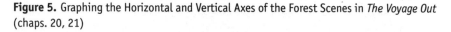

Horizontal ─────── Rachel, Terence, Helen in woods, upriver ───────▶

(chronotope of characters)

Bildungsroman		Literary
Austen		
Genesis		
Conrad		
Milton		
(etc.)		
Gender		Historical
Family		
Empire		
(etc.)		
Psychosexual		Psychic
Melymbrosia		
Woolf's *Diary*		
Woolf's *Letters*		
Woolf's "Reminiscences"		
Woolf's "22 Hyde Park Gate"		
Woolf's *A Sketch of the Past*		
(etc.)		

Vertical   (chronotopes of writer and readers)

Figure 5. Graphing the Horizontal and Vertical Axes of the Forest Scenes in *The Voyage Out* (chaps. 20, 21)

Conservative member of Parliament, shows microcosmically how interlocking narratives of gender, class, race, and empire reverberate vertically within the horizontal narrative. The scene's heavy parodic effect depends on a dramatic irony created by the (vertical) intertextual resonances of which the characters (in horizontal space and time) remain unaware. As readers, we see not only the exchange between Rachel and Richard (horizontal) but also Woolf's dialogic play with cultural scripts in which Richard figures as synecdoche for patriarchal, imperialist capitalism (vertical). The interplay between these horizontal and vertical narrative functions gives the scene its satiric punch.

Transfixed by Richard's powerful presence, Rachel asks him "big questions" about life such as, "What *is* your ideal?" His answer points simply to "the English." In spite of his attempt to distance himself from old-fashioned chauvinism, he reinvokes the cultural narratives of class, race, and gender on which the British Empire depended:

> I grant that the English seem, on the whole, whiter than most men, their
> records cleaner. But, good Lord, don't run away with the idea that I

don't see the drawbacks—horrors—unmentionable things done in our very midst! I'm under no illusions. Few people, I suppose, have fewer illusions than I have. . . . Well, when I consider my life, there is one fact I admit that I'm proud of; owing to me some thousands of girls in Lancashire—and many thousands to come after them—can spend an hour every day in the open air which their mothers had to spend over their looms. (64–65)

Mr. Dalloway's patronage of the factory girls reappears in his patronizing of Rachel, which depends on the Victorian separation of spheres for middle- and upper-class men and women. When Rachel exclaims to him, " 'I know nothing!' . . . 'You ought to make me understand,' " he responds: " 'I never allow my wife to talk politics. . . . If I have preserved mine [his ideals], . . . it is due to the fact that I have been able to come home to my wife in the evening and to find that she has spent her day in calling, music, play with the children, domestic duties' " (65). Rachel is able to question how his vision of progress addresses the intangible needs of human beings only in the hesitant form of an image: "There's an old widow in her room, somewhere, let us suppose in the suburbs of Leeds. . . . [She] goes to her cupboard and finds a little more tea . . . or a little less tea. . . . Still, there's the mind of the widow—the affections; those you leave untouched" (66). His response combines ideological narratives of the state, industrial economy, progress, and empire: "I can conceive no more exalted aim—to be the citizen of the Empire. Look at it this way, Miss Vinrace; conceive the state as a complicated machine; we citizens are parts of that machine; some fulfill more important duties; others (perhaps I am one of them) serve only to connect some obscure parts of the mechanism, concealed from the public eye. Yet if the meanest screw fails in its task, the proper working of the whole is imperilled" (66).

Rachel's interior response unwittingly exposes the racial narrative that underlies Dalloway's vision of the perfect machine of the British Empire: "It was impossible to combine the image of a lean black widow, gazing out of her window, and longing for some one to talk to, with the image of a vast machine, such as one sees at South Kensington, thumping, thumping, thumping" (66). Rachel's unvoiced thought unconsciously counters Dalloway's odd phrase, "the English seem . . . whiter than most men," with her own inexplicable transformation of a widow in black mourning clothes into "a lean black widow." The vertical narrative links Dalloway's conflation of Englishmen/white/clean with Rachel's condensation of widow-in-black to black widow, a kind of metonymic displacement in each case that marks the spot of the racial, as well as class and gender, scripts that undergird the British Empire.[13]

The scene between Rachel and Richard closes when Mrs. Dalloway joins them just as two warships of the Mediterranean Fleet pass nearby. "Richard raised his hat," while "convulsively Clarissa squeezed Rachel's hand. 'Aren't you glad to be English!' she said" (69). Completing the circuit of surrogate parents and child, the warships mark them all as "English," as beneficiaries of empire. The public sphere of state and the private sphere of family interpenetrate in this moment of satiric convergence between the horizontal and vertical narratives. Embedded within the innocent conversation of the characters who move through the novel's horizontal space and time is a veritable "mosaic of quotations," a vertical citational strategy that Woolf employs so as to warn the reader subterraneously of Richard's impending sexual assault of Rachel and to explode through parodic mimicry the cultural narratives of British patriotism, gender divisions, race, class, and empire.

The literary aspect of the vertical narrative in *The Voyage Out* centers first in the novel's status as a bildungsroman, a genre that for women has been dominated by the marriage plot. For many women writers and certainly for Woolf, Jane Austen's novels were prototypical: the narrative drive (kinesis) centered in courtship; narrative closure (stasis) achieved in engagement and immanent marriage.[14] Rachel's voyage out of girlhood—somewhat delayed at age twenty-four by Victorian protectionism and the absence of a mother—is structured around a series of initiations that bring her ever closer to marriage, still the teleology of a proper young woman's life in the Edwardian period. The novel's constant dialogue with other literary texts highlights these initiations and at the same time signals the text's resistance to these conventional scripts. Horizontal and vertical narratives sometimes converge in this regard, for the characters themselves are always reading and talking about books.[15] Embedded within their conversations, however, is a vertical dimension in which Woolf's novel as a whole invokes and revokes precursor texts. For example, the Dalloways try to persuade Rachel to read Austen (57–58, 62), and their parting gift to Rachel is a copy of Austen's *Persuasion*, inscribed with their London address, with its implicit invitation for social debut (70). These gestures at Austen represent their delicately mannered attempt (in the horizontal narrative) to "persuade" Rachel to enter the marriage market under their tutelage, to fulfill in life the plot scripted in the novel. " 'Why do people marry?' " Rachel asks Clarissa; " 'That's what you are going to find out,' Clarissa laughed" (60). Rachel's distaste for Austen—"She's so—so, well, so like a tight plait" (58)—presages her unconscious resistance to the courtship plot she later acts out and ultimately rebels against. Here the vertical narrative of dialogue with Austen's *Persuasion* mirrors and thus reinforces the Dalloways' attempted persuasions in the horizontal narrative.

At other times, however, the writer signals the novel's literary dialogism to the reader, who becomes the "narrator" of a story of which the characters in the horizontal narrative remain unaware. For example, the excursion upriver, where the British tourists feel the primeval rhythm of the current and witness the ever more "primitive" native life in the tropics, echoes Conrad's *Heart of Darkness*. "They seemed to be driving into the heart of the night," Woolf writes about the travelers, "for the trees closed in front of them, and they could hear all round them the rustling of leaves. The great darkness had the usual effect of taking away all desire for communication by making their words sound thin and small" (265). The irony, of course, is that Kurtz's cry, "The horror, the horror," at the end of Marlow's trip structurally parallels the penultimate courtship scenes in the forest, where Rachel and Terence become engaged. In "telling the story" of this dissonance between *The Heart of Darkness* and *The Voyage Out*, the reader begins to "narrate" a discomfort with the courtship that exists at this point only in trace form in the horizontal narrative.

The reader's dis-ease with the engagement is further intensified by the forest scene's evocation of the story of the Fall in Genesis. As Christine Froula points out, the tropical forest heavy with scent and sunlight reinscribes Eden. The warning to watch out for snakes, Terence's play with a piece of red fruit, and noises of beasts and birds all recapitulate biblical iconography to suggest through juxtaposition that the declaration of love constitutes a fall of sorts that will expel the young people from paradise (270–72). This intertextual foreshadowing seems borne out when Rachel falls sick while Terence reads to her from Milton's *Comus*. Vertically beneath the horizontal presence of *Comus* lies the text's dialogue with Milton's *Paradise Lost*, a text both invoked and revoked as a narrative about sin. Such intertextual warnings help the reader see where the horizontal narrative will end up. Just when the fruit of the romance plot appears ready to ripen for plucking, the horizontal narrative makes a sudden swerve toward death, one in some sense predicted by the vertical narrative.

The psychic dimension of the vertical narrative intensifies the troubling undercurrents established by the text's literary and historical dialogism. We can begin to locate this psychic dimension, this textual unconscious, first, by identifying eruptions of the semiotic into the surface of the text and, second, by examining the compositional history of the text, that is, by moving to the chronotope of the writer.

The Voyage Out both thematizes and performs aspects of the Kristevan semiotic—linguistic spaces that foreground the pre-symbolic and pre-oedipal. Rachel's nightmares and hallucinations, which exist as part of the horizontal narrative, have a double vertical dimension: first, as disguised articulations of Rachel's unconscious fears and desires, never fully narrated in the text; and second, as enigmatic dream-texts that disrupt the progression of the marriage plot and foreshadow its dissolution. From these moments, the reader can construct a subterranean story of fear and longing at Rachel's entrance into the adult world of sexuality.

The first nightmare comes after Richard Dalloway suddenly assaults Rachel in the midst of a raging storm at sea. She dreams of being pursued by "barbarian men" with moaning voices and desiring eyes and snuffling noises (75–77). During her fevered delirium, Rachel has three major hallucinations that echo her nightmare and end with her death. The first hallucination images Rachel walking through a damp, oozing tunnel under the Thames, "where there were little deformed women sitting in archways playing cards," who gradually become Helen and the nurse whispering at the window (331). Rachel's second hallucination comes repeatedly in the form of "a little old woman" rolling about with knives (333). Her final appearance comes with Terence's kiss: Rachel opens her eyes to see "an old woman slicing a man's head off with a knife" (339). Rachel's final hallucination is an image of herself whisking through spaces, times, and sounds that seem, without clear signification, to relive her "voyage out." Then she sees herself falling into "a deep pool of sticky water which eventually closed over her head." Hearing only booming sounds and seeing only a play of light and dark, Rachel curls up at the bottom of the sea, lifeless but not dead (341).

The pursuing men, the old women in the oozy tunnel, the old woman with the knife, and the womb/tomb of the sticky sea represent a movement backward through time from the oedipal, through the pre-oedipal, to the prenatal; from the father who terrifies, to the mother who wields the father's power, to the prenatal death-in-life. That Terence's kiss should turn into the phallic mother's castrating slice condenses an image of maternal horror and revenge on men (a reverse castration) that expresses the daughter's longing for her dead mother and anger at her loss. Read vertically, these scenes of terror and pre-symbolic sensation recapitulate in reverse order a psychosexual narrative that begins in the bliss of the maternal body and moves inexorably and terrifyingly into the Law of the Father.[16]

A relational reading strategy based in the compositional history of *The Voyage Out* also provides access to the psychic dimension of the vertical narrative.[17] According to Leonard Woolf, Virginia wrote some fifteen to twenty drafts of the novel from about 1908 until 1913, of which nine exist in partial form. Louise DeSalvo assembled one extant draft, written between 1909 to 1910, and published it under Woolf's original title, *Melymbrosia*. After completing this version in 1910, DeSalvo argues, Woolf became ill in the summer of 1911, at least partially because of her fear of making the blunt social criticism in the novel public (Introduction). She set aside this manuscript and completed a final revision during the period of her courtship, engagement, and marriage to Leonard, from 1911–13. Intermittent illness during the completion of *The Voyage Out* led to her suicide attempt in September 1913 and severe illness until 1915, the year the final 1913 draft was published.

The various drafts of *The Voyage Out* continue to exist vertically within the horizontal narrative of the published text. Read intertextually, they demonstrate the constitution of the text's subjectivity as the result of a textual process—a linguistic subjectivity that refers autobiographically back to Woolf, the writer, without being her equivalent. DeSalvo and other critics implicitly narrate the sequence of revisions as a plot of self-censorship. The overt feminism and social critique of *Melymbrosia* are muted in *The Voyage Out*. As many have noted, Rachel changes significantly in the process of revision, in general from what Elizabeth Heine calls "an intelligent, outspoken, critical young feminist" to "a vague and innocently naive dreamer" (294). "The writing of the novel itself," DeSalvo writes, "was becoming a voyage out—a voyage *away from* the bluntness, the candor, the openness, and even the subtlety—with which Woolf had handled her material in this version" (*First Voyage*, 66). Evidence for self-censorship is compelling, especially in the context of Woolf's later changes in such manuscripts as *The Years* and of similar patterns in the work of other modernist women writers.[18] Revision in women's writing in the modern period often involved a sometimes conscious, sometimes unconscious negotiation between the desire to speak and the need to repress what is forbidden in their narratives of modernity. As a result, final drafts of texts often contained highly disguised forms of desire and social critique to which we have partial access through a vertical reading of all the drafts as a composite text.

However, the vertical narrative that emerges from the text's compositional history is not solely limited to the story of self-censorship. This plot does not fully address how Woolf's repeated return to the scene of writing the novel functioned within her construction, through writing, of a new subjectivity—how, in other words, the story of Rachel's failed *Bildung* relates to Woolf's efforts to make her own development a success. Her numerous revisions engaged Woolf in a "writing cure" in which the transferential scene of writing gradually constitutes a new subjectivity.

Within this context, Woolf's difficulty in completing *The Voyage Out* signals the transferential return of the repressed. The change in Rachel from a sharply critical young woman into a relatively more passive one suggests that in the later version, Woolf was able to confront what she had repressed in the earlier drafts. The Rachel of *The Voyage Out*, whose resistance to the marriage plot speaks increasingly only through somatic symptom, has more in common than the bolder Rachel of *Melymbrosia* with the Woolf who experienced delirium in 1910, ambivalence and anxiety during her courtship and engagement, and intermittent illness in 1911–13. In *The Voyage Out*, Woolf may have been exploring more directly than she could yet do in *Melymbrosia* the roots and dimensions of her illness by examining the psychodynamics of a less critical, more passive Rachel. In the final months before her suicide attempt, Woolf may also have been engaged in an attempt to "kill off" that part of herself whose resistance to patriarchy takes the symptomatic form of madness.

WHY SPATIALIZE NARRATIVE?

What do we learn by conceptualizing the narrative of *The Voyage Out* in spatial terms? In contrast to typological approaches, spatialization emphasizes the psychodynamic, interactive, and situational nature of narrative processes; it also provides a fluid, relational approach that connects text and context, writer and reader. Spatialization is not, of course, the only way to produce such readings. Other interpretative strategies have long gained access to a text's literary and historical resonances without resort to spatial tropes. Other critics, such as Ross Chambers, have developed ways of reading what he calls "not the actual historicity of texts, but the markers, within them, of historical situation" (10). His analysis of a text's contractual appeal and adaptation of Clifford Geertz's "thick description" represent a different route to reach some of the same objectives. James Phelan's distinction between the mimetic and synthetic dimensions of character as the reader experiences it represents yet another. For Phelan, the mimetic aspect suppresses the reader's awareness of the character as authorial construction, whereas the synthetic foregrounds this construction as part of a communication between author and reader (1–27, 115). For him, it is the play between the mimetic and the synthetic that accounts for narrative progression, a theory that assumes, like spatialization of narrative axes, that the text operates on an interplay between two different chronotopes—the mimetic world of the characters, and the synthetic realm of the author and reader.

Spatialization can, however, go beyond these other methods by facilitating some new readings of narrative that might not otherwise exist. The notion of a vertical axis embedded in the horizontal suggests the way in which historical, literary, and psychic intertextualities constitute more than resonances attached to the text associatively, suggestively, or randomly. Instead, they initiate *stories* themselves—dialogic narratives "told" by the reader in collusion with a writer who inscribes them in the text consciously or unconsciously. This, I would argue, is the contribution made by Kristeva's graph of the writer/reader (horizontal axis) and text/context (vertical axis). Moreover, the concept of interactive horizontal and vertical narrative axes allows for a relational reading of the two that produces a "story" not present in either axis by itself. For example, reading the horizontal narrative of *The Voyage Out* in relation to its vertical axis in the form of *Melymbrosia* can produce another narrative that is not fully present in either of the texts read alone.

Let us take for illustration the climactic scene in which Helen learns of Rachel's engagement in *The Voyage Out* and its vertical intertext in *Melymbrosia*.[19] In both texts, the announcement takes place at the end of the second walk in the tropical forest upriver. In both, the wild grasses enfold the bodies with sensuous murmuring and breezy touch. In *The Voyage Out*, Rachel and Terence walk together and verbalize their love for the first time. Helen comes upon them suddenly and so startles Rachel with her touch that Rachel falls into the grass, stares up into the looming faces of Helen and Terence, watches them kiss, and vaguely understands that he is telling Helen about the engagement (283–84). But in *Melymbrosia*, Rachel walks with Helen, not Terence, and their jaunt suddenly turns into a wild chase at the end of which they fall onto the ground rolling in each other's arms. Rachel tells her great secret about Terence, and Helen stuffs grass into Rachel's mouth and makes a surprise declaration of her love for Rachel, who is so like her dead mother Theresa, whereupon Terence arrives (207–9).

The mechanisms of Freud's dreamwork help "narrate" the "story" that emerges from a relational reading of the horizontal narrative (*Voyage Out*) and its vertical intertext (*Melymbrosia*). The two-page scene in *Melymbrosia* is condensed into two paragraphs in *The Voyage Out*, and the diffuse point of view, into Rachel's subjectivity. The eroticism is displaced from a lesbian dyad in *Melymbrosia* (Helen and Rachel) into heterosexual pairs in *The Voyage Out* (first Rachel and Terence, and then Helen and Terence as the parental pair to an oddly infantilized Rachel). Theresa functions in both texts as the absent figure of desire. In *Melymbrosia*, Helen's invocation of Theresa completes the circuit of her love for Rachel, with Terence as the disruptive third party. But in *The Voyage Out*, Theresa disappears, present only through condensation in Terence's name, which suggests that he substitutes for the lost mother (an association contravened by his family name "Hewet," with its proverbial echo of "hack and hew"). Linguistic traces of the *Melymbrosia* scene remain in *The Voyage Out*, giving palimpsestic depth to the surface of the later text. For example, the grasses that Helen stuffs into Rachel's mouth in *Melymbrosia* reappear cryptically in this sentence in *The Voyage Out*: "She fell beneath it, and the grass whipped across her eyes and filled her mouth and ears" (283). The two women's erotically rolling in the grass in *Melymbrosia* reappears in disguised form in *The Voyage Out*: "Helen was upon her. Rolled this way and that, now seeing only forests of green, and nigh the high blue heaven, she was speechless and almost without sense" (283). Finally, the scene in *The Voyage Out* is a secondary revision of the one in *Melymbrosia*, (re)shaping the original site of pre-oedipal, pre-symbolic, and homoerotic desire into one of oedipal, symbolic, and heterosexual desire. This revision represents a progression that itself recapitulates Rachel's own terrifying transition into a heterosexual economy of desire ruled by the Law of the Father.

The climax of both scenes read relationally produces a new "story" not present in either text by itself. In *Melymbrosia*, the sublimated eroticism of Helen's and Rachel's romp in the grass ends tellingly in a confession of love and a discussion about Theresa. Rachel's exclamation that "I love Terence better" unravels the repressed story of desire:

> The inevitable jealousy crossed Helen's mind as she saw Rachel pass almost visibly away into communion with someone else. "I've never told you, but you know I love you, my darling," she said, flushing as she spoke. "Sometimes," the words were spoken with Rachel pressed to her—"You're so like Theresa, and I loved her."
> "Why did she die?" said Rachel. . . .

"The great thing is love" said Helen. They were both pressed by the sense that the others were coming near. (*Melymbrosia*, 208–9)[20]

In *The Voyage Out*, this scene undergoes significant condensation, displacement, and secondary revision. Rachel becomes the only center of consciousness, the confession of love disappears, Helen becomes Theresa, and the lover becomes the father. As Rachel becomes "speechless and almost without sense," the dead mother returns in the form of Helen, who kisses her lover/father:

> At last she lay still, all the grasses shaken round her and before her by her panting. Over her loomed two great heads, the heads of a man and woman, of Terence and Helen.
>
> Both were flushed, both laughing, and the lips were moving; they came together and kissed in the air above her. Broken fragments of speech came down to her on the ground. She heard them speak of love and then of marriage. Raising herself and sitting up, she too realized that Helen's soft body, the strong and hospitable arms, and happiness swelling and breaking in one last wave. . . . For the moment she could not remember who they were. (*Voyage Out*, 283–84)

In this version, Rachel reverts to a pre-oedipal state—hearing the semiotic, senseless babble ("broken fragments of speech") above her, happy in the powerful/strong arms of the maternal body. Yet in the condensation of hallucination, the scene also represents an entrance into the oedipal period, where the talk "of love and then of marriage" and the flush of kissing faces signify the child's experience of triangulated desire. Rachel's lover becomes Helen's lover; Terence becomes the father before the child's very eyes. Within this hallucinatory frame, Rachel's engagement to Terence suggests a kind of double incest: first with the father, and then, vicariously through him, with the mother. For Rachel (as perhaps for Woolf, inducted into heterosexuality by incestuous assaults from her half-brothers), heterosexual love and incest psychically interpenetrate and ultimately terrify.[21] After this scene, Rachel becomes increasingly silent, passive, and withdrawn into the wordless security of her piano, all of which serve as foreshadowing symptoms that culminate in her fever, hallucinations, and death.

These scenes from *Melymbrosia* and *The Voyage Out* can surely be interpreted separately and without reference to horizontal and vertical narratives, but spatializing narrative allows for the possibility of what cannot be read in either text by itself. Reading *Melymbrosia* as part of the vertical narrative of *The Voyage Out* suggests a multiplicity of "stories" that can be "narrated" by the reader who engages with the spatialized text. One such story is the narrative of self-censorship that takes place in the revision process. The text Woolf suppressed openly examines lesbian eroticism, its relationship to an absent mother, and the potential bisexual oscillation of sexual orientation in women's psyches. *The Voyage Out* represses this story and replaces it with the heterosexual plot of the conventional woman's *Bildung*. From this perspective, *Melymbrosia* gives us some access to the forbidden story of female desire, the textual and political unconscious of the horizontal narrative in *The Voyage Out*.

The second story that emerges from a relational reading of the two scenes is the narrative of Woolf's transferential repetition and working through of deeply conflictual issues as she wrote and rewrote her first novel. Within the context of Woolf's constant return to the scene of writing, *The Voyage Out* begins to narrate the story of somatic symptom and illness that is more repressed in *Melymbrosia*. The scene in *The Voyage Out* probes the terror of heterosexuality that Rachel increasingly feels, the terror as well that Woolf herself perhaps felt at the tyranny of the marriage plot that she was both writing and living out at the time she completed her final draft in 1913. The story of Rachel's verbally mute, hysteric resistance to the engagement that supposedly makes her so happy is not fully narrated in *Melymbrosia*, whereas in *The Voyage Out*, it is. The later text, then, reveals the textual and political unconscious of the earlier text.

The opposition between the first and second stories that emerges from spatialized reading suggests yet a third story: the story with which I began of how *The Voyage Out* tells a double tale of defeat and liberation. The horizontal narrative of *The Voyage Out* is the story of failure, the *Bildung* that ends in death. The vertical narrative, reconstructed by the reader, is the story of rebellion, Woolf's successful "voyage out," which, for all the psychic pain it caused, did lead out of the drawing room and into the world of letters as an initial declaration of independence from the dominant literary and historical narratives of the early twentieth century. The confrontation between vertical and horizontal narratives itself constitutes a story that is not told in either axis taken in isolation.

A reading strategy based in the identification of horizontal and vertical narrative axes fosters relational readings, discourages "definitive" and bounded interpretations, and encourages a notion of the text as a polyvocal and dynamic site of repression and return. Such spatialized readings also allow us as readers to construct a "story" of the fluidly interactive relationship between the surface and palimpsestic depths of a given text—taking into account all the historical, literary, and psychic resonances that are embedded within the horizontal narrative and waiting to become narrated in the reading process. Ideally such a story is made up of a sequence of relational readings that at every point in the horizontal narrative examines its vertical component. The richest insights produced by a spatialized reading strategy may well reside in the way it potentially produces interpretations of the textual and political unconscious of a given text or series of texts. But, in general, spatializing narrative gives us a systematic way of approaching the various forms of narrative dialogism and of (re)connecting the text with its writer and world. In Kristeva's words, spatialization suggests an interpretive strategy that regards a text as "a dynamic . . . *intersection of textual surfaces* rather than a *point* (a fixed meaning), as a dialogue among several writings: that of the writer, the addressee . . . , and the contemporary or earlier cultural context" (*Desire*, 65).

NOTES

An earlier version of this essay was presented at the International Conference on Narrative Literature in Nice, France, June 1991. Portions of the theoretical argument appeared in *Narrative* (1993) as "Spatialization: A Strategy for Reading Narrative."

1. For my purposes here, I am not suggesting a masculine/feminine binary for time as space, as do Kristeva in "Women's Time" and de Lauretis in *Alice Doesn't* (143). See also Winnett's critique of Brooks's model.

2. Other examples of dissonant narratives include Charlotte Brontë's *Villette*, George Eliot's *Mill on the Floss*, Kate Chopin's *The Awakening*, Charlotte Perkins Gilman's "The Yellow Wallpaper," Emile Zola's *Germinal*, Zora Neale Hurston's *Their Eyes Were Watching God*, and Nella Larsen's *Passing*.

3. This and subsequent figures are intended as pedagogical aids rather than as pseudoscientific topologies. They represent the kind of visualization of abstract ideas that I and many others commonly use in the classroom. The two-dimensional space of a board or page cannot represent with accuracy the multidimensional intersections that I posit for narrative configurations of space and time.

4. See, for example, Barthes's "Introduction to the Structural Analysis of Narratives"; Genette; Chatman; Phelan; and Brooks's discussion of spatialization in Russian Formalism and French structuralism (16).

5. See their distinctions between the "narrative audience" (which accepts the story as "real") and the "authorial audience" (which covertly remains "aware of the synthetic"—that is, constructed—nature of the narrative) (Phelan, 5). Rabinowitz proposed the original distinction that Phelan develops extensively in relation to his work on the rhetorics of character and progression.

6. See, for example, DuPlessis; Brooks; Gates; Bersani; Chambers; and de Lauretis.

7. This is, of course, a founding principle of psychoanalysis, made as early as Josef Breuer and Freud's jointly written *Studies on Hysteria* (1895). See also Freud's "Repression."

8. See especially *Revolution* (13–106), "From One Identity to an Other" (*Desire*, 124–47), and "Motherhood according to Bellini" (*Desire*, 237–70). For other formulations of the textual unconscious, see Culler; Felman; Riffaterre; and Jameson.

9. See especially Kristeva, *Revolution* (13–106), and "From One Identity to an Other" (*Desire*, 124–47).

10. For a different attempt to move textual criticism beyond the teleological search for the "definitive" text, see Jerome McGann's *A Critique of Modern Textual Criticism*.

11. I have made this argument more fully in "Return of the Repressed in Women's Narrative."

12. Like H.D.'s Madrigal Cycle, the different versions of the Dedalus narratives can be read both ways, with early as well as late texts serving as the textual unconscious for the others in the series. See my "(Self)Censorship and the Making of Joyce's Modernism" in *Joyce: The Return of the Repressed*. The essays in this collection provide examples of reading the vertical narrative axis in its literary, historical, and psychic dimensions.

13. The opposition of the "whiter" Englishmen and the "black widow" anticipates other mysterious gendered confrontations in Woolf's writing, such as in the essay "Mr. Bennett and Mrs. Brown"; the lonely widow also anticipates the enigmatic old woman whom Clarissa identifies with the mysteries of the human soul in *Mrs. Dalloway*. My thanks to Jane Marcus, who suggested to me that "black widow" referred to mourning weeds, and to J. M. Coetzee, whose essay "The Spread of Racist Thinking: Metaphors of Metonymy" suggests that metonymic displacement is endemic to racist thinking. For another discussion of race, class, gender, and empire in *The Voyage Out* in relation to *Heart of Darkness*, see Marianne DeKoven, *Rich and Strange*, 85–138.

14. For discussions of the marriage plot, see, for example, DuPlessis; Nancy Miller; Gilbert and Gubar; Abel, Hirsch, and Langland; Boone; and D. A. Miller.

15. For the importance of reading in *The Voyage Out*, see especially Froula; Schlack, *Continuing Presences*; and Friedman, "Pedagogical Scenes."

16. Woolf constructs this same narrative more directly in "A Sketch of the Past" (64–72).

17. For the compositional history of *The Voyage Out*, see DeSalvo, "Sorting" and Introduction to *Melymbrosia*.

18. See also Schlack, "Novelist's Voyage," and Friedman, "Return of the Repressed."

19. In *Writing beyond the Ending*, DuPlessis briefly calls attention to these scenes (211); see also DeSalvo, *Virginia Woolf's First Voyage* (56–57).

20. This scene anticipates Freud's theory that lesbian desire is based in a never relinquished, pre-oedipal longing for the mother. See "Psychogenesis" (1920) and "Femininity" (1933). See also Marcus's "Virginia Woolf and Her Violin" (*Languages*, 96–114), in which she argues that Woolf's strong attachments to and

sometimes passions for older women played out Woolf's "great romance with her dead mother" (96).

21. For accounts and interpretations of sexual abuse in the Stephen family, see, for example, Woolf, "A Sketch of the Past" and "22 Hyde Park Gate" in *Moments of Being* (68–69, 162–78); Quentin Bell, *Virginia Woolf* (43–44, 78, 95–96); DeSalvo, *Virginia Woolf*. According to Bell, Woolf's half-brother George Duckworth repeatedly molested Virginia, possibly after the death of Julia Stephen (when she was thirteen), but more likely after the death of her father in 1904 and then again after her first social debut (when she was about seventeen) (43–44). Gerald Duckworth, her other half-brother, stood her on a ledge and "explored my private parts," which led, she believed, to her shame about her body and her looking-glass phobia ("Sketch," 68–69). According to DeSalvo, incest and sexual abuse were part of the climate of the Stephen family and affected Virginia's sisters, Stella and Vanessa (1–70).

WORKS CITED

Abel, Elizabeth, Marianne Hirsch, and Elizabeth Langland, eds. *The Voyage In: Fictions of Female Development*. Hanover: University Press of New England, 1983.

Bakhtin, M. M. "Forms of Time and Chronotope in the Novel." *The Dialogic Imagination*. Ed. Michael Holquist. Trans. Caryl Emerson and Michael Holquist. Austin: University of Texas Press, 1981. 84–258.

Barthes, Roland. "Introduction to the Structural Analysis of Narratives." 1966. *Image-Music-Text*. Trans. Stephen Heath. New York: Hill and Wang, 1977. 79–124.

Bell, Quentin. *Virginia Woolf: A Biography*. New York: Harcourt Brace Jovanovich, 1972.

Bersani, Leo. *A Future for Astyanax: Character and Desire in Literature*. New York: Columbia University Press, 1984.

Boone, Joseph Allen. *Tradition Counter-Tradition: Love and the Form of Fiction*. Chicago: University of Chicago Press, 1987.

Breuer, Josef, and Sigmund Freud. *Studies on Hysteria*. 1895. Trans. James Strachey. New York: Basic Books, n.d.

Brooks, Peter. *Reading for the Plot: Design and Intention in Narrative*. New York: Vintage, 1984.

Chambers, Ross. *Story and Situation: Narrative Seduction and the Power of Fiction*. Minneapolis: University of Minnesota Press, 1984.

Chatman, Seymour. *Story and Discourse: Narrative Structure in Fiction and Film*. Ithaca: Cornell University Press, 1978.

Coetzee, J. M. "The Spread of Racist Thinking: Metaphors of Metonymy." Paper delivered at the International Conference on Narrative Literature. Nice, France, 14 June 1991.

Conrad, Joseph. *The Heart of Darkness*. 1899. London: Heinemann, 1921.

Culler, Jonathan. "Textual Self-Consciousness and the Textual Unconsciousness." *Style* 18 (1984): 369–76.

DeKoven, Marianne. *Rich and Strange: Gender, History, Modernism*. Princeton: Princeton University Press, 1991.

De Lauretis, Teresa. *Alice Doesn't: Feminism, Semiotics, Cinema*. Bloomington: Indiana University Press, 1984.

DeSalvo, Louise A. Introduction. *Melymbrosia*. By Virginia Woolf. New York: New York Public Library, 1982. xiii–xliv.

——. "Sorting, Sequencing, and Dating the Drafts of Virginia Woolf's *The Voyage Out*." *Bulletin of Research in the Humanities* 82 (1979): 271–93.

——. *Virginia Woolf: The Impact of Childhood Sexual Abuse on Her Life and Work*. Boston: Beacon, 1989.

——. *Virginia Woolf's First Voyage: A Novel in the Making*. Totowa, NJ: Rowman and Littlefield, 1980.

DuPlessis, Rachel Blau. *Writing beyond the Ending: Narrative Strategies of Twentieth-Century Women Writers*. Bloomington: Indiana University Press, 1985.

Felman, Shoshana. "Turning the Screw of Interpretation." *Yale French Studies* 55/56 (1977): 94–207.

Frank, Joseph. "Spatial Form in Modern Literature." *Sewanee Review* 53 (Spring, Summer, Autumn 1945).

——. *The Widening Gyre*. Bloomington: Indiana University Press, 1968.

Freud, Sigmund. "Femininity." *New Introductory Lectures on Psychoanalysis*. Trans. James Strachey. New York: Norton, 1965. 112–35.

——. "Further Recommendations in the Technique of Psychoanalysis: Recollection, Repetition, and Working Through." 1914. *Therapy and Technique*. Ed. Philip Rieff. New York: Collier, 1963. 157–66.

——. *General Psychological Theory*. Ed. Philip Rieff. New York: Collier, 1983. 207–13.

——. *The Interpretation of Dreams*. 1900. Trans. James Strachey. New York: Avon, 1965.

——. "A Note upon the 'Mystic Writing-Pad.'" 1925. *General Psychological Theory*. 207–12.

——. "The Psychogenesis of a Case of Homosexuality in a Woman." *Sexuality and the Psychology of Love*. Ed. Philip Rieff. New York: Collier, 1963. 133–59.

——. "Repression." 1915. *General Psychological Theory*. 104–15.

Friedman, Susan Stanford. "Return of the Repressed in Women's Narrative." *Journal of Narrative Technique* 19 (1989): 141–56.

——. "(Self)Censorship and the Making of Joyce's Modernism." *Joyce: The Return of the Repressed*. Ed. Susan Stanford Friedman. Ithaca: Cornell University Press, 1993. 21–57.

——. "Spatialization: A Strategy for Reading Narrative." *Narrative* 1 (1993): 12–24.

——. "Virginia Woolf's Pedagogical Scenes of Reading: *The Voyage Out*, *The Common Reader*, and Her Common Readers." *Modern Fiction Studies* 38 (Spring 1992): 101–25.

Froula, Christine. "Out of the Chrysalis: Female Initiation and Female Authority in Virginia Woolf's *The Voyage Out*." *Tulsa Studies in Women's Literature* 5 (1986): 63–90.

Gates, Henry Louis, Jr. *The Signifying Monkey: A Theory of African-American Literary Criticism*. Oxford: Oxford University Press, 1988.

Genette, Gérard. *Narrative Discourse: An Essay on Method*. Trans. Jane Lewin. Ithaca: Cornell University Press, 1980.

Gilbert, Sandra M., and Susan Gubar. *The Madwoman in the Attic: The Woman Writer and the Nineteenth-Century Literary Imagination*. New Haven: Yale University Press, 1979.

Heine, Elizabeth. "The Earlier *Voyage Out*: Virginia Woolf's First Novel." *Bulletin of Research in the Humanities* 82 (1979): 294–316.

Jameson, Fredric. *The Political Unconscious: Narrative as a Socially Symbolic Act*. Ithaca: Cornell University Press, 1985.

Kristeva, Julia. *Desire in Language: A Semiotic Approach to Literature and Art*. Ed. Leon S. Roudiez. Trans. Thomas Gora, Alice Jardine, and Leon S. Roudiez. New York: Columbia University Press, 1980.

——. *Revolution in Poetic Language*. 1974. Trans. Margaret Waller. New York: Columbia University Press, 1984.

Lacan, Jacques. "Signification of the Phallus." *Ecrits: A Selection*. Trans. Alan Sheridan. New York: Norton, 1977. 281–91.

McGann, Jerome J. *A Critique of Modern Textual Criticism*. Chicago: University of Chicago Press, 1983.

Marcus, Jane. *Virginia Woolf and the Languages of Patriarchy*. Bloomington: Indiana University Press, 1987.

Miller, D. A. *Narrative and Its Discontents: Problems of Closure in the Traditional Novel*. Princeton: Princeton University Press, 1981.

Miller, Nancy K. "Emphasis Added: Plots and Plausibilities in Women's Fiction." *Subject to Change: Reading Feminist Writing*. New York: Columbia University Press, 1988. 25–46.

Phelan, James. *Reading People, Reading Plots: Character, Progression, and the Interpretation of Narrative*. Chicago: University of Chicago Press, 1989.

Rabinowitz, Peter. "Truth in Fiction: A Reexamination of Audiences." *Critical Inquiry* 4 (1977): 121–41.

Ricoeur, Paul. "Narrative Time." *On Narrative*. Ed. W. J. T. Mitchell. Chicago: Chicago University Press, 1981. 165–86.

Riffaterre, Michael. "The Intertextual Unconscious." *Critical Inquiry* 13 (1987): 371–85.

Schlack, Beverly Ann. *Continuing Presences: Virginia Woolf's Use of Literary Allusion*. University Park: Pennsylvania State University Press, 1979.

——. "The Novelist's Voyage from Manuscripts to Text: Revisions of Literary Allusions in *The Voyage Out*." *Bulletin of Research in the Humanities* 82 (1979): 317–27.

Winnett, Susan. "Coming Unstrung: Women, Men, Narrative, and Principles of Pleasure." *PMLA* 105 (1990): 505–18.

Woolf, Virginia. *Melymbrosia*. Ed. Louise DeSalvo. New York: New York Public Library, 1982.

——. "Modern Fiction." *The Common Reader: First Series*. 1925. New York: Harcourt Brace and World, 1953. 150–58.

——. "A Sketch of the Past." *Moments of Being*. Ed. Jeanne Schulkind. 2d ed. New York: Harcourt Brace Jovanovich, 1985. 61–160.

——. *The Voyage Out*. 1915. New York: Harcourt Brace Jovanovich, 1948.

the rhetoric of

feminist conversation

Virginia Woolf and the Trope of the Twist

melba | cuddy-keane

N|ot long ago, I heard a young woman scholar refer to her articles as a "series of conversations with other critics"; a male colleague disapproved, thinking that her words implied lack of rigor and seriousness. Back in 1910, when Virginia Woolf was embarking on some "humbler" mechanical work for the cause of Adult Suffrage, she lamented, "How melancholy it is that conversation isn't enough!" (*Letters* 1:421). By conventional standards, Woolf's remark would, I suppose, seem even more frivolous than the female academic's and would be taken once again to demonstrate Woolf's proclivity for apolitical aestheticism. Yet today most feminist critics would identify, in these isolated episodes, a rhetorical tradition in which "conversation" is conscientious political action—thoroughly serious and developing in time its own rigorous poetics. Writing for a collection on feminist narratology, I am obviously going to support the latter view, yet I am also going to propose that the dynamics of conversation are such that the conventional view cannot be entirely excluded. Conversation focuses on the *exchange* of different views: *conversare*—"to turn around frequently"; in Woolf's words, a "turn & turn about method" (*Diary*, 2:247). Thus, as a rhetorical mode, it is particularly well suited to a woman writer who seeks an alternative to the authorial/authoritative dominance of patriarchal discourse. But to eschew authority is to incur vulnerability; by refusing to *impose* its own seriousness, conversation leaves itself open to the popular construction of it as "light" discourse. In a feminist context, of course, light does not imply "lightweight," but the difficulty is that because conversation by nature encodes opposing views, the culturally dominant view can easily be privileged by the naïve or resisting reader/listener. The radical writer who rejects authorial dominance takes the risk that a conventional reading will dominate instead.

To see the effects of such cultural investments of power, we have only to compare the relative stature today of Woolf and Bakhtin as literary theorists. To write conversation, to turn and turn about, is to engage other voices, so that the technique I am discussing is related to what we now call—after Bakhtin—the dialogic, or double-voice discourse. But I have introduced the subject through Woolf's vocabulary because I am interested in "conversation" as a feminist strategy and in its reception by an audience whose assumptions have been formed by a dominant male ideology. The (still) prevailing cultural evaluations distinguish "conversation" from such genres as "lecture," "(formal) essay," or "tract," identifying the first as private, casual, spontaneous, informal, and fluid, and the others as public, serious, informed by tradition, premeditated, and goal-oriented. In 1929, in an essay entitled "Discourse Typology in Prose," Mikhail Bakhtin advanced the idea of double-voice discourse through formalist analysis and within a well-recognized tradition of expository argument.[1] In 1923, Woolf proposed her own version of the dialogic by casting a review of Joseph Conrad in a narrative and dramatic form: two fictionalized readers, in a garden setting, debate the relative merits and limitations of Conrad's works. Entitled "Mr. Conrad: A Conversation," the dialogue maintains a "turn & turn about" nature by presenting a genuine exchange of equally valid views; in addition, neither speaker adopts a unilateral or monologic position. The form was, in Woolf's eyes, a crucial breakthrough; she considered restructuring all the essays for *The Common Reader* as conversations (*Diary*, 2:261), and although she did not *literally* effect this plan, conversation became the informing trope of her critical prose. Yet though synchronically Woolf and Bakhtin were engaged with similar ideas, Woolf is now in the ironic position of being rediscovered in Bakhtinian terms; Bakhtin's essay has been enshrined as a seminal work on the "dialogic," whereas Woolf's conversational mode was ignored in her time and remains relatively unnoticed today.[2] I am not suggesting that Woolf articulated her ideas as fully as did Bakhtin or that the recognition of his work is inappropriate. What interests me is the astonishing disparity between Bakhtin's secure place in the contemporary critical canon and the lack of recognition and, indeed, understanding accorded to Woolf's equally provocative approach. Surely some of this difference has to do with cultural assumptions involving power and genre: that reviews are not serious criticism, that narratives are not serious reviews, that conversation is not a serious rhetorical mode.[3]

But the success of any rhetorical strategy depends on responsive reading, and the conversational mode requires a pliancy and elasticity that readers in Woolf's day did not anticipate—or did not anticipate as an element in critical prose. "Mr. Conrad: A Conversation" was greeted with deafening silence in Woolf's immediate circle. But the response did not deter Woolf from her method. Quite the opposite; she recorded: "To be dashed is always the most bracing treatment for me.... It also has the effect of making me more definite & outspoken in my style" (*Diary*, 2:265).[4] Firmly convinced that conversation was for her the right mode, she decided to be less literal in her approach. To avoid the distracting intrusion of personalities and fictional settings, Woolf located the dialogue directly in the essayist's voice: "Characters are to be merely views." But a less obviously mediated dialogue creates a greater challenge for the reader. No longer situated as a spectator witnessing a debate, the reader undergoes repeated repositionings; it is as if the reader had just got comfortably settled in one easy chair only to be told to shift to another on the opposite side of the window. The strategy has sometimes been interpreted as one of accommodation, of conciliation, since one of the easy chairs is frequently made from the stuff of conventional assumptions, traditional thinking, and patriarchal attitudes. But the reader who is alert to the subsequent shift will not see Woolf's gesture as conciliatory; not only is a new point of view introduced, but the new perspective also exposes the first one from a new angle. Furthermore, repeated shifts foreground the process of shifting; that is, repeated redefinition prompts the reader to consider the significance of interpretative structures in the creation of meaning, in the assigning of value. Woolf's leap forward in her method thus led her to a new perspective on her subject matter; in the same diary entry, she notes that "a new aspect, never all this 2 or 3 years thought of, at once becomes clear.... To curtail, I shall really investigate literature with a view to answering certain questions about ourselves." Shifting position thus becomes the method and the matter of Woolf's style.

A narratological analysis of such prose would thus need to describe the text with reference to a destabilized reader and to chart the plot as, at least in part, a trajectory of different value systems (or positionalities) and changing points of view (or focalizations).[5] In her analysis of the poem "Female Ingenuity," for example, Susan Lanser demonstrates the way "narrative meaning" is "a function of narrative circumstance" (355) and describes a plot that is "generated by the relationship between narrator and narratee" (357). Although Lanser's poetic example works explicitly with multiple readers—there are two intradiegetic readers, addressed by the overt and the coded texts, and a third extradiegetic reader who sees the relation between the other two—her approach applies equally well to the text whose multiple readers are implicitly inscribed through shifting focalizations. And, as we shall see, these shifts can be as structurally crucial in nonfictional as in fictional forms.

In its emphasis on multiple relations between writer and reader, my approach aligns itself with recent developments in speech-act theory that address the complex expressive context of a linguistic act. At the outset, speech-act theory introduced a significant move from the study of autonomous linguistics to the examination of language in its social context. As Mary Louise Pratt has argued, however, most speech-act theorists adopted a simple model of "one-to-one speech" as the norm, posited verbal interaction as an equal exchange between unified subjects, and judged verbal utterances according to assumed common standards of truth and falsehood. In contrast, Pratt urges the need to develop beyond the privatized context of "THE text" and "THE reader." Speech-act approaches should consider various "readerships, kinds of readers, and kinds of readings"; they should examine "how texts are constructed to address mass and multiple readerships or to place a single reading subject in multiple roles at once" (61); and they should analyze how speaking subjects are themselves positioned in a variety of ways. The resulting mode of analysis recognizes differing and multiple motivations and assumptions in both author and reader and situates the speech act within the complicating dynamics of unequal power relations. The relevance of Pratt's observations becomes strikingly clear when we consider the rhetorical strategies in Virginia Woolf's essay "On Not Knowing Greek."

Approximately two months after her renewed commitment to the conversational method, Woolf was in the middle of writing an essay for her first collection of criticism, *The Common Reader* (1925) (*Diary*, 2:276). Although the apparent subject of the essay is Greek *literature*, the title "On Not Knowing Greek" foregrounds the issue of how we read. More specifically, the title alludes to a distinction separating middle- to upper-class male readers from women and middle- to lower-class men: knowing, or not knowing, Greek. For despite the gradual introduction of English Literature into the university curriculum, in the 1920s the educational foundation of the public boys' schools and the Oxbridge universities continued to be a firm grounding in the classical languages.[6] In this respect, education produced different discursive communities according to class and gender—a discrimination of particular concern for feminism. Beginning with its title, Woolf's essay engages this power structure, in which different readers are differently situated.

The essay opens with an image of hierarchical ranking on a scale of knowledge and the writer's disarmingly candid admission that "our ignorance" places us "at the bottom of any class of schoolboys" (*Essays*, 4:38). Whether we read the first-person plural as editorial or consensual, Woolf's relation to her readers bifurcates according to two different reading communities. Readers who are conscious of the inadequacies of their knowledge of Greek—and presumably this group could include the third-class Oxbridge graduate—are disempowered by their consciousness of "superior" readers but brought into community with the writer; the privileged reader who knows Greek is elevated above the text and allowed a measure of complacent superiority. But from this point on, the essay enacts a series of shifts, twists, and reversals that serve first to modify, then to question, and finally to undo the initial ordering.[7]

A close examination of the opening sentence shows how our feet are first firmly planted on a solid platform, only to experience first slight and then growing sensations of tremor: "For it is vain and foolish to talk of knowing Greek, since in our ignorance we should be at the bottom of any class of schoolboys, since we do not know how the words sounded, or where precisely we ought to laugh, or how the actors acted, and between this foreign people and ourselves there is not only a difference of race and tongue but a tremendous breach of tradition" (*Essays*, 4:38). After its humble opening, the sentence embarks on a series of redefinitions that gradually alter and ultimately reverse the initial signification of "knowledge." At the beginning, "knowledge" signifies the acquisition of a foreign language, the knowledge any (privileged) schoolboy might be expected to have; the first subsequent definition—"how the words sounded"—could still be compatible with a schoolboy's training, *if* all that is meant is the pronunciation of words. In the next definition, however, the word "precisely" signals the possibility of ironic intention, for identifying humor is scarcely as "precise" as parsing a sentence. Each subsequent idea takes us increasingly further from "schoolboy" knowledge, until our ignorance of Greek is located in the untransversable chasm of the difference of tradition—what we would now describe as a recognition of "otherness." The sentence thus encapsulates a distinctive feature in Woolf's "turn & turn about" technique: the text adopts a focalization and then disrupts it, and this disruption alters the positioning of different readers in relation to the text. In this example, the privileged reader situated outside the perspective of the implied author in the first part of the sentence is brought inside her perspective at the end: both are equally ignorant in the larger interpretative scheme. Conversely, by the end of the sentence, the uneducated reader is no longer marginalized by her ignorance, since ignorance is shared by all.

The rhetorical signification here is undoubtedly tricky, and for its effect, it requires us to perceive that the slippage in each definition introduces an increasing discontinuity, that the discontinuity effects a reversal, and that the doubleness of view both acknowledges a power structure among different readerships and works to undo it. One might prefer a sentence that unfolds in a more accessible, straightforward way, but the advantage of Woolf's technique is that it destabilizes the reader's relation to the text and so foregrounds the role played by the reader in any interpretation of the text's meaning. And such destabilization is indeed Woolf's subject; in a further enactment of the twist, the essay on "*not* knowing" turns out to be about *knowing*—the whole question of interpretation—and the reversal in its initial sentence is repeated on a larger scale in the structure of the essay as a whole.

On a first reading, most readers are unlikely to be fully aware of the rhetorical shifts in the opening sentence; the more probable reaction is a subliminal uneasiness, a premonition of uncertainty. But the narrative repositionings become increasingly blatant as the essay progresses. The initially subservient role of the "ignorant" narrator is subverted when Woolf begins not only to quote Greek in the original but also to compare the effect of the original with its translations. Yet the "privileged" position of knowing the language is then undercut as the essayist points out that no one in the twentieth century has firsthand knowledge of the society or the climate of ancient Greece or—and now Woolf goes beyond the issue of phonetic pronunciation—really knows how these words sounded when spoken freely and naturally in their original context. But next, our inability to know the Greek world because of cultural and historical difference is overturned by the hypothesis that what we discover in this literature is the stable and permanent—the clear outline of the "type" or original human being who transcends the particularity of context. At this point, we seem to have returned to the stable ground of "knowing," abandoning the uneasy perch of a postmodernist theory of alterity for the comfortable chair of traditional liberal humanist assumptions and the touchstone of universal human nature.

But just as we have shifted position, Woolf again changes course to argue that, rather than revealing a universal absolute, our reading of Greek teaches us to know ourselves. Our passion for pure outlines is but the reflection of the "vagueness" and "confusion" of the twentieth century; what we seek in the literature of the Other articulates our own lack. From this perspective, "not knowing" refers to the subjectivity of all knowledge: "Back and back we are drawn to steep ourselves in what, perhaps, is only an image of the reality, not the reality itself, a summer's day imagined in the heart of a northern winter" (*Essays*, 4:48). But just as this image problematizes any attribution of "truth" to Greek literature, so the word "perhaps" casts uncertainty over any assertion of relativity. The constant turning-about means that any view can be interrogated by its opposite, so that Woolf's reading of Plato stands perhaps as a better description of her own technique: "What matters is not so much the end we reach as our manner of reaching it" (*Essays*, 4:46). For the significance of the essay is not just that such questions are raised; it is equally important that they are raised through a process of settling and unsettling, as we are urged simultaneously to form opinions and never to allow opinion to harden into "truth." Ultimately the effect is to dissolve the conventional either/or oppositional relation between knowing and not knowing and to hold these apparent opposites together in an ironic tension.

"On Not Knowing Greek" thus illustrates how Woolf transforms the explicit dialogue of "Mr. Conrad: A Conversation" into a subtle technique that achieves the rhetorical effect of conversation through a single voice that undergoes constant shifts in focalization. But because this "turn about" technique constantly defers its own authority, and perhaps because Woolf once posited its origins in her "tea-table training" ("Sketch," 150), readers have often assumed that it is merely feminine "charm," employed to be gracious and deferential. "On Not Knowing Greek," however, reveals the close tie between Woolf's rhetoric and her theory of interpretation—a theory that is not conciliatory but assimilative and transformative; that is, it neither compromises with nor accedes to the opposing view but rather engages it within a new perspective and, in so doing, reconstitutes it in new terms. For Woolf addresses conventional scholarly expectations—advancing theories, for example, about the distinctive characteristics of Sophocles, Euripides, and Aeschylus—while she simultaneously disempowers the authoritative stance by situating her interpretation within an ongoing process of provisionality and exploration. She confronts and acknowledges discriminatory differences in education relating to class and gender, but she also engages larger equalizing contexts that unite readers in what they share. In this light, the conversational shift—or what we might call the trope of the twist—becomes a distinctive conflict strategy—one that is indeed assertive, even while it looks for common ground on which to accommodate difference.

In contrast, Woolf consistently objects to monologic prose because it allows for no such negotiation. In *A Room of One's Own*, the authoritative voice of the patriarchal male writer darkens his text with a "shadow shaped something like the letter 'I'" (150), shutting the reader out and preventing any possibility of active creative dialogue between narrator and narratee. The absence of the dialogic leaves the reader vulnerable to domination— the political consequences of which become clear as Woolf goes on to ridicule the idea of a "Fascist poem" as an impossible contradiction in terms (155). Fascism (the subjugation of the crowd to the desire of the leader) is antithetical to poetry (liberator, through its multiplicity and suggestivity, of the minds of responsive readers).[8]

But with her faith in the reader's active engagement, Woolf rejects monologic peroration because she also believes it fails to be rhetorically persuasive. Our ideas, she asserts, tend to develop through resistance and reaction; thus, for example, after her initial disappointment with the reception of her Conrad article, she rebounds with even more vigor to her task. And reviewing a book that aimed to stir children to a revolutionary passion "to redress the wrongs of the world," Woolf points to the limitation of the writers' well-intentioned but simpleminded didactic approach.[9] So natural, she suggests, is the human tendency to resist imposed instruction that "the truth may be that if you want to breed rebels and reformers you must impress upon them from the beginning the virtues of Tories and aristocrats" (*Essays*, 2:196). Preaching locks the reader into either a passive or an oppositional role; the alternative is a discourse that defines a space for exchange and negotiation, a discourse that acknowledges and incorporates the active and reactive nature of our thinking. In another review, Woolf is even more specific about assessing communicative strategies in terms of the possibilities they construct for response, and again she uses an example from childhood to illustrate her point.

Reviewing *Joan and Peter*, a novel by H. G. Wells, Woolf faults the novelist for being so caught up in his attack on the educational system that he forgets the priority of narrative, of fiction, of character. The passionate cause deteriorates to a harangue by a man who is "sore and angry and exaggerated and abusive," with the result that he alienates his reader, who withdraws in boredom. But the most fascinating part of the review is the first paragraph, where, as is often the case, Woolf prefaces her discussion of a specific work with some question of a general theoretical nature. Here the theory concerns what we might call the interpersonal dynamics of conflict talk: "The moralists of the nursery used to denounce a sin which went by the name of 'talking at,' and was rendered the more expressive by the little stress which always fell upon the 'at,' as if to signify the stabbing, jabbing, pinpricking nature of the sin itself. The essence of 'talking at' was that you vented your irritation in an oblique fashion which it was difficult for your victim to meet otherwise than by violence" (*Essays*, 2:294). By way of general theory, Woolf directs our attention to the way speech defines the possibilities for reply. To harangue is to stab or jab and will be answered in kind; the alternative to "talking *at*" is, by implication, talking *to* or "talking *with*"—a preferable mode not because it lends a "nicer" construction to the speaker but because it converts confrontation and violence into dialogic negotiation. The nursery thus becomes a linguistic *ur*-text illustrating the relation between speech and conflict situations.

Perhaps not too surprisingly—given her own links between child and adult speech—Woolf's use of conversation as conflict strategy is strikingly illuminated by recent linguistic studies of children's handling of disputes in play situations. In one way it is, of course, a preposterous leap from Virginia Woolf to middle-class, preschool American children in the late 1980s and early 1990s, even given the likely persistence of nursery admonitions against "talking at." But these examples of child speech offer a clear demonstration of the way conversational turns can be used in negotiation, while the conclusions drawn from the study help to caution us against relegating Woolf's manner to a simple "feminine charm."[10]

In an analysis of conflict episodes in the play of preschool children, Amy Sheldon proposes a theory of "double-voice discourse" that, while drawing on Bakhtin for terminology, sounds remarkably like Woolf's conversational mode. A problem with much existing research in the area, according to Sheldon, is that it adopts a simple model of binary opposition, polarizing boys' goals of self-assertion against girls' objectives of interpersonal harmony. Arguing that these studies assess girls' language against a masculine norm in which assertiveness is equated with brute force aggression, Sheldon posits an alternative model in which the girls' self-assertion coexists with an orientation toward the other. In this style of conflict talk, acknowledging the other's view is not a sign of "weakness" in negotiation but a powerful maneuver "to tone down coercion and domination, to bring about adjustment and accord": "The orientation to others does not mean that the speaker necessarily acts in an altruistic, accommodating, or even self-sacrificing manner. It means, rather, that the speaker pays attention to the companion's point of view, even while pursuing her own agenda" (99). These strategies can be highly effective in achieving one's goals and illustrate "the imaginative and elaborate ways in which girls are self-assertive and powerful."

Any attempt to summarize Sheldon's data misses both the wonderfully shifting logic of the children's talk and Sheldon's own intricate analysis of the twists. In a play scenario of making dinner, for example, two little girls argue because one of them is offering a half pickle instead of a whole one (having kept half for herself), but the one "serving" the pickle asserts that she *is* providing a whole pickle—that is, a whole *half* pickle. (In contrast, the little boys' pickle conflict becomes a forceful and threatening confrontation over ownership.) In another incident, a little girl who doesn't want to pretend to answer a telephone—because, in her fantasy, she is driving a car and therefore couldn't hear the phone ring—is drawn by her companion into a second level of play-narrative that allows her to *pretend* that she can hear the telephone ring in the house, even though in her own play-narrative she is driving a car. What emerges in example after example is that twists, disjunctions, and shifts to a different level of meaning are used so that the speaker accomplishes her own desires against those of an opposing or resisting person, while still "script[ing] a part for both of them to play" (111). Sheldon relates her own observations to the work of other researchers who study interaction in girls' or women's groups and who describe the linguistic strategies with such terms as "reciprocal play," "collaborative narrative," and "cooperative competition" (99–100).

The prevalence of such interactive strategies in female groups raises the question of a specifically female discourse. Sheldon does not, however, essentialize double-voice discourse as a female mode: boys will also use it—though in a more limited way—if they are functioning in groups in which the tasks are relational.[11] The context of the social interaction, rather than the gender of the speaker, determines the strategy. Where gender *does* play a significant role is in the observers' tendency to judge double-voice discourse, when it occurs in *female* speech, as signifying only such mitigating gestures as "compromise, evasion, acquiescence, and clarification of intent" (97). The issue is less how women speak than how we read women's speech.

Perhaps the most fruitful connection to be drawn, then, between the girls' play and Woolf's discourse is the need to avoid gendered assumptions about female speech; more specifically, we need to resist the assumption that conversational turns are simply conciliatory gestures because they differ from the direct confrontational tactics of the masculine norm. Further, Sheldon's analysis of the girls' conflict talk suggests a remarkably close parallel to Woolf's rhetorical tactics. Despite the vast difference in cultural and linguistic sophistication, Woolf's discourse similarly reveals a "dual orientation" in which "self-assertion is enmeshed with addressee-oriented mitigation" and in which use is made of the "pretend frame" and "conversational turns" (Sheldon, 95).[12] But a significant difference is that, addressing a broader and more diverse audience, Woolf has to negotiate not just with conflicting desires or agenda but also with different linguistic assumptions. Establishing a reciprocal or interactive conversation is for her a rather more complicated task.

As Sheldon's examples illustrate, the success of double-voice discourse as conflict talk depends on both sides "playing" according to the same rules. The conversational twist tends not to work when the interlocutor employs the single-voice discourse of competitive, unproblematized aggression. In part, as I suggested earlier, the problem is that a nonauthoritarian mode is vulnerable to the natural tendency of the already-dominant to maintain domination. Double-voice discourse assumes a cooperative and collaborative reader and, like any style, it can have its resisting readers too. In my next example, a published exchange between Woolf and a male editor illustrates the difficulties encountered when the reader refuses to "play."

In 1920, Woolf was involved in a male/female dialogue that developed as follows: Woolf published an article in the *Woman's Leader* challenging an editorial by H. W. Massingham ("Wayfarer") in the *Nation*; Massingham in turn wrote a letter to the *Woman's Leader* criticizing Woolf's article, and Woolf responded once again the following week. What is particularly of interest here is Massingham's complete failure to "read" Woolf's first rhetorical strategies and her switch—almost, but not completely—to his mode of language in her second communicative attempt.

Massingham's original editorial concerns the defeat of a parliamentary bill to end the violently cruel trade in egret feathers. But after decrying the cruelty and documenting the threat to the species, Massingham suddenly turns his attack on women, ending, "But what do women care? Look at Regent Street this morning!" (464). Picking up Massingham's words, Woolf takes him to task for his unconscious gendered assumptions, using at first her "turn & turn about" technique.

The opening sentence of Woolf's article, like the beginning of "On Not Knowing Greek," both adopts a focalization and subjects it to a wobble. In paraphrasable content, the meaning is straightforward, running something like this: "Even though I have since childhood always adhered to the principle of never contributing to the harm of the egret, after reading 'Wayfarer' I am angry enough to go and buy an egret feather and put it in my hat." But this apparently simple opening encodes contradictory implications. Although Woolf situates herself in angry opposition to Massingham, her constructed voice imitates the image of women in Massingham's text: emotional, irrational, self-centered, and defensive of their right to fashion, offended at any imputation of blame. In Woolf's actual sentence, however, linguistic twists signal that this "voice" is simply a role: "If I had the money and the time I should, after reading 'Wayfarer,' in the *Nation* of 10 July, go to Regent Street, buy an egret plume, and stick it—is it in the back or the front of the hat?—and this in spite of a vow taken in childhood and hitherto religiously observed" (*Essays*, 3:241). The phrase "If I had the money and time" separates Woolf from the shoppers on Regent Street; her abrupt question about the feather's placement, plus the crude words "stick it," further transgress Massingham's construct of women by establishing both ignorance of and disdain for fashion, and in a not entirely ladylike way. Thus, although Woolf poses as the traditional "woman," at the same time she subverts and disrupts the markers that inscribe this woman's role. The result is a double positionality: Woolf takes the part of the fashionable, leisured women, while she repudiates any involvement in their acts.

The multiple implications of the sentence are further complicated by the question of multiple readerships. Since Woolf's article was written for the *Woman's Leader* at the request of Ray Strachey, the primary audience—unlike that of the *Nation*—would be female and feminist, followed by male readers concerned about equality between the sexes and issues "of special interest to women."[13] But since the article was also a reply to Massingham, another significant readership is the male—or possibly female—reader who has yet to arrive at any perception of the problematic nature of gender assumptions. And the general readership might include, of course, the women whose purchase of egret feathers initiates the debate.

Woolf's multilevel discourse allows these different readers to enter her text from different positions. Let me try hypothetically to sketch their most likely reactions. The woman of fashion would be brought into complicity with the writer through shared anger but would also feel challenged by

Woolf's religiously taken vow. Readers like Massingham would likely respond with shocked disdain at Woolf's apparent rejection of a worthy cause, but they might also feel a measure of uneasiness at the hints of subversive mockery in her tone. The feminist reader would sympathize with both the anger and the vow but might well be puzzled, if not chagrined, by Woolf's seemingly childish response. But whatever their differences, all *careful* readers would perceive a wobble—a significant premonition that this article will not proceed in a straightforward way. And it is precisely this wobble that enables Woolf to combine self-assertion—her angry gesture—with scripting a *negotiable* role for the other to play. By itself anger would polarize readers into those who share the anger and those who are affronted by it; the wobble makes it harder for readers to become entrenched in fixed positions, for Woolf's prose is itself destabilized by the element of performance in her angry stance.

As in "On Not Knowing Greek," the doubleness encoded in the first sentence of "The Plumage Bill" unfolds in the structure of the essay as a whole. Woolf proceeds to paint a harsh portrait of the unthinking, self-indulgent woman of fashion—the buyer of the feather—presenting her in a way that seems astonishingly to corroborate Massingham's critical view. But then, in another twist, she renders a far more devastating portrait of men—the hunters and merchants who turn killing into a commodity and the male Parliament that fails to pass the Plumage Bill prohibiting the trade. Readers who follow Woolf's twists to this level will see that *without denying Massingham's criticism of the women who purchase the feather*, Woolf has asserted another perspective in which the actions of men are much more reprehensible.

But the next and more significant twist relates to the very ground of our inquiry, since Woolf prompts us to read the subject of Massingham's article not as the violence done to birds but as Massingham's violence to women. Beyond the question of apportioning blame for the torture of egrets lies the question of our discriminatory assumptions about gender: the difference in social attitudes to women's instincts as opposed to men's. And here Woolf's attack is as much on the readers who have read Massingham's words without protest as it is on Massingham for having written them. But how can Woolf get her audience to see that the social code unconsciously condemns women's pleasures—their love of beauty—as sin, whereas men's pleasures—their lusts for hunting, women, and money—are accepted, even valorized? Again the twist becomes a crucial strategy: if she can get her readers to reverse the terms and imagine a similar attack on men's instincts, they will see how discriminatory the social encoding of gender is: the universal standard of justice leads a double life.[14]

Rather than directly attacking Massingham's assumptions, Woolf echoes—imitates—Massingham's final words but enacts a twist by reversing his reference to gender. Massingham had tried to expose women's insensitivity to the birds and especially to the young by evoking the cultural association of women with children, the cultural assignation of nurturing as a *female* quality: "They [the birds] have to be shot in parenthood for child-bearing women to flaunt the symbols of it. . . . But what do women care? Look at Regent Street this morning!" (463–4). Having documented men's participation in violence—the Regent Street shop windows, for example, contain guns and boots as well as flowers and dresses—and having demonstrated that it is men who have failed to prohibit the trade, Woolf writes, "But what do men care? Look wherever you like this morning! Still, one cannot imagine 'Wayfarer' putting it like that. 'They have to be shot for child-begetting men to flaunt the symbols of it. . . . But what do men care? Look at Regent Street this morning!' Such an outburst about a fishing rod would be deemed sentimental in the extreme. Yet I suppose that salmon have their feelings" (*Essays*, 3:243). The ironies both indict men for violence and, at the same time, problematize this indictment. For, on one level, Woolf's statement is *more* valid than Massingham's, but on another level, it is—just like Massingham's—not valid at all. Woolf prompts her readers to reexamine "male" behavior—to question, for example, whether "child-begetting" should make one any less nurturing than "child-bearing"—but then, *scripting a reciprocal as opposed to an adversarial role for Massingham to play*, she implies the ridiculousness, the reductiveness, of a wholesale condemnation of men. The repetition of "But what do men care?" enacts this further twist, shifting from a reasonable question to an unjust categorization. And the second meaning allows Massingham to share Woolf's mockery of her "outburst"—but only at the cost of similarly repudiating his own words. Woolf thus asserts her own views while creating a space for her disputant to join her in a critique of all gender assumptions, no matter which sex's characteristics are at stake.

Woolf's conversational turns therefore have the potential of functioning as effective conflict strategies, chastising her adversaries while turning them into allies. A first difficulty is, of course, that the reader must have the ability to grasp rhetorical complexity. But the greater difficulty, I think, is the challenge of seeing what we are not prepared to look for—of understanding what our conditioning has predisposed us not to see. For it appears that readers who would have had no difficulty with Swift's "A Modest Proposal" nevertheless failed to detect satire from a woman's pen. In the sequel, Massingham (and not only Massingham and not only men, as a similar letter from a female correspondent indicates) is oblivious to Woolf's irony. He sees the wobble but does not get much further in reading it than his own confusion, which he then attributes to Woolf: she has written an "ambiguous article" and "should have made herself clearer" (588). He understands that she is raising the question of the difference between the sexes but mistakenly concludes that her defense of women is *for the purpose* of putting the blame (for the killing of birds) on men. He notices the twist but thinks it works detrimentally to "obscure the issue," failing to see that the twist redefines the very issue itself.

In answering Massingham a second time, Woolf rewrites her first response with little alteration in content but with a radical change in style. Because she now addresses her remarks to readers who failed to follow her twists, she adopts their monolinear style: as she says of Massingham, "His meaning is plain enough." And so Woolf proceeds to "clear up some at least of [her] ambiguities," meaning that she rewrites her previously rich, layered, and ironic sentences as unproblematized statements of univocal intention: "To torture birds is one thing, and to be unjust to women is another, and it was, I hope, plain to some of my readers that I was attacking the second of these crimes and not the first. . . . It seems to me more necessary to resent such an insult to women as Wayfarer casually lets fall than to protect egrets from extinction" (245). But Woolf's response also leaves no doubt that in thus clarifying her meaning she experiences a drop. Her earlier article she had thought was written with "sufficient plainness"; in writing it, her strategy had been to "denounce as forcibly as [she] could." Merely to condemn Massingham's remark is to deal with a symptom; Woolf can address the root of the problem only if she can get him to reexamine the things he take for granted, to *experience* the effects of unconscious discrimination by trying life out the other way around. But there is little possibility for reciprocity in the unproblematized discourse of direct combat. Massingham is now entrenched in an oppositional position: either his words will be "forced down [his] throat" or he must "justif[y them] up to the hilt."

But having descended to the level of didacticism, Woolf once again employs a twist to return to polyvocality. The univocal discourse addressed to Massingham—or the reader he represents—is set in a "narrative" frame addressed to the editor, established by the salutation "Madam" and the opening of the penultimate paragraph, "Had you placed six columns of your paper at my disposal." But the conclusion also returns to ironic, multilayered discourse. Having written the body of the letter in a curt, assertive, and instructional voice, Woolf shifts to pose as the conventional "woman": humble, chastised, apologetic. Other textual elements then ironize this voice, but this time her strategy works to differentiate between, rather than to draw together, her diverse readerships.

In mocking apology, Woolf expresses regret for any damage she might have done to the cause of the egret and offers "to make whatever reparation [she] can." But then Woolf enacts a twist that wickedly constructs Massingham as naïve reader, while it unites with the cooperative, collaborative readers who are willing and able to "play": "Plainly with this example of my own ambiguity as a writer before me, it would never do to write another article solely from the birds' point of view. But I will give myself the pleasure of spending whatever sum I receive for my article, not upon an egret plume, but upon a subscription to the Plumage Bill Group. With prayers to you therefore to make it as handsome as possible" (*Essays*, 3:245). On the overt level, Woolf assumes the voice of a submissive penitent; on the first ironic level—blatant enough even for Massingham to detect—her penitence is undercut by what *appears* to be satiric mockery of his humane concerns. But the twist comes when such obvious irony is subverted by a further ironic level, where the laughter is directed at the naïve moralist who can be tricked into thinking that Woolf is satirizing a concern for birds, whereas she is actually satirizing his (or her) inability to follow the twists and turns. By teasing with her *pretended* mockery of the Plumage Bill, Woolf taunts the baffled simpleminded reader while she flirts with those alert enough to follow her drift. Further, by so thoroughly and outrageously transgressing the code of the "proper lady," she invokes, with *some* readers, a feminist complicity in the shared—and somewhat nasty— joke.

The Plumage Bill exchange thus reveals what can happen when Woolf's negotiations break down. Because the strategies depend on a flexible reader who can both detect and experience the twists, the effect can be merely confusing for an uncomprehending or resisting reader who adheres to the single-voice mode. To see Woolf's rhetoric as conflict strategy is therefore not always to see it as successful; however, by analyzing it in the context of its reception, we can begin to understand both how it works and why it sometimes fails. Then, perhaps even more important, this exchange demonstrates that, while Woolf was certainly capable of expressing her anger or exasperation directly, her *preference* was to employ the conversational turn because of its greater potential for persuasive effect. The difference in her two responses to Massingham suggests that she employs wobbles, shifts, and twists not to tone down anger but to make the best *use* of anger for changing the way the reader thinks. The expression of anger in women's writing has been a controversial issue in feminist criticism; and in a survey of the critical reception of anger in Woolf's texts—a history that begins with a refusal even to recognize its presence—Brenda Silver concludes that more recent opinion is divided as to whether Woolf's "control" of anger is "self-editing" or "self-censorship."[15] It might well be more accurate, however, to use the term "self-positioning," thereby circumventing the either/or binary nature of the debate and suggesting that judicial self-editing can make use of the tendency to self-censorship, in a skillful *performance* of anger.

Once we accept the conversational turn as a significant conflict strategy, we can then go further to distinguish its different uses, depending on the nature of the confrontation. The two essays I have considered here, for example, suggest a subtle but important distinction between the projects of enabling polyphonic thinking in the individual reader and challenging the monologic societal voice. The relative emphasis on these two audiences is reflected again in the different textual strategies of *A Room of One's Own* and *Three Guineas*, in a way that once more demonstrates the significance of the reader to the trope of the twist.

In *A Room of One's Own*, the intradiegetic readers are the women who attended Woolf's original talks. The extradiegetic readers make up an unlimited number of possibilities, but whoever we are, we read *through* the audience of young university women in the late 1920s.[16] Addressed to these intradiegetic readers, the text's primary goal is to prompt them to forget the male censor and critic and to develop "the habit of freedom and the courage to write exactly what [they] think" (171). The resistance to be overcome is the women's internal encoding of the social prescriptions against their freedom; therefore the rhetorical strategies, like those of "On Not Knowing Greek," seek to undo the restrictive habits of mind that inhibit the ability to think of things in new ways, to entertain new positionalities. For the most part, the new ways involve authenticating their experiences as women—something they have learned not to do, or at least not to do in their writing. While there are hints of another less binary mode beyond such gendered thinking, Woolf leaves that for a later stage. Now, if her project is to liberate women to be themselves, then laughter may be more enabling than anger; laughter may be a better strategy for diminishing the specter of the male to its proper size. But the trope of the twist is still crucial for Woolf's enabling project, for Woolf asks her audience to shift out of the role to which they have been consigned.

Discussing, for example, a hypothetical new novel by a woman writer, Woolf remarks: " 'Chloe liked Olivia . . .' Do not start. Do not blush. Let us admit in the privacy of our own society that these things sometimes happen. Sometimes women do like women" (123). If, like Alex Zwerdling, we assume that Woolf is writing for a male audience and repressing her anger, we may agree with him that "the comic technique of this passage makes what might have been disturbing to men more tolerable" (256). But if we read the passage as addressed to women, it has a rather different effect. In this light, Woolf *plays the role* of the playfully charming woman but then twists this role into a mocking imitation of male expectation—in effect, a mocking as well of the repression and silence that have prevented women from writing the truth about their lives. Then, in the multiple ironies encoded in the fully ambiguous "sometimes women do like women," Woolf laughs at both the man who thinks that female friendship must imply lesbianism and the man who assumes that it doesn't. For Woolf begins this section with a fantasy about an eavesdropping male played by Sir Charles Biron, a name that Woolf doesn't have to identify to her immediate audience as that of the presiding judge in the Radclyffe Hall trial. The laughter thus becomes bonding laughter at the expense of the male censor, who is imaged like the naïve Polonius foolishly duped behind the curtain, while Woolf evokes in her audience a sense of the power and variety of female friendship despite its occlusion in written narratives because of male ignorance and fear. The extradiegetic reader can choose to "hear" with Biron or "hear" with the young women; if the reader can do both then she or he will understand both the social encoding and the liberation. Anger is occasionally useful in *A Room of One's Own* as a separation device, but it is largely through laughter that Woolf gets her audience to shift into a different and freer space.

Three Guineas, however, like "The Plumage Bill," is an oppositional text that focuses on *dis*abling the power of patriarchal attitudes in society, specifically those assumptions that make war conceivable. Woolf's contemporaries who failed to see that she *was* answering the question of how to prevent war must simply have repressed one of her most powerful rhetorical strategies—the reiterated reference to the pictures of "dead bodies and ruined houses" that document the ongoing war in Spain. Cited ten times throughout this text, these photographs make, in our visual imagination, the semiotic counterplot to the procession of literal photographs documenting the social inscription of power: the valorization of dominance in the patriarchal hierarchy exacts the inevitable cost in civilian homes and lives. However forceful Woolf's direct expression of anger in this text, perhaps there is nothing so powerful as the horror that accumulates around the wartime photographs as Woolf draws wider and wider circles of the spreading poison and the implicated guilt that lie behind them. And the twist in *Three Guineas* involves getting us to shift positionality in relation to this picture: first, to get us all to see the *same* picture, to see it and only it—not even such comforting sentiments as defending the freedom of England—as the real meaning of "war"; second, to make us reexamine our own position in relation to the competitive, hierarchical dynamics which have produced this picture and which will reproduce it over and over—no matter which "side" is responsible—in the coming battle.

In terms of positionality, this reexamination has much to do with how we situate ourselves as extradiegetic readers in relation to the intradiegetic reader encoded in the text. It is easy to see Woolf's direct attack on the heads of society's institutions; but what of the reader who is Woolf's ostensible correspondent, the figure whom Zwerdling describes as the symbolic representative of "the confused, liberal, established men with feminist sympathies" (259)? Zwerdling reads this intradiegetic reader as a buffer in Woolf's attack on the establishment, a device to avoid "offending the males in her audience so seriously that they will stop reading the book" (259). Perhaps I might say that the text *permits* this approach as one way for a reader to enter its concerns, but I suggest that Woolf's discourse works progressively to redefine this reader and to challenge us to separate ourselves from his naïve—though well-meaning—complicity in the dominant and dominating symbolic order. Woolf's last reference to the war picture connects it with the voice of Creon and so with a long and pervasive history of the inscription of dominance in Western culture. "And Creon," she writes, "brought ruin on his house, and scattered the land with the bodies of the dead. It seems, Sir, as we listen to the voices of the past, as if we were looking at the photograph again, at the picture of the dead bodies and ruined houses that the Spanish Government sends us almost weekly. Things repeat themselves it seems. Pictures and voices are the same today as they were 2,000 years ago" (*Three Guineas*, 161–62). Though anger accumulates around the description of the picture, possibly even greater anger is encoded in that little word "Sir." In the positionality at the beginning of *Three Guineas*, "Sir" could be taken at its currency in Woolf's society—a mark of respect, of courtesy, of a cordial relation between Woolf and her fictional reader to deflect the possibility of offense. But shifts in positionality involve redefinitions of language; by the end of *Three Guineas*, "Sir" has become a term of abuse. The extradiegetic reader is invited to feel its full ironic power and to separate from identification with anyone who would accept such an address—or indeed accept the convention of using it. If we really want to stop war, we must thoroughly distance ourself from its causes—and that means never to admire, never to support, never to validate the term "Sir" and its hierarchical implications again. Certainly direct anger is an important dimension of *Three Guineas*, needed for an oppositional rhetoric that was not part of the project in *A Room of One's Own*. But Woolf's "turn & turn about" discourse is as crucial a strategy in the later work as it was in the earlier. In each work, shifting positionality foregrounds the constructed nature of our values, systems, and histories, but whereas the effect in *A Room of One's Own* is liberating laughter, in *Three Guineas* it betokens implicated guilt and what is *almost* despair.

Inevitably, even in analyzing the polyvocal rhetoric of conversation, I end by appearing to propose a definitive reading. But the nature of Woolf's prose is to negotiate with different readers; what I have done is to record the conversation that I myself have with her text.[17] Also, I might echo her own ending in *A Room of One's Own*: while you have been reading, "you have been contradicting [me] and making whatever additions and deductions seem good to you" (158). Or, finally, as Woolf says elsewhere, "A book, in order to live, must have the power of changing as we change" ("Charlotte Brontë," *Essays*, 3:27). In the poetics of conversation, with its trope of the twist, perhaps the very first principle is that the discussion is always "to be continued."[18]

NOTES

1. I use this essay as representative simply to draw attention to the synchronicity of Woolf and Bakhtin in time. Bakhtin continued to write well into the forties but the English translations of his work appeared much later, and because critics usually cite only the date of the translation, Bakhtin tends to be treated as a contemporary theorist.

2. There is the danger, too, that in reading Woolf through Bakhtin, we might obscure Woolf's difference. Bakhtin situated oppositional discourse within the power structure of the discourse of authority; Woolf's conversational mode, by repeated twists and turns, situates all discourse in a relational model. Bakhtin, furthermore, developed his theory of the dialogic without reference to women writers. For a discussion of the problematic relation of Bakhtin to feminism, see Herndl.

3. The recognition accorded *A Room of One's Own* might seem to belie my point, but it was the feminist rediscovery of this work that won for it its present critical stature. The essays, which have been read primarily in the context of general literary theory, have led an obscure and marginalized existence. One need only review the table of contents in anthologies of literary theory and criticism to evidence this point.

4. Bracing treatments, like cold showers, are hardly soothing experiences, however, and we know that Woolf suffered acutely when her work was attacked. But any setbacks were purely emotional; once back at work, there was no question of taking a more conventional path. If her diary shows that she had to make a conscious effort to shake off the depression, it also indicates that she countered criticism with a greater belief in herself: "Now I think the thing to do is to note the pith of what is said . . . then to use the little kick of energy which opposition supplies to be more vigorously oneself" (*Diary*, 4:101). How well she succeeded is reflected in Leonard Woolf's comment that "the moment always came when she stiffened herself against the critics, against herself, and against the world" (*Downhill*, 57).

5. Throughout this essay, I use "focalization" to refer to the essayist's voice, and "position" or "positionality" to refer to the values and assumptions encoded in each utterance. Since I am discussing works in which shifts in focalization involve shifts in positionality, the two are obviously closely related and sometimes interchangeable.

6. For the significance of the classics in the education of Virginia Woolf's male contemporaries, see Rosenbaum, *Victorian Bloomsbury*, and for the role of the classics versus the vernacular in producing two differently gendered educational communities, see Dusinberre, "Virginia Woolf and Montaigne." The effect of such gender-inflected education is tellingly evidenced in the career of Jane Harrison, who, in her own view, gravitated toward the study of Greek religion because, having been educated at home by governesses, she lacked the philological background necessary for the textual criticism that at the time defined research in the classics at Cambridge. According to Ackerman, this deficiency in her education was also a factor in her continuing dependence, both emotionally and intellectually, on her male mentors. See Ackerman, chapter 5: "Jane Harrison: The Early Work."

7. Most critics—even postmodernist critics such as Pamela Caughie and Rachel Bowlby, both of whom comment insightfully on multiple discourse in Woolf's other works—have read "On Not Knowing Greek" as unproblematized and non-ironic. The standard reading, however, merely indicates how comfortable Woolf makes the traditional chair in this essay. For a reading of the twists and rhetorical shifts in this essay, however, see Edward Bishop and Graham Good, two critics who discuss the essay primarily in terms of its style.

8. Woolf's advocacy of dialogue as opposed to domination explains why, in *A Room of One's Own*, she refuses to exhibit her "fish" (i.e., to expound an explicit theory) and why, having analyzed women's situation in terms of gender difference, she then deconstructs such binary thinking: "Perhaps," she suggests, "to think . . . of one

sex as distinct from the other is an effort" (145), because to maintain any one state of consciousness for a long time means "unconsciously holding something back, and gradually the repression becomes an effort" (146–47). Woolf, it seems, did not need to be guided by Derrida any more than by Bakhtin.

9. The book was by Arthur Ponsonby and Dorothea Ponsonby, *Rebels and Reformers: Biographies for Young People* (George Allen and Unwin, 1917).

10. By proposing that Woolf's style is a mode of conflict talk, my approach is different from—though not incompatible with—the approach to the "tea-table manner" as a strategy for self-definition. In her study of the discourse of the "proper lady," for example, Mary Poovey draws on Gilbert and Gubar's analysis of "feminine 'swerves'"—the use of double-voice discourse as a way of presenting a "surface design" of "conformity" that is then disrupted and subverted by deeper subtextual meanings; Poovey then focuses on the way such "strategies in art" are also "strategies for living" that enable the writer to accommodate her identity—as formed both by, and apart from, the hegemony—through "the articulation of simultaneous, if contradictory, self-images" (44–46). While Poovey's analysis is certainly applicable to Woolf's divided and pluralistic sense of self, my interest here is in Woolf's response to the heterogeneity, the difference, of her readership.

11. Sheldon refers to the "self-in-relation model of feminine development" proposed by Carol Gilligan and Jean Baker Miller to help explain the greater prevalence of double-voice discourse in girls' groups.

12. Some of the techniques used by the children include "word blends," which allow the girls to reach a consensus by combining agenda; confusing and switching of pronouns to avoid inscribing the other's opposition into their speech; and invoking the pretend frame to give a playmate the chance to recast her opposition—all of which can be found in Woolf's writing too.

13. The policy of the journal states that it will "advocate a real equality of liberties, status, and opportunities between men and women. So far as space permits, however, it will offer an impartial platform for topics not directly included in the objects of the women's movement, but of special interest to women" (*Essays*, 3:526).

14. That this rhetorical turn—or the trope of the twist—is a significant feminist strategy becomes more obvious when role reversal informs the narrative plot, as it does in such varied examples as Woolf's *Orlando* (1928), Caryl Churchill's *Cloud 9* (1978), or Sydney Pollack's film *Tootsie* (1982). As Marguerite Waller points out, however, the reversal in *Tootsie* functions merely to generate sympathy for women's position; it does not challenge the "male-centered mode of signification," reveal the male perspective as "ideologically constituted," or expose the "rhetorical operations" of itself as a text (2–3). The effect of the twist in both Woolf and Churchill, on the other hand, is to shift the reader/audience into a rethinking of cultural values, assumptions, and, indeed, encoded epistemology.

15. See Silver, "Textual Criticism." For the controversies in readings of Woolf's anger in *Three Guineas*, see Silver, "The Authority of Anger."

16. The published *A Room of One's Own* is, of course, a reversioning of Woolf's original talks, which appear to be no longer extant. S. P. Rosenbaum speculates that the

more conventionally written essay "Women and Fiction," which Woolf published in the New York review *Forum*, may be "probably as close as we can now come to what Woolf said at Cambridge" (Woolf, *Women and Fiction*, xxi). However, the publication history of another important talk, "How Should One Read a Book?" suggests otherwise. As originally presented at Hayes Court, a private girls' school, the talk directly addresses and engages its audience; when Woolf developed this talk into an essay for the *Yale Review* (1926), she shifted to an impersonal assertive prose. In the last version, written for *The Common Reader: Second Series* (1932), she returned, though in a different way, to the immediate and dialogic rhetoric of conversation. The implications are that Woolf varied her style according to her audience, using a conversational style when she had a stronger sense of the collaborative potential of her audience. However, whether or not she used conversational twists in her Cambridge talks, what is significant is that she encoded a dialogic audience in *A Room of One's Own* from the very first word.

17. Perhaps the best genre for using conversation as critical discourse is the collaborative volume. In Kauffman's 1989 collection *Gender and Theory*, for example, each essay is written to "provoke controversy" and to "liberate dialogue" (4). Furthermore, "each essay is 'dialogic' in another sense; it is followed by a response which demonstrates that another logic has been put into play, one that displaces and unsettles the initial argument, and reveals its unconscious resistances" (5). Virginia and Leonard Woolf anticipated this form in their 1939 pamphlet "Reviewing," which juxtaposed Virginia's attack on reviewers of contemporary fiction with a counterargument written by Leonard. Both arguments emphasized the interactive nature of the presentation, Virginia's beginning, "The purpose of this paper is to arouse discussion," and Leonard's opening with, "This Pamphlet raises questions."

18. In her recent study of Woolf and Samuel Johnson, Beth Rosenberg approaches the dialogic elements in Woolf's writing through an exploration of Woolf's (re)reading of the conversational element in Johnson's prose. Rosenberg is quick to indicate, however, that she is not proffering a definitive study of influence: numerous factors contribute to Woolf's use of conversation, just as a variety of critical and theoretical approaches will illuminate Woolf's dialogic style. My own study can thus be taken to stand in dialogic relation to Rosenberg's, participating in the kind of "greater conversation" among Woolf's critics that Rosenberg herself invokes. I end here, for example, by happily acknowledging the many "conversations" I have already had about this paper, especially with Sally Greene, Linda Hutcheon, Kathy Mezei, Richard Pearce, and Karlheinz Theil.

WORKS CITED

Ackerman, Robert. *The Myth and Ritual School: J. G. Frazer and the Cambridge Ritualists*. New York: Garland, 1991.

Bakhtin, Mikhail. "Discourse Typology in Prose." *Readings in Russian Poetics: Formalist and Structuralist Views*. Ed. Ladislav Matejka and Krystyna Pomorska. Ann Arbor: Michigan Slavic Publications, 1978. 176–96.

Bishop, Edward. "The Essays: The Subversive Process of Metaphor." *Virginia Woolf*. Macmillan Modern Novelists. Basingstoke: Macmillan, 1991. 67–78.

Bowlby, Rachel. "Introduction: A More Than Maternal Tie." *A Woman's Essays: Selected Essays*. Vol. 1. By Virginia Woolf. London: Penguin, 1992. ix–xxxiii.

Caughie, Pamela L. "Virginia Woolf as Critic." *Virginia Woolf and Postmodernism: Literature in Quest and Question of Itself*. Urbana: University of Illinois Press, 1991. 169–93.

Dusinberre, Julie. "Virginia Woolf and Montaigne." *Textual Practice* 5 (1991): 219–41.

Good, Graham. "Virginia Woolf: Angles of Vision." *The Observing Self: Rediscovering the Essay*. London: Routledge, 1988. 112–34.

Herndl, Diane Price. "The Dilemmas of a Feminine Dialogic." *Feminism, Bakhtin, and the Dialogic*. Ed. Dale M. Bauer and Susan Janet McKinstry. SUNY Series in Feminist Criticism and Theory. Ed. Michelle A. Massé. Albany: State University of New York Press, 1991. 17–23.

Kauffman, Linda S., ed. *Gender and Theory: Dialogues on Feminist Criticism*. New York: Blackwell, 1989.

Lanser, Susan S. "Toward a Feminist Narratology." *Style* 20 (1986): 341–63.

Massingham, H. W. [Wayfarer]. "A London Diary." *Nation*, 10 July 1920, 462–64.

——. Letter. *Woman's Leader*, 30 July 1920, 588.

Poovey, Mary. *The Proper Lady and the Woman Writer: Ideology as Style in the Works of Mary Wollstonecraft, Mary Shelley, and Jane Austen*. Chicago: University of Chicago Press, 1984.

Pratt, Mary Louise. "Ideology and Speech-Act Theory." *Poetics Today* 7 (1986): 59–72.

Rosenbaum, S. P. *Victorian Bloomsbury: The Early Literary History of the Bloomsbury Group*. New York: St. Martin's, 1987.

Rosenberg, Beth Carole. *Virginia Woolf and Samuel Johnson: Common Readers*. New York: St. Martin's, 1995.

Sheldon, Amy. "Conflict Talk: Sociolinguistic Challenges to Self-Assertion and How Young Girls Meet Them." *Merrill-Palmer Quarterly* 38 (1992): 95–117.

Silver, Brenda R. "The Authority of Anger: *Three Guineas* as Case Study." *Signs: Journal of Women in Culture and Society* 16 (1991): 340–70.

——. "Textual Criticism as Feminist Practice: Or, Who's Afraid of Virginia Woolf Part II." *Representing Modernist Texts*. Ed. George Bornstein. Ann Arbor: University of Michigan Press, 1991. 193–222.

Woolf, Leonard. *Downhill All the Way: An Autobiography of the Years 1919–1939*. London: Hogarth, 1967.

Woolf, Virginia. *The Diary of Virginia Woolf*. Ed. Anne Olivier Bell. 5 vols. London: Hogarth, 1977–84.

——. *The Essays of Virginia Woolf*. Vols. 1–4 (vols. 5–6 forthcoming). Ed. Andrew McNeillie. San Diego: Harcourt Brace Jovanovich, 1986–94.

——. "How Should One Read a Book?" Holograph, unsigned, dated 18 November [1925]. In "Articles, Essays, Fiction, and Reviews," 1:179–249. Berg Collection, New York Public Library.

———. "How Should One Read a Book?" *Yale Review* 16 (1926): 32–44.

———. "How Should One Read a Book?" *The Common Reader: Second Series*. 1932. London: Hogarth, 1962. 258–70.

———. Letter. *Woman's Leader*, 6 August 1920, 608.

———. *The Letters of Virginia Woolf*. 6 vols. Ed. Nigel Nicolson. London: Chatto and Windus, 1975–80.

———. "On Not Knowing Greek." *The Common Reader [First Series]*. 1925. London: Hogarth, 1959. 39–59.

———. "Reviewing." With a Note by Leonard Woolf. 1939. In *The Captain's Death Bed and Other Essays*. Ed. Leonard Woolf. London: Hogarth, 1950. 118–34.

———. *A Room of One's Own*. London: Hogarth, 1929.

———. "A Sketch of the Past." *Moments of Being*. Ed. Jeanne Schulkind. 2d ed. London: Hogarth, 1985. 61–159.

———. *Three Guineas*. 1938. London: Hogarth, 1986.

———. *Women and Fiction: The Manuscript Versions of "A Room of One's Own."* Ed. S. P. Rosenbaum. Oxford: Blackwell, 1992.

Waller, Marguerite. "Academic Tootsie: The Denial of Difference and the Difference It Makes." *Diacritics* 17 (1987): 2–20.

Zwerdling, Alex. "Anger and Conciliation in *A Room of One's Own* and *Three Guineas*." *Virginia Woolf and the Real World*. Berkeley: University of California Press, 1986. 243–70.

the terror and the ecstasy

The Textual Politics of Virginia Woolf's

Mrs. Dalloway

patricia | matson

While contemplating the writing of a prototypical male novelist, Virginia Woolf, with her usual wit and irony, recognizes the textual dominance of the masculine subject as a phallocentric construct, designed to place/define woman as other/absence:

> It was delightful to read a man's writing again. . . . It indicated such freedom of mind, such liberty of person, such confidence in himself. One had a sense of this well-nourished, well-educated, free mind. . . . But after reading a chapter or two a shadow seemed to lie across the page. It was a straight dark bark, a shadow shaped something like the letter "I." One began dodging this way and that to catch a glimpse of the landscape behind it. Whether that was indeed a tree or a woman walking I was not quite sure. Back one was always hailed to the letter "I." One began to be tired of "I." (Woolf, *Room of One's Own*, 95)

For Woolf, this rigid masculine "I" coincides with the oppression inherent to the patriarchal dyad: woman in patriarchy is relegated to the background of his/story (is that "a tree or a woman walking"?); she occupies the position of passive, objectified other.[1]

As many of Woolf's feminist critics have suggested, deconstructing patriarchal ideology and foregrounding woman's subjectivity are central to the textual politics at play in Woolf's fiction and essays.[2] My focus here will be *Mrs. Dalloway*, which was published four years before *A Room of One's Own* and yet foreshadows and encapsulates many of the ideas expressed in the essay. In Woolf's vision, if women are going to begin to foreground our desires, to write ourselves out of absence/silence, then the construction of the subject—the treatment of "this shadow shaped something like the letter 'I' "—becomes crucial to our enterprise. In *Mrs. Dalloway*, the "freedom of mind" and "liberty of person" brandished in "a man's writing" are shown to be an illusion, a (self) fabrication: Woolf reveals that each of the novel's subjects is subjected to the dictates of the dominant discourses of the patriarchal status quo. The authority of the humanist subject and the authority of patriarchal value systems are challenged at every turn throughout Woolf's novel.[3] Through a thematic analysis of femininity and masculinity as discursive constructs, the text challenges oppressive ideologies of gender, a challenge that is paralleled and furthered by the narrative's exploration of the politics of madness. It is particularly through her creation of shell-shocked Septimus Warren Smith and society lady Clarissa Dalloway that Woolf examines the relationship between codes of oppression and the possibilities of transgression and resistance. Although these two characters never meet, their stories are strangely bound.

Woolf's narrative style and structure also pose a fundamental challenge to the reading I/eye. Whereas conventional realism often supports an "either/or, dichotomized" vision of the world dependent on "a dualism pernicious because it valorizes one side above another, and makes a hierarchy where there were simply twain," Woolf's text is inscribed with a "both/and" vision (DuPlessis, "For the Etruscans," 132). The terms of the opposition—the division, for example, between the foreground/subject and the background/object-other—are not simply reversed: they are collapsed. As Pamela Caughie suggests in *Virginia Woolf and Postmodernism*, Woolf refuses to prescribe the substitution of a new order for the old: the trick "lies not in reconciling, balancing, or choosing between two positions but in enacting, over and over again, certain ways of proceeding; not in arguing for any one position but in testing out the implications of many" (xi–xii).[4] This enactment of process, what Toril Moi calls Woolf's "textual practice" (9), is, in a sense, the subject of *Mrs. Dalloway*, a novel that involves readers in a heterogeneous, exploratory, and spiraling process. The novel's narrative structure is fundamentally political and even, in a way, anarchic, posing as it does a challenge to authority in all its various forms without ever becoming prescriptive; the "point of Woolf's continually experimental form, like the point of postmodern fictional strategies, is to resist the search for a totalizing, consistent reading" (Caughie, 14). Thus does *Mrs. Dalloway* radically undermine and revise that "shadow shaped something like the letter 'I' " and "his" conventional story and explore the possibilities of a subversive narrative.

With the character of Lady Millicent Bruton, Woolf sums up her understanding of the sexual politics of writing: despite her own position of cultural authority, Lady Bruton lacks textual author(ity): "One letter to the *Times* . . . cost her more than to organise an expedition to South Africa (which she had done in the war). After a morning's battle beginning, tearing up, beginning again, she used to feel the futility of her own womanhood as she felt it on no other occasion" (*Mrs. Dalloway*, 165).[5] At such times she turns, with appreciative need, to the honorable Hugh Whitbread, a "being so differently constituted from herself, with such a command of language; able to put things as editors like them put"—a being, that is, who is at home in the male-dominated world of letters. With his immortal silver fountain pen, Hugh Whitbread transforms Lady Bruton's nonsense—her "tangles"—into "sense."[6] He has access to the editor's grammar and sentiments—he's in the (masculine) know. The ironic crunch is never far behind, however, as Lady Bruton, on hearing the draft of a letter that she feels certain is "a masterpiece," wonders if "her own meaning [could] sound like that" (167). With this, Woolf subtly raises a question about writing and meaning, for what is Lady Bruton's meaning, and what is Hugh Whitbread doing when he transforms Lady Bruton's (feminine) tangles into (masculine) sense?

IMPOSSIBLE MEANING: THE SHIFTING OF SIGNS

In contrast to the (phal)logocentrism of the pompous and "honorable" Hugh with his virile pen, there exists, in *Mrs. Dalloway*, another (strategic) version of writing and meaning. Near the beginning of the novel, the appearance of the airplane, with its somewhat futile attempts to write a message in the sky, stands in the novel as a kind of literary clue, directing us toward a new understanding of the interconnected processes of writing, reading, meaning, and resistance: "There it was coming over the trees, letting out white smoke from behind, which curled and twisted, actually writing something! making letters in the sky! . . . But what letters? A C was it? an E, then an L? Only for a moment did they lie still; then they moved and melted and were rubbed out up in the sky, and the aeroplane shot further away and again, in a fresh space of sky, began writing a K, an E, a Y perhaps?" (29)[7] In her description of the soaring airplane, Woolf playfully offers us a "key" of interpretation. The letters—which seem never to be complete before they fade again into clouds of nothingness while another letter is begun—suggest a deconstructionist's vision of language.[8] As Gayatri Chakravorty Spivak explains Jacques Derrida's concept of signification in her preface to his *Of Grammatology*, "Such is the strange 'being' of the sign: half of it always 'not there' and the other half always 'not that' . . . one sign leads to another and so on indefinitely" (xvii). The airplane's skywriting enacts the notion that "our very language is twisted and bent even as it guides us" (xiv). It enacts, that is, the process of what Derrida calls *writing*, a practice dependent on the processes of deferral and displacement (différance) and one that scripts the impossibility of establishing absolute clarity of meaning.[9] *Writing*, in this sense, is antiauthoritarian; *writing* is concerned with process itself: it "describes relations and not appellations" (*Of Grammatology*, 26). In deconstructive defiance of the logocentrism of Western metaphysics, *writing* relies on the recognition that "nothing is ever fully present in signs" and that meaning "is . . . never identical with itself" but "is the result of a process of division or articulation, of signs being themselves only because they are not some other sign. It is also something suspended, held over, still to come" (Eagleton, 129).[10] The process of *writing* is metaphorically evoked not only by the sky-writing airplane but also later in *Mrs. Dalloway* by an image of clouds, as they metamorphose from one shape to another:

> For although the clouds were of mountainous white so that one could fancy hacking hard chips off with a hatchet . . . and had all the appearance of settled habitations assembled for the conference of gods above the world, *there was a perpetual movement among them. Signs were interchanged*, when . . . now a summit dwindled, now a whole block of pyramidal size which had kept its station inalterably advanced into the midst. . . . Fixed though they seemed at their posts . . . nothing could be fresher, freer . . . to change, to go, to dismantle the solemn assemblage was immediately possible; and in spite of the grave fixity, the accumulated robustness and solidity, now they struck light to the earth, now darkness. (210–11; emphasis added)

Although clouds might appear to have a fixed (unified, definable) shape, their constant transformation undermines this appearance as an illusion, a fiction constructed by the (ego's) desire to pinpoint meaning.

Right from its beginning, *Mrs. Dalloway* articulates an awareness of the process enacted by the skywriting airplane and the shifting signs of the clouds. Although Hugh Whitbread suffers from a confident illusion in thinking that he is in control of words and meaning, the text continually proposes that nothing can be pinpointed with any certainty. Woolf's writing celebrates the discovery of "multiplicity instead of consistency, and signifying flux instead of stable meaning" (Silverman, 246). *Mrs. Dalloway* is inscribed with an antiauthoritarian politics, a politics that is enacted through and by the writing itself.

UNDERMINING LOGOCENTRIC DESIRE: WRITING *JOUISSANCE*

As we witness each person who watches the airplane attempt to read its message, Woolf parodies the (reader's) desire to know. The spectator's (reader's) quest is not simply to accept the writing process but also to translate that process into "some ultimate 'word'" (Eagleton, 131): "'Glaxo,' said Mrs. Coates in a strained, awe-stricken voice.... 'Kreemo,' murmured Mrs. Bletchley, like a sleep-walker" (*Mrs. Dalloway*, 29). For some, the airplane represents the logos/word itself—a transcendent sign of "presence, essence, truth, or reality": "Away and away the aeroplane shot, till it was nothing but a bright spark; an aspiration; a concentration; a symbol . . . of man's soul; of his determination, thought Mr. Bentley . . . to get outside his body, beyond his house, by means of thought, Einstein, speculation, mathematics, the Mendelian theory—away the aeroplane shot" (41). Mr. Bentley's vision of the airplane as something other than what it is—as something signifying a transcendent, essential meaning of life and "man's soul"—is undercut even as it unfolds, for while indulging in his "ode to science," he is shown in the (literally) down-to-earth acts of "rolling his strip of turf" and "sweeping round the cedar tree." His vision is then immediately supplanted by another, that of "a seedy-looking nondescript man" standing "on the steps of St. Paul's cathedral." While Mr. Bentley bows to the "word of science," this man looks to the cathedral and the cross as signs of Truth and transcendence: "The cathedral offers company, he thought, invites you to membership of a society; great men belong to it; martyrs have died for it; why not enter in, he thought, put his leather bag stuffed with pamphlets before an altar, a cross, *the symbol of something which has soared beyond seeking and questing and knocking of words together* and has become all disembodied, ghostly—why not enter in?" (41–42; emphasis added). His vision coincides with Derrida's claim that the "age of the sign is essentially theological" (*Of Grammatology*, 14). While the cross is Meaning and Logos, the plane (writing) represents process, *différance*, and the impossibility of arriving at ultimate Truth. And it is this that is victorious in Woolf's text, for before he succumbs to "that plaguy [*sic*] spirit of truth seeking" and enters the cathedral, "out flew the aeroplane. . . . Unguided it seemed; sped of its own free will . . . like something mounting in ecstasy, in pure delight . . . writing" (42). The *jouissance* of (the airplane's) writing rises above and against logocentric desire, tracing (the potential of) its deconstruction: "The 'rationality' . . . which governs a writing thus enlarged and radicalized, no longer issues from a logos. Further, it inaugurates the destruction, not the demolition but the de-sedimentation, the de-construction, of all the significations that have their source in that of the logos. Particularly the signification of *truth*" (Derrida, *Of Grammatology*, 10).[11] The narrative demonstrates that this process of "a writing thus enlarged" has the potential to undermine Power and Authority, those auspices of Truth. The plane's audience, mesmerized by the ecstatic dance of smoke, fails to notice the passing of a car that is rumored to be transporting "the enduring symbol of the state" (23): " 'It's toffee,' murmured Mr. Bowley—(and the car went in at the gates and *nobody looked at it*)" (30; emphasis added). And so Woolf gives us the "key" to her transgressive textual vision: this "enduring symbol," which moments before held centerstage, has been emptied of its significance, supplanted by the inauguration of a new way of being and seeing.

OFF THE BEATEN TRACK: THE WRITING OF WRITING

Like other modernist/postmodernist writers, Woolf's own writing "involves the . . . de-construction" of (phal)logocentrism, that system of meaning/being symbolically depicted in Woolf's text by the clocks on Harley Street, which, "shredding and slicing, dividing and subdividing . . . nibbled at the June day, *counselled submission, upheld authority*, and pointed out in chorus the supreme advantages of a sense of proportion" (*Mrs. Dalloway*, 154; emphasis added). The clocks are reminiscent of a group of uniformed soldiers who earlier march through Mrs. Dalloway's London: like the regular fall of the soldiers' feet, the dogmatic ticking allows no space for "life, with its varieties, its irreticences" (77). The ticking clocks and the marching soldiers can be read not only as ideological metaphors but as metaphors for conventional form; as my reading of the skywriting airplane has indicated, form and ideology, ways of being and seeing in the world, are inextricably connected.[12] It is thus through her "exploitation of the sportive, sensual nature of language" that "Woolf rejects the metaphysical essentialism underlying patriarchal ideology, which hails God, the Father or the phallus as its transcendental signified" (Moi, 9). Inscribed as it is with a "both/and vision," her writing undoes the oppressive either/or schema implicit to phallogocentric textuality and authority.

Not only does Woolf parody and undermine the logocentric drive of the airplane's spectators but we, as readers (/spectators) of her text, are implicated in this process as well. Just as the readers of the airplane's skywriting are drawn into the production of its meaning, so Woolf's "fiction draws forth the reader's active involvement in the production and thereby calls attention to the text's construction" (Caughie, 12). As readers, "we cannot take the narrative itself for granted, for to do so is to accept the text as *about* a unified world or consciousness that exists independently of our means of constructing such unity" (76). Woolf's is a political textual practice because it calls into question the assumptions we make about ourselves and our relationships to others. In *Mrs. Dalloway*, as in much of Woolf's writing, we are permitted no safe haven, granted no assurances, no authority; as readers, we are denied stable ground and are instead caught in the often turbulent and disorienting spin of the spiral. On the one hand, Woolf's fragmented and deconstructive writing keeps the letter "I" from casting its oppressive shadow within her narrative; on the other, it poses a challenge to the reading I/eye. We are forced to work at making sense of the text, and herein lies the key to Woolf's textual politics: Woolf's text, which is "writerly," in the terms of Roland Barthes, "'dis-places' the reader or viewer, alienates him or her from the all too-familiar subject-positions of the existing cultural regime," thus calling on "us to speak rather than to be spoken . . . to participate in the production not only of meaning but of subjectivity and the larger symbolic order" (Silverman, 248–49). In this way, Woolf's writing in and of itself is an act of resistance: that is, the authority of the "patriarchs and pedagogues" is undercut and challenged at the level of syntax.

Woolf's textual practice soars and dances like the airplane, shifts and changes like the clouds, and spirals like the dissolving leaden circles of Big Ben's striking. The novel's syntax and sentence structure work against the possibility of a reading aligned with the authoritative dividing and subdividing of the clocks on Harley Street. The narrative is fraught with digressions, delays, forks in the road, and roundabouts; we, as readers, find ourselves continually displaced. Phrases abound that bear no clear syntagmatic relationship to one another. Often the point of a sentence is confused or uncertain, caught up in the rambling variances of a character's thought:

For Heaven only knows why one loves it so, how one sees it so, making it up, building it round one, tumbling it, creating it every moment afresh; but the veriest frumps, the most dejected of miseries sitting on doorsteps (drink their downfall) do the same; can't be dealt with, she felt positive, by Acts of Parliament for that very reason: they love life. In people's eyes, in the swing, tramp, and trudge; in the bellow and the uproar; the carriages, motor cars, omnibuses, vans, sandwich men shuffling and swinging; brass bands; barrel organs, in the triumph and the jingle and the strange high singing of some aeroplane overhead was what she loved; life; London; this moment of June. (*Mrs. Dalloway*, 5)

The "it" in the first sentence of this passage lacks an antecedent; not until the end do we understand what "it" is. In this way the narrative enacts the process of deferral, whereby meaning is "something suspended, held over, still to come" (Eagleton, 129). Words do not follow an orderly line of syntagmatic displacement; their relationship is connected to the processes of subjective thought that Woolf believed characteristic of "an ordinary mind on an ordinary day": "The mind receives a myriad impressions— trivial, fantastic, evanescent, or engraved with the sharpness of steel. From all sides they come, an incessant shower of innumerable atoms. . . . Life is not a series of gig lamps symmetrically arranged; but a luminous halo, a semi-transparent envelope surrounding us from the beginning of consciousness to the end" ("Modern Fiction," 154). Woolf's much-cited image of the "gig lamps symmetrically arranged" implies a realist literary convention that demands order, clarity, unity; in contrast, her modernism, like Joyce's, is intended to depict a more authentic form of consciousness, one that does not coincide with the unitary, integrated, and authoritarian subject envisioned by patriarchal humanism.[13] Clarissa Dalloway's contemplation of "why one loves it so" enacts Woolf's vision of mind, this "incessant shower of innumerable atoms" as she thinks of this and this and this, tracing the spiral pattern of Big Ben's striking in defiance of classic or readerly conventions, the regularity of a clock's ticking.

The segmentation of the text is signaled by the abundance of commas and semicolons throughout. The proliferation of phrases, one after the other in an often syntactically discordant manner, counteracts the possibility (and desirability) of a linear progression. Just as the jouissance of the airplane's skywriting defies the logocentric drive of those who watch it, so Woolf "exposes the way in which language refuses to be pinned down to an underlying essential meaning" (Moi, 9). Not only do we not know what "it" is in the above-quoted passage, but the process of deferral and displacement continues. Although one can finally establish a semblance of meaning, it is not made easily accessible. Woolf's writing draws us into the production of meaning, forces us to make connections, and refuses to grant us a position of mastery over the text.

A recognition that meaning cannot be pinpointed with any certainty is bolstered by the nebulous nature of Clarissa's love: what *does* it mean to say that what she loves is simply "this moment in June"? We have hardly reached a clear-cut closure. According to Barthes, closure—the resolution of stable meaning—is fundamental to the "readerly" text. Through it, the reading subject's desire for unity is confirmed. In *Mrs. Dalloway*, no scene or passage is unambiguously resolved (nor, in fact, is the novel's end). We are drawn, instead, into the spiraling process of a textual *différance*, which is emphasized by the recurrence of the words "for" and "but." Although these conjunctions commonly initiate an answer, explanation, or solution of some sort, in *Mrs. Dalloway* they suggest the endless process of deferral, tracing the unfolding of connections, without ever drawing that (desired) conclusion, establishing certainty of meaning (of closure). This process is confirmed by the repetition of key words or phrases in any given passage (and throughout the novel as a whole): "Was everybody dining out, then? Doors were being opened here by a footman. . . . Doors were being opened for ladies . . . ladies with bare heads. . . . Everybody was going out. What with these doors being opened . . . it seemed as if the whole of London were embarking in little boats moored to the bank. . . . as if the whole place were floating. . . . And Whitehall was skated over . . . skated over by spiders. . . . And here in Westminster was a retired Judge, presumably. . . . An Anglo-Indian presumably" (249). Stylistically imitating the image of the airplane's skywriting, repetition involves the reader again in the processes of writing, tracing a spiraling out of connections rather than a dogmatic march toward unambiguous meaning.

The mandates of realism, which require "a consistent (noncontradictory)" narrative presentation (Holly, 42)—like "gig lamps symmetrically arranged"—are further undermined with the abrupt, often incongruous changes of verb tenses. While our usual perception of time depends on a logical progression—the demarcation of past, present, and future (epitomized by the "dividing and subdividing" of the clocks on Harley Street)—the disruption of this uniform system inserts a degree of confusion (of non-sense) into the text: "He burst into tears; wept; wept without the least shame, sitting on the sofa. . . . And Clarissa *had leant* forward, taken his hand, drawn him to her, kissed him—actually had felt his face on hers" (69; emphasis added). We move from a narration of action in the past tense to the past perfect, which implies that the narration of Clarissa's consolation happened in a time before, prior to Peter's display of despair. A reading for consistency, linear causality, and clarity is thus confounded. Woolf's *writing* takes precedence over the more traditional concerns with character, plot, and story. An enactment of "traversal"—the segmentation, disruptions, and incoherencies that form her "textual practice"—keep the reader from assuming the authority of "I," a position of (sexual/textual) mastery, a position identified by Woolf throughout her work as coincidental with (patriarchal, political, and spiritual) oppression.

That Woolf has written a novel that does not comply with the dictates of phallogocentric realism—the conventions of Barthes's "readerly" text—is also manifest through her formal deconstruction of the dominant "I" (a blinding of the all-knowing eye). In *Mrs. Dalloway*, no one point of view dominates. Like the dissolving letters etched in the sky by the airplane's smoke, the narrative continuously slips from one subject's point of view to another's. So too are the dissolving circles of Big Ben's striking characteristic of the novel's pattern of focalization. Shaped by the unfolding of connections and interconnections, the narrative mirrors Clarissa Dalloway's experience: "Odd affinities she had with people she had never spoken to, some woman in the street; some man behind a counter—even trees, or barns" (231). The text repeatedly explores the "odd affinities" between characters, keeping the dominant "I" from taking root and casting its shadow across the page.

Although there are the principal focalizers—Clarissa, Peter, Rezia, and Septimus—numerous other viewpoints peep through the spaces between. Multiplicity supplants uni(form)ity as we skip quickly from one gaze, one train of thought, one snatch of observation to another; and so we move from the glove shop, to the hat shop, from Sara Bletchley, to Emily Coates, to little Mr. Bowley. We meet and share fleeting moments of "reality" with any number of characters without ever being granted the conventional satisfaction of knowing who they are or of having their roles within the narrative defined. The narrative's (and Woolf's) celebration of life's varieties and irreticences is confirmed by the absence of a ubiquitous and all-knowing (implicitly phallic) "I." Rachel Blau DuPlessis suggests that the creation of the "communal protagonist" is in itself a writing of a "both/and vision," a way of rejecting either/or. Enacting "the structures of social change in the structures of narrative," the "communal protagonist operates . . . as a critique both of the hierarchies and authoritarian practice of gender and of the narrative practice that selects and honors only major figures" (*Writing*, 163).[14] Hence this aspect of Woolf's writing also involves the textual politics of resistance and subversion.[15] The constant shift of viewpoints often involves a momentary confounding of time and space, further defying the mandates of realist/readerly conventions and reveling instead in the (spiraling) possibilities of multiplicity. The logic of the narrative is disrupted when we do not know who we are with, or where we are:

> Calmly and competently, Elizabeth Dalloway mounted the Westminster omnibus.
>
> Going and coming, beckoning, signalling, so the light and shadow which now made the wall grey, now the bananas bright yellow, now made the Strand grey, now made the omnibuses bright yellow, seemed to Septimus Warren Smith lying on the sofa in the sitting-room. (211)

A shared experience of light and shadow by two different (and seemingly unconnected) characters in two different places enables Woolf not just to shift the narrative from Elizabeth Dalloway to Septimus Smith but also to defy rational limits of time and space. Similarly, distinctions between thought and speech are not always maintained; conventional boundaries are dismissed. Thus Peter Walsh responds in his own mind to a thought of Clarissa's: "'But he never liked any one who—our friends,' said Clarissa; and could have bitten her tongue for thus reminding Peter that he had wanted to marry her. Of course I did, thought Peter" (62). It is as if Peter is responding both to what Clarissa has implied and to the narrative itself, the textual revelation of what Clarissa had almost said. This pattern continues. After a paragraph tracing Peter's thoughts of sitting on the terrace at Bourton in the moonlight, Clarissa suddenly responds: "'Herbert has it now,' she said. 'I never go there now,' she said" (63). Bourton has not been explicitly mentioned, but the "it" of Clarissa's reference becomes the "it" of Peter's thoughts. Her words too involve not only an implicit response to Peter's inner world but an explicit response to what is written in the text, engaging in a dialogue with the narrative itself. This process is repeated a few pages later, when Peter reacts again to what is unspoken by Clarissa but "spoken" in the text: "It was his silly unconventionality, his weakness; his lack of the ghost of a notion what any one else was feeling that annoyed her, had always annoyed her. . . . I know all that, Peter thought" (69). So the rug is pulled from beneath the traditional narrative desire for clarity and consistency, and as readers, we are drawn into the enigmatic twists and turns of Woolf's writing.

A GUIDING VOICE: WRITING A SPACE FOR CRITICISM

Finally, the novel's narrative design permits not only the interchange of the various characters' viewpoints but allows for Woolf's own voice—or the voice of an unknown narrator whom I will identify as Woolf—to insert itself in the gaps in between. The writer (narrator) is able to engage in a dialogue with her own fiction (narrative). At times it is possible to disentangle her voice from the others in the text, but the narrative viewpoint is often ambiguous. Sometimes a character's subjective point of view comes filtered through the voice of our narrator; at other times she remains behind the scene, responsible for the choreography but not participating in the performance. Occasionally, the narrator jumps onto center stage, not only directing the narrative movement but commenting on characters and situations as well. It is the narrator who, with her almost hyperbolic description, implicitly criticizes the public's response to the appearance of "the Proime Minister's kyar": "But now mystery had brushed them with her wing; they had heard the voice of authority; the spirit of religion was abroad with her lips gaping wide" (*Mrs. Dalloway*, 20). The narrator's is an ironic and critical tone, prone to grand, mythic metaphors: Sir William, with his goddess "Proportion, divine proportion," is one example (*Mrs. Dalloway*, 150).[16] Thus the heterogeneity of voice and vision in *Mrs. Dalloway* is not confined only to Woolf's characters—Woolf as narrator/author participates in this process as well. Hence, while she mocks the conventional authority of the omniscient narrator, she is nonetheless able to put this convention to a use of her own and further explore and critique the politics of oppression in her text.

A MAD SENSE OF PROPORTION

Woolf's antiauthoritarian vision unfolds throughout the narrative. Through the characters of Clarissa Dalloway, her husband Richard, and her former love Peter Walsh, for example, Woolf deconstructs the politics of gender and the masculine claim to privilege, ultimately suggesting the possibilities of female resistance and sexual autonomy. With her creation of the bitter, mackintoshed figure of Doris Kilman, Woolf critically investigates the politics of religious discourse and the connection between ideological oppression and personal repression. And with Clarissa's remembrance of Sally Seton, Woolf writes a space for female desire and eroticism against the grain of the patriarchal and heterosexual script. But it is with the characters of Sir William Bradshaw and Septimus Warren Smith that the text most intensely explores the relationships of power, authority, and resistance, and from this exploration emerges a further investigation of the politics of language. It is perhaps in this part of the narrative that Woolf's form and content are most inseparable: the "mad" character of Septimus Smith refers us to the crushing of the human spirit as a consequence of a dogmatic patriarchal authority, and yet Woolf's writing of this man's madness takes us into the heart of the subversive poetics at play in her text.[17]

Through the character of Sir William Bradshaw, Woolf demonstrates that patriarchy relies on discursive constructs to bolster self-serving values in the name of Truth. Sir William's divine sense of proportion is part of the same ideology that dictates the marching footfall of the uniformed soldiers (who are, Woolf reminds us, "boys of sixteen" going to war), an ideology that excites praise for "duty, gratitude, fidelity, love of England" (76) and, in the mind of Sir William, "family affection; honour, courage; and *a brilliant career*" (154, emphasis added). This cold patriarch's proclamations serve him well. Since forms "of subjectivity which challenge the power of the dominant discourses at any particular time are carefully policed" and are often "marginalized as mad or criminal" (Weedon, 91), Sir William knows that if honor and courage fail, "he had to support police and the good of society, which, he remarked very quietly, would take care . . . that these unsocial impulses, bred more than anything by lack of good blood, were held in control" (154). He is always able to rely on the discourse that constitutes and supports his power. Woolf shows us that his notions of "the good of society," "good blood," and what does or does not constitute an acceptable social impulse are discursive fabrications that keep at bay whatever threatens to disrupt the order that serves him so well. The narrator, with her wry observation that life is indeed good for Sir William—with his divine sense of proportion, his "twelve thousand a year," and his "lust . . . to override opposition"—directs us to a judgment of his dangerously selfish motivation (153–54).

Although Septimus's Dr. Holmes is more of a buffoon and is less calculating and cruel than Bradshaw, both men, with their wealth and power, represent the backbone of patriarchal oppression and authority. By questioning the behavior and motives of those who are in a (power) position to define sanity, Woolf is able to question not only the validity of their definitions but also to expose the ideological assumptions on which they are based. What, then, is madness?

WRITING THE POETIC: THE *JOUISSANCE* OF MADNESS

Ironically Septimus, like Bradshaw with his "divine proportion," assumes at times that he too holds the key to truth and meaning, that he too has the answers: "Men must not cut down trees. There is a God. (He noted such revelations on the backs of envelopes.) Change the world. No one kills from hatred. Make it known (he wrote it down)" (35). Frequently, the language of Septimus's madness is but an exaggerated imitation of the dominant and historical discourses of patriarchy, in the form of philosophy, religion, politics, and science. He counts himself, in his delusions of grandeur, among the great minds of (patriarchal) civilization: "Greeks, Romans, Shakespeare, Darwin and now himself" (101–2). Not unlike the overbearing judges of his own character, Septimus too fancies himself the possessor of truths and assumes the role of judge: "He would . . . explain how wicked people were . . . He knew all their thoughts, he said; he knew everything. He knew the meaning of the world, he said" (100). Septimus holds the key, the Word: but he asserts the primacy of sense, of reason, through an articulation of non-sense. It may in fact be that by having him mimic hegemonic and logocentric discourse within the perimeters of his madness, Woolf ridicules the catchphrases of those with power, further challenging the discursive supports of patriarchal sense.

There is, however, more to Septimus's madness than his exaggerated utterances of grandeur and spiritual authority. Nothing and no one in Woolf's text remain fixed; in fact, many of Septimus's thoughts and experiences undermine logocentrism and provide us with a few grains of the textual wisdom at play in *Mrs. Dalloway*. Unlike the other characters who stand watching the airplane skywriting and who attempt (with futility) to establish meaning—to make sense of the fading signs—Septimus responds to the airplane in a writerly rather than a readerly way: he is content to submerge himself in the process; he doesn't seek mastery over meaning. He has the "key," for he takes sublime pleasure in the movement of the writing itself: "It was plain enough, this beauty, this exquisite beauty, and tears filled his eyes as he looked at the smoke words languishing and melting in the sky and bestowing upon him in their inexhaustible charity and laughing goodness one shape after another of unimaginable beauty and signalling their intention to provide him, for nothing, for ever, for looking merely, with beauty, more beauty!" (31). In this state of heightened (un)awareness, language, in the conventional sense, ceases to exist. The letters aren't part of a syntagmatic chain of signification, a system of meaning dependent on absence, but exist for Septimus as presence (beautiful shapes in the sky). He responds to sound in a similar way: "'K . . . R . . .' said the nursemaid, and Septimus heard her say 'Kay Arr' close to his ear, deeply, softly, like a mellow organ" (32). Sound ceases to be privileged—silence (absence) becomes presence: "Sounds made harmonies with pre-meditation; *the spaces between them were as significant as the sounds*" (33, emphasis added).

These passages invoke a sense of what Julia Kristeva has called *le sémio-tique*. For Kristeva, language which involves a radical breakdown of the signifying function is associated with what she terms *the semiotic chora*. Linguistically, it can be "detected . . . in the first echolalias of infants and rhythms and intonations anterior to the first phonemes, morphemes, lexemes, and sentences" (*Desire*, 133). Once the subject enters the (post-oedipal) Symbolic, *le sémiotique* is, for the most part, repressed, and "can be perceived only as pulsational *pressure* on symbolic language," emerging "as contradictions, meaninglessness, disruption, silences and absences in symbolic language" (Moi, 162). According to Kristeva's theory of poetic language, the (textual) effects of *le sémiotique* are potentially subversive, undermining the subject's illusive claim to authority and disrupting the phallocentric discourse.

In *Mrs. Dalloway*, our first entrance into the magical mad world of Septimus Warren Smith involves an invocation of *le sémiotique*. Like Lacan's "hommelette," Septimus is frequently without ego boundaries. His vision is dominated by pre-oedipal sensations—color, light, an unmitigated immediacy of sensation—and he makes no distinction (imposes no difference) between his self and (what is) other: "But they beckoned; leaves were alive; trees were alive. And the leaves being connected by millions of fibres with his own body, there on the seat, fanned it up and down; when the branch stretched he, too, made that statement. The sparrows fluttering, rising, and falling in jagged fountains were part of the pattern; the white and blue, barred with black branches" (32–33).

As Toril Moi suggests in her discussion of Kristeva, the subject who permits unconscious pulsations—the pulsations of *le sémiotique*—to "disrupt the symbolic order . . . is also the subject who runs the greater risk of lapsing into madness" (11). Thus while Septimus's jouissance—his pleasure in the materiality of language—refers to the subversive potential of writing, it also indicates his position as a mad subject in relation to the Symbolic: "To . . . [the] demand for recognition and for the restoration of identity through language . . . [is opposed] in the figure of . . . madness . . . the dislocation of any transitive, communicative language, of 'propriety' as such, of any correspondence or transparency joining 'names' to 'things,' the blind opacity of a lost signifier unmatched by a signified, the pure recurrent difference of a word detached from both its meaning and its context" (Felman, 9). I think that with her creation of Septimus Smith, Woolf is exploring the relationship between madness and poetic language—language which permits and exploits discursive disruptions of *le sémiotique* and which therefore dislocates the (illusory) stability of the transcendent subject/ego in control of her/his meaning.

An image of *le sémiotique* is invoked in *Mrs. Dalloway* in the form of an archaic female figure. The voice of the old woman, who sings her "ancient song" opposite Regent's Park tube station, is dependent not on the rigors of signification and the logocentric drive for meaning but on the unintelligible rhythms of *le sémiotique*: "a frail, quivering sound, a voice bubbling up without direction, vigour, beginning or end, running weakly and shrilly and *with an absence of all human meaning* into 'ee um fah um so/foo swee too eem oo'" (122; emphasis added). Woolf's imaging of this "rusty pump" illuminates her vision of *le sémiotique* as a potentially subversive expression that can resist the workings of an oppressive/oppressed civilization: while this archaic voice sings, "the passing generations—the pavement was crowded with bustling middle-class people—vanished, like leaves, to be trodden under, to be soaked and steeped and made mould of by that eternal spring" (124).[18]

Kristeva opposes *le sémiotique* to *le symbolique*, which is fundamentally homogeneic and as such supports (and is supported by) what Luce Irigaray terms the "Economy of the Same," presided over by the One (the Father/Phallus). It is this order that the poetic transgresses because it defies the rigors of homogeneous meaning: "There is within poetic language . . . a *heterogeneousness* to meaning and signification. . . . This heterogeneousness to signification operates through, despite, and in excess of it and produces in poetic language 'musical' but also nonsense effects that destroy not only accepted beliefs and significations but . . . syntax itself, that guarantee of thetic consciousness (of the signified object and ego)" (*Desire*, 133).[19] There is a heterogeneity in Septimus's vision: like the plane tracing letters in the sky, his discourse refuses to be pinned down to (one) coherent, cohesive meaning; he slips from one point, one perception, to another, failing to establish the connections (logical syntax) made by the subject (who believes her/himself) in control of her/his meaning. In Kristeva's terms, poetic language "posits a thesis, not of a particular being or meaning, but of a signifying apparatus; it posits its own process as an undecidable process between sense and nonsense, between *language* and *rhythm* . . . between the symbolic and semiotic" (*Desire*, 135). Rezia's description of Septimus's revelatory rantings illustrates this process, drawing attention to the "musical" and "nonsense effects" of poetic language: "Some things were very beautiful; others sheer nonsense. And he was always stopping in the middle, changing his mind; wanting to add something; hearing something new;

listening with his hand up" (212–13). Septimus's statement that he can be counted among the great minds—akin to Shakespeare (who, according to Kristeva, is a *poetic* writer)—takes on an added irony: he is not so dissimilar from the poets and processes that Kristeva describes. He too has transgressive visions and is fascinated with words, with language, with writing things down. He too revels in the beauty of process, movement, the materiality of words (recall his response to the plane's skywriting), intuiting the possibility that "the world itself is without meaning."

The character and experience of Septimus Smith are closely connected to the processes at work within the novel as a whole: his visions, language, and experience reverberate throughout the text, finding correspondences in Woolf's writing of subjectivity and the poetic nature of her own anti-authoritarian language/style. Yet the character of Septimus, driven by a subversive creative energy, points toward the danger of poetic language. There may, after all, be a fine line between genius and insanity. On the one side are poets and writers (Woolf herself?), praised by Kristeva as artists who solicit the disruptions of *le sémiotique* as a means of transgressing the mandates of an oppressive textuality, and on the other side are psychotics, those who have plummeted into the chasm "that threaten[s] the unstable subject of poetic language" (*Desire*, 139).[20] As illuminated by the treatment of Septimus's experience in context of the novel as a whole, madness is not an absolute or an essence but exists relationally, in response to—as the result of—an oppressive order. Poetic language, Kristeva argues, "in its most disruptive form (unreadable for meaning, dangerous for the subject), *shows the constraints of a civilization dominated by transcendental rationality*" (*Desire*, 139–40; emphasis added). The subject of madness in *Mrs. Dalloway* involves, I think, an exploration (and an implicit critique) of these constraints—the constraints of a society dominated, that is, by men like Sir William Bradshaw.

A SPACE IN-BETWEEN:
THE CREATION OF CLARISSA DALLOWAY

If the patriarchs and pedagogues represent one extreme and Septimus Smith another, I would suggest that Clarissa Dalloway represents a point between the two, a point concerned with the possibilities of individual resistance to oppression. Clarissa Dalloway is, to an extent, a prisoner of the social discourse that claims her as Richard's wife, an object in her husband's home. For Woolf to choose as her "protagonist" a character who belongs to the social system that she is criticizing is not as incongruous a decision as it might at first appear, given her comment regarding the work of E. M. Forster: "He is always constrained to build the cage—society in all its intricacy and triviality—before he can free the prisoner" (*Death of the Moth*, 165).[21] When at the end of *Mrs. Dalloway* Sally Seton asks, "Are we not all prisoners?" and suggests that in life one can only scratch on the cell wall, she gives voice to Woolf's own concern with the cage and what can be done to resist and defy its oppressive enclosure. One possibility, of course, is to go the route of Septimus Smith. Clarissa reads the writing on his particular wall when she acknowledges that "death was defiance. Death was an attempt to communicate" (280). But although psychotic vision has its lure, it leads ultimately to a dead-end street. Septimus may escape the oily eye of Human Nature, but he will no longer know the beauty of life, "the triumph and the jingle and the strange high singing of some aeroplane overhead" (5). With the character of Clarissa Dalloway and her love of "this moment of June" and with the *writing* of her own text, Woolf sketches the possibility of another path of resistance, one that skirts the line between sense and non-sense, sanity and insanity, and allows life, with its varieties and irreticences, to triumph against "the constraints of a civilization dominated by transcendental rationality" (Kristeva, *Desire*, 139).

Through the occasional revelations of Clarissa Dalloway, Woolf proposes a way of being and seeing in the world, a way that contradicts the patriarchal dogma of Sir William and company without completely succumbing to the *semiotic* chaos of Septimus Smith. Unself-consciously anti-authoritarian, Clarissa recognizes the undesirability of imposing definitions: "She would not say of any one in the world now that they were this or were that" (*Mrs. Dalloway*, 11). While she knows "nothing" according to the values of an androcentric culture, she has an understanding of life that embraces the wonders of multiplicity: "She knew nothing; no language, no history; she scarcely read a book now . . . and yet to her it was absolutely absorbing; all this; the cabs passing; and she would not say of Peter, she would not say of herself, I am this, I am that" (11). Clarissa Dalloway's philosophy defies the exclusive/excluding codes of phallogocentric discourse: "Why creeds and prayers and mackintoshes? when, thought Clarissa, that's the miracle, that's the mystery; that old lady, she meant, whom she could see going from chest of drawers to dressing-table. She could still see her. And the supreme mystery which Kilman might say she had solved, or Peter might say he had solved, but Clarissa didn't believe either of them had the ghost of an idea of solving, was simply this: here was one room; there another. Did religion solve that, or love?" (193). Here was one room;

there another: difference is quietly celebrated without being encoded, entrapped within an oppressive system of binary oppositions, either/or. Clarissa experiences a sense of what it is to step beyond the discourses that support the character of Doris Kilman (creeds and prayers), but her vision also includes moments when binary oppositions are broken down and the tension of contradiction alleviated: "She felt very young; at the same time unspeakably aged. She sliced like a knife through everything; at the same time was outside, looking on" (11). Life, with all "its varieties, its irreticences" is resurrected from beneath "a pavement of monuments and wreaths" (77) and endowed with "supreme mystery"—the mystery and wonder of a heterogeneous vision.

THE TERROR AND THE ECSTASY: A CONCLUSION

The final pages of *Mrs. Dalloway* bring together, with acute and climactic reverberations, all the threads of exploration and resistance that are woven throughout the text.[22] This final tapestry of Woolf's subversive poetics begins when, immediately after hearing about Septimus's suicide, Clarissa drifts into "the little room where the Prime Minister had gone with Lady Bruton. . . . The chairs still kept the impress of the Prime Minister and Lady Bruton, she turned deferentially, he sitting four-square, authoritatively. They had been talking about India" (279). Power, authority, colonialism—the terrible drumbeat of patriarchy beats on, but at this point in the novel we hear it only as an echo. Only an emptied sign of civilization's "greatness" remains. It is into this echoing absence of the drumbeat that Clarissa walks, retreating from the social hubbub of her party to a room of her own: a space where she can turn inward, away from her sense of being a social construct—Richard's wife, a society hostess. And while the leaden circles of Big Ben's strikes dissolve "in the air," Clarissa stands looking out of the window at the night sky, "ashen pale, raced over quickly by tapering, vast clouds," and contemplates with empathy and understanding the fate of a man she never met.

While the interchange of viewpoints and connections between all the subjects—and particularly between Septimus and Clarissa—keep us from becoming entrapped in an oppressive system of meaning and being, these two characters provide a vital intertextual commentary on each other. Septimus represents that part of Clarissa which threatens her own stability as a subject within the (patriarchal) "symbolic order," and her character keeps us from being able to write off Septimus as a psychotic. Because Clarissa remains, after Septimus kills himself, to contemplate the significance of his action, his death can not be dismissed as the final, pathetic display of his madness. She recognizes him as both a potential genius and as a victim, forcing us once again to draw connections between the possibilities of the poetic, madness, and tyranny: "Or there were the poets and thinkers. Suppose he had had that passion, and had gone to Sir William Bradshaw, a great doctor yet to her obscurely evil . . . but capable of some indescribable outrage—forcing your soul, that was it—if this young man had gone to him, and Sir William had impressed him, like that, with his power, might he not then have said (indeed she felt it now), Life is made intolerable; they make life intolerable, men like that?" (281). It is because Clarissa has felt her own soul forced to comply with the dictations of the patriarchal drumbeat that she can empathize with Septimus Smith. Divided though they are by sex, age, class, and experience, the two are united throughout the novel by their struggle to protect the "privacy of the soul" from the thwarting intrusions of "human nature."[23] It is thus that Clarissa interprets Septimus's suicide as a preservation of "a thing there was that mattered" and hopes that he died "holding his treasure" (280–81).

Throughout this passage, while Clarissa's thoughts hop like a bird from one branch to another, she returns again and again to the old woman opposite, reminding us not only of the connections between subjects in the text—those "odd affinities"—but also of the significance of this old woman as a symbol of celebrated (and unthreatening) difference, the "supreme mystery" of here one room and there another. The old woman is preparing for bed, and as Clarissa watches her—this reflection of herself— she seems to have come to an acceptance of her own inevitable decline, an awareness that she too will put out her light "with all this going on." Life— "with its varieties, its irreticences"—will continue, while this old woman goes quietly to bed. Such is the nature of the spiral. Like Septimus, the old woman reminds Clarissa of the inevitability of death, but at the same time, her presence in the room opposite is an affirmation of life—the joy of life that Clarissa has experienced with a vague intensity throughout her day: "in the triumph and the jingle and the strange high singing of some aeroplane overhead was what she loved; life; London; this moment of June" (5).

NOTES

1. That women and men are culturally relegated to different positions in relation to the letter "I" is humorously depicted in *The Years* when Peggy encounters an "egotist" at a party: " 'I, I, I' he went on. It was like a vulture's beak pecking, or a vacuum-cleaner sucking. . . . I, I, I. . . . He noted her lack of sympathy. . . . 'I'm tired,' she apologized. 'I've been up all night,' she explained. 'I'm a doctor'—the fire went

out of his face when she said 'I.' That's done it—now he'll go, she thought. He can't be 'you'—he must be 'I'" (275–76).

2. See, for example, Jane Marcus, *Virginia Woolf and the Languages of Patriarchy*; Makiko Minow-Pinkney, *Virginia Woolf and the Problem of the Subject*; and Rachel Bowlby, *Virginia Woolf: Feminist Destinations*.

3. For discussion of the humanist subject as a patriarchal construct, see in particular the introduction to Toril Moi, *Sexual/Textual Politics*, and Jane Flax, "Mother-Daughter Relationships: Psychodynamics, Politics, and Philosophy."

4. Caughie identifies this emphasis on process as a principal tenet of postmodern discourse; in her view, Woolf's "formal experiments resulted in what many have come to call a postmodern narrative practice, as well as in a feminist textual politics" (7).

5. Lady Bruton, with her "reputation of being more interested in politics than people; of talking like a man; of having had a finger in some notorious intrigue of the eighties," is a phallic woman, to say the least (*Mrs. Dalloway*, 159–60). Yet although she excludes the feminine Clarissa from her luncheon and is generally known to "disapprove" of wives, the image of Lady Bruton, standing with her feet firmly planted within the courtyard of androcentric values, is undercut by the revelation that some aspect of her being emerges from behind these privileged walls and defies their power to completely define her subjectivity as a woman: "Her inquiry, 'How's Clarissa?' . . . signified recognition of some feminine comradeship which went beneath masculine lunch parties and united Lady Bruton and Mrs. Dalloway, who seldom met, and appeared when they did meet indifferent and even hostile, in a singular bond" (160–61).

6. Feminist critics Sandra Gilbert and Susan Gubar argue in their introduction to *The Madwoman in the Attic* that the pen can be read as a metaphorical penis, signifying the male prerogative to (pro)create in a sphere that precludes women's inclusion.

7. Makiko Minow-Pinkney, in *Virginia Woolf and the Problem of the Subject*, refers to this passage as an indication of "the extent to which Woolf is playing with the conventions of novelistic interpretation. . . . For this 'key' to all mythologies is doubtless the transcendental signifier or solution to the hermeneutic riddle of the novel. . . . As narrator, [Woolf] refuses an 'authoritarian' relation to her own novel. . . . Her writing makes the fixed 'I' or K-E-Y recede. It loosens the ligatures of the unifying subject so as to produce a style whose characteristics are simultaneity and fluidity" (59). Although Minow-Pinkney's analysis of subjectivity intersects at points with my own, her thematic preoccupation with the concept of "subject" is psychoanalytic and focuses primarily on the theories of Julia Kristeva; my analysis of subjectivity and Woolf's writing, in contrast, is framed by a poststructuralist concern with the politics of (sexual/textual) resistance to authority.

8. It is interesting to note, Melba Cuddy-Keane pointed out to me, that the dissolving letters *are* advertising something—the airplane and its message are implicated in the rise of a new system of meaning, a new logos: postwar consumerism.

9. More specifically, Derrida discusses *nonphonetic writing*, by which he refers to a break from the traditional connection between the breath/voice of the transcendent ego and the written word, or logos (*Of Grammatology*, 18–26).

10. The characteristics that Derrida calls *difference* and *deferral—différance*.

11. "In Kristeva's vocabulary, *'jouissance'* is total joy or ecstasy (without any mystical connotation)" (Roudiez, 16).

12. Phyllis Rose claims that "authority, the rigid imposition of form upon matter, whether that matter be subject peoples or the fictive stuff of life, is associated for Woolf with masculinity, and the critical arguments she makes in 1919 and 1924 on behalf of the innovation in fiction prefigure her feminist arguments of 1929 and 1938" (in "Modern Fiction," "Mr. Bennett and Mrs. Brown," *A Room of One's Own*, and *Three Guineas*, respectively) (100–101).

13. For a succinct explication of the principles of traditional humanism and realist form and how these principles have inculcated the negative reception of Woolf by certain Anglo-American critics, see Toril Moi's introduction to *Sexual/Textual Politics*. In alignment with Moi's discussion, my use of the term "realism" refers to a textual practice that demands clarity and distinction, life envisioned as "a series of gig lamps symmetrically arranged," which is based on the traditional humanist belief in the "whole person" and the quest for a "unified integrated self-identity" (Moi, 7). According to Marcia Holly's elaboration of a feminist aesthetic in "Consciousness and Authenticity," realism "first of all demands a *consistent (noncontradictory)* perception of those issues (emotions, motivations, conflicts) to which the work has been limited" (42; emphasis added). I am arguing that this mandate is rooted in a phallogocentric ideology and that Woolf's depiction of the marching soldiers, the clocks on Harley Street, and Sir William Bradshaw's divine sense of proportion involves an investigation of this ideology and its oppressive, life-denying consequences for both women and men.

14. Woolf's use of the communal protagonist is most fully realized in *The Waves, The Years*, and *Between the Acts* but is evident too in *Jacob's Room, To the Lighthouse*, and *Mrs. Dalloway*.

15. It is Woolf's "use of mobile, pluralistic viewpoints," her failure to comply with a "unitary vision," that exasperates critics like Elaine Showalter who, Toril Moi suggests, operate from the perspective that "good feminist fiction would present truthful images of strong women with which the reader may identify" (7–8).

16. Woolf's critical commentary has, in fact, solicited some criticism: her satirical mythic vision of Sir William's goddess, "Proportion, divine proportion," is labeled by Elaine Showalter as the unfortunate intrusion of Woolf's own voice; she claims that "personal experience explains the inartistic lack of proportion most critics have noticed as a "flaw" in this fiercely vibrant section of the novel" (277). I think it is unfortunate that Showalter couldn't resist using the phrase "lack of proportion"—its ironic relevance to the passage she is describing aligns Virginia Woolf with Sir William's "mad" victims and thus implicitly sides with Bradshaw's version of reality, the system of values that Woolf seeks to undermine and resist. Furthermore, as I have suggested, the voice and style of *Mrs. Dalloway* is heterogeneous. What Showalter considers an "inartistic lack of proportion" is but another example of the multiple and layered nature of Woolf's writing. At this point in the text, Woolf uses the discourse privileged by Bradshaw himself to critique his position; we might consider this a narrative strategy rather than a "flaw."

17. The fact that Woolf chose to make Clarissa Dalloway's "mad" double a mad*man* is another way in which she "succeeds in collapsing . . . polarities in *Mrs. Dalloway*" and "undermine[s] the myth that women . . . are associated with madness" (Beshara, 1).

18. Jane Marcus, in *Virginia Woolf and the Languages of Patriarchy*, refers to this ancient voice as one of several instances in Woolf's fiction which suggest that "other oppressed voices of race and class, of difference and colonial subjectivity, are beginning to syllable themselves" (11). Marcus claims that the presence of such old workingwomen refers us to Woolf's concern with all kinds of oppression: "Woolf does not privilege gender over class and recognizes that once the woman writer's voice finds its tongue and speaks and writes its own language, other oppressed voices will find their tongues and write the languages of class and race" (13).

19. In "Revolution in Poetic Language," Kristeva associates the thetic with the ability of the subject to "separate from and through his [*sic*] image, from and through his objects" (Kristeva, *Reader*, 98). Thetic consciousness, then, substantiates the illusion of the self as transcendent ego, the subject in control of meaning, and corresponds, again, to the ego-bound "I" described by Woolf in *A Room of One's Own*.

20. Rose, in her interpretive biography of Woolf, traces the connections between her art and madness, claiming that while "there was a close connection between her madness and the sources of her creativity . . . her creativity was her principal stay against madness" (258).

21. "I want to criticise the social system, and to show it at work, at its most intense" (*Writer's Diary*, 63); it is, in fact, Clarissa's society-lady persona that has drawn a great deal of ambivalence and criticism, including from Woolf herself when she writes in 1925 that the character seemed to be "in some way tinselly" (*Diary*, 3:32). The original Clarissa Dalloway, whom we meet in the short story "Mrs. Dalloway in Bond Street," is "tinselly" in the extreme, but Woolf "fleshes out" the character of this charming society hostess in *Mrs. Dalloway* through the invention not only of her memories but also of a lively and rebellious personal vision.

22. These last pages also resound with the dissolving patterns of Woolf's style: the sentences do not unfold in a neat syntagmatic order, leading to (an) ultimate (dis)closure, but phrases fade into one another without any logical connection. Repetition, abrupt shifts in focus, unspecified pronoun usage—all the characteristics of Woolf's *writing* reach a peak of expression while Clarissa contemplates the death of Septimus Warren Smith.

23. Rachel Blau DuPlessis, in her analysis of *Mrs. Dalloway* as an antiromance, makes the acute observation that Woolf's "structural coup" is "the creation of an unsexual, nonromantic central couple. . . . Neither of the men to whom [Clarissa] is bound in a social, legal, or romantic sense is the man to whom she is bound in the psychic sense" (*Writing*, 57). The fact that Woolf chose to cast Clarissa's double as a man, rather than a woman, may then be read as a wish to undermine the traditional heterosexual narrative. I would add that the creation of Septimus's character facilitates Woolf's exploration of the effects of war on the human spirit and that the bond between Septimus and Clarissa enables her to trace a connection between military authority and the oppression of women, as elaborated in *Three Guineas*.

Barthes, Roland. *S/Z*. Trans. Richard Miller. New York: Hill and Wang, 1974.

Beshara, Gloria. "Collapsing Polarities between Reason and Madness, Masculine and Feminine, and Inside and Outside, in Woolf's *Mrs. Dalloway*." Unpublished paper. Simon Fraser University, 1992.

Bowlby, Rachel. *Virginia Woolf: Feminist Destinations*. Oxford: Basil Blackwell, 1988.

Caughie, Pamela L. *Virginia Woolf and Postmodernism: Literature in Quest and Question of Itself*. Urbana: University of Illinois Press, 1991.

Derrida, Jacques. *Of Grammatology*. Trans. Gayatri Chakravorty Spivak. Baltimore: Johns Hopkins University Press, 1976.

DuPlessis, Rachel Blau. *Writing beyond the Ending: Narrative Strategies of Twentieth-Century Women Writers*. Bloomington: Indiana University Press, 1985.

DuPlessis, Rachel Blau, and members of Workshop 9. "For the Etruscans: Sexual Difference and Artistic Production—the Debate over a Female Aesthetic." *The Future of Difference*. Ed. Hester Eisenstein and Alice Jardine. New Brunswick: Rutgers University Press, 1987. 128–56.

Eagleton, Terry. *Literary Theory: An Introduction*. Oxford: Basil Blackwell, 1983.

Felman, Shoshana. "Women and Madness: The Critical Phallacy." Rev. of *Women and Madness*, by Phyllis Chestler; *Speculum de l'autre femme*, by Luce Irigaray; and *Adieu*, by Balzac. *Diacritics* 5 (Winter 1975): 2–10.

Flax, Jane. "Mother-Daughter Relationships: Psychodynamics, Politics, and Philosophy." *The Future of Difference*. Ed. Hester Eisenstein and Alice Jardine. New Brunswick: Rutgers University Press, 1987. 20–40.

Gilbert, Sandra M., and Susan Gubar. *The Madwoman in the Attic: The Woman Writer and the Nineteenth-Century Literary Imagination*. New Haven: Yale University Press, 1984.

Holly, Marcia. "Consciousness and Authenticity: Towards a Feminist Aesthetic." *Feminist Literary Criticism: Explorations in Theory*. Ed. Josephine Donovan. Lexington: University Press of Kentucky, 1975. 38–47.

Irigaray, Luce. *This Sex Which Is Not One*. Trans. Catherine Porter, with Carolyn Burke. Ithaca: Cornell University Press, 1985.

Kristeva, Julia. *Desire in Language. A Semiotic Approach to Literature and Art*. Ed. Leon S. Roudiez. Trans. Thomas Gora, Alice Jardine, and Leon S. Roudiez. New York: Columbia University Press, 1980.

———. *The Kristeva Reader*. Ed. Toril Moi. New York: Columbia University Press, 1986.

Marcus, Jane. *Virginia Woolf and the Languages of Patriarchy*. Bloomington: Indiana University Press, 1987.

Minow-Pinkney, Makiko. *Virginia Woolf and the Problem of the Subject*. Sussex: Harvester, 1987.

Moi, Toril. *Sexual/Textual Politics: Feminist Literary Theory*. London: Methuen, 1985.

Rose, Phyllis. *Woman of Letters: A Life of Virginia Woolf*. London: Pandora, 1978.

Roudiez, Leon S. Introduction. *Desire in Language: A Semiotic Approach to Literature and Art*. By Julia Kristeva. Ed. Leon S. Roudiez. Trans. Thomas Gora, Alice Jardine, and Leon S. Roudiez. New York: Columbia University Press, 1980. 1–20.

Showalter, Elaine. *A Literature of Their Own: British Women Novelists from Brontë to Lessing*. Princeton: Princeton University Press, 1977.

Silverman, Kaja. *The Subject of Semiotics*. New York: Oxford University Press, 1983.

Spivak, Gayatri Chakravorty. Translator's Preface. *Of Grammatology*. By Jacques Derrida. Baltimore: Johns Hopkins University Press, 1976. ix–lxxxvii.

Weedon, Chris. *Feminist Practice and Poststructuralist Theory*. Oxford: Basil Blackwell, 1987.

Woolf, Virginia. *Between the Acts*. Harmondsworth: Penguin, 1953.

——. *The Death of the Moth and Other Essays*. New York: Harcourt Brace Jovanovich, 1942.

——. *The Diary of Virginia Woolf*. Vol. 3, *1925–1930*. Ed. Anne Oliver Bell. Harmondsworth: Penguin, 1982.

——. Introduction. *Mrs. Dalloway*. New York: Modern Library Edition, 1928. v–ix.

——. *Jacob's Room*. Harmondsworth: Penguin, 1965.

——. "Modern Fiction." *The Common Reader*. New York: Harcourt Brace Jovanovich, 1953. 150–58.

——. "Mr. Bennett and Mrs. Brown." *Collected Essays*. Vol. 1. London: Chatto and Windus, 1966. 319–37.

——. *Mrs. Dalloway*. New York: Harcourt Brace Jovanovich, 1985 [1925].

——. *A Room of One's Own*. London: Triad Grafton, 1977.

——. *Three Guineas*. Harmondsworth: Penguin, 1977.

——. *To the Lighthouse*. New York: Harcourt Brace Jovanovich, 1927.

——. *The Waves*. Harmondsworth: Penguin, 1951.

——. "Women and Fiction." *Women and Writing*. Ed. Michele Barrett. New York: Harcourt Brace Jovanovich, 1979. 43–52.

——. *A Writer's Diary*. Ed. Leonard Woolf. New York: New American Library, 1968.

——. *The Years*. London: Panther, 1977.

seismic orgasm

Sexual Intercourse and Narrative Meaning

in Mina Loy

rachel blau duplessis

> *The only point at which the interests of the sexes merge—*
> *is the sexual embrace.*
> —*Mina Loy, "Feminist Manifesto" (1914)*[1]

In a little-noted observation from 1948, Dorothy Richardson—that doughty (but, alas, also doughy) critic and writer of fiction—remarks how close the interest of most novels is to the "frothy excitement" of sexuality, how the plot of the novel—its pace, tempo, shape—involves arousal and climax, linearity and disclosure (Richardson, 192). In contrast was the model for fiction she postulated, proposed, and proselytized from 1915 on: an erasure of any elements of story based on "the sex motif as hitherto seen and depicted by men"; attention to a multipointed multiplicity of narrative middle (comparable with Stein's theory and practice); and critique of telos, sequence, causality, gender polarization, and gender asymmetry (Gregory, 12). Richardson associated narrative-as-expected with gender-as-mandated (DuPlessis, *Writing*, 143–55). Richardson's vehemence about the ideological link of narrative and sexual conventions indicates how intensely these questions were under debate in early modernist work, in which the construction of a new womanhood and sometimes a new manhood seemed plausible and productive.

Currently, narrative poetics has returned to this issue—the link of narrative sequence, sexuality, gender, and pleasure. These materials have shaped certain modern narrative theory, though without Richardson's name attached. Nor that of Woolf, who tried to shift the weight of conventional gender plots in a major feminist theoretical and narrative practice. There has emerged, thanks first to Freud and then to Peter Brooks and Roland

Barthes, a suggestive discussion, with universal claims, of narrative design and sexual trajectories (Brooks, 112). The current resurgence of such models suggests that they are themselves historically related to the pressures on gender and sexuality created by feminisms. Brooks plays between the stasis/quiescence of beginnings and stimulation of endgame to name narrative middles as "imposed delay, as arabesque in the dilatory space of the text" (107–8). Brooks argues that reader pleasure in the trajectory of the text is structured by a model of cathartic sex, with the pressures and pleasures of delay building toward (one) "final discharge," with some worry over "premature discharge" (108, 109). Depending on the distance from and suspicion with which one regards this, it may or may not model itself totally on male orgasm. Although its language ("discharge") assuredly does, its general sentiment about energy and release may be unimpeachably inclusive. But, damningly, it has no curiosity about the authority of the sexual trajectories of others or about the capacities of other models (political power, spiritual crisis) to structure narratives. The (female, and so forth) reader must (if she will) bend Brooks; Brooks is disinterested. As often as one begins looking to a transhistorical and transindividual "Masterplot," one is well within the speaker-as-universal.

Barthes's related summary of oedipal plot—astonishingly, given in parentheses—"(to denude, to know, to learn the origin and the end)" ironizes its pleasures considerably (10). Teresa de Lauretis, in an extensive and synthetic narrative middle, elaborates how all structuralist and modernist theory is implicitly oedipal, enacting the minority of the question of the Sphinx, seeing female as site or obstacle, not as agent (103–57). In an elegant feminist framing of Brooks, Susan Winnett sketches alternatives to the "scenario of male pleasure," not only the orgasmic model of plot but male models of reception and reading as well and other stories beyond the sexual, all in the interests of "relativizing the Masterplot" while accepting its economy of arousal and release: "The other stories have already been written; we simply have to learn how to read them" (511, 508, 515).

And to read them contextually. What happens if one tries to insist on the social and historical construction and function of a sexualized narrative? Here I am exploring the shaping critique of Jay Clayton. Many of the critics mentioned above desire to historicize desire, "to move beyond formalism," but Clayton is succinct on the issue: the models they use are not historical, though as psychoanalytic models they are "indeed social" (39, 46). "What would it mean to think of desire as historical?" asks Clayton in a sweeping question that then evokes a bibliographic array of (historical) resources—Annales school history of consciousness, social histories of sexuality, marriage, the family, women, and feminist critique, with which one might begin to "historicize." Resisting formalist, universalizing models is a fraught process that necessitates microscale studies.

To reiterate, the formalist issues such "Masterplot" readings raise (or arouse) are incomplete without attention to the ideological and historical motivations that accompanied these issues coming into narrative poetics in the first place—in Richardson, in Woolf, in Lawrence, and in other writers for whom negotiating issues of gender, sexuality, and representation was a task with fervent practical and political meanings.[2] Among these writers is Mina Loy (1882–1966), a (British) poet, novelist, polemicist, and visual artist.[3] Issues in narrative poetics must be implicated in and completed by an understanding of "sociological poetics," in the sense given by Medvedev and Bakhtin, the postulate that literature (whether novel or poetry) is a "historical phenomenon" and that criticism is a "social evaluation" (120, 119). "Not only the meaning of the utterance but also the very fact of its performance is of historical and social significance, as, in general, is the fact of its realization in the here and now, in given circumstances, at a certain historical moment, under the conditions of the given social situation" (120). "What is involved here, consequently, is the juxtaposition of one ideological formation (literature) to other ideological formations (ethical, cognitive, religious, etc.)" (146). Susan Lanser seems to be indicating the same general concerns by asking that the definitions of the structuralist mode be made "more flexible, dynamic, adequate to the diversity of the historical material" (613). Jonathan Arac is, as are Medvedev and Bakhtin, willing to open poetry as well as fiction to this approach, to study the relation of poetic genre, rhetoric, and text to "socio-cultural codes," therefore calling for "interdiscursivity," some tentative beginning on "the historical study of the orders of language" (350).

I take this charge—to complete narrative poetics with a "sociological poetics"—as serious, difficult, and challenging. In this essay I will continue such an approach, looking at works in which sexual intercourse is not just a metaphoric rhythmic background of Masterplot but was depicted or represented repeatedly, and offer a historical and textual discussion of how and why. I am continuing to use sexual intercourse as the ground, not so much as a generalized trope, but as a contested subject of representation. Further, to indicate the mediation of text and historical moment, I link literary language to social debate in the context of narrative choices. This is but one possible tactic in the interests of resisting an exclusively formalist narratology.

Dracula (1897) sets a context for the questions of sexuality and the new woman as they come into narrative structure. The killing of entombed, but wanton, vampire Lucy occurs at midbook. The thrashing, writhing, foaming monster, so described as her fiancé hammers the Thor-like stake to penetrate her heart, is Stoker's grotesque description of a female in orgasm (or raped or "deflowered"), voyeuristically viewed by the male band of vampire hunters (258–60). *Dracula* is a distinctive contribution to the discussion of female sexual appetite and the new woman, issues that will become a large part of modernism, for one purpose of its narrative lies in separating the productive, striving, intelligent part of the new woman from the libidinous possibilities of female independence or autonomy as represented by the sucking/phallic touch of Dracula and his recruitment of Lucy, who has been overloaded with polyandry, prostitution, promiscuity. As the narrative further unrolls, after Lucy's intense death, the character Mina is represented by the author as split in two. Her striving participation in the hunt for the vampire as intelligent journalist is compromised by her incipient motherhood, for participation in professional activities damages the child-to-come. The scene in which Mina is forced to drink blood from Dracula's breast/chest as a child might force "a kitten's nose into a saucer of milk to compel it to drink" is fellatio, rape, and nursing in a lurid amalgam; it then becomes Mina's task to separate the sexual from the maternal, the active from the passive, the rebellious from the conformist (336). Stoker creates a long (and sometimes tedious) endgame to this plot in which whenever Mina withdraws from the quest to kill Dracula, the quest goes badly, and whenever she participates, it goes better, a vacillation between female power and powerlessness resolved only when she discovers she can give instructions to the hunters in a trance—so presenting useful information untainted by female intelligence and conscious will. *Dracula* puts us on notice about the narrative and cultural pressure point created by the possibility of autonomous female sexual desire (in Lucy) and autonomous female activity (analysis and correlation of texts, even literary production, in Mina) and the relation of both to motherhood. And the book makes overt the implicit link between displaced depictions of sexual intercourse and narrative climaxes.

Two works, mainly, will be discussed here; they draw directly on the discourses of new woman/free love, repeatedly narrate acts of sexual intercourse, and end with some consideration of babies. These representations focus intensely on sexual activity; we can read sexual intercourse as a site wherein various agents and cultural processes are exposed: redefinitions of morality, questions about the independence of women, the loss of verbal and physical taboo, the relation of female sexuality and maternity. They are works written about ten years apart, separated by World War I: Mina Loy's thirty-four section "Love Songs to Joannes" (1915–17) is a poem at a cultural pressure point of female subjectivity and sexual relations (Loy, LLB, 91–107).[4] Mina Loy produced a work whose depiction of sexuality is a provocation to conventional codes of the lyric, deliberately alters some of the trajectories of novelistic narrative, and alludes in its own way to social debates. "Love," as Loy tersely reports, is "the preeminent littérateur," making and contributing to ideological narratives of all sorts (107). Because of its depiction of sexual intercourse and because it is indebted to "new woman" discourse of early modernism, Loy's work is comparable with certain of Lawrence's novels. So the familiar *Lady Chatterley's Lover* (1928) will (briefly) counterpoint it.

The quasi-narrative conventions of long poems—telling a set of intersecting or mutually suggestive narratives, having a persona or point of view going on an intellectual-ethical-political-spiritual quest through a social terrain, making thematically and narratively suggestive vignettes without the back and fill of one specific or clear plot, mixing lyric mode and narrative statement—these are familiar in such works as Pound's *Hugh Selwyn Mauberley* (1920), Eliot's *The Waste Land* (1922), and, with far more essay and no plot but the reading of a cultural situation, in Williams's *Spring and All* (1923) as well. To show by implication, to narrate, "lyrically" honoring gap and fragment, to make poetry by an imagist condensation of the novel—this work was pioneered in Loy's "Love Songs."[5]

"Love Songs" is not a narrative poem in the normal discursive sense of that word, but it does "make a progression of realisations," and hence sequence is vital to it (Kouidis, 62, citing Loy). Loy traces the course of a love affair, involving open sexual desire, and her active, somewhat shamed pursuit of an apparently flagging partner, the complex of satisfactions and dissatisfactions centering on a split between sexual urge and suspicious analysis, an apparent break from her lover about which she is both cynical and wounded, and finally a passionate consideration of sexuality and reproduction. The early part of the poem shows the "Loy" figure enthralled and pursuing her lover, traveling to him, even stalking him through city streets at night, at once exhilarated by her passion and debased by it. In one of these sections, the female figure is a marionette of passion who "know[s] the Wire-Puller intimately" (Loy, LLB, 94). For if (as Nancy Cott summarizes) free love advocates "assumed that free women could meet men as equals on the terrain of sexual desire just as on the terrain of political representation or professional expertise," they found instead sexual exploitation, inequality, thralldom, and the ambiguities of serial monogamy in relation to jealousy (45). The poem negotiates the separate pulls toward sexual pleasure and emotional danger.

"In defiance of superstition I assert that *there is nothing impure in sex—* except the mental attitude toward it" (Loy, LLB, 271). Loy's forthright critique of a "mental attitude" deemed "superstition," not to speak of her forthright willingness to discuss sex (sexuality, gender, sexual intercourse are all mingled in the term) are clear statements of a New Woman position. This sexual radical position appears in the "Feminist Manifesto," a declarative prose work from the same era as the poem.[6] In her "Feminist Manifesto" Loy is unsubordinate, sexually blunt, eager to transcend and eradicate (by the power of individual agency and will) any prior world history of female servility—what Dora Marsden would call Bondwomen in opposition to the modern Freewoman behavior and what earlier feminists Charlotte Perkins Gilman and Olive Schreiner called Parasitism and Prostitution.[7] And yet Loy fiercely rejects the reforms of contemporary feminism. In Loy's manifesto view, the feminist movement is *"Inadequate"* because it depends on political reforms calling for "equality," among them, female suffrage, equal education, and professional opportunity. The issue is not reform of institutions but reform of consciousness. "Leave off looking to men to find out what you are *not*. Seek within yourselves to find out what you *are*" (LLB, 269).[8]

Loy's manifesto is situated at a crisis of historical change, indeed, at an apocalypse of apoplectic change. Yet her absolute rejection of prior female strategies and her repeated tropes of destruction protest too much; feminine consciousness is a specter haunting the poem. Loy calls, in the manifesto, for free love brought about by "intelligent curiosity and courage" in acknowledging sexual desire; the critique of "the impurity of sex"; the "surgical *destruction of virginity*" at puberty so that it could not be a bargaining chip; "the right to maternity" for all women, married or not; and the principled resistance to marriage, called "comfortable protection" (LLB, 270–71). And while the manifesto declares, "Women must destroy in themselves the desire to be loved," it continues in a pensive fragment: "The feeling that it is a personal insult when a man transfers his attentions from her to another woman."[9] Along with "the desire to be loved," presumably this insulted feeling must be extirpated too, given Loy's defiant desentimentalism, as if feelings associated with the ideology of femininity were downright toxic, part of the "rubbish heap of tradition" (LLB, 269). Thus, she argues, "Honor, grief, sentimentality, pride, and consequently jealousy must be detached from sex" (LLB, 271). As in most manifestos, there is a ferocious prevalence of "must."

This liberatory feminism is in dialogue both with general ideology and with a specific kind of Victorian and modern reforming feminism called the Social Purity movement, which combines claims for the moral superiority of women with a denial of female sexuality. Social Purity was hegemonic in the suffrage movement (1908–14), but not unchallenged. Libertarians and utopian socialists, as well as feminist sex radicals, rejected the "purity" argument; these would find chosen sexual unions a moral and ethical kind of sexual behavior and would urge the end of sexual repressions.[10] Most dramatic was the claim that women had a right to and capacity for (hetero)sexual pleasure, that women's sexual drive was equal to men's, and that no need existed for the double standard.[11] In contrast, social purity feminists made urgent allegories of gender division in sexual matters: men were lustful, women were spiritual; men needed their sexual (and the synonyms were bestial, animal) instincts curbed by women as asexual guardians of an evolutionary superiority, glossed as a minimal need for the "sexual embrace" (Mort, 148).[12]

Feminists were found among both sex radicals and social purity reformers. As DuBois and Gordon summarize, feminists have acted within two conflicting traditions about sex, one committed to analyzing its dangers, its victimizing potential—frequent pregnancy, venereal disease, exploitation, and seeking protection by enforcing those controls over men that women (in the double standard) had internalized, by insisting on chivalric honor in men and consensual sex, and by campaigning against vice (prostitution), which often was a campaign for the "containment of female sexuality within heterosexual marriage" no matter how oppressive (15). The other tradition included feminist sexual radicals who were committed to pleasure, encouraged female autonomy and sexual expression, but did not see, or thought they had transcended, power relations and the "male construction of the sexual experience available to most women" (7).

The narratives of thralldom and recovery, obsession, rupture, and painful isolation visible in "Love Songs" do conform to certain stories of the dangers of sexuality. "The desire to be loved" (one of the aspects of female servility) and the capture of the woman "in the weak eddy / of your [the man's] drivelling humanity" is confessed repeatedly in the early part of the poem and even seems to recur at the end (98). This goes far to argue that the old feminine consciousness, with its concepts such as "love," accompanied by "honor, grief, sentimentality, pride, and consequently jealousy" (271), spoils the brave new world of liberated heterosexuality; at the very least the poem stands in a contradictory relation to the manifesto. Ellen Trimberger's studies of sex radicals confirm the realities of jealousy and pain in open heterosexual relationships of contemporaneous free love advocates ("Feminism" and "New Woman").

Loy's poem is also filled with sex-radical evocations of pleasures both sexual and intellectual and the equal meeting of the partners on a sexual terrain. The poet enters into her consideration of the "wild oats / Sown in mucous-membrane" with the clear admonition, "These are suspect places" (91).[13] "Sowing wild oats" comes from a proverbial expression; "mucous-membrane" is a medical term. The mixture of dictions in this logopoeic style has its origins, as I have argued elsewhere, in the feminist critique of a foundational cluster of materials about romance in poems ("Corpses of Poesy"). The main character assumes various postures for this investigation, among them a "wise virgin" pose, holding an investigatory lantern aloft so it will not be blown out by "the bellows / Of experience." For this lantern show (like a slide show, the sections of the poem offer individual moments of a quasi-narrative montage), the poet takes her own cool, analytic "eye" as the source of light, but that analytic "lantern" is involved with inflammatory orgasmic imagery: "An eye in a Bengal light / Eternity in a skyrocket" (91).[14] Negotiating sexual and analytic passions, the poem often presents impacted and intellectualized languages of wit graphically describing sexual moments and apparatuses. The gaze of power (narrator's eye as illuminating lens) rests on the man, even—in the first view we have of him—on his genitalia as a metaphor for him: "The skin-sack / In which a wanton duality / Packed / All the completions / of my infructuous impulses / Something the shape of a man" (91–92). Despite this lucid female gaze, her completions are inside his testicles: the sperm to make her fruitful. But the "wanton duality" is not simply an abstract portrait of his genitalia, but of her double impulse toward licentious, rebellious sex and desire for male fertilization. Maternalist thinking meets free love (Weeks, 126–28).

The poem's "I-you" pronominal usages are notable. The poem is as if telegraphed to "you" to call "your" attention to the intricacy of the narrator's desire for "you." The reader, as textual substitute for the man addressed, is in a peculiarly intimate, but complex, position. First, reading is like the eroticized overhearing of a confession; certainly the pronouns produce intimacy, not distance. Second, the "I-you" pronouns instead of "he-she" suggest give-and-take, agency in both.[15] These formal choices make intellectual and ideological comment. Because of the "I-you" pronominals, similarity and contiguity are valued, and both partners seem to have both desire and suspicion (suspicion of their relationship and of each other; suspicion as well about what sexuality means). This equal intersubjectivity attempts to depict a nonhierarchical arrangement of the sexes.

"Voices break on the confines of passion / Desire   Suspicion   Man   Woman / Solve in the humid carnage . . ." (95). This set of metonymies suggests that both man and woman have desire and suspicion. In sex-radical terms, they are equal on the terrain of the sexual embrace. Further, all barriers are "solved" in that embrace, where "solved" may mean dissolved or explained, emerging as a "correct answer" to questions about modern sexuality. Sexual intercourse, that "humid carnage," is then said to override gender division, as the epigram from Loy's manifesto also suggests (269). The same phrase can also, however, be interpreted as following the lines of sexual purity binaries, as if creating two matched sets (an imaginary comma between the terms): "desire" goes with "man" and "suspicion" with "woman." The language choices suggest these latent narratives of male-female relations, which then evoke positional debates within feminism. As Nancy Cott observes, "The endorsement of heterosexual passion and pleasure was a double-edged sword for Feminists in the 1910s" because for feminists, "heterosexual liberation for women intended to subvert gender hierarchy rather than to confirm it" (152). The evidence of a debate between subversion of hierarchy and confirmation of it occurs in the language of this passage and elsewhere in Loy.

With "laughing honey / And spermatozoa / At the core of Nothing / In the milk of the Moon" and continuing for six sections, Loy composes precisely on or alluding to (hetero)sexual intercourse with a striking frankness of diction, and in a great variety of registers, including terror, danger, pleasure, resistance, lust, and controlling wit (94–95).[16] These are not, it appears from their tonal differences, narratives of one erotic encounter but rather six separate, distinct, and precisely noted representations of activities and attitudes that go with sex, with special attention to the similarities between the partners at the moment of pleasure when (according to Loy) male-female distinctions dissolve, yet a moment whose social and psychological context is precisely the dangers of that difference: "seismic orgasm" (105). For instance, the obliteration of gender distinctions seems especially keen in "humid carnage // Flesh from flesh / Draws the inseparable delight / Kissing at gasps   to catch it," and then to "welded to-gether" and "knocking sparks off each other" (95–97). With its sparks, "welded" puns on and rejects the more familiar phrase "wedded together" with an industrial metaphor. But even Loy's most distinctive phrases—"humid carnage" or "seismic orgasm"—combine pleasurable words and dangerous words. "Carnage" reaches etymologically for "flesh" and con-notively for "carnal," with a historical pun, "dying," but denotively for "mass slaughter." In "seismic," also, pleasure and danger contend; the technical term for earthquake is far fiercer than the sentimental notion that in orgasm "the earth moved."

Charming and alarming is this haiku, allusively complete in just three lines.

> Shuttle-cock and battle-door
> A little pink love
> And feathers are strewn
>
> (95)

The shuttlecock of badminton bears irresistible double overtones, and the battledore, a flat wooden paddle (and the old word for badminton itself), is provocatively respelled "battle-door" to suggest site of penetration. This first line emphasizes the physical difference between the sexes, yet the sport that can be made of these differences. "Pink love" smacks of a fond eros of knowing possession, rather than unconsummated yearning. The "feath-ers" signal a comic devastation of the "birdie" or cock, a triumph perhaps of the woman—or perhaps mutual release in plucking. Sex becomes a game, a sport, a cartoon.

Mina Loy's "Love Songs," then, contains a unique representation of sexual intercourse, along with many also imaginatively graphic descriptions of specifically sexual apparatuses. Of thirty-four sections, fourteen (about 40 percent of the poem) are arguably centered on different occasions of/ acts of sexual intercourse or may be said to mention sex prominently. And this representation is drastically a-conventional—a challenge to prudes and, more interesting, to the hegemonic romance narratives of the lyric genre, but equally well a challenge to modernist libertarian thinking. For aspects of this urgency—the turn to reproductive sexuality at the end—could be seen as radically conservative.

The next main portion of the poem (sections 16–25) narrates the appar-ent aftermath of sex and romance, with the tentative steps toward recovery and backslidings into misery, pleasure in isolated identity, bitterness about betrayal.[17] The "severing" might be of man from woman with the "heinous acerbity / Of your streetcorner smile" (99, 102). But it might be self-induced, a bitter self-imposed punishment of exile from him when her emotions (pride, jealousy, sentimentality, and so forth) could not be detached from her sexual experience and she violated the terms of her own brave "Feminist Manifesto."

A key section on the recovery is a private "green" poem of pleasure in isolation and revival—like a Marvellian pastoral.

> Green things grow
> Salads
> For the cerebral
> Forager's revival
> Upon bossed bellies
> Of mountains
> Rolling in the sun
> And flowered flummery
> Breaks
> To my silly shoes
>
> In ways without you
> I go
> Gracelessly
> As things go
>
> (100–101)

In her thinking about her long poem, Loy spoke of "Love Songs" as "the best since Sappho."[18] More than just a chipper touch of self-praise, this phrase seems to indicate both Loy's concern to situate the poem in a tradition of female lyricists and as well to hint at a playful, yet decided set of allusions to Sappho's images. These encodings occur especially, but not exclusively, in this part of the poem, which speaks of her tentative recovery from or rejection of thralldom and romance. Unlike a "sapphic" (that is, lesbian or bisexual) use of Sappho as one might see in H.D., Loy uses the Sappho of unwilling, yet persistent feelings of sexual desire: "Desire shakes me . . . it is a creeping thing and bittersweet / I can do nothing to resist" (Sappho, 78). So Loy claims Sappho as the necessary precursor in the frank and free treatment of sexual matters.

In the poem, Loy calls on certain isolated images of Sappho that have a particular aura in our poetic tradition precisely because they exist a-contextually, in randomly preserved fragments. Loy reweaves them into a sequence. There is Sappho's sweet apple, unpicked at the top of a tree, and her "cool water rustles through apple shoots" and Loy's comparably watery "apple stealing under the sea" (Sappho, 52, 4; Loy, LLB, 98). Sappho had her "feet / in many colored thongs"; Loy notes "my silly shoes," which break flowers when they walk, as do the feet of Sappho's Cretan women (Sappho, 18, 44; Loy, 101). Sappho had a vastly suggestive "dripping towel"; Loy notes how "a white towel" wipes away the sweat and yellow-white liquids of lovemaking (Sappho, 67; Loy, 104). Sappho set forth "shoots of parsley"; Loy notes how "green things grow / Salads" for her renewal (Sappho, 136; Loy, 100–101). Loy even proposed a tricky revision of a famous Homeric line, as did Sappho; in Loy's blunt terms, "The little rosy / Tongue of Dawn," part of the pink palette of the poem, wakes the lovers (Sappho, 47; Loy, 102). One section in the very final part of the poem is explicitly Sappho-like in its suggestion of loss; it is the only section that names the man: "The moon is cold / Joannes / Where the Mediterranean . . ." (Loy, 106); this brooks comparison with Sappho's "The moon / the Pleiades" fragment and may respond to—or parallel—Pound's deliberate reaction of the fragment: "spring / Too long / Gongola" (Sappho, 45; Pound, 112).

A summary set of lines thereupon moves away from the sensuous alba of romance tradition, dividing into two categories those who wake up postcoitus. The section names "some of us" still "melted" "Into abysmal pigeon-holes / Passion has bored / In warmth"; this produces an unsavory combination of the swindled female "pigeons," their wretched domestic compartments, and the duplicitous word "bored," summarizing both ennui and sexual penetration (Loy, LLB, 102). These are distinguished from "some few of us" who "Grow to the level of cool plains / Cutting our foothold / With steel eyes" (102). An analytic elite has woken up in another sense and will be able to scrutinize the situation of love and sex, examining "Nature" with intellectual dispassion, not sensual passion, misplaced morality, or curdling personal sentiments of loss. "The cerebral forager" first takes herself as a one-woman petri dish for the cultivation of sexuality and then becomes a scientist scrutinizing the growths (101). The sex-radical woman may suffer the conventional narrative of passion and loss, thralldom and aftermath, but she will rewrite that narrative by rebounding to analyze it.

Nature is then called "that irate pornographist."[19] "Irate" means angry, excited, incensed; "pornographist" makes of Nature an angry or emotional producer of texts depicting sexual intercourse. Given Loy's poem, this would put her in precise alliance with Nature; she too is an angry writer depicting sexual intercourse who had certainly "shed . . . petty pruderies." Yet in what senses does she side with Nature? Loy first argues, with naturalist panache, that we are some kind of means for Nature; Nature is a presenter of materials for our sexual arousal, and we are just those human materials on which Nature has to act, containers for natural forces, and that individual niceties, specific feelings, certain kinds of resistance are counterproductive, causing only suffering to the small speck somehow standing up in the face of these forces. Nature "knows us" with "blind eyes"—implacable, amoral (106). Women and men are, in a kind of Hardyesque fatedness—controlled like cosmic puppets by the force and overwhelming character of "nature"—sexual drives.

These "naturalist" feelings about sexuality (that the hard-won individualism of the New Woman stands in the way of and is swept away by cosmic natural drives) seem to be at issue when Loy bitterly calls for a new breed of "sons and daughters" who might have "some way of braying brassily / For caressive calling" and who might be "seduce[d]" "To the one / As simple satisfaction / For the other" (104–5).

> Let them clash together
> From their incognitoes[20]
> In seismic orgasm
> For far further
> Differentiation[21]
> Rather than watch
> Own-self distortion
> Wince in the alien ego
> (105)

The sexual life of these active and "caressive" paragons will be simple, compared to her "own-self distortion." They will have evolved to be more in accord with Nature than she, more like human animals ("braying") without twinges of bourgeois individualism.

As she represents sexual intercourse, the loss of individual gender binaries was an advantage and a pleasure, the place where disparate gender interests merge. But there is danger: a lust for orgasm necessarily overrides a sense of ego or boundaries. So the "Nirvana" is terrible/terrifying and terrific/exhilarating, as they "tumble together / Depersonalized / Identical / Into the terrific Nirvana / Me you—you—me" (97). A woman could fear that "depersonalized" erosion of identity. These metaphors of chaos or annihilation in sexual bliss show the dangerous loss of identity, perhaps reversion to a "femininity" of dissolution and passivity, defined by stereotypical gender ideas that Loy has staked herself on resisting. The pleasures and dangers of merging boundaries are in unresolvable circulation in the poem.

In the end, "seismic orgasm" has yet another function. It is necessary to the utopian building of a new female gender identity—one in which "the mistress and the mother" are not distinct (269). For Loy, autonomous sexuality and her "freewoman" brand of autonomous feminism still involved a deeply felt claim to maternity.[22] The argument toward the end of the poem ("Evolution   fall foul of / Sexual equality / Prettily miscalculate / Similitude") strongly suggests that "sexual equality" and species meliorism are at odds (104). When one factors in Loy's rejection of a feminism of equal rights and equal access, the phrase suggests that mainstream feminism is going to fall foul of natural forces but that her eugenicist feminism, proudly set forth in the "Feminist Manifesto," will not. To build better species, the sexes should remain, in certain of their aspects, strongly differentiated—(intelligent) womanly women meeting (intelligent) manly men. And yet, at the same time, the linking of sexual activity with reproduction was a potentially conservative position, when the whole history of modern struggles for the acceptance of sexual practices (whether contraception, abortion, homosexual expression, or masturbation) has been to valorize nonreproductive sex, what Richard Brown wittily dubs "copulation without population" (63).

> The prig of passion
> To your professorial paucity
>
> Protoplasm was raving mad
> Evolving us
> (Loy, LLB, 107)

They are ill-suited to continue the race. One would not want to produce "foetal buffoons" in whom the bad patterns of the generative parents get mimicked or copied *in utero* (Loy, 105). The superior candidates for "vital creation" should produce racially superior children and should "participate consciously in the evolutionary process" (Loy, 271; Weeks, 130). But the partners in this poem are characterized as too far from the origins of life— he by "paucity" (smallness, dearth)—a kind of finicky withdrawal—and she as a "prig of passion." But since she is assuredly no prude ("prig"), one looks to other meanings; she could be arrogant or smug, a plausible reading of the ways the poem tests and tempers her self-assured "Feminist Manifesto." Or, interestingly, a reading of "prig" in British slang, a pickpocket, petty thief, or pilferer: she was trying to pilfer a little passion—and more—but his "paucity" prevents her.

The second narrative that structures the end is—to baldly summarize—her rage and grief that she does not have his child, that she did not get pregnant, or that pregnancy was not allowed to happen, barred from happening by contraceptive practices or even, perhaps, by abortion.[23] This affair did not lead to "vital creation," that is, to a child (271). As she says: "The procreative truth of Me / Petered out / In pestilent / Tear drops / Little lusts and lucidities" (101). There is angry mourning for the washing away of their sperm and cyprine mixture, a "plastic" substance that was not allowed to become anything:[24]

> The hands of races
> Drop off from
> Immodifiable plastic
>
> The contents
> Of our ephemeral conjunction
> In aloofness from Much
> Flowed to approachment of — — —
> NOTHING
> There was a man and a woman
> In the way
> (103)

The next section with its white towel and images of blank whiteness characterizes his abilities at erasure: "I am burnt quite white / In the climacteric / Withdrawal of your sun" (103). Not only about thralldom, although plausibly about her wounding by the loss of his illuminating central presence, this section seems specifically about withdrawal, combining the words "climax"—a pun on an uncertain tactic of birth control—and "climacteric," or "critical change of life."

Loy parses the resistances of the "man and [the] woman / In the way" of successful conception. The "crucifixion" section (one of the final ones) seems to criticize her self as a "busybody / Longing to interfere so / With the intimacies / Of your insolent isolation" (Loy, 106). Not just a criticism of him for narcissism or uncaringness (those familiar tropes of the end of romance) or for a selfish unwillingness to become a father, this is specifically her "crucifixion" as the bearer of a new and controversial idea (she is the "Caryatid of an idea"): that women should freely bear the children of their lovers and that superior women will bear superior children in a eugenicist sense (106). The final sense of loss is not between them, only or exclusively, but between her and the missing child.

For in the "Feminist Manifesto," Loy also produced a eugenicist codicil to her maternalist hopes: "Every woman of superior intelligence should realize her race-responsibility by producing children in adequate proportion to the unfit or degenerate members of her sex" (270). It is especially ironic to construe ordinary, run-of-the-mill, conformist women as "degenerate." This is a claim that superior women like herself, through redefined sexuality and maternity, will lead the race to a "social regeneration." As she had said, in lines I only half-glossed earlier, "Where two or three are welded together / They shall become god" (97). This is not only about the new fusions in orgasm, but about a new holy family—man, woman, and fetus/ baby. Perhaps the future paragons of "caressive calling"—more modern sex radicals than she—might be able to have sex without thinking that their combined discharges and ejaculations are "human insufficiencies / Begging dorsal vertebrae" (105). But Loy exists in an angry mourning for the lack of or loss of a child from sex, a rejoining, for both radical and eugenicist reasons, of sexual intercourse and reproduction, which can be the most traditional justification for the sexual embrace. But her justification is to claim the radical identity of sexual mother.

This brief account identifies one main issue: Loy's representation of sexuality, not in a sentimental Georgian haze—certainly one dominant convention of depiction—but sexuality as a complex of events and meanings, as a site of struggle among various historically situated discourses.[25] No human act is natural in an unmediated way, and even the most apparently basic and primal (the sexual act) has been constructed of historical and ideological meanings. As Michel Foucault remarks, "It is no longer a question simply of saying what was done—the sexual act—and how it was done; but of reconstructing, in and around the act, the thoughts that recapitulated it, the obsessions that accompanied it, the images, desires, modulations, and quality of the pleasure that animated it" (63).

It is a cultural commonplace to identify poetry with "love poetry": certain conventionalized narratives of yearning and urging, distance, loss, seduction by arguments about time, beauty, and loss. Loy's satiric, ironic, wickedly learned, and passionate voice goes far to destabilize lyric assumptions about the possession of the romance plot, female silence, and objectification. Loy, a self-styled "feminist" writer, in or alluding to the lyric of romance ("the best since Sappho") and situated at a historically mobile cusp of sexual issues—free love, maternalism—faces these issues at their extreme. Loy's crisp, richly worded, intellectual poetry, the complex "ugliness," and the satiric, clinical languages of "Love Songs" demystify the gender ideologies of beauty and of love. Central to the lyric is the carpe diem invitation, itself loosely dependent on the pink and white (or red and white) beauty of the woman. To this, Loy makes ironic counteroffers. First, of many "whites": there are a male body lengthened like a plant stretching for inadequate sunlight and the colorlessness of a man's withdrawal.[26]

> White   where there is nothing to see
> But a white towel
> Wipes the cymophanous sweat
> —Mist rise of living—
> From your
> Etiolate body
>
> (104)

And, then, the pink is not that of "cherry ripe" or "rose" but of a rooting pig. "Love Songs" opens with one of its two most frequently cited sections, in which "Pig Cupid" presides over the writing and instigates the erotic and its critique. "Pig" makes a greedy, lurid, Id-filled muse, "rooting erotic garbage" rather than shooting arrows, a drastically anticonventional figure with neither the whimsy of echt Cupids nor the possible transcendences of Amor.[27] Pig Cupid is the "Spawn of Fantasies"—the ova from which fantasy arises or the offspring of reproductive encounters. He is as well a phallic or lusty disturber of the peace, sticking his snout into "erotic garbage"—those nice narratives of " 'Once upon a time.' " Pig is, in short, a fusion of male-female-child, an erotic-satyric holy family in which there is a female writer. Loy calls attention to the fictive or scripted nature of the love plot in an arch, ironic, and bitter way:

> Spawn of Fantasies
> Silting the appraisable
> Pig Cupid
> His rosy snout
> Rooting erotic garbage
> "Once upon a time"
>
> (91)

From that beginning of the poem, Loy creates an excessive or exaggerated attention to the one act hidden in the carpe diem convention, although its constant point. She makes a new kind of gender narrative, validated by historical struggles around sexuality, sexual expression, and female desire. By excess in a female voice, she swamps the convention's dependency on a certain delicacy, feminine resistance, or reluctance. She overrides the poetic convention of romance both by a sense of aggression (Carpe diem! You don't even have to ask!) where she represents herself continuously as a sexual woman, and by a sense of judgment, where she represents her skeptical, damaging analysis of what can happen after the "achievement" of bliss or completion promised in the convention of romance (Carpe diem/dies irae). A short list includes impotence or awkward, ill-paced consummations, betrayals of trust, "ephemeral conjunction[s]," jealousy, the apparently "superhuman" man reseen as a "weak eddy," "Little lusts and lucidities / and prayerful lies" (103, 98, 101).

Besides the lyric conventions of romance and love to which it is clear Loy responds, her modern sexual story differs from at least one other sex-radical author narrating sex, love, and intercourse.[28] In her work, Loy refuses the novelistic linkage of sexual climaxes and narrative climaxes. An important novel contemporaneous with the poem, *The Rainbow* (1915) by D. H. Lawrence, embeds sexual contact—kisses, courtships, and sexual acts—in a tumultuous context of *Bildung*. Sexuality, an animating drive for the characters, is thoroughly contextualized as expressive of emotional and spiritual development, and both passion and revulsion (which are versions of each other) are impelled through the novel's three generations of erotic encounters like enormous weather fronts. Sexuality is also a force programmatically set against superficial liberal meliorisms and moralities: education, regimentation, intellection, and abstraction. Lovemaking is a dark and "subtle" exercise, in which an insinuating, "stealthy," "relentless," and "fecund" male figure, by penetration, "shatters" certain resistances in a female figure, inducing her to leave off light and go into the dark. "The lighted vessel vibrated, and broke in her soul, the light fell, struggled and went dark. She was all dark, will-less, having only the receptive will" (Lawrence, *Rainbow*, 420, 422). The will-lessness of Lawrence's heroines may be construed as a response to various political assumptions and spiritual claims of female agency: it is in dialogue with feminisms. It is uncanny that Loy's trope of lighting an orgasmic yet investigatory lamp is the obverse of this blackout: creating female will, power, aggression, and judgment (Loy, LLB, 91).

This tendency to link narrative climax and sexual climax and to propose renewed heterosexuality to regulate feminism is acutely realized in Lawrence's *Lady Chatterley's Lover*. Sexual scenes in *Lady Chatterley's Lover* punctuate the book, making each orgasm a station of a sexual *via sacra* and a political affirmation not only of heterosexuality but of certain kinds of female orgasm. In the narrative middle, a bildungsplot, every sexual climax is an educational climax, but the novel ebbs out at the end with Mellors's letter and does not really have a final discharge, because it wants to make a comforting case for monogamy and marital chastity. In the first episode of intercourse between Connie and Mellors, the act occurs from compassion, without mind: just an act of lovemaking, one difficult for Connie to accept with "her tormented modern-woman's brain" (124). She has no orgasm, because she does not strive; the issue of clitoral stimulation is very fraught in Lawrence (123). The bodies initiate "free love," not only a free choice of sexual activity, but also a free choice to transcend the strictures of class, tormented intellection by women, and a social Mammon built of industrial capitalism. Their second intercourse finds her exercising judgment and resistance, envisioning the sheer silliness of the sex act and the male body, resenting his power of touch, self-conscious and awkward. But Connie still does not seek "satisfaction" in the ways she had achieved it with her love Michaelis. In the third act of intercourse, suddenly, in the woods, "the will had left her," and she experiences passive/receptive orgasm, which is dependent on the erect phallus as the centerpiece of her experience (141). Her passivity is rewarded with the "molten," the "rippling," the "flames," the "feathers"—everything "up and up to a culmination" (141–42). This is rich propaganda for the penis in an absolutely didactic mode. Her orgasm offers her a pregnancy: not of a real child, though that will come, but of "another self . . . alive in her"—the real new woman in Lawrence's scheme, who has given up "her hard bright female power" (143, 144). The lesson plan continues with an important passage in which Lawrence establishes that the phallus is not a dildo, that is not an object which a domineering woman (Baccante) can manipulate.

The fourth episode of intercourse is like a review session, in which the ideas set forth in the three prior episodes are tested and confirmed. Her rejection of touch and her intellectualized attitude to sex makes Connie "tormented"; but when the phallus hovered godlike over her waters, "she was born—a woman" (186). Her pregnancy with self culminates in birth pangs given as orgasm. The next episodes present repeated marriage scenes. In contrast to all the false (but legal) marriages in this book, Connie and

Mellors celebrate a true nuptials of their genitals, in a touching, seriocomic wedding of two members of the natural nobility, the lordly phallus John Thomas and his correspondent Lady Jane (224–27 and 242–48). For Lawrence, this is not a novel of adultery: not about secrets and disclosures and punishments. The lovers are not caught, trapped, exposed, or punished. It is, however, an oedipal narrative: the secret is, in Barthes's terms, a "denuding," by the apotheosis of his erect phallus in a nimbus of sunlight (Barthus, 10; *Lady Chatterley*, 226). It is interesting to remember than in Loy a trio of man/woman/baby was "god." Using de Lauretis's terms, one sees Lawrence making the clitoral/phallic woman an obstacle, with the creation of Connie is the resolution: "Her story . . . is [still] a question of his desire" (133).

Lawrence produces, during the apotheosis of the phallus, a remarkable attempt at a New Man. Because despite the understandable enthusiasm for male potency, the New Man also absorbs much of the language of the feminine-maidenly, in the terms that serve to describe his penis ("bud-like reticence," "tender," "frail," "pure," "lovely," "delicate," "soft," "sensitive," and "innocent"); indeed the clitoral aspects of female sexuality ("bud-like" "sensitive") seem thereby to be relocated in the male body (187, 227). The phallus is a personage with a lordly, demanding aspect and a frail, tender, feminine character.[29]

Lawrence is aware of and eloquent and polemical about clitoral sexuality. Mellors's unflattering description of the orgasms of his first wife, Bertha, shows a fervor against the active/clitoral in woman that is deeply informative (217–20). Such phallic women are willful, depraved, addicted to their sensation and, in the pièce de résistance, are really "Lesbian." Indeed, nearly all women are lesbian, if not by their clitoral "beak," by their New Woman hyperconscious cleverness, and Mellors confesses he would like to kill them all (217–19; compare 303–4). It really does recall the noble fervor of *Dracula*, where much narrative climax is expended on the right regulation of female sexuality. This fervor could be contrasted to the careful language about nonvaginal sex, for an act of heterosexual anal intercourse is the occluded climax of the sexual via sacra. This is parsed as "the end of shame." It is important to comprehend that Lawrence's curiosity and tolerance extend only to phallic sexuality (267–69). The clitoris is exorcised.

The child conceived by Connie changes in its meaning throughout the novel. First it was controlled by Clifford who was made allegorically impotent in the war but still desired an heir, a kind of *infans ex machina*. Then the child was controlled by Connie, providing a cover story for her trip to Venice to have a pretend affair, so as not to acknowledge Mellors. Finally the child is seen to belong to Mellors and Connie, as a pentacostal flame, an indicator of a better relation between men and woman along the (antifeminist) lines that the novel has proposed. Lawrence's opinions deserve longer discussion, but one can observe that for him the problem of the New Woman would be solved by a Newer Man. Lawrence powerfully offers a nonfeminist but sexual subject position for women. He tempts women who might have been burned by free love serial affairs with a concentration on purity and monogamy in Mellors's character at the end of the novel. A revolution in male sexuality will bind a new ordering of human relations that will stand against feminist and working-class revolutions—so Lawrence responds to the considerable contemporary changes in gender and class relations by his narrative proposals. The work is a continuation of the conduct book tradition in which novels educate women.

Of course, his polemic is provocative for any reader who identifies with the New Woman or her quasi independence. This is visible in Woolf's inaccurate allusions to *Lady Chatterley's Lover* in *Orlando*.[30] Woolf parodies Connie's thralldom; however, the comment "she will soon give over this pretence of . . . thinking and begin to think, at least of a gamekeeper" is inaccurate: through good sex Connie develops social and political opinions apace (*Orlando*, 175). For, among its other properties, the more Lawrentian sex Connie has, the more her social diagnoses echo those of the narrator (in free indirect discourse) and of Mellors. Woolf also parodies Mellors, who is never seen whistling under Connie's window, coming bidden to an "assignation"; this would be untypical of his "decency" and "reserve," to borrow terms from Lawrence (*Orlando*, 176; the closest scene is *Lady Chatterley*, 154). But, as her remarks about narrative in *A Room of One's Own* reveal, Woolf also wanted to invent structures to resist "the crisis"—her witty amalgam of narrative and sexual climax: "And then Alan, I thought, has passions; and here I turned page after page very fast, feeling that the crisis was approaching, and so it was. It took place on the beach under the sun. It was done very openly. It was done very vigorously. Nothing could have been more indecent. . . . 'But—I am bored!' " (*Room*, 104). Is "natural desire," Woolf asks (in *Orlando*), "what the male novelist says it is?" Or does it have other forms, many different forms, the world, happiness, dreams, the city, including—for Woolf's invocation and climax is placed just there— the birth of a child (*Orlando*, 192–93; compare Winnett). The work of Woolf and Richardson has hardly begun to be mined for feminist narrative theory.

In this novel by Lawrence, scenes of intercourse are indeed climactic: that is, they are proposed as narrative peaks. Narrative climax and orgasmic climax coincide. In contrast, Loy's representations of intercourse occur in a loosely structured plot of connection, loss, and analytic reprise; they are not climactic but various, acting to influence, and influenced by, the mixture of suspicion and desire, the playing out of equations for possibilities, which is constitutive of the sexuality depicted. Because narrative climax may not exist and certainly does not coincide with sexual climax, Loy's mode is antiseptic, less readable (indeed, less read). Because these acts provide no "crisis" in a narrative sense, they seem rather a series of repeated behaviors, conceptualized and reconceptualized, thought and rethought.

In the Loy poem, there is no "typical" or "valorized" statement about sexual intercourse. The images she does use do not concern phallic power but, as we have seen, involve a variety of attempts to figure orgasm itself ("inseparable delight") in which male is not especially differentiated from female, nor does male lead female to some realization. Loy's representations of sexual intercourse are less narrated, less sequentially filled in with a moment-to-moment or play-by-play set of ("molten") metaphors than are Lawrence's. They tend to be a fragmented narration of thought, options, or temporary, situational positions: a summary report, as if representation were precisely at issue and there were some equation to "solve." Representation, not conversion, is precisely at issue. Perhaps it is the syntactic fragmentation or obscurity of the poem, but in Loy, sexuality seems more a problem (such as in math or logic); in Lawrence, it has the status of solution or proof. Her representations are determinedly secular; allusions to sex are made with the same passionate dispassion as any other topic of the poem. There is no special, magical diction for sex, in contrast to the diction of spiritual and political renewal in Lawrence.

Finally, Lawrence confirms certain long-standing gender conventions, although acting within a libertarian sexual ideology about sexual intercourse: how the powerful magic wand of a penetrating penis (wherever it goes) transforms the female psyche.[31] Orgasm is a reconversion experience to polarized gender binaries away from modern womanhood and its terrible "beak." Loy claims, unevenly, that orgasm is the only site in which gender binaries are rendered inoperable, where men and women lose their suspicion and—both active—become just grasping flesh: the "only point at which the interests of the sexes merge." In any event, she hardly proposes heterosexuality or orgasm as means to convert women away from feminism.

Quotations from Mina Loy, "Feminist Manifesto," by permission of the Yale Collection of American Literature, Beinecke Rare Book and Manuscript Library, Yale University. Citations from Mina Loy, *Last Lunar Baedeker*, ed. Rober L. Conover (Highlands, N.C.: Jargon Society, 1982), by permission of Roger L. Conover, copyright The Estate of Mina Loy.

1. Loy, *The Last Lunar Baedeker* [henceforth LLB], 269–71; due to certain textual inconsistencies, the "Feminist Manifesto" [henceforth FM] will also be cited from its holograph version, held by the Beinecke Rare Book and Manuscript Library, Yale University.

2. My argument does not, therefore, fall within literary applications of psychoanalytic theory. However, Irigaray offers the possibility of eroding the "male oedipal/ male orgasmic" models by application of the Freudian term "bisexuality," for "once bisexuality has been admitted [by Freud], why cut short its implications?" (20).

3. British is in parentheses because Loy was active in the literary scenes in Italy and the United States and in the visual art worlds in Paris and the United States, and like many modernists, she responded to—and intervened in—several national cultures, not just her nation of origin.

4. Some attention has been paid to Loy, though not yet enough to date. The centrally useful: Roger L. Conover's introduction to his edition of the poems (Loy, xv–lxxix), the study by Virginia Kouidis, and Carolyn Burke's striking biographical, contextual, and analytic studies on Loy, which will be capped by a critical biography forthcoming from Farrar, Straus, and Giroux in 1996. See Burke, "Supposed," "Spliced," "Loy." Burke discusses elements of "Love Songs" at several junctures in her published articles to date (e.g., Burke, "Supposed" and "Spliced").

5. The theoretical challenge of this point—to look at modern long or serial poems as narrative, lyric, and essay—I will resist here because I have defined other tasks.

6. The manifesto is conjecturally dated 1914, that is, virtually simultaneous with the poem and just preceding it; possibly its critical force then is transferred to the poem "Love Songs," for although Conover notes that Loy had written on the manuscript "This is a rough draught beginning of an absolute resubstantiation of the feminist question," the manifesto is apparently not continued in these terms (269–71 and 327). Loy wrote manifestos during this era; they are part of her production of writing. A background to this feminist manifesto is an earlier (1913) "Aphorisms on Futurism."

7. As did Loy. "As conditions are at present constituted you have the choice between Parasitism, Prostitution [the private ownership of women in marriage is implied], or Negation." Loy was adamant that "economic legislation, vice-crusades and uniform education" are inadequate stops when nothing short of "Absolute Demolition" will change the sex-gender system (LLB, 272–75).

8. Loy's feminism of individual agency and will still seems to consider women as a group and indeed still uses the term "feminist." In contrast, Dora Marsden was

highly resistant to any consideration of Woman-as-type, by which she meant both stereotypes of women and any analysis considering woman in the mass—that is, analyses by gender. She announces her principles as follows: " 'Woman,' spelt with a capital, Woman-as-type, had no existence; that it is an empty concept and should be banished from language" ("Views and Comments," July 1913, 24). Marsden also insisted that " 'Feminism' was the natural reply to 'Hominism,' " suggesting that both were inadequate and unnecessary because a higher and more specific individualist urge replaced these political positions—"[woman] can be as 'free' now as they have the power to be" ("Views and Comments," December 1913, 244). This latter editorial announces the end of the "new freewoman" title, so that the review would no longer emphasize female specificity but be for "individualists of both sexes." The name change was precipitated by a letter from such male contributors as Ezra Pound, Allen Upward, and Richard Aldington.

9. This is in the manuscript, not the published version.

10. For almost contemporaneous redefinitions of morality, purity, and virtue that reflect the consolidation of the sex-radical position, see the articles in Kirchwey.

11. A review in the *New Freewoman* stated that there was no difference between men's and women's "sex-feelings" (Low, 36).

12. For the analysis of the sexual debates, I am indebted to Mort; Weeks; DuBois and Gordon; Cott; and Trimberger, "Feminism" and "New Woman." My use of British and American materials for the British Loy occurs because the poem "Love Songs," also called "Songs to Joannes," was first published in the United States and made quite a splash in avant-garde circles (first partially published in *Others* [July 1915], the whole poem was later issued as a chapbook: see *Others* 3.6 [April 1917]). Burke's essay—an important study of the link of free verse and free love—traces the considerable impact of Loy on the *Others* group and the New York avant-garde as well as the impact on Loy of Margaret Sanger's birth control activism ("New Poetry").

13. I accept two revisions to the Conover edition in this first section. Kouidis (64 n. 20) follows the manuscript and the 1917 *Others* publication. "Silting" (for "sitting") is one such revision; "these" (for "there") is the other. In addition, Loy ideally wanted each section to be followed by a reciprocal page of blank space with a "large round" in it, but I am reluctantly ignoring the issue of visual presentation.

14. A Bengal light is firework with a brilliant blue light sometimes used for signaling. The combination of orgasmic connotations with images of scrutiny and signage symbolizes Loy's work in this poem.

15. Burke ("Supposed," 136) warns not to take any of Loy's "I's" as easily autobiographical, for part of her modernism depends on "evasive self-presentation" and a "tension between concealment and revelation in uses of the first person."

16. Not only this set of materials but yet another at the end of the poem (sections 24–30) returns to intercourse as its topos and ground.

17. Both section 16 and section 25 mention the Arno River, which tends to frame this part of the poem. The narrative middle shows the "I" enmeshed in certain thralldoms in phrases such as "at your mercy"; "Is it true / That I have set you apart";

"to love you most"; and after the fall, "I store up nights against you / Heavy with shut-flower's nightmares" (95, 98, 100).

18. In a letter to Carl Van Vechten (c. 1915) held at the Beinecke Library, Yale University, cited by Conover (Loy, LLB, 326), Kouidis (85), Burke ("Supposed," 137), and Schreiber (ts. 1). I have not yet seen the context for this remark within the whole letter and Loy's and Van Vechten's correspondence.

19. Section 26 (102) reads in toto: "Shedding our petty pruderies / From slit eyes / We sidle up / To Nature / —that irate pornographist." The dashes derive from the 1917 *Others* publication of the poem.

20. They have no identity, have false names, unlike herself. Or perhaps like herself, who changed her family name from the ethnic/Jewish freight of Lowy to Loy in 1903.

21. I take this as the development of a new species within a genus or the development of specialized organs, a word used of embryos or fetuses.

22. To recall, "Every woman [i.e., married or unmarried] has a right to maternity"; indeed, "Woman must become more responsible for the child than man"—the latter is either the most banal of her propositions, since it recapitulates what is, or the most radical in proposing dyadic families and sexual mothers (270, 271).

23. Schreiber (ts.) suggests that within this poem Loy narrates an abortion.

24. I follow Susanne de Lotbinère-Harwood's suggestion (made in translating Nicole Brossard), that Anglophones use a modified version of the French word *cyprin* for a word apparently missing in English (145–48).

25. Compare another depiction of sexual intercourse in a poem: "My body was one tremulous sense / Of her slight body's eloquence. // I was a drowned man in the sea / Of her immaculate melody" (Ficke, 675). The contrast of this euphemistic poetic cupcake with Loy's work could not be more acute.

26. Kouidis briefly discusses the red-white-green imagery of this poem (81–82); it is important to see how traditional these colors are to love poetry and to pastoral. Yellow or yellow-white ("cymophanous" means just that) then becomes Loy's modernist, franker color of sex, as we see also in Williams, "Love Song": "the stain of love / Is upon the world! / Yellow, yellow, yellow / It eats into the leaves, / Smears with saffron / The horned branches" and later "a honey-thick stain" (53–54; see also 106–7).

27. "Root" could be a dialect form of the verb "rut," meaning to be in a state of sexual excitement.

28. Although I do not cite them, my knowledge of Lawrence's sex-radical odyssey has been informed by Simpson and Siegel.

29. This is related to an important scene of the female gaze at the very beginning of the novel, in which Connie sees Mellors half-naked: many of the adjectives are feminine descriptors (68).

30. Although it is a little difficult to figure out how these allusions got there. *Orlando* went to the printer on 1 June 1928 and was published on 11 October; Lawrence's book was not published until July, but it had been finished since March (Woolf, *Diary*, 183, 199, 217; Lawrence, *Lady Chatterley*, xiii, xv, xvi). One guess is that

Woolf heard about the Lawrence novel early in 1928. A second, more likely guess is that the remarks on Lawrence were inserted in page proof during the late summer. Woolf's diary, from whence the dates above, shows that by January 1929 she had read and repeatedly discussed *Lady Chatterley's Lover*.

31. Stephen Heath has spoken about this dominant discursive convention of love-making in twentieth-century fiction (he calls it "the sexual fix"), which frames the penis-vagina connection, with its male-female binary, and makes a large "primordial and cosmic investment in 'sexuality'" as "culminations of a life and a novel": "Writing love-making is again a problem of complicity with and support for the sexual fix, going over and over the standard pattern. Here if anywhere, one might think, differences would be fundamental, a plurality of positions and inscriptions would be possible. Yet here [he speaks in fact of a passage from *Lady Chatterley's Lover*] precisely the same is made and remade, the very fact of these scenes determined by the myth and its repetition; with the difficulty of writing otherwise, outside that repetition, immense" (130, 131, 126).

WORKS CITED

Arac, Jonathan. "Afterword: Lyric Poetry and the Bounds of New Criticism." *Lyric Poetry: Beyond New Criticism*. Ed. Chaviva Hosek and Patricia Parker. Ithaca: Cornell University Press, 1985. 345–55.

Barthes, Roland. *The Pleasure of the Text*. 1973. Trans. Richard Miller. New York: Hill and Wang, 1975.

Brooks, Peter. *Reading for the Plot: Design and Intention in Narrative*. New York: Alfred A. Knopf, 1984.

Brown, Richard. *James Joyce and Sexuality*. Cambridge: Cambridge University Press, 1985.

Burke, Carolyn. "Getting Spliced: Modernism and Sexual Difference." *American Quarterly* 39.1 (Spring 1987): 98–121.

——. "Mina Loy (1882–1966)." *The Gender of Modernism: A Critical Anthology*. Ed. Bonnie Kime Scott. Bloomington: Indiana University Press, 1990. 230–38.

——. "The New Poetry and the New Woman: Mina Loy." *Coming to Light: American Women Poets in the Twentieth Century*. Ed. Diana Middlebrook and Marilyn Yalom. Ann Arbor: University of Michigan Press, 1985. 37–57.

——. "Supposed Persons: Modernist Poetry and the Female Subject." *Feminist Studies* 7.1 (1985): 131–48.

Clayton, Jay. "Narrative and Theories of Desire." *Critical Inquiry* 16 (Autumn 1989): 33–53.

Cohen, Ralph, ed. *Studies in Historical Change*. Charlottesville: University Press of Virginia, 1992.

Cott, Nancy F. *The Grounding of Modern Feminism*. New Haven: Yale University Press, 1987.

de Lauretis, Teresa. "Desire in Narrative." *Alice Doesn't: Feminism, Semiotics, Cinema*. Bloomington: Indiana University Press, 1984. 103–57.

DuBois, Ellen, and Linda Gordon. "Seeking Ecstasy on the Battlefield: Danger and

Pleasure in Nineteenth-Century Feminist Sexual Thought." *Feminist Studies* 9.1 (Spring 1983): 7–25.

DuPlessis, Rachel Blau. " 'Corpses of Poesy': Some Modern Poets and Some Gender Ideologies of Lyric." *Feminist Measures*. Ed. Lynn Keller and Cristanne Miller. Ann Arbor: University of Michigan Press, 1994. 69–95.

——. *Writing beyond the Ending: Narrative Strategies of Twentieth-Century Women Writers*. Bloomington: Indiana University Press, 1985.

Ficke, A. Davison. "A Note on the Poetry of Sex." *Sex in Civilization*. Ed. V. F. Calverton and S. D. Schmalhausen. New York: Macaulay, 1929. 659–76.

Foucault, Michel. *The History of Sexuality*. Vol. 1, *An Introduction*. New York: Viking, 1980.

Gregory, Horace. *Dorothy Richardson: An Adventure in Self Discovery*. New York: Holt, Rinehart and Winston, 1967.

Heath, Stephen. *The Sexual Fix*. 1982. New York: Schocken, 1984.

Irigaray, Luce. *Speculum of the Other Woman*. 1974 Trans. Gillian Gill. Ithaca: Cornell University Press, 1985.

Kirchwey, Freda. *Our Changing Morality: A Symposium*. New York: Albert and Charles Boni, 1924.

Kouidis, Virginia M. *Mina Loy: American Modernist Poet*. Baton Rouge: Louisiana State University Press, 1980.

Lanser, Susan S. "Towards a Feminist Narratology." 1986. *Feminisms: An Anthology of Literary Theory and Criticism*. Ed. Robyn R. Warhol and Diane Price Herndl. New Brunswick: Rutgers University Press, 1991. 610–29.

Lawrence, D. H. *Lady Chatterley's Lover*. 1928. New York: Bantam, 1968.

——. *The Rainbow*. 1915. London: Martin Secker, 1928.

Lotbinère-Harwood, Susanne de. *Re-Belle et infidèle / The Body Bilingual: Translation as a Rewriting in the Feminine*. Montreal: Women's Press, 1991.

Low, Barbara. "A New Altar." *New Freewoman* 2.1 (1 July 1913): 36.

Loy, Mina. "Feminist Manifesto." Holograph. Yale Collection of American Literature. Beinecke Rare Book and Manuscript Library, Yale University, New Haven, Conn.

——. *The Last Lunar Baedeker*. Ed. Roger L. Conover. Highlands, N.C.: Jargon Society, 1982.

Marsden, Dora. "Views and Comments." *New Freewoman* 2.1 (1 July 1913): 24.

——. "Views and Comments." *New Freewoman* 2.12 (15 December 1913): 244.

Medvedev, P. N., and M. M. Bakhtin. *The Formal Method in Literary Scholarship: A Critical Introduction to Sociological Poetics*. 1928. Trans. Albert J. Wehrle. Baltimore: Johns Hopkins University Press, 1978.

Mort, Frank. *Dangerous Sexualities: Medico-Moral Politics in England since 1830*. London: Routledge and Kegan Paul, 1987.

Pound, Ezra. "Papyrus." 1915. *Personae: The Collected Poems of Ezra Pound*. New York: Boni and Liveright, 1926. 112.

Richardson, Dorothy. "Novels." *Life and Letters* 56 (March 1948): 192.

Sappho. *The Poems of Sappho*. Trans. Susy Q. Groden. New York: Bobbs-Merrill, 1966.

Schreiber, Maeera. " 'The Best since Sappho': Mina Loy's *Love Songs*," 39 pp. ts.

Siegel, Carol. *Lawrence among the Women: Wavering Boundaries in Women's Literary Traditions*. Charlottesville: University Press of Virginia, 1991.

Simpson, Hilary. *D. H. Lawrence and Feminism*. DeKalb: Northern Illinois University Press, 1982.

Stoker, Bram. *Dracula*. 1897. London: Penguin, 1979.

Trimberger, Ellen Kay. "Feminism, Men, and Modern Love: Greenwich Village, 1900–1925." *Powers of Desire: The Politics of Sexuality*. Ed. Ann Snitow, Christine Stansell, and Sharon Thompson. New York: Monthly Review, 1983. 131–52.

——. "The New Woman and the New Sexuality: Conflict and Contradiction in the Writings and Lives of Mabel Dodge and Neith Boyce." *1915: The Cultural Moment*. Ed. Adele Heller and Lois Rudnick. New Brunswick: Rutgers University Press, 1991. 98–115.

Weeks, Jeffrey. *Sex, Politics, and Society: The Regulation of Sexuality since 1800*. London: Longman, 1981.

Williams, William Carlos. *The Collected Poems of William Carlos Williams*. Vol. 1, *1909–1939*. Ed. A. Walton Litz and Christopher MacGowan. New York: New Directions, 1986.

Winnett, Susan. "Coming Unstrung: Women, Men, Narrative, and Principles of Pleasure." *PMLA* 105 (1990): 505–18.

Woolf, Virginia. *The Diary of Virginia Woolf*. Vol. 3, *1925–1930*. Ed. Anne Oliver Bell with Andrew McNeillie. New York: Harcourt Brace Jovanovich, 1980.

——. *Orlando*. 1928. New York: New American Library, 1960.

——. *A Room of One's Own*. 1929. New York: Harcourt Brace and World, 1957.

ironies of politeness in

anita brookner's *hotel du lac*

janet | giltrow

otel du Lac is a romance of a familiar type: an unattached woman, Edith Hope, is courted by a high-status man, Mr. Neville. It is also an ironic romance. For one thing, Edith is herself a writer of romances of this type. She says she writes them on behalf of the timid and negligible, on behalf of women who have no grounds to anticipate such success. Yet her stories are enjoyed by Mrs. Pusey and her daughter Jennifer—fellow hotel guests who are not timid at all but lush and confident in the social and sexual regard that flows their way. Then there is the greater irony that while Mr. Neville's marriage proposal satisfies the terms of Edith's own stories, it in fact demeans rather than promotes the beloved.

And it is not only the story of *Hotel du Lac* that is ironic. Its style is ironic too—a membrane of refined surfaces stretched over other actualities. Investigating this ironic voice and its replicas of a certain way of speaking, I found in *Hotel du Lac* dense populations of these linguistic features: (a) presupposing expressions, which assume rather than assert; (b) agentless expressions, which suppress mention of actors; and (c) modality and projection, which assign statements as issuing from contingent conditions. These features travel unrestricted from narration across the threshold of Edith's reported thoughts and speech and other characters' reported thoughts and speech. They are also not immediately explicable in terms of irony.

To prepare to offer, eventually, a glimpse of the ironic profile of these linguistic forms, I will first propose that they contribute to a larger set of expressions: "politeness" expressions. I analyze politeness as including not only courtesies but suppressions too, as well as tacit gestures by which people recognize one another in their range of social distinction, by which people indemnify themselves and sustain advantage. In analyzing politeness this way, I am informed by Pierre Bourdieu's account (1991) of the "economy of linguistic exchanges" and his observations on politeness wordings, euphemization, and other "attenuations." He says that command of such constructions goes to speakers at higher levels of the social order. And he says that speakers and listeners, by speaking and listening to one another, enact the interests and hierarchies implicit in their habits of address—identification, deference, domination. "Form," he says, "and the information it imparts condense and symbolize the entire structure of the social relation from which they derive their existence and efficacy" (80).[1] Ways of speaking enact the social order.

Being the kind of romance it is, *Hotel du Lac* puts the social order in a certain light, illuminating women's service to it. Efforts of address go toward a particular social distinction: a woman's fitness for marriage. In this context, a woman is interpretable through the practice of linguistic habits or the reading of supplementary codes of dress or posture. Language situates a woman in the social order and urges her toward incorporation.

Bourdieu says that linguistic "form" imparts "information" symbolic of social relations. This claim raises some questions. How does form do this? What are the forms? What is the information? In *Hotel du Lac*, the information is about the destiny of women, their sexual fate and the use of their sexuality. Politeness—a system for enacting deference and domination as well as solidarity—is the mechanism by which such information is conveyed through "form." And, in *Hotel du Lac*, the forms themselves are the features I have named and will demonstrate. But another question remains. Why are *these* forms—linguistic resources that have developed within English for communicative purposes—such eligible contributors to politeness? How are speakers repaid for the expense of such syntactic refinements of statements? Alone, in isolation, these forms seem to be socially neutral and not symbolically informative. But together, in *Hotel du Lac* and elsewhere in our experience of speaking and listening, they combine in symbolic formation. I will try to establish that each form donates its separate capacity to figure tacitness, mutual understanding, compelling but unspoken assumptions; each offers its capacity to achieve indirection, to erect invisible blocks to conduct, to at once baffle and sustain the flow of power—and thus together furnish the very materials of politeness. And I will show that these wordings operate beyond the expressions that are normally studied as politeness expressions—that is, honorifics, thanks, face-saving requests, compliments, and so on. I will show these wordings gathering in utterances beyond conversational exchange, behind the front lines of good manners, in narration and description, and I will suggest that they render these utterances equally symbolic of social advantage, deference, and order.[2] *Hotel du Lac* shapes interlocutory spaces where politeness arises to locate people in relation to one another, so they know their place. And study of the language of *Hotel du Lac* illuminates Brookner's sense of a particular set of social positions, those constituting marriage, as it recruits the unattached woman to the service of systems of domination and deference.

I focus on two passages. One (Appendix A) is the book's first two paragraphs. Describing a scene of "mysterious opacity," these paragraphs introduce Edith and locate her at the hotel. The other passage (Appendix B) occurs a few pages later. It accounts for the operation of the hotel itself, telling how things are done there, telling about the policies and protocols that govern this very polite world, a model of tact and propriety. To this setting, Edith has been dispatched, to be reabsorbed into the accepted orders of female sexuality.

PRESUPPOSING EXPRESSIONS

Technically speaking—and roughly—elements presupposed rather than asserted survive negation: they are removed from the domain of contradiction, sequestered from controversy.[3] Practically speaking, presupposed elements are those which the writer assumes to be in some way *familiar* to the reader. Presupposition marks shared knowledge, indicates conditions that are well known in some circles. These social circles are in effect maintained or created by the presupposing utterance itself and figured in it.

The beginnings of fiction often presuppose things. Characters are named as if the reader knows who they are; entities are referred to with definite determiners as if they are known to the reader. For example, the following could be the first sentence of a story:

Ramona walked out of the office with the man who promised to change her life.

Although the definite expressions mark the assumed familiarity of the three entities *Ramona*, *office*, and *man*, readers will not in fact know this person, what office this is, or who the man is. But they can *infer* the existence of Ramona, the office, and the promise by which the man is identified.

There is some efficiency to arrangements for inference—to presupposing rather than asserting the existence of entities. Even in everyday speech, efficiencies are achieved by presupposing rather than asserting. I can tell a new acquaintance—say, from a milieu that would typically include readers of this essay—"My cat brings in snakes and mice," entirely aware that she doesn't know I have a cat, but allowing her to *infer* that I do from the definiteness of the possessive determiner "my." In everyday speech, the ease or nonsurprisingness of the inference is a check on excessive presupposition: we can all easily assume a world in which people like me are apt to have a cat. It is a politeness to presuppose rather than assert—an acknowledgment of shared experience *not* to assert. By not asserting, I politely construct the listener as knowing the world in a certain way, a way that I share with her.[4]

At the beginning of *Hotel du Lac*, many entities are presupposed. In the first two sentences, readers must infer the existence of a particular "window," "garden," "lake," "brochure":

> From the window all that could be seen was a receding area of grey. It was to be supposed that beyond the grey garden, which seemed to sprout nothing but the stiffish leaves of some unfamiliar plant, lay the vast grey lake, spreading like an anaesthetic towards the invisible further shore, and beyond that, in imagination only, yet verified by the brochure, the peak of the Dent d'Oche, on which snow might already be slightly and silently falling. (7)

By consulting common knowledge of travel, readers can use "brochure" to infer that the window and garden belong to a hotel, this slender inference supported by the book's title and by "the tourists" and "the rates" in the third sentence. Sometimes the presupposing expressions themselves contain the material for inferring an identity for the things referred to. For example, "the dense cloud that descended for days at a time and then vanished without warning to reveal a new landscape, full of colour and incident" is like "the man who promised to change her life." Although we don't know the cloud or the man, we can consult the expressions themselves (their restrictive relatives) and first infer that there were descents and there was a promise and then use these inferences to infer the identity of cloud and man.

The first paragraph presupposes a lot, and calls for a lot of inferencing—but not to a degree uncommon in fiction. Actually, the sensation of inferencing may arouse a familiar feeling of beginning a story. But the second paragraph, in collusion with the narrative that follows, extends presupposition to an extreme that *is* uncommon—and, I will suggest, commandingly polite. In sentence 5 (s5), a referring expression introduces an event-entity as known: "the unfortunate lapse which had led to this brief exile." Yet nothing explains or enables us to infer what constituted the "lapse." Occurring in Edith's reported thought, other references to this event are equally opaque: "my lapse" (s7), "that apparently dreadful thing" (s11). Just as readers are constructed as having at hand resources for identifying "the window" or "the garden," they are now constructed as knowing how to identify an event that is first a "lapse" and then a "thing." In the first paragraph, we can gather materials for inferring that the window and garden belong to a hotel. But the second paragraph provides no practical materials for inference. Nor does the third paragraph or the fourth—or subsequent chapters, until, much later, chapter 9 begins with "the day of her wedding" (118), which is itself a presupposing expression requiring inference ("her wedding" » she had a wedding). Then, finally, we learn the nature of the lapse. Before she came to the hotel, before she met Mr. Neville and the Puseys, Edith had a wedding that she failed to attend. She backed out of marriage.

In this long-winded reluctance to assert, presupposition is suppression, a strategic shift from assertion to assumption, a knowing gesture toward an event so intensely regarded, so intensely interpreted that it evades mention, as politeness precludes mention of a *faux pas* but by the very preclusion observes it. So this paragraph has a confidential quality, the hushed tacitness of mutual understanding around a deeply regarded marriage behavior. These polite understandings are also constraints on readers, at their most extreme in the withholding of the wedding story, leaving readers with the unmistakable sensation of not knowing what Edith did but having to go on as if they do know.

Presupposing postures—which we might call presumption and recognize as a social stance—appear elsewhere in the narrative, too, enforcing similar constraints. The presupposing posture of definite expressions like "the unfortunate lapse" often appears in references to social conditions closely associated with the affairs of the privileged classes:

> What [the Hotel du Lac] had to offer was a mild form of sanctuary, an assurance of privacy, and *the protection and the discretion that attach themselves to blamelessness.* (14; emphasis added)

> [The Hotel du Lac] would never refuse a reasonable request from a new client, provided that the new client had *the sort of unwritten references required from an hotel of this distinction.* (15–16; emphasis added)

> [T]here seemed to be a sudden emanation of a rosy scent, signalling *the sort of preparation made by someone with a proper sense of her own presence.* (24; emphasis added)

[Alain] had *the set expression and also the expertise of a much older servant, a gentleman's gentleman.* (37; emphasis added)

[Mrs. Pusey and Jennifer] were extensively familiar with *the kind of resort which had recently but definitively gone out of fashion.* (42; emphasis added)

[Mrs. Pusey and Jennifer] were invariably to be found in the small salon that connected [their bedrooms] and which was agreeably filled with *the amenities which confident people accord themselves in strange places: a colour television, a basket of fruit, flowers, several splits of champagne.* (43; emphasis added)

In real life, speakers who sustain this way of talking can dominate others with calculated assumptions, presuming common ground to be taken for granted. At the same time as talk of this kind shields propositions from contradiction, it can intimidate listeners into compliance or pretense or silence them in fear of betraying their lack of privileged experience. (What *is* "the kind of resort" now "out of fashion"?)[5]

AGENTLESS EXPRESSIONS

As presupposing expressions assume rather than assert information, so other features suggest a tacitness, something known about conduct and social practice. Both passages resort often to passive constructions and particularly to agentless passives. The agentless passive suppresses an element of the proposition, namely, the doer of the action. Suppression leaves the reader to supply the agent from her knowledge of the world—for example, in "the rates were reduced" (s3) or "a land of prudently harvested plenty" (s4) in Appendix A, general knowledge of the hotel trade or agriculture enables us to infer who reduced the rates or who harvested crops. Agentlessness marks the action as in some way well known in the community assumed by the writer and, like presupposition, can achieve some efficiencies. But just as presupposition can contribute to politeness by not asserting, so do agentless passives have the potential to do this. Politeness operates in the choice of, for example,

The door was left unlocked

over

You left the door unlocked.

The agentless version depends on shared (but unspoken) knowledge of the doer of this action, and the unspokenness has the effect of arousing tacit knowledge of personal obligation. Although the first version is the more polite, it is also the more strategic, moving the addressee to contribute more from her knowledge of the world to the intention of the utterance.

In the first two paragraphs of *Hotel du Lac*, the passive voice appears at least once in every sentence but the last two, and in five of these eleven sentences, it occurs more than once. Passives occur continuously across both the paragraph boundary that separates the description of location from character and story as well as the threshold of Edith's reported thought: sentences 7–11 present an incidence of passives similar to that of s5–s6 or s1–s6. Moreover, agentlessness is a preferred form: twelve of seventeen passives are agentless (in sentence fragments below, emphasis added).

Paragraph 1   s1   all that could *be seen* (agentless)

                s2   It was to *be supposed* (agentless)
                         yet *verified* (agent: by *the brochure*)

                s3   the rates *were reduced* (agentless)
                         inhabitants . . . *were* frequently *rendered* taciturn (agent: by *the dense cloud*)

                s4   a land of prudently *harvested* plenty (agentless)

Paragraph 2   s5   she had *been presented* (agentless)
                         she had *been promised* (agentless)
                         she could *be counted upon* (agentless)

                s6   she . . . had allowed herself *to be driven* (agent: by *her friend and neighbour, Penelope Milne*)

                s7   I am not *to be allowed* (agentless)

                s8   I . . . *am judged* (agent: by *my friends*)
                         anything that *is put* (agentless)

                s9   I was not *to be allowed* (agentless)

               s10   My profile *was deemed* (agentless)
                         it *was agreed* (agent: by *those who thought they knew me*)

               s11   I shall *be allowed* (agentless)

The first paragraph's agentless forms depend on readers' knowledge of resort towns and harvests—a shared understanding of the world politely assumed. But the second paragraph's agentless forms move toward other domains of experience: circumstances of judgment, obligation, and permission surrounding the unattached woman. Whereas agented forms would expose the sources of such circumstances, agentlessness puts them out of reach. Politeness often has just this effect of withdrawing elements from areas of contest, leaving contradiction with no focus. And, as they appear to *distribute* force generally, as an atmospheric condition, agentless expressions diffuse or muffle the point of contact between the executors of the social order and the individual acted upon.[6] But contact is made nevertheless and executed through elliptical sites of shared understanding: like presupposition, agentlessness leaves an imprint of mutual assumptions.

The hotel passage in Appendix B is similarly saturated with agentless expressions, assuming rather than asserting the agents of practice at this very "traditional" establishment. The missing agents are hotel guests—"if [prolonged drinking were] thought" and "[drinking should] be conducted" (s7); "was heard" and "were glimpsed" (s8); "was known" (s18); and "be hired" and "be taken" (s26). These agents are hotel staff—"was implied" (s7); "be silenced" (s8); "were treated" (s13); "was made" (s14); "were provided for" and "[were] perused" (s15); "was assumed" (s16); "be dealt with" (s17); and "guaranteed" (s18). Or the missing agents can be guests and staff together, such as in "if any problems were encountered" (s17). Referring to tacit "standards" (s16), life at the hotel (where Edith is sent for a sort of reverse honeymoon, to get realigned with marriage values) lodges in the agentless passive, which takes for granted the actors in this orderly setting. And, whereas the hotel staff and the guests disappear from the surface of the sentence, mutely assumed in the hush of corridors and public rooms, the outside world is overt, and the agents of reckless doings are explicitly expressed: "the young of all nations hurtled off to the sun and the beaches, jamming the roads and the airports" (s28). These people do not stay at the Hotel du Lac.

MODALITY AND PROJECTION

Like presupposing and agentlessness expressions, modality and projection are linguistic resources available for communicative efficiencies. And, like presupposing and agentless expressions, they have qualities that make them generous contributors to politeness.

Most accounts of modality look for a unifying explanation of the modal auxiliaries—words such as *might*, *should*, and *could*. Beyond these, consistent explanations are sought for modal adverbs—words like *possibly, certainly, no doubt*, and *probably*—and for modalizing verbs such as *seem* and *appear* and, still more extensively, for projecting clauses that modalize propositions—*I believe / think / suppose*. Propositions are assigned to certain interested or contingent perspectives—*I see / know / understand*. Here, I draw on several sources to offer a simplified account designed to explain modality's contribution to politeness.[7]

Modal auxiliaries themselves fall into three categories: dynamic (estimates of capability (I *can* swim)); deontic (estimates of obligation and permission (I *should* swim)); epistemic (estimates of possibility (That *might* be a mountain)). Each type deflects statements from straight validity, from straight yes or no; each attenuates the claim. Halliday calls this attenuation "indeterminacy" (86); others (Sweetser, Talmy) have described it as registering *resistance* associated with the process or state described in the proposition or with the process of producing the statement itself. Some force pushes the claim away from straight yes or no, depositing blocks in its path and deflecting it to indirectness. So, in "all that *could* be seen" (rather than simply "all that was seen"), *could* modalizes the process of seeing by indicating its encounter with potential resistance to the process. The modality marks the statement as a speaker's estimate of the physical order—an individual agent's capabilities and the physical laws of the speaker's universe. In "she *should* be at home," *should* registers resistance to the subject's conduct. The modality marks the statement as an estimate of the social order—the community's regulation of behavior. In "snow *might* already be falling" (rather than "snow was already falling"), *might* registers resistance to the speaker's conviction: the speaker works from a situation of incomplete information, blocked from outright assertion and forced into indeterminacy. Such epistemic modality can be seen, according to Sweetser (51), as a "metaphorical mapping" of sociophysical experience onto mental process; it is an estimate of probability. So each modality is a reckoning—or, as Halliday says, an "opinion" (86) or, as I would say, an estimate or an inference from a certain position. But the premises that produce the estimate are suppressed (compare Chafe, 266). For example, in "she should be at home," the represented speaker consults principles to produce the modalized statement of appropriate behavior, but the principles themselves remain tacit and unspoken. (Speakers whose utterances cultivate a heavy incidence of deontic modals may enjoy particularly ready access to principles of social obligation and judgment.) Or, for another example, when Edith first observes the woman who will be identified as Mrs. Pusey, she sees her greeted by another woman: " 'Here I am,' carolled a young voice, and into the salon came a girl wearing rather tight white trousers (rather too tight, thought Edith) which outlined a bottom shaped like a large Victoria plum. 'There you are, darling,' cried the lady, who was, who *must* be her mother" (18; emphasis added). Epistemic modal *must* claims the highest probability for the proposition *the lady was her mother* but nevertheless reduces the proposition's determinacy by representing it as a product of inference from unspoken premises.

Projections (as in "rather too tight, *thought Edith*") identify the inferring agent (although not the premises). So modalized "you might be too late" becomes "I *think* you are too late," and tardiness or tightness a reckoning from an identified position and contingent on that point of view.

Modality and projection are both widely observed as contributing to politeness expressions in English. For example, modalities can join projection to make a command more deferential, inscribing the relative positions of speaker and listener: "*I wonder* if you *would be able* to feed my cat." Or epistemic modality can join an agentless passive to soften bad news and prepare the statement for work in the social network: "*It seems* that your application *has been rejected*." At first these statements appear to be modalized on behalf of the listener. Using the little blocks that attenuate the utterance, the speaker offers to secure the listener from insistence or repudiation by reducing the determinacy of her own statement, and taking herself as blocked and impeded. But politeness modalities can protect the speaker as much as they respect the listener, investing the expression with advantages for the speaker or confirming advantages the speaker already enjoys. As Bourdieu's account of linguistic exchanges suggests, politeness is more than respectfulness (83–85): it is an imprint of social distinction and hierarchy, and frequently offerings are actually appropriations. So the range of politeness modality stretches from apparent deference to intimidation—depending on the position from which the statement is produced. Advantageously positioned, an official at a desk can summon the implicit legitimacy of the bureaucratic order with this modal of certainty: "You have *no doubt* completed the necessary forms." While the modality of *no doubt* registers epistemic limitations—the official doesn't *know* whether the listener has completed the forms—he suggests that *his* understanding of the world leads him to infer that she has (the filling out of forms is a universal obligation to which all reasonable people submit). Or a uniformed constable can use projection to work toward domination: "I understand that you have been causing trouble." The literal surface of these two statements attenuates or partially blocks the proposition. But through another level accessible from knowledge of the social order, the modalities actually enforce and dominate. For a listener who recognizes the desk, the uniform, and the "social relation" in question and contributes this knowledge to interpretation of the utterance, the linguistic forms symbolize the interests and distinctions inherent in the situation.

Modality and projection contribute to politeness the silent inferences that estimate resistance to action and knowledge—resistances perhaps naturally continuous with the framing of the social order, for the blocks to directness are symbolically and strategically deployed in politeness, to be interpreted in light of social understandings of speakers' and listeners' relative positions, to be read along the scale from deference to domination. At the same time, both modality and projection locate statements as contingent—as coming from somewhere, as having been produced by someone interested in their reception. These syntactic refinements extend speakers along vectors of value out into the social space where the statements operate.

The two paragraphs that begin *Hotel du Lac* are impeccably outfitted in modality and projection, groomed and ready for polite company, their statements attenuated, contingent, indirect (in all fragments below, emphasis added):

Paragraph 1	S1	all that *could* be **seen**
	S2	It was *to be* **supposed**
		which *seemed* to sprout
		snow *might* already be . . . falling
	S3	—
	S4	—
Paragraph 2	S5	an access of good will *could* pierce
		she *could* be counted upon
		this *apparently* unpopulated place
		she *should* have been at home
	S6	—
	S7	I am not *to be* allowed . . . she **thought**
		why *should* I be
	S8	who *should* **know** better and am **judged** . . . I **understand**
	S9	I was not *to be* allowed
	S10	was **deemed** . . . was **agreed** . . . it *should* stay that way
		who **thought**
	S11	*no doubt* . . . I **notice**
		I *shall* be allowed
		that *apparently* dreadful thing
		frankly
	S12	—
	S13	—

This is a domain of resistances, physical and social obstructions, epistemic occlusions, estimates of the world from unexpressed premises and contingent positions, each position itself an object of interpretation, just as the position of the constable or the official is such an object, except that here the context for interpretation is not bureaucracy or policing but marriage. Seemingly beyond conversational exchanges of requests, offers, or small articles of talk, the statements of these paragraphs are nevertheless fully indexed for social use. In the account of the view from the hotel and of Edith's recent error and its correction, propositions are blocked and deflected into indeterminacy by modalities and projections, so many of these projections themselves agentless and thus dispersed into the social atmosphere. Finally the exchange value of these polite wordings emerges outright in Edith's reported thoughts: "I make no claims for my particular sort of writing, although *I understand* that it is doing quite well" (s8; emphasis added). Despite privacy, Edith's estimate of her own worth is dressed up for the social occasions immanent in the language surrounding her marriage "lapse." The projecting clause deflects Edith's claim for herself, making it a more acceptable article of exchange, executing the universal politeness strategy of self-humbling.

At the hotel itself (Appendix B), the practice that refers to tacit "standards" (s16) is consolidated in modalities of obligation: "prolonged drinking . . . was not *comme il faut*, and if thought absolutely necessary *should* be conducted [elsewhere]" (s7; emphasis added to "should"); "all household noises *had to* be silenced" (s8; emphasis added). Deontic modals express a social inference, with both agent of inference and premises suppressed (Who imposes these rules? From what principles have they been derived?) But even then they can still be rather direct-sounding, unless further deflected and distributed by suppression of the agent of the action, as here: Who is liable to drink or to make noises? Erased from the surface of the expression, drinkers and noisy people are left to identify their personal obligation themselves, in this way contributing to the intention of the utterance.

But beyond the sound of syntactic deflection, we may hear something else, something arranged for our appreciation. Just within earshot is the irony of the moralization of the hotel business. These rules are pretentious—as well as being morally inflationary. A community that spends so much of its ethical currency on minor conduct may find that currency seriously devalued.

And still within earshot are the ironies of the passage's epistemic modalities. In the epistemically modalized statements, the resistance to the proposition, the force working against it, remains as strong as—and maybe stronger than—the proposition. For example, the modality of "naturally" registers the proposition that follows as predictable from the speaker's experience, encoding that experience as shared with the listener: "*Naturally*, no attempt was made to entertain [hotel guests]" (s14; emphasis added). But, despite the force of "naturally," it is still not so inevitable that the hotel provide no distractions. Many people might not be captured by this offer of common ground and might still expect a resort to offer amusements. Similarly, the modality of "of course" suggests that, from a point of view that the speaker politely constructs as shared by the listener, the qualities attributed to the Hotel du Lac are good ones: "And *of course* it was an excellent hotel" (s23; emphasis added). Yet many people still might not consider this hotel so "excellent." Although we are told "of course," we still entertain resistance to its claim—and think perhaps not so entirely excellent.

"Of course" is the most noticeable of epistemic modalities in *Hotel du Lac*—and at the Hotel du Lac. Writing to her lover, Edith reports the obligations that emanate from Mrs. Pusey on her birthday: "And of course we could hardly leave Mrs Pusey on her own after dinner" (108). On Edith's unfulfilled wedding day, "she was condemned out of hand, of course" (132). But as an instrument of presumption, "of course" belongs most fittingly to Mrs. Pusey, the excellent hotel's most excellent guest: " 'Of course, I have everything delivered,' she added" (41). "As most of Mrs Pusey's sentences began with the words 'of course,' they had a range of tranquil confidence which somehow occluded any attempt to introduce an opinion of [Edith's] own" (55). Of all the adverbs of modality, "of course" is one of the most strategic. At one level it says, "You know *x*—this is knowledge we share." But at another level it says, "*Behave* as if you know *x*." The compelling signal registers the speaker's perception of potential resistance and dominates or disarms that resistance, imposing constraints on the listener to profit the speaker. While "of course" appears to offer common ground, it is actually an appropriation of the listener's experience. Mrs. Pusey and "of course" are ironically ascendant.

Features of these passages—presupposing and agentless expressions, modality and projection—furnish the materials of politeness, refining statements for public use, those refinements ordering social relations. In this kind of romance, marriage is the conclusive social relation, as it is in forerunners of the modern version, in "Cinderella," for example, or "The

Goose Girl." Marriage is the means by which the community can recognize and incorporate the unattached woman of doubtful origins. At the brink of marriage, Edith turns away, and this gesture of sexual self-determination excites the full force of the social order, enacted in all the wordings that encode deference and domination. But how is it that politeness expressions can drift so effortlessly to irony? Perhaps, and simply, politeness in itself always has ironic possibility. And the novel of manners (so often taking marriage as its concern) naturally cultivates this ironic possibility.

As a syntactic tissue that smoothes over social obtrusions and sharp edges of power, politeness removes rank and submission from overt places, from areas of contest where disturbances can erupt. In so doing, politeness locates meaning below the surface, at tacit levels where irony lives, nourished by experience of incongruous pretenses. Accordingly, presupposition can knowingly register its opposite: a presumptuous speaker can know very well that her listener is not familiar with "the kind of resort which had recently but definitively gone out of fashion." And the listener can know that the speaker knows and still silently collaborate in the pretense, having no purchase on means of contradiction, left with only ironic awareness that power is at work. Similarly, while agentless expressions appear to impersonalize and disinterestedly distribute the expression of obligations and precepts, they in effect overtake their object all the more efficiently by preserving, just out of reach, the well-understood advantage of the speaker. Habits of deference can ironically enact domination—this condition being most tangible in the way the hotel's service to its patrons actually recruits them to the service of its own distinguished reputation. And, while modality and projection block propositions from direct routes, seemingly to secure the listener at the expense of the speaker, they can actually be deployed to the profit of the speaker: each attenuation of an advantaged speaker's statements can push the advantage into interlocutory spaces and fill them up. So, indeterminacy can in fact determine, as it does here, where M. Huber, proprietor of the Hotel du Lac, reads the register and interprets the entries according to long-standing but unspoken premises: "One new arrival. Hope, Edith Johanna. An unusual name for an English lady. *Perhaps* not entirely English. *Perhaps* not entirely a lady. Recommended, *of course*. But in this business one never knew" (23; emphasis added). Epistemically modalized, M. Huber's inferences produce indeterminate statements, delicately noncommittal, suitable for polite gossip. But this indeterminacy is only a surface phenomenon. Deeper, Edith's status is confirmed. One does know.

With an ear for discrepancies between polite surfaces and other levels, we can hear ironies in all the refinements and courtesies that attend compulsion and judgment. But the irony of style goes further. Bourdieu's ideas of language and symbolic power predict that the dominated person will contribute herself and her speech to the scheme of domination. This in itself is a radically ironic condition and a cruel disappointment of normal hopes. It is demonstrated in Edith's work as a writer of women's romance. And it is more broadly demonstrated in the way the language of politeness colonizes even Edith's own mentality.

The wordings that render Edith's own thoughts belong to the same idiom as the hotel's traditional assumptions and estimates of "character." Like the language of the book's beginning and the account of hotel life, Edith's reflections on, for example, the Puseys returning from a day of shopping are modalized and projected, referring tacitly to assumed standards that she applies on behalf of public interests, minimizing and attenuating her judgments in ways that increase their politeness values:[8] "Jennifer was a splendid specimen, *she acknowledged*, an effortless testimonial to her mother's care. Her large fair face, *perhaps a little too* sparsely populated by a cluster of *rather small* features, shone with the ruddy health of an unsuspecting child. . . . Her *rather plump* body was, *Edith saw*, set forth by clothes which were *far from* artless and *possibly too narrow*" (54; emphasis added). Edith's observations start out by applying unexpressed standards for the proportions of the female face and then verge toward propriety and moral measure: Jennifer has dressed herself not quite blamelessly. Edith is similarly exacting in calculating the success of Mrs. Pusey's nearly excessive birthday clothes (105).

These standards that Edith politely exercises also take her as their object. Her cardigan is wrong; her wedding outfit is looked over by "friends." And Mr. Neville, having measured Edith, finds her eligible for his proposal. Describing his household, he tells her, " 'You would *fit* perfectly into that setting' " (164; emphasis added). Yet the fit is ultimately insulting, the marriage proposal a bleak forecast of polite occlusions and suppressions.

Although Edith does not benefit from these standards, she enlists in their service, reproducing as well as she can from her disadvantaged position the assumptions and moral disposition of the Hotel du Lac. But, even with its archive of unwritten references and blameless behaviors, the Hotel du Lac is, after all, only a public lodging house, a place where people rent rooms, and its traditions only the practice of a certain kind of housekeeping, sustained by a presumptuous way of speaking. This language cannot address the heart of Edith's predicament—her memories of her mother.

The wordings of politeness, and the romance mode itself, urge unattached Edith toward incorporation in the social order. But athwart the urge toward incorporation lies another trajectory, one originating in experience prior to the social order, in childhood and the temper of the parental bond. This original experience is often a concern in Anita Brookner's novels, rendered as haunting persistences: the child-mother in *Providence*, mild partner in a scarcely consummated life; the parents' obliteration in *Latecomers*; the dingy, heedless home in *A Start in Life*; the flooding misery of unspeakable pain in *A Friend from England*; even the vestigial serenity of early memories in *Brief Lives*. In *Hotel du Lac* the discharge of this original experience is not absorbed by the language of polite exchange.

One night, in a letter to her lover, Edith "[writes] up" the Puseys, entertainingly, lightly. But the writing up fails to dispose her recent view of "the two women lovingly entwined as they saw her to the door to say good-night," and early memories intrude, prior and "painful" (48). They arrive unwelcome, rough guests unacclimatized to the atmosphere of the Hotel du Lac, syntactically abrupt at the heels of the recollection of the Puseys at their door:

> For there was love there, love between mother and daughter, and physical contact, and collusion about being pretty, none of which she herself had ever known. Her strange mother, Rosa, that harsh disappointed woman, that former beauty who raged so unsuccessfully against her fate, deliberately, willfully letting herself go, slatternly and scornful, mocking her pale silent daughter who slipped so modestly in and out of her aromatic bedroom, bringing the cups of coffee which her mother deliberately spilled. And shouting, "Too weak! Too weak! All of you, too weak!" Sighing for Vienna, which had known her young and brilliant, and not fat and slovenly, as she was now. And weeping for her dead sister, Anna. (48)

"Her strange mother" trails three appositives—"Rosa," "that harsh disappointed woman," and "that former beauty"—the last extending to a long restrictive relative. But "her strange mother" is itself syntactically stranded: that is, it bears no structural relation to the preceding sentence.[9] From this abrupt beginning—unanchored in its surroundings, syntactically foreign, gauche—the long relative "who [had] raged so unsuccessfully against her fate" spawns three subjectless nonfinite clauses, the first two taking "mother" as subject, and the third, "daughter": "willfully letting herself go," "mocking her pale silent daughter," and "bringing the cups of coffee." The three fragments which follow are each governed by this syntactic pattern of subjectless nonfinite clauses: "And shouting," "Sighing for Vienna," and "And weeping." With each participial fragment, "her strange mother" is reactivated as subject, as if, after each attempt at closure, the mother is resurgent, claiming more territory.

Once these tough, blunt pieces of sentences arrive, the story of Edith's childhood then comes out over the next two pages (48–50)—without the modalities and agentless and presupposing expressions that characterize the account of life at the Hotel du Lac. The story of the mother's "aromatic bedroom" and Grossmama's "grim apartment," the rage and fury of hard-bosomed women, and the tears of "seven-year-old Edith" cannot be assumed in tacit language. Nor is this story susceptible to the modalities and projections that attenuate attributes and events. It defies polite speech, like a rude remark amid courtesies.

Women who back out of marriage make men laughingstocks. Edith's bridegroom Geoffrey becomes one (131) when Edith goes right by the registry office; Mr. Neville's wife made him ridiculous (166) when she too obviously looked for her pleasure elsewhere. Amid the laughter, neither courtesies nor tacit gestures can retrieve the man from his ignominy. But soon enough the laughter dies down, and the rumors of polite speech resume, in *Hotel du Lac* situating women properly in relation to marriage, the institution that (along with shopping, according to Bourdieu [71, 83]) most efficiently incorporates them into the social order.

Edith's sudden departure removes her from the course of talk at the Hotel du Lac. By some measures, this is a costly decision—not only in terms of forsaken status but also in terms of the loneliness she thereby embraces as she turns her back on Mr. Neville's proposal and goes home to the intermittent attentions of a married lover. Whether Edith in her solitary state is more or less vulnerable to the harsh memories of childhood, I would not say, for she has no history or future except as linguistic matter and the interpretive recognition it can excite in readers. But insofar as that recognition reproduces experience of the social uses of language, Edith's circumstances might call on us to witness the failure of adulthood—a state concerned with social distinction and systems of advantage or surrender—to redeem the woeful child. Prior to politeness, voiced in another style, syntactically driven by original forces rough and obscure rather than refined and opaque, the memories of childhood abandon Edith to the strange (but perhaps not altogether rare) status of adult orphanhood. She inherits sayings of which she is custodian but which she can scarcely use to social advantage. She inherits her father's maxim: "This is when character tells"—"character" used in a sense different from that current at the Hotel du Lac. And his resigned valediction, preliminary to death: "'Just clearing the decks.'" And her mother's shrieks, in another tongue, "*Schrecklich! Schrecklich! . . . Ach, du Schreck!*" (49).

APPENDIX A

[1.] From the window all that could be seen was a receding area of grey. [2.] It was to be supposed that beyond the grey garden, which seemed to sprout nothing but the stiffish leaves of some unfamiliar plant, lay the vast grey lake, spreading like an anaesthetic towards the invisible further shore, and beyond that, in imagination only, yet verified by the brochure, the peak of the Dent d'Oche, on which snow might already be slightly and silently falling. [3.] For it was late September, out of season; the tourists had gone, the rates were reduced, and there were few inducements for visitors in this small town at the water's edge, whose inhabitants, uncommunicative to begin with, were frequently rendered taciturn by the dense cloud that descended for days at a time and then vanished without warning to reveal a new landscape, full of colour and incident: boats skimming on the lake, passengers at the landing stage, an open air market, the outline of the gaunt remains of a thirteenth-century castle, seams of white on the far mountains, and on the cheerful uplands to the south a rising backdrop of apple trees, the fruit sparkling with emblematic significance. [4.] For this was a land of prudently harvested plenty, a land which had conquered human accidents, leaving only the weather distressingly beyond control.

[5.] Edith Hope, a writer of romantic fictions under a more thrusting name, remained standing at the window, as if an access of good will could pierce the mysterious opacity with which she had been presented, although she had been promised a tonic cheerfulness, a climate devoid of illusions, an utterly commonsensical, not to say pragmatic, set of circumstances—quiet hotel, excellent cuisine, long walks, lack of excitement, early nights—in which she could be counted upon to retrieve her serious and hardworking personality and to forget the unfortunate lapse which had led to this brief exile, in this apparently unpopulated place, at this slowly darkening time of the year, when she should have been at home. . . . [6.] But it was home, or, rather, "home," which had become inimical all at once, so that she had acquiesced, rather frightened at what was happening to her, when her friends had suggested a short break, and had allowed herself to be driven to the airport by her friend and neighbour, Penelope Milne, who, tight-lipped, was prepared to forgive her only on condition that she disappeared for a decent length of time and came back older, wiser, and properly apologetic. [7.] For I am not to be allowed my lapse, as if I were an artless girl, she thought; and why should I be? [8.] I am a serious woman who should know better and am judged by my friends to be past the age of indiscretion; several people have remarked upon my physical resemblance to Virginia Woolf; I am a householder, a ratepayer, a good plain cook, and a deliverer of typescripts well before the deadline; I sign anything that is put in front of me; I never telephone my publisher; and I make no claims for my particular sort of writing, although I understand that it is doing quite well. [9.] I have held this rather dim and trusting personality together for a considerable length of time, and although I have certainly bored others I was not to be allowed to bore myself. [10.] My profile was deemed to be low and it was agreed by those who thought they knew me that it should stay that way. [11.] And no doubt after a curative stay in this grey solitude (and I notice that the leaves of that plant are quite immobile) I shall be allowed back, to resume my peaceable existence, and to revert to what I was before I did that apparently dreadful thing, although, frankly, once I had done it I didn't give it another thought. [12.] But I do now. [13.] Yes. (7–9)

APPENDIX B

[1.] The Hotel du Lac (Famille Huber) was a stolid and dignified building, a house of repute, a traditional establishment, used to welcoming the prudent, the well-to-do, the retired, the self-effacing, the respected patrons of an earlier era of tourism. [2.] It had made little effort to smarten itself up for the passing trade which it had always despised. [3.] Its furnishings, although austere, were of excellent quality, its linen spotless, its service impeccable. [4.] Its reputation among knowledgeable professionals attracted apprentices of good character who had a serious interest in the hotel trade, but this was the only concession it made to a recognition of its own resources. [5.] As far as guests were concerned, it took a perverse pride in its very absence of attractions, so that any visitor mildly looking for a room would be puzzled and deflected by the sparseness of the terrace, the muted hush of the lobby, the absence of piped music, public telephones, advertisements for scenic guided tours, or notice boards directing one to the amenities of the town. [6.] There was no sauna, no hairdresser, and certainly no glass cases displaying items of jewellery; the bar was small and dark, and its austerity did not encourage people to linger. [7.] It was implied that prolonged drinking, whether for purposes of business or as a personal indulgence, was not *comme il faut*, and if thought absolutely necessary should be conducted either in the privacy of one's suite or in the more popular establishments where such leanings were not unknown. [8.] Chambermaids were rarely encountered after ten o'clock in the morning, by which time all household noises had to be silenced; no vacuuming was heard, no carts of dirty linen were glimpsed, after that time. [9.] A discreet rustle announced the reappearance of the maids to turn down the beds and tidy the rooms once the guests had finished changing to go down to dinner. [10.] The only publicity was the word of mouth recommendations of patrons of long standing.

[11.] What it had to offer was a mild form of sanctuary, an assurance of privacy, and the protection and the discretion that attach themselves to blamelessness. [12.] This last quality being less than attractive to a surprising number of people, the Hotel du Lac was usually half empty, and at this time of the year, at the end of the season, was resigned to catering for a mere handful of guests before closing its doors for the winter. [13.] The few visitors who were left from the modest number who had taken their decorous holiday in the high summer months were, however, treated with the same courtesy and deference as if they were treasured patrons of long standing, which, in some cases, they were. [14.] Naturally, no attempt was made to entertain them. [15.] Their needs were provided for and their characters perused with equal care. [16.] It was assumed that they would live up to the hotel's standards, just as the hotel would live up to theirs. [17.] And if any problems were encountered, those problems would be dealt with discreetly. [18.] In this way the hotel was known as a place which was unlikely to attract unfavourable attention, a place guaranteed to provide a restorative sojourn for those whom life had mistreated or merely fatigued. [19.] Its name and situation figured in the card indexes of those whose business it is to know such things. [20.] Certain doctors knew it, many solicitors knew it, brokers and accountants knew it. [21.] Those families who benefit from the periodic absence of one of their more troublesome members treasured it. [22.] And the word got round.

[23.] And of course it was an excellent hotel. [24.] And its situation on the lake was agreeable. [25.] The climate was not brilliant, but in comparison with other, similar, resorts, it was equable. [26.] The resources of the little town were not extensive, but cars could be hired, excursions could be taken, and the walking was pleasant if unexciting. [27.] The scenery, the view, the mountain, were curiously unemphatic, as if delineated in the watercolours of an earlier period. [28.] While the young of all nations hurtled off to the sun and the beaches, jamming the roads and the airports, the Hotel du Lac took a quiet pride, and sometimes it was very quiet indeed, in its isolation from the herd, knowing that it had a place in the memory of its old friends, knowing too that it would never refuse a reasonable request from a new client, provided that the new client had the sort of unwritten references required from an hotel of this distinction, and that the request had come from someone whose name was already on the Huber family's files, most of which went back to the beginning of the century. (13–16)

NOTES

1. Bourdieu's sense of politeness in many ways matches what Brown and Levinson describe in their exhaustive and groundbreaking work on "politeness phenomena." Like Bourdieu, they insist on the social significance of styles of expression: "We believe that patterns of message construction, or 'ways of putting things,' or simply language usage, are part of the very stuff that social relationships are made of (or, as some would prefer, crucial parts of the expressions of social relations)" (60). But their theoretical assumption of mutuality ("In general, people cooperate [and assume each other's cooperation] in maintaining face in interaction, such cooperation being based on the mutual vulnerability of face" [66]), which is essential and productive in the context of their research, directs attention away from the reciprocal of deference—domination. Bourdieu's core insights are more sympathetic to my purposes. Nevertheless, Brown and Levinson's inventory of politeness offers many valuable supports to my analysis of the occurrence of the forms I have identified in *Hotel du Lac*.

2. Although Brown and Levinson concentrate on speech acts that call on the addressee to act or react in some face-threatening situation—that is, one in which positive wants (desire for approval) or negative wants (desire to be unimpeded) are at stake—they acknowledge that the conventions which render these speech acts polite can appear where wants are not so obviously at stake: "*The wants . . . are [not] the only motivation for using these linguistic means*. Indeed, there are very general social motivations for using various techniques of positive politeness and negative politeness; they operate, respectively, as a kind of social accelerator and social brake for decreasing or increasing social distance in relationships, regardless of [Face Threatening Acts]" (98; emphasis in original), and "We should . . . stress that the wants . . . are not the only motivations a speaker may have for using the linguistic realizations characteristic of negative politeness. The outputs are all forms useful in general for social 'distancing' (just as positive-politeness realizations are forms for minimizing social distance); they are therefore likely to be used whenever a speaker wants to put a social brake on to the course of his interaction" (135). Each of these observations, however, has to do with contexts of exchange, where speech is directly addressed, as in conversation or letters.

3. For example, the statement,

> The examination is scheduled for Tuesday.

presupposes

> There is an examination.

If the sentence is negated, the presupposition is not defeated:

> The examination is not scheduled for Tuesday.

still presupposes "There is an examination." My account of presupposition develops from Prince, Clark and Marshall, Levinson, Sperber and Wilson, and Green, relying in particular on Prince's account of assumed familiarity.

4. It would be a slightly different matter perhaps if I said "My ocelot brings in snakes and mice," without first asserting that I have an ocelot. This might sound presumptuous or showy, as if this remarkable circumstance is taken for granted where I come from.

5. Such presupposing expressions abound in a wide range of everyday genres. Recipes, for example, can instruct you to "Ask your fishmonger to scale the bass," when in fact you have no fishmonger and begin to feel the lack. Or academic discussions can presuppose a realm of experience—"the sort of argument Derrida favors"—as a standard for membership in the social circle circumscribed by the utterance.

6. Identifying impersonalization as a politeness strategy, Brown and Levinson observe that the "passive coupled with a rule of agent deletion is perhaps the means *par excellence* in English of avoiding reference to persons involved in [Face Threatening Acts]" (199). Among the examples they offer is the transformation of "I expect" to "It is expected." Developing their observations, we can see that the transformation also has the effect of appearing to distribute the source of the condition beyond the (suppressed) agent—to something like "it is *generally* expected." Agentlessness has this effect especially when the passivization acts on a verb of mental process. In the transformation of, say, "I know the Hotel is a fine establishment" to "the Hotel du Lac is known to be a fine establishment," the proposition *the Hotel du Lac is a fine establishment* seems to get distributed as much more widely held, so that a single position spreads to general authority.

7. These sources are Halliday, Chafe, Latour and Woolgar, Talmy, Palmer, and Sweetser.

8. Brown and Levinson remark on minimizing as a politeness strategy (181–83). An imposition can be minimized in, for example, an elaborate wording such as, "I just want to ask you if I can borrow a tiny bit of paper" (182). Such strategies are also familiar in the kinds of transformations that would take, for example, "your trousers are too short" and project and modalize to produce "I see that your trousers might possibly be too short." Although both statements (politely) assume a taken-for-granted standard for trouser length, the second carries the speaker's application of the standard right to its target, courteously.

9. Fragments are not uncommon elsewhere in the narrative, but rarely if ever are they

this kind of intrusion. Typically, they are continuations of previous sentences, broken off from them but still structurally governed by them or, as in the passage cited above from M. Huber's reported thoughts on hotel register, although elliptical, easily supplied with the missing materials.

WORKS CITED

Bourdieu, Pierre. *Language and Symbolic Power*. Ed. John B. Thompson. Trans. Gino Raymond and Matthew Adamson. Cambridge, Mass.: Harvard University Press, 1991.

Brookner, Anita. *Brief Lives*. London: Jonathan Cape, 1990.

——. *A Friend from England*. London: Grafton, 1987.

——. *Hotel du Lac*. London: Triad Grafton, 1985.

——. *Latecomers*. London: Grafton, 1988.

——. *Providence*. London: Jonathan Cape, 1982.

——. *A Start in Life*. London: Jonathan Cape, 1981.

Brown, Penelope, and Stephen Levinson. "Universals in Language Usage: Politeness Phenomena." *Questions and Politeness: Strategies in Social Interaction*. Cambridge: Cambridge University Press, 1978.

Chafe, Wallace. "Evidentiality in English Conversation and Academic Writing." *Evidentiality: The Linguistic Coding of Epistemology*. Ed. W. Chafe and J. Nichols. Norwood, NJ: Ablex, 1986. 261–72.

Clark, Herbert, and Catherine Marshall. "Definite Reference and Mutual Knowledge." *Elements of Discourse Understanding*. Ed. A. Joshi, B. Webber, and I. Sag. Cambridge: Cambridge University Press, 1981. 10–63.

Green, Georgia M. *Pragmatics and Natural Language Understanding*. Hillsdale, NJ: Lawrence Erlbaum, 1989.

Halliday, M. A. K. *An Introduction to Functional Grammar*. London: Edward Arnold, 1985.

Latour, Bruno, and Steve Woolgar. 1979. *Laboratory Life: The Construction of Scientific Fact*. Princeton: Princeton University Press, 1986.

Levinson, Stephen C. *Pragmatics*. Cambridge: Cambridge University Press, 1983.

Palmer, F. R. *Modality and the English Modals*. London: Longman, 1990.

Prince, Ellen. "Toward a Taxonomy of Given-New Information." *Radical Pragmatics*. Ed. Peter Cole. New York: Academic Press, 1981. 223–55.

Sperber, Dan, and Deidre Wilson. *Relevance: Communication and Cognition*. Cambridge, Mass.: Harvard University Press, 1986.

Sweetser, Eve E. *From Etymology to Pragmatics: Metaphorical and Cultural Aspects of Semantic Structure*. Cambridge: Cambridge University Press, 1990.

Talmy, Leonard. "Force Dynamics in Language and Cognition." *Cognitive Science* 2 (1988): 49–100.

angela carter's new eve(lyn)

De / En-Gendering Narrative

alison lee

n Jeanette Winterson's *Written on the Body*, the narrative voice is of indeterminate gender and, despite various clues, remains undecidable throughout the novel. At one point, describing lovemaking, the narrator makes an address to "you," a you who could be either the lover or the reader or maybe both, and the language of the encounter is the language of torture: "Who taught you to write in blood on my back? Who taught you to use your hands as branding irons? You have scored your name into my shoulders, referenced me with your mark" (89). It is almost impossible to read this novel without making some guesses as to whether the narrator is male or female, yet to do so is to reveal one's own assumptions about language, perception, voice, and narrative structure and whether any of them reveal maleness or femaleness. When gender is an inscription written on the body, it becomes also a form of violence, and for this reason the narrator prefers to be covert: "Written on the body is a secret code only visible in certain lights; the accumulations of a lifetime gather there. In places the palimpsest is so heavily worked that the letters feel like braille. I like to keep my body rolled up away from prying eyes. Never unfold too much, tell the whole story" (89).

Angela Carter, in *The Passion of New Eve*, foregrounds similar problems of gender identification, but here sex and gender are overt and yet still unstable. This novel about a man who is surgically changed into a biological woman does indeed "tell the whole story," and does so by making the violence of gender inscription on the body quite clear. Nonetheless, the reader, even with the whole story in front of her or him, is in a similarly perplexing position if she or he tries to pin down whether the narrative voice or the focalization is male or female. This is not to suggest, in either case, that the narrator is female because the narrator is indeterminate or absent or lacking some firm direction. Instead, both novels are examples of what Rachael Blau DuPlessis defines as a feminist writing practice:

> One may assert that any female cultural practice that makes the "meaning production process" itself "the site of struggle" may be considered feminist. These authors are "feminist" because they construct a variety of oppositional strategies to the depiction of gender institutions in narrative. A writer expresses dissent from an ideological formation by attacking elements of narrative that repeat, sustain or embody the values and attitudes in question. So after breaking the sentence, a rupture with the internalization of the authorities and voices of dominance, the woman writer will create that further rupture . . . breaking the sequence—the expected order. (34)

Indeterminacy in *The Passion of New Eve* is a challenge to the reader to recognize where the ruptures occur, where centers cannot hold, and where ideological formations are undermined in the narrative. Given that the narrator, Eve, has been male and is female, it is not surprising that the narrative voice should also be a site of struggle: "Masculine and feminine are correlatives which involve one another. I am sure of that—the quality and its negation are locked in necessity. But what the nature of masculine and the nature of feminine might be, whether they involve male and female . . . that I do not know. Though I have been both man and woman, still I do not know the answer to these questions. Still they bewilder me" (149–50).

Just before his unwilling transformation into a biological woman, Evelyn asks: "Does a change in the coloration of the rind alter the taste of a fruit?" (68). Despite the assurance of one of his captors that a "change in the appearance will restructure the essence" (68), the novel is much less certain. It explores the problems of appearance and essence, examining the process by which Evelyn learns to adapt his female body to his male history. Eve, as Evelyn becomes, has to learn to be a woman because she is seen by others—and eventually sees herself—as a woman.

Beulah (in Hebrew, marriage), the underground technological womb from which Eve is born, is a city of single-breasted women in the service of Mother, "the Great Parricide . . . the Castratrix of the Phallocentric Universe" (67). Her plan to make New Eve the virgin mother of the "Messiah of the Antithesis" (67) by impregnating Eve with Evelyn's sperm has the larger goal of the "feminisation of Father Time" (67). To this end, Mother seeks to help Evelyn into his womanhood through a program of rudimentary "psycho-surgery" (68). The process suggests that appearance alone is not quite enough to produce essence. Evelyn's education consists of video-tapes of "every single Virgin and Child that had ever been painted," of nonphallic imagery "such as sea anemones opening and closing," and, "to subliminally instil the maternal instinct," of images of "cats with kittens, vixens with cubs" (72). It involves telling stories about men's treatment of women's bodies: female circumcision, foot binding, suttee, "the horrors my old sex had perpetrated on my new one" (73), as Eve puts it. But most of all and particularly because Eve's new form is one "taken from a con-sensus agreement on the physical nature of an ideal woman drawn up from a protracted study of the media" (78), the psychosurgery involves showing the movies of Tristessa St. Ange, "the most beautiful woman in the world" (5). Eve thus learns to be woman as cinema spectacle, framed, as it were, "by the look of the camera as icon, or object of the gaze: an image made to be looked at by the spectator, whose look is relayed by the look of the male character(s)" (de Lauretis, 139). In effect, Eve learns that she must accept being looked at as Evelyn looked at women.

In *Alice Doesn't*, Teresa de Lauretis makes the point that "The project of feminist cinema . . . is not so much 'to make visible the invisible,' as the saying goes, or to destroy vision altogether, as to construct another (object of) vision and the conditions of visibility for a different social subject" (67–68). Such a project would entail an articulation of "the relations of the female subject to representation, meaning and vision" (68) and would raise the question of how to "reconstruct or organize vision from the 'impossi-ble' space of female desire . . . and how to represent the terms of her double identification in the process of looking at her looking" (69). Arguably, de Lauretis's comments on film—and film theory in general—might also find a useful application in theorizing a feminist narratology. *The Passion of New Eve*, in which the narrator (Eve) tells her/his story as both a man and a woman, in which she looks at him looking at women, and in which she learns to be a woman from the way she is looked at, seems an appropriate example from which to begin theorizing.

Given the importance of who sees and who is seen in the novel, the aspect of narratology particularly pertinent to an examination of gender as Carter presents it is focalization. Rimmon-Kenan points out that focaliza-tion retains some of the "optical-photographic connotations" of point of view; however, in broadening the term "to include cognitive, emotive and ideological orientation[s]," she maintains a semiotic distinction between "perspective and narration" while suggesting, as Susan Lanser does, that narrative can be studied "in relation to a referential context" (345). In *On*

Story-Telling, Mieke Bal also points to an ideological aspect of focalization and connects this aspect to the term's "critical potential" (3). Creating a framework for focalization, as opposed to what she sees as Gérard Genette's "unsystematic and rather unworkable definition" (3), Bal seeks to "accommodate the indispensable ideological counterpart, the other's eye, or the ideological mimesis that Bakhtinians emancipate" (3). Looking at looking as an important part of gender construction is central to *The Passion of New Eve*, and *ideological* focalization creates a political framework through which to examine how Eve/lyn sees and is seen.

Carter is a postmodern writer who critically revisits and re-visions the history of Western literary representation. Intertextual references are drawn from the Bible, Greek and other mythologies, *Great Expectations*, *Wuthering Heights*, *Orlando*, Poe, Sade, Wagner, and Mahler, among others. The list provides a proliferation of voices and stories against which the transformation of Evelyn into Eve is effected. As Susan Suleiman points out, Carter "multiplies the possibilities of linear narrative and of 'story,' producing a dizzying accumulation that undermines the narrative logic by its very excessiveness" (137). The novel's intertextuality complicates linear narrative and linear time because readers have to read on many different levels at once. For Mother, linear time is a "phallic projectory," and feminizing time involves a "journey backwards to the source" (Carter, 53). Moreover, she assumes that the source is attainable as something stable, and this, as the novel makes clear, dooms her project to failure.

The multiplication of narrative possibilities crosses paths with focalization in the thrice-repeated phrase "persistence of vision" that is always directly associated with Tristessa. The term comes from nineteenth-century attempts to explain why the eye perceives motion in film when there is, in fact, "nothing but a succession of still images" (Anderson and Anderson, 85). The explanation at the time was that "a positive after-image from the first flash of a two-flash display is assumed to be still present when the second flash occurs. The continued existence of a positive after-image . . . makes possible the perception of continuous movement" (Anderson and Anderson, 79). The persistence of the retinal image gives the illusion of movement, and although this is now considered an inadequate explanation of motion perception, it is interesting to consider the ideological implications that Carter seems to find in the term. As Lederman and Nichols suggest, "Innumerable commentators have cited the impression of movement as a fundamental part of any cinematic appeal based on realism" (299). Persistence of vision, here, however, is not realist. Like metaphor, it carries over from one image onto another; Carter uses it to emphasize a relationship rather than an inexorable forward movement. Indeed, the phrase is used in the novel to suggest a cinematic method of temporarily cheating time, of maintaining an appearance as essence: "For you [Tristessa] were just as beautiful as you had been twenty years before, would always be so beautiful as long as celluloid remained in complicity with the phenomenon of persistence of vision; but that triumph would die of duration in the end, and the surfaces that preserved your appearance were already wearing away" (5).

But persistence of vision also acts on characters as well as on the reader. Rather like the rabbit/duck drawing that can be either but not both at once, persistence of vision encourages a back-and-forth reading. It recontextualizes earlier images in terms of later ones, and later, in terms of earlier. The reader's apprehension of intertexts works in this manner, and because the "origin" for the referent is Carter's text, historical origins and progression are problematized. Such is the case with Evelyn's change of gender, particularly the moment at which Evelyn misrecognizes his image in a labyrinthine reworking of Lacan's mirror-stage: "But when I looked in the mirror, I saw Eve; I did not see myself. I saw a young woman who, though she was I, I could in no way acknowledge as myself, for this one was only a lyrical abstraction of femininity to me, a tinted arrangement of curved lines. I touched the breasts and the mound that were not mine; I saw white hands in the mirror move, it was as though they were white gloves I had put on to conduct the unfamiliar orchestra of myself. I looked again and saw I bore a strong family resemblance to myself" (74). This is Evelyn's first experience of gender as performance, and as I will argue later, this notion has implications for narrative. On one level, Evelyn is the narrator-focalizer, and Eve, the focalized object: "Let the punishment fit the crime, whatever it had been. They had turned me into the *Playboy* center fold. I was the object of all the unfocused desires that had ever existed in my own head. I had become my own masturbatory fantasy. And—how can I put it—the cock in my head, still, twitched at the sight of myself" (75). Designating Eve as a *Playboy* centerfold seems to indicate the male gaze, and yet the various permutations of who is looking at whom are dizzying. To assume the male gaze would suggest that Evelyn's persistence of vision is unidirectional, which, in its every other appearance in the text, it is not. To determine *literally* who sees in this passage, one would have to enter into an unresolvable debate between mind and body. Here, as in many other parts of the novel, the "I" who speaks or sees is indeterminate: "I" is simultaneously "not-I." Therefore, on another level, one could argue that the retrospective narrator, Eve, is narrating while Evelyn focalizes on Eve. But in this case, the male gaze is outwitted because Eve looks back; as both narrator and character, she actively returns the gaze while looking at herself being looked at.

My interpretation of persistence of vision as a relationship rather than a "phallic projectory" (53) has implications for the construction of subjectivity, which seems very much at issue here. Eve is not *born* but *made* a woman, and some of Evelyn's gestures and inflections (101) remain until the moment when Eve learns to look at, touch, and explore herself as a woman (146). The subject, either of the narration or of the character, is formed in relationship, as is the narrative itself, which comes to the reader, for example, already interpreted through the remarkably dense weaving of intertexts. The constantly shifting and often ambiguous focalization, the multiple "voices" of the intertexts, and the temporal indeterminacy of persistence of vision point out not only the multiplicity of narrative but also multiply the possibilities for gender beyond the absolutes of maleness and femaleness suggested by the one-eyed, one-legged, sterile character Zero and the eight-breasted character Mother.

The fluidity of gender is made most apparent and most ambiguous in the first five chapters, in which Evelyn's story is narrated through Eve's retrospective eye. When the British-born Evelyn lands in New York to take up a teaching position, he finds himself in a chaotic fragmented world in which former centric factions such as "the blacks" and "the Women" fight for control. The city itself is a narrative of discontent, "scribbled all over with graffiti in a hundred languages expressing a thousand different griefs and lusts and furies" (12). Evelyn becomes an innocent abroad in a Mad Max landscape inhabited by gun-toting thugs and rats "fat as piglets" (17). The city, he says, is a "metaphor for death," and as the "movie [runs] towards its last reel" (15), he meets Leilah, a black prostitute who arouses his most savage desires. Their increasingly vicious erotic games are terminated by her pregnancy, which causes Evelyn to lose interest in her. An illegal abortion sends the bleeding Leilah into hospital and eventual sterility, while Evelyn rushes to escape to the California desert on a quest for "that most elusive of chimeras, myself" (38). When Evelyn focalizes, especially on Leilah, his vision is to some extent determined by Eve's looking back on him looking at women. Since Eve is a woman when she tells Evelyn's story, her narration, of course, is tinged with the knowledge of what it is to be both the subject and the object of such a look.

The most interesting aspect of this section of the novel is the complication of the narrative level and extent of participation. To some degree, the novel imitates the narrative structure of one of its intertexts—*Great Expectations*—in that Eve is narrating in retrospect, yet she is both the I and the not-I narrator. Determining narrative level in the section of the novel that tells Evelyn's story depends entirely on whether the reader sees Eve as a man in a woman's body or as a woman—on whether a change in the coloration of the rind changes the essence. To use Rimmon-Kenan's terms, Eve is extraheterodiegetic if she has indeed become a woman separate from Evelyn, but intrahomodiegetic if Evelyn is still part of Eve. Given that hetero- and homodiegesis are determined by a narrator's participation in the story either not at all or "at least in some manifestation of his 'self'" (Rimmon-Kenan, 95), it is worth noting that "self," here, is a liminal concept of which neither Evelyn nor Eve is very sure. Indeed, the issue is complicated because there are "feminine" qualities in Evelyn even before his metamorphosis and "masculine" qualities in Eve after it: "As I have told you, I was slender and delicately made; now I was dressed like this girl, I looked like this girl's sister, except that I was far prettier than she" (55). Evelyn recognizes in himself "a fatal lack" (34), one that he thinks is reflected by Leilah. Eve, who is "literally in two minds" after her operation (77), comments, "I would often make a gesture with my hands that was out of Eve's character or exclaim with a subtly male inflection. . . . Although I was a woman, I was now also passing for a woman, but, then, many women born spend their whole lives in just such *imitations*" (101; emphasis added). And as Eve becomes "almost the thing I was" (107), she comments that remembering her life as Evelyn "was like remembering a film I'd seen once whose performances did not concern me. Even my memories no longer fitted me, they were old clothes belonging to somebody else no longer living" (92).

There is no marked change of "voice" between the parts of the novel that concern Eve and Evelyn, although in both sections comments are made about women's speech being incomprehensible. Leilah's speech is reported indirectly, and the narrator comments that "her argot or patois was infinitely strange to me, I could hardly understand a word she said" (26). The women in Zero's harem are forced to utter animal noises because "Zero believed women were made from a different soul substance from men, a more primitive, animal stuff" (87), and so "our first words every morning were spoken in a language we ourselves could not understand" (97). And yet this too is reported speech which the reader does not read.

However, even the direct discourse cannot be easily assigned either to male or female. The first sentence, for example, appears to be spoken by Evelyn: "The last night I spent in London, I took some girl or other to the movies and, through her mediation, I paid you a little tribute of spermatozoa, Tristessa" (5). Logically, the speaker is Evelyn, since only Evelyn could pay such a tribute. Yet it could also be argued that the speaker is an Evelyn who has been temporarily remembered by Eve, whose distance from an "actual" Evelyn is made clear in the formality, almost parody, of the phrase "tribute of spermatozoa." At this point of retrospective telling, neither Tristessa nor Evelyn "exists" except in Eve's memory; each is re-created by Eve, who soon makes her presence known. The way in which she does so imitates Leilah's erotic journey through the labyrinthine New York streets. As Evelyn, consumed with desire, follows Leilah, she leaves behind an Ariadne's thread of clothing dropped on the street for Evelyn to pick up: her dress, crotchless knickers, fur coat, and stockings. When Eve narrates the opening chapters, her narration becomes itself a kind of striptease, when she drops clues about her voice and plot: "Tristessa. Enigma. Illusion. Woman? Ah!" (6). Eve continues, "The black lady never advised me on those techniques when she fitted me up with a uterus of my own" (9), and, "There was a seventeenth-century print, tinted by hand, of a hermaphrodite carrying a golden egg that exercised a curious fascination upon me, the dual form with its breasts and its cock, its calm, comprehensive face. (Coming events?...)" (13). Although these clues, Tiresias-like, prophesy something of the future, they complicate the narrative. Like the discarded articles of clothing, Eve's snippets of information dropped along the way for the reader to pick up make it clear that the narrator is, and is not, Evelyn. However, while tempting the reader to pursue the erotic game, Eve's discarded clues do not lead the reader to a fulfillment of desire. The clues are clues about how not to read the various labyrinths appearing in the novel, and this includes the narrative itself. At the heart of each labyrinth is something that seems to be a center or a culmination but is in fact a dual, if not multiple, being: Leilah, Mother, and Tristessa. But centers fluctuate: Leilah becomes Lilith, Mother goes mad, Tristessa is revealed to be male and female. Eve's journey through a space-time labyrinth at the end of the novel moves to its center but does not center at the beginning of time. Although she looks for Mother, all she finds are some relics from her own past and the echo of her own voice:

I have come home.
The destination of all journeys is their beginning.

I have not come home.

I emitted, at last, a single, frail, inconsolable cry like that of a new-born child. But there was no answering sound at all in that vast, sonorous place where I found myself but the resonance of the sea and the small echo of my voice. I called for my mother but she did not answer me.

"Mama—mama—mama!"

She never answered. (186)

There is no return to the womb as fulfillment and no harmonious concatenation of opposites; the novel does not suggest androgyny as a satisfactory alternative.

When, as a member of Zero's harem, Eve is subjected to Zero's violent coupling, she says: "And more than my body, some other equally essential part of my being was ravaged by him for, when he mounted me with his single eye blazing like the mouth of an automatic, his little body imperfectly stripped, I felt myself to be, not myself but he; and the experience of this crucial lack of self, which always brought with it a shock of introspection, forced me to know myself as a former violator at the moment of my own violation" (101–2). The phrase "not myself but he" points back to Eve's life as Evelyn, suggesting that she recognizes herself as both self and other. This is not to suggest that Eve, or the novel, puts any store in an absolute unity. Eve is both and neither male and female. Indeed, the fluidity of gender in the novel in both the transsexual Eve and the transvestite Tristessa accounts for some of the difficulties in ascribing levels of narrative and focalization. Gender does not determine narrative; it makes narrative identity as complex as gender identity. Both Eve and Tristessa learn to *perform* their genders, and the very act of performance suggests a liminality that would seem to argue against an original essence. The "double-drag" wedding, in which Tristessa plays the bride and Eve the groom is the culmination of the performative images: "But this masquerade was more than skin deep. Under the mask of maleness I wore another mask of femaleness but a mask that now I never would be able to remove, no matter how hard I tried, although I was a boy disguised as a girl and now disguised as a boy again" (132). That this is also a description of the narrative in the first five chapters of the novel further confounds attempts to determine the narrative level and implies that the narrative itself is a conscious performance that reflects the shifting identities of the narrator.

Judith Butler, in *Gender Trouble*, makes the point that gender "is the repeated stylization of the body, a set of repeated acts within a highly rigid regulatory frame that congeal over time to produce the appearance of sub-stance, of a natural sort of being" (33). Mother's fondest wish—to kill time and live forever—is perhaps an effort to eliminate precisely those frames that regulate gender. But it is also clear that her project will fail, because although Mother, like Eve, is a technological construction, she believes in the essence of what her appearance conveys. For both Tristessa and Eve, gender is an "ongoing discursive practice" (Butler, 33); for Mother, it is a "concrete fact" (Carter, 58).

Nowhere is the stylization of the body made more apparent than in the presentation of Tristessa, although both s/he and Eve make the "mistake" of being "a little too emphatically feminine" (101). Zero, who thinks of himself as the "concrete fact" of machismo assumes that to be too much like a woman is to show "signs of the tribade" (101). With "almost a jeweller's eye" (106) he examines Eve, who sees "almost pure envy in his eyes for mother had made me unnatural only in that I was perfect" (107). Zero's sterility, however, he blames on Tristessa, "Queen of Dykes" (101), whose apparently female gaze has symbolically castrated him: "He'd been watching her in a revival of Emma Bovary in an art-house in Berkeley and Tristessa's eyes, eyes of a stag about to be gralloched, had fixed directly upon his and held them. He'd been on mescaline; she'd grown, grown to giant size, and her eyes consumed him in a ghastly epiphany. He'd felt a sudden, sharp, searing pain in his balls. With visionary certainty, he'd known the cause of his sterility. He was like a man who could not cast a shadow, and that was because Tristessa had sucked his shadow clean away" (104). The "woman's" active gaze, then, as Zero sees it, is not just a threat. When the woman looks back, she does so with "toothed" eyes.

Tristessa constructs his feminine appearance as "the shrine of his own desires"; he "had no function in the world except as an idea of himself" (128). Specifically, this ideal woman is a *femme fatale*, a combination of beauty and suffering, "romantic dissolution, necrophilia incarnate" (7). The irony here is that the *femme fatale* has herself ambiguous connotations, which Mary Ann Doane describes as "the fact that she never really is what she appears to be" (1). Tristessa, despite his feminine manners and ap-pearance, is more fully androgynous than Eve. Eve does come to see herself as a woman through Tristessa's mediation, but Tristessa's gender remains a far more ambiguous performance. He parodies the feminine but does not become it. Lilith describes him as "too much of a woman already" to undergo Mother's surgical transformation, but notes, too, "the awfully ineradicable quality of his maleness" (173). He symbolizes the fabrication of gender that even he cannot put into narrative. When Tristessa narrates his own story, he distances himself from its subject, calling himself both "I" and "she" and creating for himself a "fictive autobiography" designed to "make him suffer" (152). But even here there is no suture of identity; Tristessa's gender remains double: " 'What if Tristessa made you pregnant?' [Lilith] said. 'Your baby will have two fathers and two mothers' " (187).

What is clear about both Tristessa and Eve, however, is the lack of an "original" gender. Butler argues that gender parody, as in transvestism, "is *of* the very notion of an original . . . so gender parody reveals that the original identity after which gender fashions itself is an imitation without an origin." In such "fluidity of identities," she sees an openness to "resignification and recontextualization; parodic proliferation deprives hegemonic culture and its critics of the claim to naturalized or essentialist gender identities" (138). Zero and Mother are characters who, despite their self-construction as male and female incarnate, do see an essential identity. Each has eliminated, or wishes to eliminate, the "other." For Eve and Tristessa, though, gender cannot help being performative because its liminality provides multiple possibilities.

In Carter's novel, this multiplicity is reflected in the narrative and in the shifting voice and look of the narrator. It seems to me that the ideological possibilities of "Who speaks?" and "Who sees?" give narratology a critical potential, to use Bal's term, one that can combine the semiotic and the referential. Susan Lanser's intriguing arguments for a feminist narratology include the suggestion that narratology might provide a model for determining whether there is a "woman's writing" (346). She makes the point that the "precision and abstraction of narratological systems offers [*sic*] the safety for investigation that more impressionistic theories of difference do not" (346). In a novel such as *The Passion of New Eve*, however (and I want to make this point for Winterson's *Written on the Body* as well as for many other feminist texts by women writers), the narrative system can be shown to be neither abstract nor precise, depending on the questions one asks of it, and it is this that makes it most fruitful for feminist study. I do not mean to suggest that the opposite of "abstract and precise" in itself makes anything feminist or typical of women's writing—such an assertion would simply fall back on silly stereotypes—but it is the heteroglossia, the multiplicity, the undermining of binaries that make a text like Carter's feminist in both its narrative structure and its story. The self-consciousness of the text points to an equal self-consciousness in the narrative; like many postmodern novels, *The Passion of New Eve* inscribes its own suggestions for reading and

co-creating, and it points to the very process of meaning-production that is
so important in feminist writing.

WORKS CITED

Anderson, Joseph, and Barbara Anderson. "Motion Perception in Motion Pictures."
  The Cinematic Apparatus. Ed. Teresa de Lauretis and Stephen Heath. London:
  Macmillan, 1980. 76–95.
Bal, Mieke. *On Story-Telling: Essays in Narratology*. Ed. David Jobling. Sonoma, CA:
  Polebridge, 1991.
Butler, Judith. *Gender Trouble: Feminism and the Subversion of Identity*. New York:
  Routledge, 1990.
Carter, Angela. *The Passion of New Eve*. London: Virago, 1982.
de Lauretis, Teresa. *Alice Doesn't: Feminism, Semiotics, Cinema*. Bloomington: Indiana
  University Press, 1984.
Doane, Mary Ann. *Femmes Fatales: Feminism, Film Theory, Psychoanalysis*. New York:
  Routledge, 1991.
DuPlessis, Rachel Blau. *Writing beyond the Ending: Narrative Strategies of Twentieth-
  Century Women Writers*. Bloomington: Indiana University Press, 1985.
Lanser, Susan S. "Towards a Feminist Narratology." *Style* 20.3 (1986): 341–63.
Lederman, Susan J., and Bill Nichols. "Flicker and Motion in Film." *Ideology and the
  Image: Social Representation in Cinema and Other Media*. Ed. Bill Nichols.
  Bloomington: Indiana University Press, 1981. 293–301.
Rimmon-Kenan, Shlomith. *Narrative Fiction: Contemporary Poetics*. London:
  Routledge, 1983.
Suleiman, Susan Rubin. *Subversive Intent: Gender, Politics, and the Avant Garde*.
  Cambridge: Harvard University Press, 1990.
Winterson, Jeanette. *Written on the Body*. Toronto: Alfred A. Knopf Canada, 1993.

queering narratology

susan s. lanser

he narrator of Jeanette Winterson's *Written on the Body* (1992) is in love with a married woman. Hardly a new topic, hardly tellable by some narratological criteria, but for the novel's narrative voice. For the unnamed autodiegetic narrator of *Written on the Body* is never identified as male or female. That silence and the extent to which it destabilizes both textuality and sexuality drive this novel at least as much as its surface plot. As I contemplate the field of feminist narratology which has emerged in the past decade and which comes of age with this volume, *Written on the Body* leads me to new and similarly destabilizing inquiries. In what ways, I wonder, might this text's silence be a matter for narratology? How, indeed, might sex, gender, and sexuality function as elements of a narrative poetics, and why have these categories remained on the margins of narratological inquiry?

To be sure, over this decade narratology has become more complex in its understandings of textual production and correspondingly more flexible about what constitutes its field. Yet the sex and gender (let alone the sexuality) of textual personae have not been graciously welcomed as elements of narratology; they have been relegated to the sphere of "interpretation," which is often considered a "temptation" into which narratology must be careful not to "fall."[1] Even feminist narratology, my own work included, has tended to focus on women writers or female narrators without asking how the variables "sex," "gender," and "sexuality" might operate in narrative more generally.

Taking my cue from a 1995 essay by Gerald Prince to which I have responded elsewhere, I want to argue here for the inclusion of sex, gender, and sexuality as important, intersecting elements of narrative poetics, even within conventional definitions of the field.[2] I will claim that just as Proust's *A la recherche du temps perdu* fostered Genette's identification of certain narrative conventions and transgressions and Balzac's "Sarrazine" fostered Barthes's formulation of narrative codes, *Written on the Body* points to aspects of narrative that are "proper" to narratology in its classical sense, that is, to "the (structuralist-inspired) theory of narrative," which "studies the nature, form, and functioning of narrative (regardless of medium of representation)" and examines "what all and only narratives have in common (at the level of story, narrating, and their relations) as well as what enables them to be different from one another, and it attempts to account for the ability to produce and understand them."[3] Setting aside the phrase "all and only" as a criterion that, as Prince himself has asserted, has been consistently violated even by the earliest and most renowned of narratologists,[4] I will argue that the categories sex/gender/sexuality interact with other narratological elements from narrative person to paralipsis to reliability in ways that I will only begin to suggest here. At the same time, the "application" of the categories of sex, gender, and sexuality to actual texts calls profoundly into question the separation of text from context and grammar from culture and threatens the viability of binary systems on which narratology "proper" tends to insist.

The complexities posed by sexual categories begin to emerge in the very attempt to define them for narratological purposes. Feminist theorists of the 1970s and 1980s usually distinguished "sex" from "gender" by designating "sex" as a biological category and "gender" as a social one. More recent theorists such as Judith Butler have successfully deconstructed this opposition by arguing that "sex" is itself a culturally constructed category as much constituted by "gender" as "gender" is constituted by sex.[5] Language, I suggest, further complicates this dynamic—and differently so according to whether and how sex is grammatically and hence culturally marked. When I say "she" in English, I am usually referring to animate creatures or sometimes to objects that have been grammatically gendered through cultural practice (for example a ship, a country, the moon). When I say "elle" in French or "ella" in Spanish, however, I may be referring to any number of objects, animate or inanimate, even to objects that might be biologically sexed as male; for example, "personne" (person) in French is feminine. And in German I might use the neuter form, nonexistent in French and Spanish and used in English almost exclusively (except derogatorily) for nonhumans, to name a young or unmarried female (das Mädchen). These linguistic phenomena, which obviously have ramifications far beyond the scope of this inquiry, are already, I submit, ever so slightly *queer*: sexually transgressive, undercutting their own apparent binaries.

Keeping this fluidity in mind, for the purposes of this essay I will use the term "sex" to designate the formal identification of a represented human entity as male or female. I will use "gender" to designate characteristics constructed in and by texts that implicate—but do not prove—a male or female identity by drawing on cultural codes that conventionally signify masculinity or femininity: codes such as proper names and metonymic references to clothing, activities, and behaviors. And I will use "sexuality" to designate erotic orientation or identity particularly with respect to object choice. I am assuming that readers routinely attribute a sex to narrators and characters and that they do so both through explicit linguistic markers such as "he" and "she" (or "the man" and "the woman"), through gendered codes that vary historically and culturally but are nonetheless present at least in all language cultures of the so-called West, and sometimes also through presumptions of (hetero)sexuality. Although the narrator's *sex* is never identified in *Written on the Body*, for example, that absence surely does not stop readers from looking for *gender* markers through which to constitute that narrator's sex and with it his/her sexuality—and hence to stabilize the text. It so happens that in this case Winterson has elided from the novel virtually every possible gendered identifier; only the most conventional of readers—readers unable to imagine that a woman could wield a hammer, urinate out-of-doors, deride marriage, hit a man, or make love to other women—would insist that this narrator is gendered male. For other readers, the markings of gender in *Written on the Body* will be as elusive as the markings of sex.

In positing a process by which readers use gender and sexuality to infer the sex of an author, narrator, or character, I want also, then, to stress the instability of such a project. To take a mundane example, someone reading a book's acknowledgments for clues to the sex of an author with an ambiguous first name might look for a thank-you to the author's husband or wife. That gay and lesbian couples sometimes now use these spousal designations undercuts any construction of sex that the reader might make on such a basis and shows that it is as tenuous to infer sex from sexuality or gender as it is to infer gender from sex or sexuality. But this only complicates and does not halt the project by which readers, I argue, conventionally seek to attribute sex to textual personae, if only to be able to speak about them in a binary-inflected language, but probably also from profound anxiety. This anxiety is precisely what makes *Written on the Body* so compelling a narrative.

Taking sex, then, to mean very simply the linguistic marking of a textual persona as male or female, I want to argue that sex is a far more integral and important component of narrative than narratologists have recognized.

For, as *Written on the Body* starkly reminds us, there is not only the question of which sex is designated but also the prior question of whether sex is designated at all. Sex is surely a common if not constant element of narrative, in other words, once we include its *absence* as a narratological variable. Once sex becomes a category for narratology, we can identify different modes of narrative according to the ways in which they conventionally deploy or elide markings of sex.

I will begin this enterprise by suggesting that sex is intimately connected to the narratological category that Gérard Genette has called narrative "person" and is differently constituted in homodiegetic and heterodiegetic narratives, at least in European language texts. Let me posit a basic narrative convention: a narrator's sex is normatively unmarked in heterodiegetic narratives and normatively marked in autodiegetic texts. That is, the vast majority of heterodiegetic narrators of European-language texts do not mark themselves on the basis of sex. This absence of sex marking does not mean that sex and gender fail to signify in heterodiegetic texts, for as I have been suggesting, there is also the question, to which I return below, of the *reader's* construction of sex through what s/he takes to be signs of gender. Moreover, cases in which heterodiegetic narrators mark their sex do exist; the narrators of *Tom Jones* and *Vanity Fair* explicitly refer to themselves as men. But even a heterodiegetic narrator who employs first-person pronouns may, in virtually all European languages, safely employ a range of *narrative* acts without identifying him- or herself by sex. The narrator of *Northanger Abbey*, for example, undertakes a broad range of speech acts without designating her sex, though arguably she does implicate a gender identity by deriding the productions of men and praising the works of women novelists. Some of George Eliot's early narrators, in contrast, adopt gendered allusions to implicate themselves as male.

Although the narrator's sex is normally unmarked in heterodiegetic texts, sex is routinely marked in most homodiegetic and virtually all autodiegetic narratives of any length. Granted, all of us could construct brief autodiegetic texts in which the narrator's sex is not manifest, but it is rare for an extended autodiegetic narrative to elide all markers of both sex and gender. Not all autodiegetic narratives mark the narrator's sex explicitly; names, clothing, and physical attributes—characteristics of *gender*—do indeed, as I have been suggesting, allow or encourage readers to construct assumptions about a narrator's *sex*. I would suggest, however, that while *sex* may appear initially as an open question, heterosexual presumptions operate as designators for a narrator's or character's *sexuality* unless an alternative sexuality is explicitly marked. In order to test and expand these assumptions about narrative, one might fruitfully classify and study autodiegetic narratives for their various configurations—and elisions—of markers of sex, gender, and sexuality.

My reading of *Written on the Body* suggests that a considerable degree of information has to be omitted from an autodiegetic narrative for both sex and gender to remain unmarked. Such information—including, of course, the primary omission of sex itself—would seem to constitute what Genette has called a *paralepsis*: the underreporting of information that would conventionally be provided by a particular narrator or focalizer. Paralipsis (or ellipsis in general) then becomes, along with narrative person, another narratological category that interacts with sex, gender, and sexuality. In *Written on the Body*, for example, we never learn the narrator's name, his/her physical appearance, or physical details about how his/her lovers make love to him/her, though we know the names and sexes of the lovers, their physical appearances, and physical details about how he/she makes love to them. Since much of *Written on the Body* is *about* the body, the elided physical descriptions of the narrator are not insignificant, a fact of which the narrator is well aware: "Written on the body is a secret code only visible in certain lights; the accumulations of a lifetime gather there. In places the palimpsest is so heavily worked that the letters feel like braille. I like to keep my body rolled up away from prying eyes. Never unfold too much, tell the whole story."[6]

The absence of information about a narrator's sex raises productive questions too about the relationship readers construct between the narrator and the implied author of a text. I have suggested elsewhere my own perplexity as to whether and when the marking of an author's sex (on the title page or book cover) serves implicitly to mark the sex of a sexually unmarked narrator or whether a normative masculinity overrides that link. For example, if *Pride and Prejudice* is "by a lady," is the narrator assumed to be female, or is even a narrator constructed by a female author read as male? (Or, I would now add, is such a narrator conceptualized in this age of electronic voice-synthesis as a sexless "it"?) And what about the case of autodiegetic narrators, whom college-trained readers of literature, at least, have learned not to equate with their authors? Would *Written on the Body*, for example, be assumed to have a female narrator because it is written by "Jeanette Winterson"? If so, would the text from the start be read as a lesbian narrative? Or would normative heterosexuality prevail, particularly for a reader unfamiliar with Winterson's previous novels, such that the unsexed narrator would be read as male and, for the first half of the novel, the question of a possible lesbian relationship would never arise?

I allude to the first half of the novel because *Written on the Body* also takes a narrative swerve in which sexuality ruptures the conventional system by which readers attempt to determine sex on the basis of gender clues. For readers who recognize that the narrator's sex is unmarked (rather than simply constructing the narrator as a heterosexual male or as a lesbian woman), *Written on the Body* creates a tension between two narrative scenarios. In both the beloved is married, and narrative conflict centers first around whether Louise will leave her husband Elgin, a brilliant cancer researcher, and later on the effects of the narrator's decision to flee from Louise when she/he hears that Louise has leukemia so that Louise will return to Elgin, who claims that she will die without the care that he has the power to arrange or to obstruct. For a reader open to the possibility of both narratives, the tension between the two narrative scenarios rises and falls, I suggest, according to the represented content: rising, for example, during a physical fight between the narrator and Elgin, during the narrator's musings about the negative aspects of marriage in general, or during descriptions of lovemaking, and falling, perhaps, when the focal issue is whether Louise will leave Elgin. To the extent that sex and gender matter for interpretation, the nonmarking of sex yields, in some sense, two narrative texts. Moreover, the narrative opens questions about the relationship between sex and gender in ways that allow the reader to test his or her own assumptions repeatedly.

Then, at a point midway through the novel, the text takes another informational swerve: the narrator who is in love with Louise talks about a male boyfriend called "Crazy Frank." Now we do have certain information, not about the narrator's sex, but about his/her bisexuality. The non-marking of sex yields somewhat in importance to a new category, sexuality, that had been hitherto unmarked. How does the insertion of this new formal element—undeniable queerness—affect the signification of the narrator's unmarked sex and gender? Little, perhaps, if the narrator had been read originally as lesbian; more, perhaps, if the narrator had been read as a straight man. For the new information erases the possibility that *Written on the Body* is the story of a strictly heterosexual male in love with a married woman and hence erases one standard age-old scenario of Western literature. *Written on the Body*, whatever the sex of its narrator, is a queer novel with a queer plot.

For me, *Written on the Body* also ruptures presumed links between sex, gender, and sexuality with respect to other, seemingly more conventional texts. I said earlier that in autodiegetic narratives the narrator's sex may be marked explicitly, or it may be capable of construction through markings of gender. But what if these gender markings *do not signify* the conventionally implied sex? What if the narrator in pants is a woman or the narrator named Mary a drag queen? Lesbian and gay writers have indeed exploited these possibilities of gender-bending for cover or for play; is it not possible that readers have made conventional assumptions about sex and sexuality in texts that do not explicitly mark these categories? What if we are dealing in these cases with "queer" narratives that we have been duped into constructing as sexually conventional on the basis of binary oppositions or gendered conventionalities? What if a straight-seeming narrative lends itself to a queer reading? A sexually conscious narratology offers the possibility of identifying texts according to the intersecting systems of sex, gender, and sexuality that they do and do not make possible.

The categories of sex, gender, and sexuality raise questions about narrative reliability as well. Prince argues in "On Narratology," for example, that a narrator's geographical information may be "no less correct" for his being a psychopath. But there are myriad other, grayer areas of "fact"—for example, the narrator's "factual" statement about another character's behaviors—on which doubt might well be cast were the narrator a psychopath. Prince further suggests that a narrator's authority is weakened by a "point of view designated as (suspiciously) subjective." But what determines the suspicious subjectivity of that narrative voice? Certainly, as early criticism of a novel like *Jane Eyre* gives evidence, there was a time not far distant when all women narrators were suspect for presumed subjectivity. If a heterosexual and heterosexist reader were to construct the narrator of *Written on the Body* as queer whatever his/her sex, that reader might also decide that the point of view of the narrator was suspiciously subjective about everything to do with love and desire—which are what this book is all about. Would that reader not perhaps consider unreliable the narrator's claim to have left Louise in hopes that she would in this way be able to benefit from her husband's medical connections and expertise?

Sex/gender/sexuality might also, then, constitute a category of reliability—or, conversely, reliability might be another subcategory of sex/gender/sexuality that works itself out in narratological terms. Indeed, narratological definitions of reliability, including the one I offered in *The Narrative Act*, are perilously tautological: if a reliable narrator is one who behaves "in accordance with the implied author's norms" and an unreliable narrator is one "whose values (tastes, judgments, moral sense) diverge from those of the implied author" (Prince, *Dictionary*, 101), how, in the ordinary processing of narrative, would one know the implied author's norms *except* by constructing them oneself from the values one *thinks* this author *ought* to hold? A sexually conservative reader of *Written on the Body*—fortified, perhaps, by the evidence of Winterson's previous novels, *Oranges Are Not the Only Fruit* (1985), *The Passion* (1988), and *Sexing the Cherry* (1989)—might well decide that the norms of the implied author "Jeanette Winterson" are decadent or diseased and the author's judgments therefore unreliable. In this case a narrator who would technically be considered reliable by standard definitions—because the narrator's norms are consistent with those of the implied author—might well be judged unreliable by readers whose values diverge from those of "Winterson."

Narratological distinctions of sex, gender, and sexuality may also differentiate texts by both language and medium. European languages permit considerably greater sexual ambiguity in the construction of narrators than of represented characters because the first person is less sex-specific than the third. But even with regard to narrators, the language of representation is a significant variable. *Written on the Body* is an Anglophone text, and I imagine that translators will have difficulty rendering it into any number of languages. On the very first page, for example, the narrator says, "I am alone"; in many Indo-European languages this simple clause would require a masculine or feminine adjective, as subsequent clauses would require numerous other sex-specific adjectives and predicates that are not inflected in the English text. Such languages might, then, require even deeper ellipses for maintenance of the text's silence about its narrator's sex. Languages without grammatical gender, on the other hand, might allow much more latitude than English in constructing an autodiegetic narrator without a sex. American Sign Language would give even the represented character a gender-neutral identity, because it does not use gendered pronouns at all.

And while I would not want to insist that the absence of sex marking in autodiegetic narrative is exclusive to verbal texts, I think it would be extremely difficult to maintain such an absence in a visual text. Two recent films, *Orlando* and *The Crying Game*, are instructive even though their ambiguities of sex, gender, and sexuality occur not in narrators but in characters. Most viewers of the film version of *Orlando* to whom I have spoken had difficulty imagining Tilda Swanson as a male either in voice or body; only the "ellipsis" of never representing the "male" Orlando without full dress maintained the illusion that Orlando was a man. In Woolf's novel, on the other hand, there is not only no difficulty naming Orlando as male, but there is none of the prolepsis (foreshadowing) that occurred for viewers of the film who recognized (or knew ahead of time) that the person playing Orlando was female. *The Crying Game* represents a related if somewhat different case: in the film, Dill, the cross-dressed male marked as "she," appeared visually—at least to most viewers—to be female. Dill is revealed only midway through the film to be biologically male: thus Dill is marked mimetically as female in *gender*, although Dill's body comes to be marked as male in *sex*. This queering of the filmic narrative occurs with the unveiling of the body; what the film does not permit is for Dill to be *un*known in sex in a way that a written account might have allowed—I think, for example, of Balzac's "Sarrazine." All of which is simply to say that what Prince calls the "expressive possibilities" of different "media of manifestation" (79) are fascinatingly addressed by the insertion of sex/gender/sexuality as questions for narratology. How, indeed, would *Written on the Body* be translated into film?

The narrative complexities that result from sex, gender, and sexuality also bear on the question of tellability that some narratologists have addressed. *Written on the Body* entails three plot possibilities, two by inference ("The man loves a married woman" and "The woman loves a married woman") and one empirically verifiable ("A person of indeterminate sex loves a married woman"). Of the three, the first version seems to me the least conflict-intense for a homophobic culture, the second more conflict intense, and the third different in kind because it inserts a metaplot in which additional narrative tension is generated precisely by the excitement to know whether the narrator in love with the married woman is male or female.

My point in raising these possibilities is not to suggest that narratology can *decide* these questions, just as it cannot decide the effects of metalepsis or unreliability. My point is that sex, gender, and sexuality constitute narratologically significant elements that intersect with other textual aspects to illuminate "the nature, form, and functioning of narrative," to describe commonalities and differences among narratives, and to account for readers' "ability to produce and understand them." But narratological attention to sex, gender, and sexuality also makes a strong case for a *contextual* poetics: for the impossibility of reading any narrative without considering the cultural conventions in which the narrative operates. Narratology has been nervous about such a blurring of the sharp boundaries of textuality, as it has been nervous about the related "slide" from poetics to interpretation to which the strong narratologist will not "yield." Is it possible that these resistances—to interpretation, contextuality, and sex/gender/sexuality—stem from the same anxiety?

With one last, playful evocation of *Written on the Body*, I want to suggest that narratological practice has to do not only with science but also with desire. What we choose to support, to write about, to imagine—even in narratology—seems to me as much a function of our own desire as of any incontrovertible evidence that a particular aspect of narrative is (im)proper or (ir)relevant. By resisting the notion that the text is merely an agglomeration of formal elements, the introduction of sex and gender, like the introduction of contextuality and with it of questions that have previously been associated only with interpretation, threatens the "purity" of the narratological enterprise. For some of the most interesting elements of narrative are indeed as maddeningly difficult to pin down as Winterson's narrator's sex. Perhaps, then, to embrace questions of sex, gender, and sexuality is to end up "queering" narratology in another sense: to let it deviate from the straight-and-narrow path of structuralism's binaries into a more dauntingly indeterminate terrain. Indeed, if, as some postmodern theorists contend, sex has been the binary on which all other binaries have been constituted, then the dismantling of this binary through the recognition of queerness—a queerness that, I have suggested, is already implicated in the grammars of apparently binary languages—threatens all other binaries and with it other structural certainties.

At this time when lesbian, gay, and queer studies are burgeoning, *Written on the Body* leads me to imagine that there might eventually be a queer narratology in which questions of sexuality and the challenges sexuality poses to conventions of sex and gender become a telescope through which to seek narrative elements not before attended to or attended to differently. In this context, I can't resist noting that the texts on which Barthes and Genette expend their own narratological energies, respectively *Sarrazine* and *A la recherche*, are, like *Written on the Body*, queer texts, and I would suggest that both Genette and (especially) Barthes "yield to the interpretive temptation" (Prince, 82) in delightful and illuminating ways. Instead of worrying about poetical improprieties, I hope we will welcome other such efforts much as biologists might welcome the opportunity for deep-water expeditions or accounts of them, reveling in what can be learned and experienced and willing to worry later about sifting the theoretical from the praxeological, the textual from the contextual, the narratological from the interpretive. Or, to close with the final words of Jeanette Winterson's narrator, whose sex is forever a mystery: "Hurry now, it's getting late. I don't know if this is a happy ending but here we are let loose in open fields" (190).

NOTES

1. See, for example, Diengott, "Narratology and Feminism," and Prince, "On Narratology: Criteria, Corpus, Context."
2. In "On Narratology: Criteria, Corpus, Context," Prince endorses in theory the inclusion of "gender" as an element of narrative poetics but stops short of embracing feminist narratology. For my response to this essay, see "Sexing the Narrative: Propriety, Desire, and the Engendering of Narratology."
3. Prince, *Dictionary of Narratology*, 65.
4. As Prince has recognized in his own more recent work, one element of the classical definition has been observed consistently in the breach (and, I would add, evoked only to keep certain issues fenced out of narratology): the dictate that narratology explore "what *all and only* narratives have in common" (emphasis added). To follow such a dictum would long ago have reduced narratology to a far more restrictive science than its most classical practitioners have constructed; as Prince notes, key narratological elements such as focalization, character, and description are hardly restricted to narrative. Nor, indeed, is voice: a lyric poem, for example, is said to manifest "voice," although the "speaker" is conventionally called a "persona" rather than a "narrator." Prince seems to propose a criterion of significance in place of distinctiveness: elements called into play in the relationship between story and discourse, or elements such as focalization and voice that are relevant to the "nature, form, and functioning of narrative," are worth the attention of narratologists. Likewise, narratology has always paid attention to many features that do not necessarily appear in all narratives. Such transgressive elements as metalepsis and paralepsis, which Gérard Genette has identified and discussed at some length, occur in relatively few narratives—far fewer, I hope to demonstrate, than are implicated by questions of sex.
5. Butler, *Gender Trouble: Feminism and the Subversion of Identity*, 6–9, 36–38, and passim.
6. Winterson, *Written on the Body*, 89. Further references to this novel will appear in the text.

WORKS CITED

Butler, Judith. *Gender Trouble: Feminism and the Subversion of Identity*. New York: Routledge, 1990.
Diengott, Nilli. "Narratology and Feminism." *Style* 22.1 (1986): 42–50.
Lanser, Susan S. *The Narrative Act: Point of View in Prose in Fiction*. Princeton: Princeton University Press, 1981.

——. "Sexing the Narrative: Propriety, Desire, and the Engendering of Narratology." *Narrative* 3.1 (January 1995): 85–94.

Prince, Gerald. *Dictionary of Narratology*. Lincoln: University of Nebraska Press, 1987.

——. "On Narratology: Criteria, Corpus, Context." *Narrative* 3.1 (January 1995): 73–84.

Winterson, Jeanette. *Written on the Body*. New York: Alfred A. Knopf, 1993.

coda. incredulity toward metanarrative

Negotiating Postmodernism and Feminisms

linda | hutcheon

> *It was conservative politics, it was subversive politics, it was the return*
> *of tradition, it was the final revolt of tradition; it was the unmooring of*
> *patriarchy, it was the reassertion of patriarchy . . .*
> —*Anne Friedberg,* Window Shopping

When Jean-François Lyotard defined the postmodern condition as a state of incredulity toward metanarratives, he helped set the stage for a series of ongoing debates about the various narrative systems by which human society orders and gives meaning, unity, and "universality" to its experience. Lyotard himself, in debate with the defender of the "unfinished project" of *modernity*, Jürgen Habermas, took on what he saw as the dominant metanarratives of legitimation and emancipation, arguing that postmodernity is characterized by no grand totalizing master narrative but by smaller and multiple narratives which do not seek (or obtain) any universalizing stabilization or legitimation (3–15). Fredric Jameson has pointed out that both Lyotard and Habermas are really, in fact, working from "master narrative" positions—one French and (1789) revolutionary in inspiration and the other Germanic and Hegelian; one valuing commitment, the other consensus (Jameson, vii–xxi).[1] Richard Rorty, in turn, has offered a trenchant critique of both positions, ironically noting that what they share is an almost overblown sense of the role of philosophy today (181–97).

Overblown or not, this issue of the role and function of metanarratives in the discourses of knowledge is one that has demanded attention. Various forms of feminist theory and criticism have come at it from a particular angle: the metanarrative that has been their primary concern is obviously patriarchy, especially at its point of imbrication with other major master narratives of our day—capitalism, imperialism, and liberal humanism. In their form of critique, feminisms[2] have overlapped in concern with Marxist and poststructuralist theories and with what has been called postmodern art—art that is paradoxically both self-reflexive and historically grounded, both parodic and political: the photographic art of Barbara Kruger and Victor Burgin or the fiction of Angela Carter and Graham Swift. Such art is ironic, not nostalgic in its engagement with history and with art history. It works to "de-doxify" the "doxa"—what Roland Barthes called public opinion or the "Voice of Nature" and consensus (47).

But there is a catch here: because of its use of parody as a strategic discursive structure, postmodernism manages both to inscribe and to subvert its target. In addition, from its first manifestations in architecture to the present, postmodern art has juxtaposed and given equal value to the inward-directed world of art and the outward-directed world of history and experience. The tension between these apparent opposites finally defines the paradoxically "worldly" "texts" of postmodernism. In response to the question of metanarrative, postmodernism's stand is one of wanting to contest cultural dominants (patriarchy, imperialism, capitalism, humanism, and so forth) and yet knowing it cannot extricate itself completely from them: there is no position outside these metanarratives from which to launch a critique that could avoid self-implication. And this sparks, just as powerfully, the no less real (if, ultimately, inevitably ambivalent) politics of the postmodern. Indeed, it is its compromised position that makes this political stand recognizable and even familiar to us.

It is over this paradox of the postmodern complicitous critique of metanarrative that feminisms and postmodernism part company. Of course, many commentators have recently pointed to the maleness of the modernist tradition and therefore to the implied maleness of any postmodernism that is either in reaction to or even a conscious break from that modernism. Feminisms have been resisting incorporation into the postmodern camp, and with good reason: they have felt that their political agendas would be endangered or at least obscured by the double coding of that complicitous critique; their historical particularities and relative positionalities might even risk being subsumed (though both should be protected by the postmodern contesting of universalization in the name of the local and particular). Both enterprises work toward an awareness of the social nature of cultural activity, but feminisms are not content with exposition: art forms cannot change unless social practices do. Exposition may be the first step, but it cannot be the last. Nevertheless, feminist and postmodern artists do share a view of art as a social sign inevitably and unavoidably enmeshed in other signs within systems of meaning and value. But I would argue that feminisms usually want to go beyond this to work to *change* those systems, not just to "de-doxify" them.

There is yet another difference between the two phenomena. Barbara Creed has put it this way: "Whereas feminism would attempt to explain that crisis [of legitimation that Lyotard has described] in terms of the workings of patriarchal ideology and the oppression of women and other minority groups, postmodernism looks to other possible causes—particularly the West's reliance on ideologies which posit universal truths—Humanism, History, Religion, Progress, etc. While feminism would argue that the common ideological position of all these "truths" is that they are patriarchal, postmodern theory . . . would be reluctant to isolate a single major determining factor" (52). "Reluctant to" because it cannot—not without falling into the trap of which it implicitly accuses other ideologies: that of totalization. Creed is right in saying that postmodernism offers no privileged, unproblematic position from which to speak. Therefore, she notes, "the paradox in which we feminists find ourselves is that while we regard patriarchal discourses as fictions, we nevertheless proceed as if our position, based on a belief in the oppression of women, were somewhat closer to the truth" (67). But postmodernism's rejection of a privileged position is as much an ideological stand as this feminist taking of a position. By ideology here, I mean that all-informing complex of social practices and systems of representation that so much of current theory has been concerned to delineate and debate. The political confusion surrounding postmodernism—rejected and recuperated by both the left and the right—is not accidental but a direct result of its double encoding as complicity and critique. While feminisms may use postmodern parodic strategies of deconstruction, they never suffer from this confusion of political agenda, partly because they have a position and a "truth" that offer ways of understanding aesthetic and social practices in the light of the production of—and challenges to—gender relations. This is their metanarrative. This is also their strength and, in some people's eyes, their necessary limitation.

Although feminisms and postmodernism have both worked to help us understand the dominant modes of representation at work in our societies, feminisms have focused on the specifically female subject of representation and have begun to suggest ways of challenging and changing those dominants in both mass culture and high art. They have taught us that to accept unquestioningly any fixed representations—in fiction, film, advertising, or whatever—is to condone social systems of power that validate and authorize some images of women (or blacks, Asians, lesbians, and so on) and not others. Cultural production is carried out within a social context and an ideology—a lived value system—and it is to this fact that feminist work has made us pay attention. Feminisms have, in this way, had a very profound effect on postmodernism. It is no accident that the postmodern coincides with the feminist reevaluation of noncanonical forms of narrative discourse, that a very postmodern autobiography, *Roland Barthes by Roland Barthes*, and a very postmodern family biography, Michael Ondaatje's *Running in the Family*, have a lot in common with Christa Wolf's *A Model Childhood* or Daphne Marlatt's *Ana Historic*. They all challenge not only what we consider to be literature (or, rather, Literature) but also what was once assumed to be the seamless, unified narrative of representations of subjectivity in life-writing. Victor Burgin has claimed that he wants his photography and his art theory to show the meaning of sexual difference as a *"process of production*; as something mutable, something historical, and therefore something we can do *something* about" (108; emphasis in original). Postmodernism cannot *do* that something, however; it can try to *un-do* but, without a metanarrative to direct its political agenda, that is all it can do.

Feminisms, on the other hand, can do more. For instance, in granting new and emphatic value to the notion of "experience," they have given a different angle on a very postmodern question: What constitutes a valid historical narrative? And who decides? This has led to the current reevaluation of personal or life narratives—journals, letters, confessions, biographies, autobiographies, self-portraits. In Catharine Stimpson's terms, "Experience generated more than art; it was a source of political engagement as well" (226). If the personal is the political, then the traditional separation between private and public history must be rethought. This feminist rethinking has coincided with a general renegotiation of the separation of high art from the culture of everyday life—popular and mass culture—and the combined result has been a reconsideration of both the context of historical narrative and the politics of representation and self-representation.

There is, in fact, a two-way involvement of the postmodern with the feminist: on the one hand, feminisms have successfully urged postmodernism to reconsider—in terms of gender—its antimetanarrative challenges to that humanist "universal" called "Man" and have supported and reinforced its "de-doxifying" of the separation between the private and the public, the personal and the political; on the other hand, postmodern parodic and ironic representational strategies have offered feminist artists an effective way of working within and yet challenging dominant patriarchal metanarrative discourses. That said, there is still no way in which the feminist and the postmodern—as cultural enterprises—can be conflated. The differences are clear, and none so clear as the political one. Chris Weedon opened her book on feminist practice with the words, "Feminism is a politics." Postmodernism is not; it is certainly political, but it is politically ambivalent, doubly encoded as both critique and complicity, undermining any fixed metanarrative position. Because of their necessary notion of "truth," as Creed argued, feminisms are not incredulous toward their own metanarrative, even if they do contest the patriarchal one. Feminisms will continue to resist incorporation into postmodernism, largely because of their revolutionary force as political movements working for real social change. They go beyond making ideology explicit and deconstructing it, and do so to argue a need to change that ideology, to effect a real transformation of art that can come only with a transformation of patriarchal social practices. Postmodernism has not theorized agency; it has no strategies of real resistance that would correspond to the feminist ones. It cannot. This is the price to pay for that incredulity toward metanarrative.

NOTES

1. See also Herman, "Modernism versus Postmodernism: Toward an Analytic Distinction," 59–67 especially.
2. I use the real, if awkward, plural here because there are as many feminisms as there are feminists and no clear cultural consensus in feminist narratological thinking on questions of representation. As Catharine Stimpson has argued, the history of feminist thought on this topic includes the confrontation of dominant representations of women as misrepresentations, the restoration of the past of women's own self-representation, the generation of accurate representations of women, and the acknowledgment of the need to represent differences among women (of sexuality, race, age, class, ethnicity, nationality), including their diverse political orientations (223). As a verbal sign of difference and plurality, feminisms (in the plural) would seem to be a useful collective term to designate not a consensus but a multiplicity of points of view that nevertheless do possess at least some common denominators when it comes to the notion of the *politics* of narrative representation.

WORKS CITED

Barthes, Roland. *Roland Barthes by Roland Barthes*. Trans. Richard Howard. New York: Hill and Wang, 1977.

Burgin, Victor. *The End of Art Theory: Criticism and Postmodernity*. Atlantic Highlands, NJ: Humanities Press International, 1986.

Creed, Barbara. "From Here to Modernity: Feminism and Postmodernism." *Screen* 28.2 (1987): 47–69.

Friedberg, Anne. *Window Shopping: Cinema and the Postmodern*. Berkeley: University of California Press, 1993.

Habermas, Jürgen. "Modernity—An Incomplete Project." Trans. Seyla Ben-Habib. *The Anti-Aesthetic: Essays on Postmodern Culture*. Ed. Hal Foster. Port Townsend, WA: Bay Press, 1983. 3–15.

Herman, David J. "Modernism versus Postmodernism: Toward an Analytic Distinction." *Poetics Today* 12.1 (1991): 55–86.

Jameson, Fredric. Foreword. Jean-François Lyotard, *The Postmodern Condition: A Report on Knowledge*. Trans. Geoff Bennington and Brian Massumi. Minneapolis: University of Minnesota Press, 1984. vii–xxi.

Lyotard, Jean-François. *The Postmodern Condition: A Report on Knowledge*. Trans. Geoff Bennington and Brian Massumi. Minneapolis: University of Minnesota Press, 1984.

Marlatt, Daphne. *Ana Historic: A Novel*. Toronto: Coach House, 1988.

Ondaatje, Michael. *Running in the Family*. Toronto: McClelland and Stewart, 1982.

Rorty, Richard. "Habermas, Lyotard, et la postmodernité." *Critique* 442 (Mars 1984): 181–97.

Stimpson, Catharine. "Nancy Reagan Wears a Hat: Feminism and Its Cultural Consensus." *Critical Inquiry* 14.2 (1988): 223–44.

Weedon, Chris. *Feminist Practice and Postculturalist Theory*. Oxford: Blackwell, 1988.

Wolf, Christa. *A Model Childhood*. Trans. Ursula Molinaro and Hedwig Rappolt. New York: Farrar, Straus, and Giroux, 1980.

select bibliography on feminist narratology

Kathy Mezei

Abel, Elizabeth. "Narrative Structure(s) and Female Development: The Case of *Mrs. Dalloway.*" *The Voyage In: Fictions of Female Development.* Ed. Elizabeth Abel, Marianne Hirsch, and Elizabeth Langland. Hanover: University Press of New England, 1983. 161–85.

Bal, Mieke. *Femmes imaginaires: L'ancien testament au risque d'une narratologie critique.* Montreal: Éditions HMH, 1985.

——. "Notes on Narrative Embedding." *Poetics Today* 2.2 (1981): 41–59.

Barry, Nora, and Mary Prescott. "Beyond Words: The Impact of Rhythm as Narrative Technique in *The Left Hand of Darkness.*" *Extrapolation* 33.2 (1992): 154–65.

Barwell, Ismay. "Feminine Perspectives and Narrative Points of View." *Aesthetics in Feminist Perspective.* Ed. Hilde Hein and Carolyn Korsmeyer. Bloomington: Indiana University Press, 1993. 93–104.

Booth, Alison. *Famous Last Words: Changes in Gender amd Narrative Closure.* Charlottesville: University Press of Virginia, 1993.

Booth, Wayne. "Control of Distance in Jane Austen's *Emma.*" *The Rhetoric of Fiction.* Chicago: University of Chicago Press, 1961. 243–70.

Brewer, Mária Minich. "A Loosening of Tongues: From Narrative Economy to Women Writing." *Modern Language Notes* 99.5 (1984): 1141–61.

Brinton, Laurel J. "The Historical Present in Charlotte Brontë's Novels: Some Discourse Functions." *Style* 26.2 (1992): 221–43.

Cave, Marianne. "Bakhtin and Feminism: The Chronotopic Female Imagination." *Women's Studies* 18 (1990): 117–27.

Clements, Patricia, and Isobel Grundy, eds. *Virginia Woolf: New Critical Essays.* London: Vision, 1983.

Curnutt, Kirk. "Direct Addresses, Narrative Authority, and Gender in Rebecca Harding Davis's 'Life in the Iron Mills.'" *Style* 28.2 (Summer 1994): 146–68.

Diengott, Nilli. "Narratology and Feminism." *Style* 22.1 (1988): 42–51.

DuPlessis, Rachel Blau. "Feminist Narrative in Virginia Woolf." *Novel* 21.2–3 (1988): 323–30. Rpt. in *Why the Novel Matters: A Postmodern Perplex.* Ed. Mark Spilka and Caroline Flesher McCracken. Bloomington: Indiana University Press, 1990. 341–48.

——. *Writing beyond the Ending: Narrative Strategies of Twentieth-Century Women Writers.* Bloomington: Indiana University Press, 1985.

Fishburn, Katherine. *The Unexpected Universe of Doris Lessing: A Study in Narrative Technique.* Westport: Greenwood, 1985.

Friedman, Susan Stanford. "Craving Stories: Narrative and Lyric in Contemporary Theory and Women's Long Poems." *Feminist Measures: Soundings in Poetry and*

Theory. Ed. Lynn Keller and Cristanne Miller. Ann Arbor: University of Michigan Press, 1994.

——. "Lyric Subversion of Narrative in Women's Writing: Virginia Woolf and the Tyranny of Plot." *Reading Narrative: Form, Ethics, Ideology*. Ed. James Phelan. Columbus: Ohio State University Press, 1989. 162–85.

Gates, Henry Louis, Jr. "Color Me Zora: Alice Walker's (Re)Writing of the Speakerly Text." *Intertextuality and Contemporary American Fiction*. Ed. Patrick O'Donnell and Robert Con Davis. Baltimore: Johns Hopkins University Press, 1989. 144–67.

——. "Zora Neale Hurston and the Speakerly Text." *The Signifying Monkey: A Theory of Afro-American Literary Criticism*. New York: Oxford University Press, 1988. 170–216.

Gautier, Gary. "Fanny's Fantasies: Class, Gender, and the Unreliable Narrator in Cleland's *Memoirs of a Woman of Pleasure*." *Style* 28.2 (Summer 1994): 133–45.

Gordon, Jan B. "A-filiative Families and Subversive Reproduction: Gossip in Jane Austen." *Genre* 21 (1988): 5–46.

Haggerty, George E. "'Romantic Friendship' and Patriarchal Narrative in Sarah Scott's *Millenium Hall*." *Genders* 13 (1992): 108–22.

Hirsch, Marianne. *The Mother/Daughter Plot: Narrative, Psychoanalysis, Feminism*. Bloomington: Indiana University Press, 1989.

Hite, Molly. *The Other Side of the Story: Structures and Strategies of Contemporary Feminist Narrative*. Ithaca: Cornell University Press, 1989.

Hoesterey, Ingeborg. Introduction. *Neverending Stories: Toward a Critical Narratology*. Princeton: Princeton University Press, 1992. 3–14.

Homans, Margaret. "Feminist Fictions and Feminist Theories of Narrative." *Narrative* 2.1 (January 1994): 3–16.

Howells, Coral Ann, and Lynette Hunter, eds. *Narrative Strategies in Canadian Literature: Feminism and Postcolonialism*. Milton Keynes, Eng.: Open University Press, 1991.

Ingham, Patricia. "Fallen Woman as Sign, and Narrative Syntax in *Tess of the d'Urbervilles*." *Tess of the d'Urbervilles/Thomas Hardy*. New York: St. Martin's, 1993. 80–89.

Jacobs, Naomi. "Gender and Layered Narrative in *Wuthering Heights* and *The Tenant of Wildfell Hall*." *Journal of Narrative Technique* 16.3 (1986): 204–19.

Kristeva, Julia. *Desire in Language: A Semiotic Approach to Literature and Art*. New York: Columbia University Press, 1980.

Langland, Elizabeth. "Dialogic Plots and Chameleon Narrators in the Novels of Victorian Women Writers: The Example of Charlotte Brontë's *Shirley*." *Narrative Poetics: Innovations, Limits, Challenges*. Ed. James Phelan. Columbus: Ohio State University Press, 1987. 23–37.

——. "The Voicing of Feminine Desire in Anne Brontë's *The Tenant of Wildfell Hall*." *Gender and Discourse in Victorian Literature and Art*. Ed. Anthony H. Harrison and Beverly Taylor. DeKalb: Northern Illinois University Press, 1992. 111–23.

Lanser, Susan S. *Fictions of Authority: Women Writers and Narrative Voice*. Ithaca: Cornell University Press, 1992.

———. *The Narrative Act: Point of View in Prose in Fiction*. Princeton: Princeton University Press, 1981.

———. "Sexing the Narrative: Propriety, Desire, and the Engendering of Narratology." *Narrative* 3:1 (January 1995): 85–94.

———. "Shifting the Paradigm: Feminism and Narratology." *Style* 22.1 (1988): 52–60.

———. "Toward a Feminist Narratology." *Style* 20.3 (1986): 341–63.

Leonardi, Susan J. "Recipes for Summer Reading: Summer Pasta, Lobster à la Riseholme, and Key Lime Pie." *PMLA* 104 (1989): 340–47.

McConnell-Ginet, Sally, Ruth Borker, and Nelly Furman, eds. *Women and Language in Literature and Society*. New York: Praeger, 1980.

Maclean, Marie. "Narrative and the Gender Trap." *Journal of the Australasian Universities Language and Literature Association* 74 (November 1990): 69–84.

———. "Oppositional Practices in Women's Traditional Narrative." *New Literary History* 19.1 (Autumn 1987): 37–50.

Matus, Jill. "Proxy and Proximity: Metonymic Signing." *University of Toronto Quarterly* 58.2 (Winter 1988/89): 305–26.

Mezei, Kathy. "'And It Kept Its Secret': Narration, Memory, and Madness in Jean Rhys' *Wide Sargasso Sea*." *Critique* 28.4 (Summer 1987): 195–210.

Miller, Nancy K. "Emphasis Added: Plots and Plausibilities in Women's Fiction." *PMLA* 96 (1981): 36–48.

———. *The Heroine's Text: Readings in the French and English Novel, 1722–1782*. New York: Columbia University Press, 1980.

Nelson, Dana. "Sympathy as Strategy in Sedgwick's *Hope Leslie*." *The Culture of Sentiment: Race, Gender, and Sentimentality in Nineteenth-Century America*. Ed. Shirley Samuels. New York: Oxford University Press, 1992. 191–202.

Newman, Beth. "Narratives of Seduction and the Seduction of Narrative: The Frame Structure of *Frankenstein*." *ELH* 53.1 (1986): 141–63.

———. "The Situation of the Looker-On: Gender, Narration, and Gaze in *Wuthering Heights*." *PMLA* 105 (1990): 1029–41.

Palmer, Paulina. *Contemporary Women's Fiction: Narrative Practice and Feminist Theory*. Hertfordshire: Harvester Wheatsheaf, 1989.

Prince, Gerald. "Narratology, Narratological Criticism, and Gender." Paper delivered in honor of Lubomír Doležel at the colloquium "Fiction and Worlds." University of Toronto. Toronto, Spring 1990. In Colin Mihailescu and Walid Hamarneh, eds., *Fiction Updated: The Theory of Fictionality and Contemporary Humanities*. Toronto: University of Toronto Press, forthcoming.

———. "On Narratology: Criteria, Corpus, Context." *Narrative* 3.1 (January 1995): 73–84.

Rainwater, Catherine, and William J. Scheick, eds. *Contemporary American Woman Writers: Narrative Strategies*. Lexington: University of Kentucky Press, 1985.

Robinson, Sally. *Engendering the Subject: Gender and Self-Representation in Contemporary Women's Fiction*. Albany: State University of New York Press, 1991.

Ronen, Ruth. "Review of Mieke Bal's *Introduction to the Theory of Narrative*." *Canadian Review of Comparative Literature* (May–June 1989): 188–92.

Say, Elizabeth A. *Evidence on Her Own Behalf: Women's Narrative as Theological Voice*. Savage, MD: Rowman and Littlefield, 1990.

Schabert, Ina. "The Authorial Mind and the Question of Gender." *Telling Stories: Studies in Honour of Ulrich Broic on the Occasion of His 60th Birthday*. Ed. Elmar Lehmann and Bernd Lenz. Amsterdam: Grüner, 1992. 312–29.

Senf, Carol. "*The Tenant of Wildfell Hall*: Narrative Silences and Questions of Gender." *College English* 52.4 (April 1990): 446–56.

Shires, Linda M. "Narrative, Gender, and Power in *Far from the Madding Crowd*." *The Sense of Sex: Feminist Perspectives on Hardy*. Ed. Margaret R. Higonnet. Urbana: University of Illinois Press, 1993. 49–65.

Silver, Brenda R. "The Reflecting Reader in *Villette*." *The Voyage In: Fictions of Female Development*. Ed. Elizabeth Abel, Marianne Hirsch, and Elizabeth Langland. Hanover: University Press of New England, 1983. 90–111.

Singley, Carol J., and Susan Elizabeth Sweeney, eds. *Anxious Power: Reading, Writing, and Ambivalence in Narrative by Women*. Albany: State University of New York Press, 1993.

Suleiman, Susan Rubin. *Authoritarian Fictions: The Ideological Novel as a Literary Genre*. New York: Columbia University Press, 1983.

Sweeney, Susan Elizabeth. "Formal Strategies in a Female Narrative Tradition: The Case of *Swann: A Mystery*." *Anxious Power: Reading, Writing, and Ambivalence in Narrative by Women*. Ed. Carol J. Singley and Susan Elizabeth Sweeney. Albany: State University of New York Press, 1993. 19–32.

Travis, Molly Abel. "*Beloved* and *Middle Passage*: Race, Narrative, and the Critic's Essentialism." *Narrative* 20.3 (October 1994): 179–200.

"Vers une narratologue féministe/Toward Feminist Narratology." *Tessera* 7 (Fall 1989).

Warhol, Robyn R. *Gendered Interventions: Narrative Discourse in the Victorian Novel*. New Brunswick: Rutgers University Press, 1989.

——. "Narrating the Unnarratable: Gender and Metonymy in the Victorian Novel." *Style* 28.1 (Spring 1994): 74–94.

——. "'Reader, Can You Imagine? No, You Cannot': The Narratee as Other in Harriet Jacob's Text." *Narrative* 3.1 (January 1995): 57–72.

——. "Toward a Theory of the Engaging Narrator: Earnest Interventions in Gaskell, Stowe, and Eliot." *PMLA* 101 (1986): 811–18.

Winnett, Susan. "Coming Unstrung: Women, Men, Narrative, and Principles of Pleasure." *PMLA* 105 (1990): 505–18.

Winterhalter, Teresa. "Narrative Technique and the Rage for Order in *Wide Sargasso Sea*." *Narrative* 20.3 (October 1994): 214–29.

Woods, Gurli, ed. *Isak Dinesen and Narrativity*. Ottawa: Carleton University Press, 1994.

notes on the contributors

Melba Cuddy-Keane has published numerous essays on Joyce Cary and on Virginia Woolf in such journals as *Contemporary Literature, Cultural Critique, Journal of Modern Literature, PMLA,* and *Studies in the Novel.* She is associate professor of English at the University of Toronto, where she also serves as vice-principal and associate dean of the Scarborough Campus. She is a founding member of the Joyce Cary Society and president of the Virginia Woolf Society. Her current project is a book-length study entitled "Poetics in Praxis: Virginia Woolf's Literary Theory."

Denise Delorey has taught at Brandeis, MIT, and Boston University. She recently received her Ph.D. from Brandeis. Her dissertation is on gender and the uses of allegory in the (post)modern novel.

Rachel Blau DuPlessis has recently published *The Pink Guitar: Writing as Feminist Practice* (1990), *Tabula Rosa* (1987), and *Drafts 3–14* (1991). She edited *The Selected Letters of George Oppen* (1990) and, with Susan Stanford Friedman, coedited *Signets: Reading H.D.* (1990). DuPlessis is the author of *Writing beyond the Ending: Narrative Strategies of Twentieth-Century Women Writers* (1985) and *H.D.: The Career of That Struggle* (1986) and teaches in the English Department at Temple University.

Susan Stanford Friedman is the Virginia Woolf Professor of English and Women's Studies at the University of Wisconsin-Madison. She is the author of *Penelope's Web: Gender, Modernity, H.F.D.'s Fiction* (1990) and *Psyche Reborn: The Emergence of H.D.* (1981); coauthor of *The Women's Guide to Therapy* (1979); editor of *Joyce: The Return of the Repressed* (1993); and coeditor of *Signets: Reading H.D.* (1991). She was president of the Society for the Study of Narrative Literature (1992) and has published several articles on narrative theory.

Janet Giltrow teaches in the English Department at Simon Fraser University. She has published articles on Canadian and American literature, on rhetoric and composition, on linguistic-pragmatic approaches to style, and on genre in *American Literature, Postmodern Studies, Style, Canadian Literature,* and *Technostyle.* Her textbook, *Academic Writing,* has recently appeared in a revised edition (1995), along with a companion anthology, *Academic Reading* (1995).

Linda Hutcheon is professor of English and comparative literature at the University of Toronto. She is the author of *Narcissistic Narrative: The Metafictional Paradox* (1980; rpt. 1984); *A Theory of Parody: The Teachings of Twentieth-Century Art Forms* (1985); *A Poetics of Postmodernism: History, Theory, Fiction* (1988); *The Politics of Postmodernism* (1989); and *Irony's Edge: The Theory and Politics of Irony* (1995). She has also published a number of studies of Canadian culture, including *The Canadian Postmodern* (1988); *Splitting Images: Contemporary Canadian Ironies* (1991); and, with Mark Cheetham, *Remembering Postmodernism: Trends in Recent Canadian Art* (1991).

Susan S. Lanser is professor of English and comparative literature and affiliate professor of women's studies at the University of Maryland. She is author of *The Narrative Act: Point of View in Prose in Fiction* (1981) and *Fictions of Authority: Women Writers and Narrative Voice* (1992) and coeditor of *Women Critics, 1660–1820: An Anthology*. Her essays have appeared in *Feminist Studies, Style, Frontiers, Eighteenth-Century Life, NWSA Journal*, and *Semeia* and in several edited books. Her current project is a study of eighteenth-century representations and self-representations of spinsters, sapphists, and romantic friends.

Alison Lee is assistant professor of English at the University of Western Ontario. She is the author of *Realism and Power: Postmodern British Fiction*, and her current research is on violence in postmodern women's writing.

Patricia Matson is teaching at Douglas College, Vancouver, B.C., and has published stories in *Room of One's Own* and *West Coast Review*. She is also the coauthor of an educational video on gender stereotyping in the media, "What's Wrong with This Picture?"

Kathy Mezei is the chair of the English Department at Simon Fraser University and a founding editor of *Tessera*. She has published articles on Canadian and Quebec literature, translation studies, and British women writers in *Canadian Literature, Critique, University of Toronto Quarterly, Essays on Canadian Writing, The Yearbook of English Studies*, and in edited books on Canadian literature and feminism. Her *Bibliography of Criticism on English and French Literary Translations in Canada* was published in 1988.

Christine Roulston completed her Ph.D. in comparative literature at the University of Toronto on the eighteenth-century epistolary novel, was recently a postdoctoral fellow at Cambridge University, and is now assistant professor in the French Department at the University of Western Ontario. She is working on the relation between women and confession within literary narratives.

Robyn Warhol is associate professor and director of the graduate program in English at the University of Vermont. She is the author of *Gendered Interventions: Narrative Discourse in the Victorian Novel* (1989) and coeditor with Diane Price Herndl of *Feminisms: An Anthology of Literary Theory and Criticism* (1991) and with George Perkins and Barbara Perkins of *Women's Work: An Anthology of American Literature* (1994). She has published articles on feminist narratology in *PMLA, Novel, Style*, and *Narrative*.

index

Absence: in Woolf's works, 96–97, 100, 106–7; of mothers, 128–31, 229–31; of dialogic, 144–45, 153, 162–63; of information about narrator's gender, 250, 252, 254, 257–58. *See also* Other; Silence

Ackerman, Robert, 157 (n. 6)

Agentless expressions, 15, 215, 220–22, 224, 226–28, 231

A la recherche du temps perdu (Proust), 250, 259

Alice Doesn't (de Lauretis), 240

Ambiguity (indeterminacy): as feminist narratology focus, 2, 10, 238–61; about gender, 15, 71, 72, 76–79, 83–86, 88 (n. 20), 238–60; Austen's, about marriage, 58–59; of free indirect discourse, 67–69, 71, 72; about gender roles, 70–71; in *Hotel du Lac*, 228. *See also* Parenthetical

Ana Historic (Marlatt), 265

Androgyny, 246, 247

Anger, 153–56

Anonymity (of narrator), 88 (n. 21)

Arac, Jonathan, 189

Ardis, Ann, 7

Aristotle, 17 (n. 3)

Armstrong, Nancy, 52

Art. *See* Writing

Asphodel (H.D.), 119

Auerbach, Erich, 104–5

Austen, Jane: as feminist writer, 1, 7, 10, 21–66, 70–75; gendered implications of focalization by, 11–12, 22–38, 66, 72–78; class versus gender solidarity in, 12–13, 33–34, 40–64; marriage plots in works by, 34, 45–46, 49, 73–75, 87 (n. 13), 123–24; narrators

in works by, 58, 69, 77, 82, 83, 86. *See also* titles of individual works

Author: feminist narratology's study of, 2; parallels between textual subject and its, 13, 126–27; implied, 66, 69, 78, 254; struggles between narrator, character, and, 66, 67, 69, 70–81. *See also* Narrator; Self-censorship

"The Authorial Mind and the Question of Gender" (Schabert), 11

Authority: women writers' reactions to, 10, 66; Austen's, 58, 82; narrative, 58, 66, 68, 70, 74–77, 82; Forster's, 77–79, 82; Woolf's alternatives to, 81–86, 139–59, 163–86. *See also* Author; Narrator

Autobiography, 5, 119, 265

Autodiegetic realm, 250, 253–54, 256, 257

The Awakening (Chopin), 9

Bakhtin, Mikhail: theories of narrative discourse by, 2, 4, 6, 7, 9, 13, 55, 67, 75, 111, 118, 189, 241; gender erasure in analysis by, 11, 12, 40–64; chronotope concept of, 13, 110, 112–13; on double-voiced discourse, 14, 68–69, 84, 138, 145–47, 158 (n. 10); and Woolf, 14, 138, 156 (nn. 1, 2); on free indirect discourse, 68–70

"Bakhtin and Feminism: The Chronotopic Female Imagination" (Cave), 9

Bal, Mieke, 2, 5–6, 8, 67, 72, 241, 248

Bally, Charles, 67

Balzac, Honoré de, 250–51, 258, 259

Banfield, Ann, 67, 69

Barthes, Roland, 2, 11, 118, 168, 170,

Fall, the, 124

Famous Last Words (Booth), 75

Fathers, 45, 62 (n. 8), 130

Felman, Shoshana, 117

Feminism: eugenicist, 200–202; Lawrence's response to, 204–8; variety of views within, 262–63, 266 (n. 2). *See also* Feminist film theory; Feminist literary criticism; Feminist narratology; "New Woman"

Feminist film theory, 6, 25, 34, 240

Feminist literary criticism, 1, 5–7, 9, 153, 262–63

"Feminist Manifesto" (Loy), 14, 187, 192, 195, 197, 200–202

Feminist narratology: as contextualization, 1–18; definitions of, 6–7, 21; history of, 6–11, 250; and focalization, 25

Ferguson, Suzanne, 88 (n. 24)

Fictions of Authority (Lanser), 10, 11

Fictions of Discourse (O'Neill), 4

The Fictions of Language and the Language of Fiction (Fludernik), 67

FID. *See* Free indirect discourse

Finch, Casey, 62 (n. 9), 63 (n. 14), 64 (nn. 23, 24, 26)

Flaubert, Gustave, 69, 71

Flavin, Louise, 22, 87 (n. 12)

Fludernik, Monika, 67

Flynn, Elizabeth, 6

Focalization: as "indifferent to gender," 8; Austen's use of female, 22–38; versus free indirect discourse, 70, 139–40; shifts in, 140–44; definition of, 157 (n. 5); multiple, 171–72; gender indeterminacy of, 238, 240–43

Focalizer. *See* Character

Fontanille, Jacques, 16 (n. 3)

Formalism, 2, 3, 5–8, 94–95, 138, 188–89. *See also* Structuralism

Forster, E. M., 12, 15, 66, 69, 71, 76–81, 85, 95, 179

Foucault, Michel, 27, 202

Frank, Joseph, 111

Free indirect discourse (FID): as site of gender and textual ambiguity, 12–13, 67–71; Austen's use of, 22, 28, 33, 62 (n. 9), 72–76, 86; definition of, 68

Free love, 190, 191–94, 205, 207, 210 (n. 12)

Freud, Sigmund, 117–19, 187

Friedberg, Anne, 262

Friedman, Ellen G., 17 (n. 8)

Friedman, Susan Stanford, 11, 13, 88 (n. 20), 109–36

A Friend from England (Brookner), 230

Froula, Christine, 124

Fuchs, Miriam, 17 (n. 8)

Furbank, P. N., 76, 80

Gagnon, Madeleine, 8

Gallop, Jane, 37–38

Garner, Margaret, 117

Garnett, David, 72

Gates, Henry Louis, Jr., 5, 70, 116

Gaze: as narrative device in *Persuasion*, 12, 22, 25–26, 56, 194; and construction of femininity, 239–43. *See also* Focalization; Looking

Geertz, Clifford, 127

Gender: as narrative context, 4–11; as one of subject's multiple identities, 5; as produced *through* narrative structures, 10, 238–49; and Bakhtin's assumptions, 11, 12, 40–64; versus class in *Emma*, 12–13, 40, 48–51, 59–61; ambiguity about narrator's, 15, 71, 72, 76–79, 83–86, 88 (n. 20), 238, 250, 252, 254–60; multiplicity in, 15, 238–49, 256, 259; different uses of "looking" according to, 26–30; Woolf's challenges to ideologies of, 120–23, 163–86; and education, 141, 144; reversals of, 158 (n. 14); defini-

121; Loy's use of, 202–3; in post-modernism, 263, 265

Jacob's Room (Woolf), 81, 86, 88 (n. 20); paradox of containment in, 13, 94, 95–100, 105, 107
James, Henry, 117
Jameson, Frederic, 117, 262
Jane Eyre (Brontë), 256
Jealousy, 192–94
Jesperson, Otto, 67
Joan and Peter (Wells), 144–45
Johnson, Claudia, 26, 27, 63 (n. 16), 64 (n. 27)
Johnson, Judith Van Sickle, 34
Johnson, Samuel, 158 (n. 18)
Jones, Gayl, 10
Journal of Narrative Technique, 4
Joyce, James, 93, 116, 119, 169

Kaplan, Caren, 5
Kauffman, Linda S., 159 (n. 17)
Kirchhoff, Frederick, 67, 69
Knowledge (females' access to), 12, 22, 24, 27, 55–56, 58, 99
Knutson, Susan, 9
Kouidis, Virginia M., 211 (n. 26)
Kristeva, Julia, 6, 7, 13, 110–13, 115, 117, 118, 125, 132, 176–78
Kruger, Barbara, 263

Lacan, Jacques, 118, 176, 242
Lady Chatterley's Lover (Lawrence), 14, 191, 205–8
Language: gaze as alternative to, 12, 23, 31–32; gender differences in, 43, 44, 251, 257; as site for class and gender struggles, 43–59; transformative power of, 54–59; politics of Woolf's, 173, 175; symbolic, 176, 177. *See also* Conversation; Discourse; Gossip; Politeness; Silence; Voice(s)
Lanser, Susan: as founder of feminist

narratology, 1, 8–10; on feminist narratology, 7, 17 (n. 7), 240, 248, 250–61; on narratology's male bias, 11; on female narrative authority, 88 (n. 15), 139–40, 189, 250–61
Lascelles, Mary, 38 (n. 3)
Latecomers (Brookner), 230
Laughter, 153–54, 156
Lawrence, D. H., 14, 93, 116, 189, 191, 204–8
Leclerc, Annie, 8
Lederman, Susan J., 241
Lee, Alison, 15, 238–49
Lesbianism, 128–31, 133 (n. 20), 173, 254–55
Lessing, Doris, 10, 86 (n. 4)
Levinson, Stephen, 235 (nn. 1, 2), 236 (nn. 6, 8)
Lips, Marguerite, 67
Lodge, David, 62 (n. 12)
Looking: as constructive of gendered subjectivity, 15, 26–28, 239–43; in *Persuasion*, 22–38; empowerment of heroines through, 26–28, 30–35, 38; in *Jacob's Room*, 97, 99. *See also* Gaze
"A Loosening of Tongues" (Brewer), 7
Lorck, Etienne, 67
"Love Songs to Joannes" (Loy), 14, 191, 193, 194, 196, 197, 203
Loy, Mina, 11, 14, 187–214
Lyotard, Jean-François, 262, 264

McGowan, John, 38 (n. 6)
McHale, Brian, 3, 4, 67, 68, 70
Madame Bovary (Flaubert), 69, 71
Madness, 163, 173–81, 184 (n. 17)
The Madwoman in the Attic (Gilbert and Gubar), 9, 182 (n. 6)
Mansfield Park (Austen), 56
Marcus, Jane, 133 (nn. 13, 20), 184 (n. 18)
Marlatt, Daphne, 265

Narrative strategies, 1, 6–7, 9, 14. *See also* Ambiguity; Discourse; Irony; Spatialization; Transgression

"Narrative Time" (Ricoeur), 110

Narratology: formalism in, 2, 3, 5–8, 188–89; history of, 2–11; resistance of, to feminism, 6, 11, 250–51; importance of including gender, sex, and sexuality in, 250–60. *See also* Feminist narratology

Narrator, 2; in Woolf's works, 7, 81–86; gender ambiguity of, 15, 71, 72, 76–79, 83–86, 88 (n. 20), 238, 250, 252, 254–60; as shield for author's controversial views, 70, 71, 73–76, 80–81, 83–85, 95–96; intrusive, 76, 77–79, 81, 88 (n. 21); in Woolf's works, 95–100, 107, 172–73; reliability of, 256–57. *See also* Author; Self-censorship; Voice(s)

Nation, 147, 148

Negotiation, 145–53

Nelson, Scott R., 88 (n. 18)

Neumann, Anne, 68

Neverending Stories (Hoesterey), 7

New Criticism, 3

New Freewoman, 210 (nn. 8, 11)

Newman, Beth, 10

"New Woman," 187, 190, 191, 199, 207

Nichols, Bill, 241

Northanger Abbey (Austen), 27, 34, 253

La nouvelle Héloïse, (Rousseau), 62 (n. 8)

Novels: bildungsroman genre of, 13, 94–96, 100, 116, 123–31, 204, 205; romantic, 13, 75, 184 (n. 23), 215–16, 227–28; feminocentric, 21; of sensibility, 26, 27; sentimental, 41–43, 47, 52, 54, 61, 63 (n. 22); Woolf's alteration of conventions of, 94, 95–97, 100–101, 109, 123–24, 128–31, 184 (n. 23), 187

Of Grammatology (Derrida), 165

Oltean, Stefan, 88 (n. 25)

Ondaatje, Michael, 265

O'Neill, Patrick, 4

"On Narratology" (Prince), 256

"On Not Knowing Greek" (Woolf), 140–44, 148, 153, 157 (n. 7)

Onorato, Richard, 107 (n. 4)

On Story-Telling (Bal), 241

Orange, Michael, 22

Oranges Are Not the Only Fruit (Winterson), 257

Orgasm, 11, 14, 85, 187–212

Orlando (film), 257–58

Orlando (Woolf), 158 (n. 14), 207, 241, 258

Other: Austen's depiction of women as each other's, 50–51; ancient Greek culture as, 141, 142–43; women regarded as, 162

Others publication, 210 (nn. 12, 13)

Paint It To-Day (H.D.), 119

Pamela (Richardson), 43, 46, 52, 63 (n. 22)

Paradise Lost (Milton), 124

Paralepsis, 254, 260 (n. 4)

Parenthetical, the, 13, 94–108

Pascal, Roy, 67

The Passion (Winterson), 257

The Passion of New Eve (Carter), 15, 238–49

Passive voice. *See* Agentless expressions

Patriarchy, 46–50, 262, 264; alternatives to discourse of, 14, 137–59, 162–86

Pavel, Thomas, 16 (n. 2)

"Persistence of vision," 15, 241–43. *See also* Looking

Persuasion (Austen), 1, 5, 7, 11–12, 21–38, 87 (n. 14), 123–24

Phelan, James, 4, 115, 127–28

Plato, 143

Pleasure: gender differences in, 11, 149;

females' access to, 12, 22, 193, 194;
plot trajectory and reader's, 187–212.
See also Sexuality

Plot, 5; trajectory of, similar to orgasm,
11, 14, 34, 139–40, 187–212, 258. *See
also* Marriage plots; Master plots

PMLA, 10

Poetics Today (journal), 3, 4

Point of view. *See* Focalization

Politeness, 88 (n. 27), 215–37

Polyvocality. *See* Voice(s): multiple

Poovey, Mary, 158 (n. 10)

A Portrait of the Artist as a Young Man
(Joyce), 116, 119

Postmodernism, 4, 16, 167, 241, 248,
259, 262–67

Poststructuralism, 5–7, 10, 38, 263

Pound, Ezra, 191, 198

Pratt, Mary Louise, 140

Preschoolers, 145–46

Presupposing expressions, 15, 215,
217–20, 227, 228, 231

Prince, Gerald, 2, 4, 8, 18 (n. 11), 24, 25,
250, 251, 256–58

Private versus public sphere: in *Emma*,
12, 24, 38, 44–45, 49–50, 52–61;
Bakhtin on, 41–43, 59; in *The Voyage
Out*, 123; conversation's place in, 138;
literary forms associated with, 265

"The Problem of Speech Genres"
(Bakhtin), 55

Projection, 15, 215, 222, 224–29

Proust, Marcel, 250, 259

Providence (Brookner), 230

Psychoanalysis, 4, 11, 25, 117–18

Public versus private sphere. *See* Private
versus public sphere

Queer theory, 5, 6, 15–16, 250–61

Rabelais and His World (Bakhtin), 43

Rabinowitz, Peter, 115

Race, 5, 121–23

The Rainbow (Lawrence), 204

Reader response criticism, 11

Readers: feminist narratology's study of,
2; destabilization of, 16, 75, 139–40,
142, 155–56, 168, 252, 253; interpreting of free indirect discourse by, 72,
74–75; response of, to conflicting
narrative closures, 110; as "narrators"
of submerged plot, 124–25, 127–28,
131, 142; writing for multiple, 148–
49; pleasure of, 187–88; constraints
on, 219, 227; interpretation of gender
by, 254–55. *See also* Reading practices

Reading for the Plot (Brooks), 110

Reading practices, 10, 11; "spatialized,"
13, 109–34; in *Northanger Abbey*,
27; in *Emma*, 46, 48–49; Woolf on,
140–44. *See also* Looking

Realism: of sentimental novels, 41–43,
47, 62, 72; Woolf's undermining of,
170–72, 183 (n. 13), 241

Recent Theories of Narrative (Martin), 3

"Reviewing" (Woolf), 159 (n. 17)

Revolution in Poetic Language (Kristeva),
118

Richardson, Dorothy, 14, 107, 187, 189

Richardson, Samuel, 43, 52, 100, 101,
104, 116

Ricoeur, Paul, 110

Rimmon-Kenan, Shlomith, 16 (n. 2), 70,
240, 244

The Rise of the Novel (Watt), 61 (n. 2), 72

Robinson, Sally, 9–10

Roby, Kinley E., 88 (n. 19)

Roland Barthes by Roland Barthes, 265

Roman à clef, 94

Romance (discourse of), 46–47, 51. *See
also* Marriage; Marriage plots; Novels:
romantic

Ronen, Ruth, 3, 4, 17 (n. 6)

A Room of One's Own (Woolf): feminist
aesthetic in, 93, 100, 144, 207; polemics of, 95, 96, 108 (n. 6); rhetorical

strategies in, 97, 144, 153–54, 156; *Mrs. Dalloway* and, 100, 101–3, 157 (n. 3), 162

Rorty, Richard, 262

Rose, Phyllis, 184 (n. 20)

Rosecrance, Barbara, 77, 88 (nn. 17, 19)

Rosenbaum, S. P., 158 (n. 16)

Rosenberg, Beth, 158 (n. 18)

Roulston, Christine, 11, 12, 14, 40–65

Rousseau, Jean-Jacques, 62 (n. 8)

Running in the Family (Ondaatje), 265

Russian formalists. *See* Formalism

Sanger, Margaret, 210 (n. 12)

Sappho, 197–98, 203

"Sarrazine" (Balzac), 250–51, 258, 259

Schabert, Ina, 11, 87 (n. 10)

Scholes, Robert, 11

Schorer, Mark, 63 (nn. 14, 17)

Schreiner, Olive, 192

Schuelke, Gertrude, 67

Schweickart, Patrocinio, 6

"Seismic orgasm," 11, 14, 195–96, 200

Self-censorship, 118, 126–27, 131, 153. *See also* Censors

Semiotics, 2, 7, 17 (n. 9), 118, 125, 176–77, 179

"Sensationalism," 23, 38 (n. 4)

Sense and Sensibility (Austen), 26

Sex (as narratology category), 251–60. *See also* Gender; Sexuality

Sexing the Cherry (Winterson), 257

Sexuality, 5; plot an imitation of trajectory of, 11, 14, 34, 187–212; and Woolf, 13, 14, 101–4, 125–26; ambiguity of, in *Written on the Body*, 15, 250–60. *See also* Chastity; Desire: sexual; Marriage

Sheldon, Amy, 145–47

"Shifting the Paradigm" (Lanser), 8

Showalter, Elaine, 6, 183 (nn. 15, 16)

Sibling relations, 64 (n. 25), 130

The Signifying Monkey (Gates), 116

Silence: narratology's interest in, 5, 117; about gender, 15, 250, 252, 254, 257–58; Bakhtin's, about gender difference, 40–43; as transgression, 50–51; about domestic abuse, 53; Austen's, about Emma's marriage proposal, 58–59, 87 (n. 13); as form of control, 71, 220; in *Mrs. Dalloway*, 175. *See also* Absence; Language

Silver, Brenda, 153

Slavery, 50, 116–17

Smith, Barbara Herrnstein, 107 (n. 3)

Smith, Sidonie, 5

Social Purity Movement, 193, 195

Sons and Lovers (Lawrence), 116

Spacks, Patricia Meyer, 5, 55, 58

"Spatial Form in Modern Literature" (Frank), 111

Spatialization: of narratives, 109–34

Spivak, Gayatri Chakravorty, 106, 164–65

Spring and All (Williams), 191

Stanzel, F. K., 67

A Start in Life (Brookner), 230

Stein, Gertrude, 187

Stephen Hero (Joyce), 119

Sterne, Laurence, 26

Stimpson, Catharine, 265, 266 (n. 2)

Stoker, Bram, 190, 206

Story. *See* Narrative

Stout, Janis, 23

Strachey, Ray, 148

Structuralism, 2, 3, 5, 10, 111, 189. *See also* Formalism

Subject: positions of, 5, 10, 27, 45–49, 148–53; decentered or elusive, 10, 81, 94, 95, 105–7, 163, 167. *See also* Author; Character; Narrator; Readers

Subjectivity, 162–63

Suleiman, Susan, 241